SCHOOL OF ORIENTAL AND AFRICAN STUDIES

SINHALESE
AN INTRODUCTORY COURSE

SECOND EDITION

[redacted]

SINHALESE

AN INTRODUCTORY COURSE

Second Edition

C.H.B. REYNOLDS
Formerly lecturer in Sinhalese,
School of Oriental and African Studies,
University of London

SCHOOL OF ORIENTAL STUDIES
UNIVERSITY OF LONDON
1995

Published by the School of Oriental and African Studies
(University of London), Thornhaugh Street, Russell Square,
London WC1H 0XG

First edition 1980
Second edition 1995

British Library Cataloguing in Publication Data
A catalogue record for this book is available from the British Library

ISBN 0 7286 0240 7

Typeset by PDQ Typesetting and printed in Great Britain
at the Alden Press, Oxford.

PREFACE TO THE FIRST EDITION

The island of Sri Lanka, formerly officially known as Ceylon*, contains about 14 million inhabitants (1978), the majority of whom speak the official language Sinhala (pronounced with the middle vowel *short*), more generally known in English as Sinhalese. (In the 19th century, the spelling 'Cingalese' was common.)

Most of the remainder of the population speak Tamil, an unrelated Dravidian language which is spoken principally in southern India. Sinhalese, which is an Indo-European language, is spoken only in Sri Lanka, and its closest relative is the language of the Maldive Islands.

In Lanka the spoken and the written language differ considerably – very much more than they do in English. For example, most verb forms have quite different terminations in the written language. This book is concerned solely with the spoken language.[1] It is intended to give a general introduction to the language in a form which can be used, if necessary, without a teacher. It is essential, in that case, to use the accompanying set of tapes, which can be obtained from the School of Oriental and African Studies, Thornhaugh Street, London WC1H 0XG. If tapes are not available, particular attention should be paid to the phonetic Introduction.

Each lesson contains two exercises for practice, the first (headed A) in translation from Sinhalese into English, the second (headed B) in translation from English into Sinhalese. At the end of the book are given suggested Sinhalese versions of the B sentences, and these also appear on the tapes, after each group of A sentences; they do not, of course, represent the only correct ways of translating the sentences in question. Lessons 7, 16, 24 and 31 are primarily revision lessons, and contain less new material than the others.

The course is written in a romanized transcription throughout, but the first seventeen lessons contain a graded scheme of instruction in the Sinhalese script, which is invariably used in Sri Lanka.

This course is designed for westerners, and therefore gives fuller comment and explanation than any existing course known to the compiler, and includes also some incidental notes about life in Ceylon in general, where the relevant facts are likely to be

---

1. Written forms are occasionally mentioned in the footnotes.

unfamiliar to the reader. It should provide an essential introduction to further study of the language and its literature.

This course was originally written in 1963–66 in collaboration with Dr Tissa Rajapatirana, now of the Australian National University, Canberra, who provided nearly all the sentences. He gave further assistance in 1967, and my debt to him is very great. I am also deeply indebted to Mr. S.B. Bandara, at present of the University of the West Indies, Mona, who helped in a revision of the whole course in 1968–70 and recorded the sentences on tape. I am grateful also to Mrs I.P. Jayasekara, Dr B.S.S.A. Wickramasuriya and Professor J. Tilakasiri of the University of Sri Lanka, and to Mr Kumara Ratnayaka of the Sri Lanka Broadcasting Corporation. The arduous job of typing was ably carried out by Winnie Garland and Susan Madigan. I should like to thank the Publications Committee of the School of Oriental and African Studies for meeting the cost of publication.

CHRISTOPHER REYNOLDS
London, May 1978.

---

*This book was basically completed in 1967, and therefore it used the familiar name 'Ceylon' throughout. It has not always seemed worth changing this name (which originates from the word **Sinhala** and is in no way derogatory), especially as the name Ceylon is still frequently used in Sri Lanka itself. Prices of goods quoted in the sentences may also refer to the 1960s.

PREFACE TO THE SECOND EDITION

This course, basically written in 1967, was submitted for publication in 1978. Stocks of the first issue being now exhausted, I am very grateful to the School of Oriental and African Studies for the opportunity to reissue in a corrected and improved form. The Course, as originally designed, consisted of 38 Lessons, but as it was only possible to include 31 Lessons in the first printing, I have taken this chance to add two further Lessons and an appendix. I am particularly glad that through the great courtesy of Dr David Walton of the University of Sussex, I am now enabled to give the script sections of Lessons 1–18 in a printed form, as I had originally intended.

I have benefited from the detailed comments of Professor K. Matzel of the University of Regensburg which appeared in *Indo-Iranian Journal* 24(1982), and in subsequent correspondence with him, though I have not thought it right to make as many adaptations of the text as he would have wished (especially in the transcription of final open vowels).

I have received welcome help from a number of other people, especially Ven. K. Piyatissa, Dr Asoka Premaratne, Professor G. D. Wijayawardhana, Professor A.V. Suraweera, Professor J. B. Disanayaka, Professor W. M. Gunatilaka, and Professor P. B. Meegaskumbura. Naturally I have also benefited from the study of other Sinhala courses of a similar kind to mine; these include D. Garusinghe: *Sinhalese, the spoken idiom*, Munich, H. Hüber 1962; M. W. Sugathapala de Silva and D. D. de Saram: *Spoken Sinhalese for the beginner*, Colombo, Ceylon University Press 1963; K. Matzel: *Einführung in die singhalesische Sprache* (in German), Wiesbaden, Harrassowitz 1966, 1983, 1987; G. H. Fairbanks, J. W. Gair and M. W. S. de Silva: *Colloquial Sinhalese*, 2 vols. Ithaca, N.Y., Cornell University 1968; D. D. de Saram: *An introduction to Spoken Sinhala*, University of Sri Lanka, 1977; J. B. Disanayaka: *Say it in Sinhala*, Colombo, Lake House, 1974, 1981.

I have kept the original title, 'Sinhalese'. Although the Sinhalese form 'Sinhala' is often used nowadays, Europeans usually distort it by lengthening and accenting the middle syllable. I have also left the familiar and friendly name 'Ceylon' in a few places (the current English form of the indigenous name is /Srilæŋkə/, rather than the more correct Srii Laŋkaa). There seems also no point in trying to update measurements and prices of a bygone or disappearing era. Although cents are hardly used nowadays (even the price of one cigarette – cigarettes are often sold singly – is about Rs.1/50), the point of the sentences containing such examples is to show how compound figures are expressed, not to give a guide to prices, which in any case are never stable for long. And, as in England, the metric system has been introduced with adaptations.

It may be worth pointing out that where, in a few places, the word 'colloquial' is used, this refers to something more vulgar than the ordinary spoken language.

CHRISTOPHER REYNOLDS
London, June 1994

CONTENTS

INTRODUCTION

Pronunciation

Vowels

a aa i ii u uu e ee o oo æ ææ

a, i, u, e, o and æ are short vowels; aa, ii, uu, ee, oo, ææ are long.

1. **a** is pronounced in two different ways, here called full and reduced. In the initial syllable of a word, and in all closed syllables (i.e. those ending in a consonant), it is full, and resembles a continental **a**, or the vowel in standard English **cut**. Elsewhere it is reduced to a neutral vowel ə, much as in unaccented syllables in English, e.g. **a**rise, m**a**chine.

mala (flower), pron. [malə]

malak (a flower), pron. [malak] (not [malək])

The sequence **aha** is however not realized as **ahə**- or **əhə**[1] but as **aha**- or **-əha**. Thus **ahasa** (sky) is pronounced [ahasə],[2] **maha** (great) is [maha] (not [mahə]), **egoḍaha** (that side) is [egoḍəha] (not [egoḍəhə]).

For the sequences **ayi** and **avu**, see under semivowels, below.

In the case of the very common verb **karanavaa** (do), and all its conjugational variants, the vowel in the initial syllable is realized as ə ([kərənəva]). This is the only purely Sinhalese word where this sound occurs in an initial syllable, but Sanskrit loan-words beginning with a double consonant often show this same feature.

prayoojana (use, n.), pron. [prəyoojənə]

dvaya (pair), pron. [dvəyə]

(English loan-words may also have the sound ə in places not covered by the general rule, e.g. nars (nurse), pron. [nərs], rabar (rubber), pron. [rabər]).

It is important to remember that **a** in an initial syllable in Sinhalese does not become reduced in quality when the second syllable is a closed one, e.g. **Mahinda** (name of the apostle of Buddhism in Ceylon, and of a well-known school in Galle) must not be pronounced [Məhində], but [Mahində]. To English ears this gives the

---

1. Except in certain literary verb-endings, e.g. giyaha (they went), pron. [giyəhə].
2. See also Consonants 4, below.

effect of an accent on the first syllable, where English speakers might tend to stress the second; in Sinhalese, accent is not significant, but the quality of the vowel **a** is; the vowel scheme of English words such as **balloon** is highly unusual in Sinhalese (and words of this type, when they appear in Sinhalese as loans, almost always use **æ** instead of **a** for the (unaccented) first syllable: **bælun**).

Where the full **a** sound is heard in final open syllables, it is normally written **aa** (i.e. as a long vowel). This convention avoids the ambiguities that would otherwise arise in realizing final open **-a**. (But Sinhalese spelling is not consistent here.)

The second portion of a compound word is sometimes treated as a separate word: Kataragama, pron. [Katərə-gamə].

2. **aa** resembles the **a** in **father**. In a final open syllable, and before declensional terminations or before the particles **da**, **lu** and **ma** it is normally shortened in duration, while retaining the same quality (except in disyllables where the first syllable is short, e.g. babaa). Sinhalese spelling is not consistent here.

lamayaa, lamayaage, lamayaaṭa (child, of child, to child), pron. [laməya, laməyage, laməyaṭə].

yanavaa, yanavaada (go, go?), pron. [yanəva, yanəvadə];

but

babaage, giyaada, (of baby, went?) pron. [babaage,[1] giyaadə].

This shortening is occasionally found in other words, e.g. takkaali (tomatoes), artaapal (potatoes), Hoomaagama, Varakaapola (place-names), pron. [takkali, artapal, Hoomagamə, Varəkapolə].

Otherwise, the vowel length of **aa** is appreciably greater than that of **a**.

baala (young), pron. [baalə].

3. **i, ii** and **u**, **uu** form two pairs, each containing a long and a short vowel. There is little difference in quality between the long **ii** and the short **i**, the important difference being one of length. The different vowel-sounds of **soot** and **boot** in standard English will serve for Sinhalese **u** and **uu**, but the Sinhalese **i** resembles a shortened form of the vowel-sound in **sheep**, rather than the **i** in **ship**.

In final open syllables **ii** and **uu** are normally pronounced as if written **i** and **u**.

English speakers must be careful to avoid diphthongs in pronouncing these

---

1 But ammaage is pronounced [ammage] and neither [amməge] nor [ammaage]. To English speakers this may sound as if it had two accents, on syllables 1 and 2.

vowels, especially before consonants such as **l**, **r**. **nuul** (thread) must not be pronounced [nuəl], **biira** (beer) must not be pronounced [biərə].

4. **e, ee, o, oo**. Here again the difference between the vowels in each pair is one of length, rather than quality. English speakers must be careful to avoid a diphthong (as in **rain**) when pronouncing Sinhalese **ee**, which is a pure vowel as in Italian **mese** or French **é**. **e** is the shortened equivalent of this vowel-sound, and is not the same as the **e** in English **met**, though the difference is not very great. The sound in English **rain** is similar to that of Sinhalese **eyi**, which is clearly distinguishable from **ee** to Sinhalese ears, though English ears may find the distinction difficult.

oo is a closer vowel than the sound in Eng. **pork**. It is entirely unlike the diphthong in **note**, but is a pure vowel as in Italian **Roma**. **o** is the shortened equivalent of this vowel-sound, and is not the same as the **o** in Eng. pot; the vowel-sound in Sinh. **pot** (books) is much more rounded.

Be careful therefore with such words a **meeka** (this), **ooka** (that), to pronounce as [meekə] (not [meikə]), [ookə] (not [oukə]).

In final open syllables, **ee** and **oo** are normally pronounced as if written **e** and **o**. Before declensional terminations, **ee** is generally shorted in speech where the previous syllable is heavy, e.g. iskooleeʈa (to the school) is pronounced [iskooleʈə], but kaḍeeʈa (to the shop), Yaapaneeʈa (to Jaffna), remain [kaḍeeʈə,[1] Yaapəneeʈə].

5. **æ, ææ** are like the vowel sounds in Eng. **cat**, **jam**. In final open syllables, no difference of length is normally audible; in polysyllabic words in such positions both **æ** and **ææ** are sometimes realized as ə, e.g. oonæ (must) may be heard as [oonə].

Consonants

      k g ŋ c j ñ ʈ ḍ t d n p b m y r l v s h ḥ ñ m̆

1. Stops
k, g, b sound as in English **kid, good, book**.

In many Indian languages, aspirated consonants have to be distinguished from un-

---

1. Sometimes realized, however, as [kaḍeʈʈə].

aspirated consonants, e.g. in Hindi there is a significant difference between **k** and **kh**. In Sinhalese this is not so, although there are in the Sinhalese script two separate characters representing **k** and **kh** in Sanskrit and Pali loan-words. In normal speech, Sinhalese initial **k-** often has slight aspiration, as in English. Intervocalically, there is sometimes little contact audible,

e.g. **ṭikak** (a little) may sound as [ṭiak],
dekakaṭa (to two) as dehekəṭə].

p as in English apple.

When initial, there is not usually much aspiration, so that it may sometimes be heard as **b** by English ears.

c, j are palatal stops, resembling palatalized **t′**, **d′** in Russian.

English **ch** as in **church** and **j** as in **judge** will do, but the initial consonant-sounds in **tube** and **duke**, as pronounced by many people in English, are perhaps better equivalents.

ṭ, ḍ are retroflex stops.

That is to say, the tip of the tongue is curled backwards where it touches the top of the mouth. This usually gives a characteristic hollow sound to the adjacent vowels, which is clearly noticeable with many Sinhalese or Indians when they are speaking English. The top of the tongue is not generally curved back so far when speaking Sinhalese as it is when speaking Tamil, for instance; but the characteristic retroflex sound should be clearly audible. ṭ and ḍ seldom stand initially, and never finally, in pure Sinhalese words.

t and **d** are true dental stops.

That is to say, the tip of the tongue must actually touch the teeth, or even be visible between them. English **t** and **d** are neither dental or retroflex; they are represented in Ceylon by ṭ, ḍ because they are clearly not dental, though most English speakers usually feel that they resemble more nearly the dental **t**, **d** (which are used in Ceylon to represent English **th**, as in **thick, then** – sounds which do not occur in Sinhalese). English speakers will find considerable difficulty in hearing a distinction between ṭ, ḍ and **t**, **d**, but they must make special efforts to pronounce them so that they are easily distinguishable to a Sinhalese listener.

k, **p** (less common) and **t** are the only stops which occur in final position at the end of a word.

2. Nasals

m, **n** sound as in English mat, not. When final in a word both these sounds are often replaced in speech, and sometimes in writing, by **ŋ** (as in **singer**). Thus **gan** and **gam** will both frequently sound as **gaŋ** (especially in isolation).

ŋ itself occurs in loan-words, or at the end of a word, where nasals, whether written **n**, **m**, or **ŋ**, are usually realized as **n** or **m** in correspondence with a following initial consonant; e.g. **maŋ balanavaa** (I look), **maŋ dækkaa** (I saw), where **maŋ** is realized as [**mam**] and [**man**] respectively.

n between two vowels is often very lightly pronounced, e.g. the first **n** in words such as **aninavaa, penenavaa, paniṭṭuva**. There is a tendency for vowels following nasal consonants to be nasalized; this is the case with all present-tense verbal endings in **-navaa**, where the whole ending is nasalized, e.g. **balanavaa**; contrast this with past-tense forms, e.g. **bæluvaa** (looked), where the ending is never nasalized.

ñ (as in Spanish) occurs normally as an allophone of **n** when a palatal consonant follows, and in such cases the orthography is not fixed, so that **n**, **ñ** and **ŋ** may all be found, e.g **punci, puñci** or **puŋci** (little). In a few words this sound also occurs before a vowel, e.g. **ñaav** (miaow), and it may also occur doubled intervocalically: **karaññam** (will do), **karapiñña** (curry leaf).[1]

3. Liquids

l is clear, and never has the 'dark' sound which occurs in Eng. **pull, milk**. American speakers may find this especially difficult.

r is normally realized very much as in standard (southern) English. A French or Northumbrian **r** is not intelligible in Ceylon, i.e. a word containing that sound may not be understood.

Be careful with the pronunciation of **r** immediately followed by another consonant; **karma** ('action') must not be pronounced like **kaama** (desire).

1. Also **karannam** and **karapiñca**.

When initial, **r** is fairly strongly aspirated, i.e **rææ** (night) sounds as [**hrææ**]. In pure Sinhalese words **r** does not occur as a final consonant.

4. Fricatives

s is usually much as in Eng. **sit**, but when followed by another consonant it is often very lightly pronounced, and sometimes hardly audible. An initial consonantal group beginning with **s-** (occurring only in loan-words) is preceded by **i-** in normal speech, though this is not usually written,[3] e.g. **strii** (woman), pron. [istri].

The English **sh** sound is not a significant phoneme in Sinhalese, but a palatal ʃ which may resemble an English **sh** is heard from some speakers in some contexts.

h is as in English **hit**. Between two similar vowels it is lightly pronounced, e.g. **ahasa** (sky) may sound as [**aasə**], **ehet** (but) is usually heard as [**eet**], **kihipayak** (several) may be written as **kiipayak**. (Beware of laying a stress on the second syllable of **kihipayak**.)

In many cases **h** in modern Sinhalese has developed from an older **s**, and the two letters often alternate in inflexional forms.

ḥ occurs finally in a few interjections, such as **caḥ**, and sounds as **ch** in Scottish **loch**.

5. Semivowels

y is like **y** in **yet**, but in intervocalic positions it is very lightly pronounced; **iyi** for instance will sound as **ii**. **a-** vowels before and after **y** tend to become closer, i.e. more like **e** or **æ**. The sequence -əyə in rapid speech tends to be realized as -**ee**.

v is a very lax fricative, something between Eng. **v** and **w**. Thus it will sound to an Englishman sometimes like **v**, but more often like **w**. This consonant often occurs at the end of a word; here it always resembles Eng. **w** more than **v**, e.g. **W** (double-u) is normally written in Sinhalese **ɖabliv**. The sequence **-əvə** in rapid speech tends to be realized as **-oo**.

Intervocalic **y** and **v** often represent glide-sounds, and may even be interchangeable, e.g. **tiyunaa** and **tivunaa** may both be written for a sequence of sounds which, but for the conventions of Sinhalese script, might well be written **tiunaa**.

The diphthongal sounds **ai** and **au** (resembling the vowel-sounds in Eng. **hide**

---

3. It is written in this book, however.

and **crown**) are conventionally written **ayi** and **avu** in Sinhalese. Thus **naṭayi** (dances), pron. [naṭai], **pæṭavu** (young ones), pron. [pæṭau]. These spellings conflict with the general rules for the pronunciation of **a**, as given above, which would be satisfied if these sounds were represented by the closed syllables **ay** and **av** respectively. **av** is also often written in such words (**pæṭav**), but **ay** hardly ever. In fact **y**, whatever vowel may precede it, is hardly ever written without a vowel after it, though e.g. **æyi** (why) might be equally logically written **æy**.

6. **Half-nasals**

Peculiar to Sinhalese* is the half-nasal. This is found before voiced stops, where **n̆ga**, **n̆ja**, **n̆ḍa**, **n̆da**, **m̆ba** are significantly different from **nga**, **nja**, **nḍa**, **nda**, **mba**. (**n̆ja** occurs very rarely). Each of these half-nasal combinations counts as one letter, and has a special symbol in the script. They do not, therefore, lengthen a preceding syllable, i.e. in **kanda** (hill) there is a heavy (long) syllable **kan-**, followed by a short one **-da**, but in **kan̆da** (tree-trunk) there are two light syllables only, **ka-** and **n̆da**.

The half-nasal sound is sometimes hardly audible except as a nasalization of the preceding vowel. A half-nasal combination is always followed immediately by a vowel.

7.

The Sinhalese script has a complete set of aspirated stops

kh, gh, ch, jh, ṭh, ḍh, th, dh, ph, bh,

which are often used in writing Sanskrit and other borrowed words, but they are not pronounced in a significantly different way from the unaspirated k, g, c, j, ṭ, ḍ, t, d, p, b.

Similarly, the script has separate symbols for retroflex ɳ and ɭ , and for palatal and retroflex ʃ, ʂ, but these are not realized in a significantly different way from **n**, **l**, **s**. Sometimes however spelling may usefully differentiate between homophones; **kala** (time), **kaɭa** (pots) – also **kaɭa** (done), but pronounced [kələ]; **balalaa** (having looked), **baɭalaa** (cat).

8.

A sound **f** (usually bilabial) may occur in the pronunciation of certain borrowed

*And Maldivian.

words. It is felt to be a kind of **p**, and is frequently replaced by **p.**

The English letter **z**, though it is used in the romanizing of some Sinhalese surnames such as Zoysa, Zylva, is pronounced as an **s**; the English letter itself is referred to in Sinhalese as **isæḍ**.

Neither **f** or **z** exist in the Sinhalese script.

9. **Doubling**

Except for **h**, **ḥ** and half-nasals, all consonants may be doubled, though double **rr** and **ŋŋ** are never written in the script. When a consonant is doubled it must be so pronounced, e.g. **kk** as in Eng. **bookcase**, **ll** as often heard in Eng. **wholly**. (Doubling a consonant has no effect, as it has in English, on the preceding vowel.) Apart from doubled consonants, the only consonant clusters that occur in proper Sinhalese (i.e. non-borrowed) words consist of nasal + voiced stop or c. Nasal + other unvoiced stops occur at internal junctions, e.g. Gam-pola.

Where a word ending in a consonant is immediately followed by a word beginning with a vowel, the consonant is pronounced (though not written) double. Here a final **-n** or **-m** is usually realized as **ŋŋ** (see on **n** above).

ekak æti (there is one thing),	pron. [ekakkæti]
ekat ekaṭa (perhaps),	pron. [ekattekəṭə]
kaar-eka (the car),	pron. [kaarrekə]
æyi ee (why is that?),	pron. [æyyee] (see on **y** above).
vam ata (the left hand),	pron. [vaŋŋatə]

The word **maŋ** (I) is sometimes an exception to this rule:

maŋ aavaa (I came),	pron. [maŋaava].

10.

In pronouncing final stopped consonants, especially before a pause, the breath is often continued after the tongue is removed from the place of utterance, which may produce a kind of nasal aftersound. This is confusing at first, but very easy to get used to. For example, **bat** (rice) may sometimes sound to the English speaker like Eng. **button**. In reciting poetry or music, when a closed syllable of this kind has to be prolonged ('dragged', as they say), the vowel itself is not lengthened but the prolongation is attached to the nasal aftersound[1], and this may also occur in the

1. E.g. not mala-a-a-ak, but malakn-n-n.

middle of a word between two consonants (e.g. a Pali word such as **Buddhassa** may sound as [Budn-hasn-sə]). Final **-k** is often not released and therefore inaudible; in the common termination **-ak**, its presence can be known by the quality of the preceding **a** vowel.

11.
In rapid speech, many assimilations and abbreviations occur; in particular, a final consonant is often assimilated to an initial consonant in the following word or particle.

kekkak tanaa (having constructed a hook) → kekkat-tanaa
mokak-da (what) → mokad-da

Where a final -**a**(ə) is followed by an initial **a**-, the vowel-sounds generally coalesce and sound as long **aa**; diga + arinavaa → digaarinavaa (open out). Final -**a**(ə) followed by initial **u**- (as in ata ussanna, raise your hand) often gives the effect of an English diphthongal **o**. In formal recitation, e.g. of poetry, where one word ends in a vowel and the following word begins with a vowel, a glottal stop is often put between.

Accent

Accent is not a significant feature of the Sinhalese language. The effect of this to English ears, which find it almost impossible to hear sound-sequences without also hearing accents, will be that the same word may appear to be sometimes accented on one syllable and sometimes on another. The same thing occurs, for example, with French. Any syllable of a Sinhalese word may be prolonged for special emphasis, but this does not constitute an accent. The prolongation of an ə-vowel sounds surprising to most people, as when **eekaṭa** (to that) is heard as [eekəṭəə], or **hoňdaṭa** (well, adv.) as [hoňdəəṭə].

It is possible to say, however, that certain words or particles, such as **da**, **ne** are usually spoken without stress. Initial short vowels are often spoken at a lower pitch than the subsequent syllable, which may tend to make especially initial **u**- difficult to distinguish.

LESSON 1

hadanavaa	make, mend
balanavaa	look (at)
yanavaa	go
enavaa	come
bonavaa	drink
dæn	now
ada	today
heṭa	tomorrow
hæmadaama	every day
mama, maŋ	I
api	we
pota	book
puṭuva	chair
tee	tea
lamayaa	child, boy
minihaa	man, person
ammaa	mother
taattaa	father
mahattayaa	gentleman, Mr (following the name)
eyaa	he, she
ee gollo,[1] **ee gollan**	they (lit. those people)

(a) All verbs end in the present tense in **-navaa** (always nasalized in speech), and are usually listed in this form in dictionaries. The vowel preceding **-navaa** is either **a**, **i** or **e**; **bonavaa** is the only verb which forms an exception to this. In a very small number of verbs, **-navaa** is preceded by another **n** (e.g. dannavaa).

1. Some speakers prefer the form **ee golla** or **ee gollaa**. There should be more stress on **ee** than on **golla**.

This verb-form is used without change in all three persons, both singular and plural, and in meaning it may refer, according to text, either to an action actually being done, or to one which is done habitually, or to one which will be done shortly; i.e. **maŋ yanavaa** may mean:

(1) I am actually on the way
(2) I go (e.g. on Tuesdays)
(3) I will go soon (as in English we say 'I am going tomorrow' as well as 'I will go tomorrow').

(b) The order of words in a Sinhalese sentence is very variable, almost any order often being possible, though with difference of emphasis. There is a general preference for the order: subject, adverb, object, verb. Alterations to this pattern tend to give special emphasis to the word displaced, e.g. if the verb is placed at the beginning it receives special emphasis, though the actual stress placed on individual words also plays a part here.

taattaa puṭuva hadanavaa	father is mending the chair
	(normal order)
puṭuva taattaa hadanavaa	**father** is mending the chair
taattaa hadanavaa puṭuva	father is mending the **chair**
hadanavaa taattaa puṭuva	father is **mending** the chair

or –

ammaa dæn tee bonavaa	mother is drinking tea now
	(normal order)

where all of the 23 possible variants on this order are possible, in certain circumstances.

(c) The vocabulary above contains no equivalent for 'you'. There is no generally acceptable word for 'you' in Sinhalese. Between friends and intimates, **oyaa** (lit. 'that person') is very commonly used, or sometimes **mee lamayaa** (lit. 'this child'); when addressing a superior or a stranger it is usually best to use the 3rd person, e.g.

taattaaṭa oonæda?	does father want (it)?
	i.e. do you want it, father?
Gunapaala mahattayaa ehema hitanavaada?	does Mr. Gunapaala think so?
	i.e. do you think so, Mr. Gunapaala?

In the plural, **oya gollo** ('those people') may be used for 'you all'.

It is modern policy to favour the use of **mahattayaa** (Mr) by itself as an equivalent for 'you' (of males) in all formal cases:

mahattayaaṭa hoňdaṭa ninda giyaada iiye?	did Mr (i.e. did you) sleep well last night?

Some people may use **tamuse** in this fashion, but this is not recommended. Village folk may use **unnæhæ**, **unnæhe** or **ohe** in respectful contexts, and **uṁba** or **bola(ŋ)** in more intimate contexts. Other equivalents for 'you' sometimes heard in certain contexts include **tamunnaanse**, **obatumaa** (both respectful) and **baŋ** (intimate).

The foreigner should of course be respectful whenever he is in any doubt. It is nearly always possible to manage without using any second personal pronoun at all.

api (we) is not infrequently used of oneself alone, instead of **maŋ**.

(d) **hadanavaa** (make, mend) may also mean 'try' in certain contexts; or 'bring up' (children etc.). **tee hadanavaa** to 'make' tea, usually refers to the 'making' of an individual cup, and therefore corresponds more nearly to Eng. 'pour out' – whereas **tee vakkaranavaa**, to 'pour' tea, may refer to the whole process of preparing tea, and therefore correspond more nearly to Eng. 'make tea'.

balanavaa also has to be translated in various ways. Of animals, and sometimes also of human beings, it is 'to examine', e.g. of a doctor and his patient; of persons, it is often 'to look after', or just 'to see'. Of things – but not of persons – it can be 'to look at', and sometimes 'to look for'. Also it may, like **hadanavaa**, mean 'to try' to do something.

Sentences headed A are for practice in translating Sinhalese into English.

A.
ammaa tee hadanavaa — mother is making/pouring tea
lamayaa pota balanavaa — the boy is looking at the book
Soomapaala mahattaya tee bonavaa — Mr S is drinking tea
minihaa puṭuva hadanavaa
5 ammaa lamayaa balanavaa
taattaa heṭa enavaa
heṭa ee gollo enavaa
minihaa hæmadaama enavaa
eya ada enavaa
10 minihaa ada puṭuva hadanavaa

Note: Be careful not to stress the second syllable of verbs such as hadanavaa, balanavaa (see Introduction). The vowel-sound in the second syllable is ə, not a.

Sentences headed B are for practice in translating English into Sinhalese.

B

The boy is going
Father is coming
We are drinking
They are coming
5 I am looking at the book (reading the book)
He is drinking tea
The man will mend the chair tomorrow
We drink tea every day
Mother pours out the tea every day
10 We are going now

Script

Sinhalese is always written in a script of its own. Although we use here a systematic transcription in roman letters, in Lanka itself such transcriptions are not generally used or understood. It is therefore essential for the beginner who wishes to learn to read and write to learn the script as soon as possible.

Sinhalese script, like all Indian scripts, is syllabic; that is to say each sign normally represents not a letter but a syllable. There is a separate basic sign connected with each consonant; these when used by themselves represent that consonant followed by the vowel **a**. They can be modified in various ways to indicate that other vowels may or may not follow that consonant.

E.g. ම = ma, මි = mi, මු = mu, ම් = m, etc.

Here we shall start with five simple consonants, each of which includes the vowel **-a**.

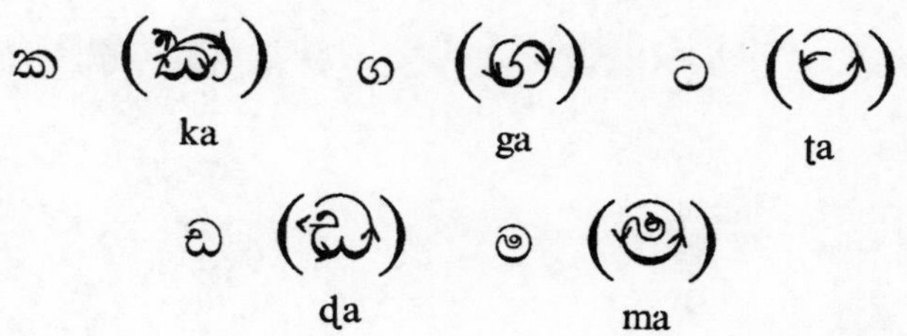

(Arrows mark the direction in which the letter is formed).

Sinhalese letters are not joined together in cursive writing, and there are no capital letters.

Where a letter begins with a 'platform', as in ඩ , the platform is made first , followed by the rest of the letter ඩ.

කග	මඩම	කමකට	මඩමකටම
කට	මටම	ගමකට	
කම	කටට	මගකට	
කඩ	ගමට	කටකට	
ගම gama	මගට	මඩමක	
මඩ	කටක	කටටම	
මට mata	ගමක		
මග	මගක		
ටක			
මම mama			

LESSON 2

denavaa	give (lend, sell, pay)
liyanavaa	write
koo?	where?
mehe	here
nææ, næhæ	(there) is not; no!
maṭa	to me, for me
apiṭa[1]	to us, for us
eyaaṭa	to him/her, for him/her
ee gollanṭa	to them, for them
liyuma	letter (missive)
gama	village
salli	money
gedara	home, house
iskoolee	school
eka	one
heṭaṭa	(for) tomorrow
dænaṭa	for the time being
adaṭa	(for) today

(a) The dative case of a noun always ends in **-ṭa.** This form is also used in connection with verbs of motion, e.g. to go **to the village**. Notice the forms **maṭa, gollanṭa.** With certain common words, such as **gedara, iskoolee, -ṭa** is often omitted with the verbs **yanavaa, enavaa. gedaraṭa** in rapid speech may be pronounced **[gedəṭṭə]**, and **gedara enavaa** as **[gedərenəva]**. A final **-aaṭa** is often pronounced **-aṭə** (but **not** -əṭə), e.g. lamayaaṭa, ammaaṭa, pr. **[laməyaṭə, ammaṭə]** (see Introduction).

-ṭa can also be added to **ada, heṭa, dæn** (notice the form **dænaṭa**). Here the difference of meaning is not always obvious.

(b) There are no separate words in Sinhalese corresponding to Eng. 'a' and 'the', but there is a suffix **-k** which gives the effect of the indefinite article 'a'. In the case

1. Also apaṭa (which is the written form).

of animate nouns, i.e. those denoting a living being, the final **-aa** of the noun is changed to **e** before this **-k**.

pota	book, the book
mahattayaa	gentleman, the gentlemen
potak	a book
mahattayek	a gentleman

The dative suffix **-ṭa** can be added after this indefinite **k**; here a connecting vowel is needed, which is **-a-** in the case of inanimate nouns and **-u-** in the case of animate nouns.[1]

potakaṭa	to (for) a book
mahattayekuṭa	to (for) a gentleman

For 'a mother', 'a father', **ammaa kenek, taattaa kenek** are more respectful than **ammek, taattek**. (**kenek** means 'a person').[2] **Tee** and **salli** are plural words; **tee-ekak** (lit. 'a one tea') means 'a cup of tea', and **salliyak** means 'a coin' (originally half a cent).

When **eka** (one) is used before a noun, the suffix **-k** is required after the noun; **eka liyumak**, one letter.

(c) The suffix **-t** adds the meaning of 'also' or 'even'.

mamat / maat yanavaa	I will go too
apiṭat denavaa	will give to us also
gamakaṭat yanavaa	will even go to a village

Before **-t**, a final long vowel is shortened (except in monosyllables); **eyat**, he also.

Where **-t** is added to a word ending in a consonant, **-u-** is inserted; **dænut**, even now.

(d) **koo** in the meaning 'where?' can only be used with a noun. In such sentences no verb 'to be' is required.

koo pota? / pota koo?	where (is) the book?

Answer:

pota nææ	the book is not (here)
pota mehe	the book (is) here

---

1. This **-u-** however is sometimes hardly audible.

2. **mahattayan kenek** is sometimes used for **mahattayek**. For **kenek**, see lesson 11.

No word for 'is' is required here either. But where the sentence contains a verbal form ('where are you going?'), **koo** cannot be used in this sense.

(e) Be careful with the pronunciation of words such as pota – potak – potakaṭa – potakaṭat. They are pronounced [**potə – potak – potəkəṭə – potəkəṭat**] respectively (see Introduction). Remember that the second vowel in **potakaṭa** must be realized as ə, not as **a**.

A.

koo lamayaa?
taattaa koo?
koo ammaa?
ammaa nææ
liyuma mehe nææ
api dæn gamaṭa yanavaa
lamayaa ammaaṭa liyumak liyanavaa
taattaa minihaaṭa salli denavaa
ammaa ee gollanṭa tee denavaa
lamayaa heṭa iskoolee yanavaa
lamayaa ammaaṭat liyumak liyanavaa
mamat tee bonavaa
mama teet bonavaa
taattaa minihaaṭa sallit denavaa
api heṭa gedara yanavaa
lamayek potak balanavaa
mahattayaa tee-ekak bonavaa
eyaa dæn mehe nææ
mehe puṭuvak nææ
ammaa, maṭat kee too?

Note that **minihaa** or **ee minihaa** (that man) are often used where Eng. would say simply 'he'. (Similarly **ee gææni** (that woman) is used for 'she').

Notice the following:

lamayaa mehe yanavaa enavaa (the verbs usually in this order), the child is coming and going, i.e. often comes, here.

taattaa ada heṭa enavaa, father will come to-day (or) tomorrow, i.e. in the near future.

minihaa dæn dæn mehe enavaa, he is on his way here now.

Words in round brackets in B sentences do not need to be put into Sinhalese.

B. Where is the letter?
Where is (there) a chair?
Father will come to the village tomorrow.
The boy is going home.
5 Father gives the man money (=pays him) for a book.
At the moment I am writing a letter.
We are going home for (the day) tomorrow.
Father will give the man money for a chair also.
We will come home tomorrow also.
10 We also are going home tomorrow.
Father is mending a chair also.
A man is making a chair.
The man is looking (over) here.
They will come here tomorrow.
15 The book is not (here).
Mother gives tea to a child also.
I am making a chair for the boy also.
He is writing a book.
The child looks at the book every day.
20 A man also is coming here.

Note: In 13 and 14 above, where the word 'here' seems to imply motion ('hither'), **mehe** can still be used.

Script

ත  ද  න 

ta da na

ප  බ 

pa ba

To lengthen the **a** vowel, a sign ා (called **ælapilla**, side-mark) is placed after the consonantal sign.

තා	නා	පා	බා
taa	naa	paa	baa

daa has a special form දා. The ælapilla is not considered a separate letter, but to form part of the previous symbol.

In handwriting, ත and න are usually as indistinguishable as u and n in English handwriting. Even in printed books, they often look very similar.

තද	කාට	ගනන	දාගබ	බදාදා
තන	පාට	මතක	මානන	පතාකා
දාන	බාග	බතට	පාගන	පනදා
දාත	නාග	පනත	පානම	බාගදා
පන	පාත	ගමන	කාටද	
පත	පාන	කපන	මාමාට	
පට	දාන	මකන	පතාම	
බන	තාම	පතන		
නම	පාප			
කන	ගගා			
කද	කකා			
නානා	පගා			
මාමා	කනා			
පාගා	කඩා			
මාතා	බබා			
බඩ	පනා			
	තමා			
	තබා			
	කාම			

LESSON 3

livvaa	wrote
dunnaa	gave
bæluvaa	looked (at)
hæduvaa	made
bivvaa	drank
giyaa	went
aavaa	came
iiye	yesterday
mage	my
ape	our
eyaage	his, her
ee gollange	their
mokak-da (pron. [**mokaddə**])	what?
ballaa	dog
balalaa	cat
gonaa	bullock, bull
sudu	white
ratu	red
loku	big
puŋci, **poḍi**	little
mee	this
ee, **oya**, **ara**	that
ehe, **ohe**, **arahe, ahare**	there

(a) All verbs end in the past tense in **-aa**. This ending is always pronounced very short (**-a**, but not -ə), and never nasalized.

(b) **-ge**[1] is a gentitive case-ending, which is only applicable to animate nouns. A connecting vowel **u** is needed after an indefinite **k** suffix;[2] **ballekuge**, of a dog. Notice the special form **ape**, our.[3] **mage, eyaage** and other such genitive forms are often pronounced **maye, eyaye** etc., in rapid speech (i.e with a glide-sound instead of inter-vocalic **g**). Final **-aage** is often pronounced **-age** (but not **-əge**), e.g. **lamayaage, ammaage**, pr. [laməyage, ammage] (see Introduction).

(c) **-yi** when added to a predicative word has the effect of the copular verb 'to be'; **pota lokuyi**, the book is/was big. The converse of this is **pota loku nææ**, the book is not big; here **-yi** is not required. **loku** cannot be separated from **nææ** without changing the meaning (see (d) below), so that the only other possible order of words is **loku nææ pota**.

This **-yi** must be added after adjectival words ending in **-a** or **-u**. Where such a word ends in **-i, -yi** is usually added in writing, but is hardly audible in speech. It is not used after words ending in a consonant.

For the pronunciation of final **-yi**, see Introduction (**-uyi** is pronounced **-uy** and **-ayi** is pronouned **-ay**).

pota puŋci(yi)	the book is small
mee mage puʈuva	this is my chair
mee potak	this is a book
mee mage potak	this is a book of mine

Notice here that the **k** suffix may still be added even if the previous word has a **-ge** ending.

Before **-yi**, a final long vowel is shortened, except in monosyllables: **eyayi**, (it) is he. **-yi** should not be added after an interrogative word (e.g. **mokakda**); no copular is required here.

mee mokakda?	what is this?

nææ cannot be used to negate nouns or pronouns (such as **mage**); a different word must be used in saying 'not mine', 'not a chair' (Lesson 8).

(d) Where adjectival words are not predicative, they must immediately precede their noun.

---

1. In books, usually written **-gee**.

2. This **-u** however is sometimes inaudible.

3. To make clear the distinction between **api** and **ape** it is necessary to stress or lengthen the **-e**.

puŋci pota	the small book
pota puŋci(yi)	the book is small

The same rule applies to genitive case-forms, which must precede the noun they qualify.

ape ballaa	our dog
ballaa ape	the dog is ours.

(e) Of the three words corresponding to 'that', **oya** represents something near, or connected with, the person who is spoken to,[1] **ara** represents something more distant, and **ee** is a general term used in reference to something previously mentioned. These words are used adjectivally; as nouns, 'that (thing)' can be represented by **eeka**, **araka**, **ooka** (lit. 'that one'; ooka = oya + eka), and 'this thing' by **meeka** (lit. 'this one').

When asking and answering the question What is this/that? the normal forms will be mee/ara mokakda? oya/ee potak, though meeka/araka mokakda? ooka/eeka potak are also used. (Notice the correlation of **mee** and **oya**). But with adjectival predicates, a noun-ending is needed in the subject; thus for 'that is mine', **oya mage** alone is insufficient; we must say **ooka** (or **oya eka**) mage, or else oya **mage eka**, 'that is my one', and similarly with 'that is for me' **ooka maṭayi.**

The adjectival forms **mee** etc. are also often used before verbs:[2]

taattaa ara enavaa	there's father coming.

The words **menna**, **onna**, **aanna** (or **anna**) mean 'look here', 'look there', or 'here is', 'there is'. These words are sometimes shortened to **meeŋ**, **aaŋ**.

aanna taattaa enavaa	look, there's father coming
onna oya puŋci sudu pota mage	that little white book there is mine
menna salli	here's the money.

(f) An animate noun which is the direct object of a verb may have -va added to it.[3]

maŋ ballaava[4] bæluvaa	I examined the dog

This **-va** may also be added after the indefinite suffix **k**. An intervening -u- is often inaudible.

api ballekuva bæluvaa	we examined a dog

1. Hence **oyaa** means 'you', while **eyaa** means 'he'.
2. Particularly in the incomplete form (lesson 4) and in commands (lesson 6).
3. See also lesson 13 **a**.
4. Pron. [**ballavə**] (see Introduction).

-va is also added after pronouns. In the case of the pronoun **mama**, I, the form **maava** is used.

Apart from the optional use of this termination, there is no distinction between a subject case and an object case in Sinhalese, and the term 'direct case' is used in this book for all forms in which a grammatical subject or object appears.

(g) **gonaa**, normally translated 'bull', is the ordinary draught animal of Ceylon, used for pulling carts. It is often very small, and has a hump on its neck. It is not at all dangerous, and is a by-word not for fierceness but for stupidity. **ballaa** (dog) as a term of abuse is considered insulting.

A.
mama iiyet potak bæluvaa
ee puʈuva puŋci(yi)
mee ballaa suduyi
mee puʈuva mage
mage ee poɖi pota nææ
ee minihaa mee dæn giyaa
ape loku lamayaa gamaʈa giyaa
sudu mahattayek iiye mehe aavaa
mage pota ratu ekak
mage eka puŋci puʈuvak
ee mahattayaa iiye ape iskooleeʈa aavaa
eyaa loku nææ, puŋci(yi)
taattaage tee-eka ammaa bivvaa
oya mage eka
ratu eka mage
puŋci ammaage lamayaa gedara giyaa
mage puʈuva(yi) ee
mamayi lamayaage taattaa
minihaa gonaava balanavaa
ara mokakda? ee puʈuvak
mee mokakda? oya salliyak
mee maŋ
maŋ heʈa ohe enavaa
oya pota taattaage
oya ratu pota maʈayi

B. My book is red.
The boy drank tea.
The man went to the village.
Mother came home.
5 I looked at that book.
Father gave me (some) money yesterday.
He mended the chair.
That is mine.
This one is a big chair.
10 That big white bullock is ours.
That is for father.
Where is my chair?
Where is the boy's father?
This book is that child's.
15 Their bullock is not here.
The cat is white.
Our boy is big now.
This is my father.
He gave me his dog.
20 The mother looks after the child.
We went home yesterday.
He is my father.
The boy is going home.
That one belongs to that boy.
25 That big dog over there is ours.

Notes

A. 4 mage or mageyi.

5 'is not here' – may perhaps be lost; 'my book has gone'. Remember that this cannot mean 'is not mine'.

6 mee dæn, 'just this minute'.

9 ratu ekak, 'red one'. Notice that **eka** here is used just as in English; cf. 14 below, mage eka, 'my one'.

11 iskoolee here adds **-ṭa** because it is not being used in the specialized sense of 'to go to school' (i.e. as a pupil). A similar distinction occurs

in English ('to school' and 'to the school'). iskooleeṭa is pronounced [**iskooleṭə**], see Introduction. It is normal to say ape iskoolee, rather than mage iskoolee; so also ape gedara, our house, not mage gedara.

12 Literally, 'he is not big, (is) little'. No word corresponding to Eng. 'but' is required.

16 The brothers of a father are not referred to by the word usually translated 'uncle', nor are the sisters of a mother referred to by the word usually translated 'aunt'. Instead, these relatives are regarded as a kind of father and of mother respectively, and their spouses conversely as kinds of mother or of father. A distinction is made however as to whether these relatives are older or younger than the real parents; **puŋci ammaa** or **kuɖammaa** is the younger sister of the mother, the elder one being called **loku ammaa**. Similarly a father's brothers will be called either **loku taattaa** or **puŋci taattaa**: the latter is also called **baappaa**.[1]

18 mamayi or maŋ. lamayaage is pronounced [**laməyage**], see Introduction. For the context, see B13 below.

22 'It's me!'

23 **ohe** means 'in your direction', 'your way'.

24 'This book is father's'. This may mean 'This book is yours, father' (see lesson 1 c).

B. 8 See (e) above.

13 This kind of expression is sometimes used in contexts where we might ask 'Where is your husband?' Words meaning 'husband' or 'wife' are generally avoided in Lanka, often even when speaking English.

18 My: **mage** and **ape** are equally acceptable here (cf. note on A11 above).

20 Note that **balanavaa** alone is insufficient to give the meaning 'look at' a person (see lesson 1, note).

---

1. Alternative names for these uncles are **loku appaa** or **mahappaa**, and **kuɖappaa**. **appaa** by itself however is not generally used for 'father', but **appacci** is used in Kandyan districts. **kuɖaa** is a literary word for 'little', and **maha** for 'great'.

Script ච  ජ 

ca ja

To remove the inherent vowel **-a** from a consonantal sign, two symbols are used (called **al-kiriima** signs), ..්.. and ..්... The second is used over letters which end by curving upwards to the left.

ක් ග් ට් ඩ් ම් ත් ද් න් ප් බ් ච් ජ්

These now represent consonants without any vowel.

තට	මන්ද	පප්පඩම්
ජඩ	බන්ඩා	තමන්ට
පච	කාක්කා	තට්ටම
ජප	තාත්තා	කප්පන්න
මත	බාප්පා	ජනතා
ගන	පප්පා	නග්ගන්නා
ජන	දන්නා	මක්කාද
ගජ	කන්නක්	කඩන්ට
දන්	ගන්නත්	කපන්ඩ
ගම්	කන්ද	නටන්න
බක්	නන්ද	මකන්නට
නම්	පච්ච	තමාම
පත්	මම්ම	දමන්නා
කත්	චන්ද	තකන්නාට
චාම්	කම්ම	තබ්බන
පාන්	නාන්න	මඩ්ඩන
තාක්	දන්න	තම්බන
මාත්	මාන්න	කන්කානම
පාත්	දන්න	

බත්	ජපන්
දත්	දන්ඩ
කන්	මතක්
ටක්	කමත්
මද	ගබක්
මජ්ජ	තට්ට
	බද්ද

LESSON 4

kohoma-da	how?
mokada	what?
monavaa-da (pl.)	what?
æyi **mokada**	why?
kavda	who?
kaage-da	whose?
kaaʈa-da	to whom? for whom?
kavadaa-da	when?
kohe-da **kotana-da**	where?
væɖa	work (in general)
væɖee	specific piece of work
væɖakaarayaa	servant
nama	name
aliyaa	elephant
karanavaa	do
keruvaa	did
metana	here
etana **otana** **atana**	there

(a) In interrogative sentences, an interrogative particle **-da** is usually found (though sometimes intonation alone may suffice to indicate a question, as in Eng. 'you are going?'). The particle **-da** may sometimes be added directly to the verb. If however it is added to any other word in the sentence, then the incomplete form of the verb, which is explained below, must be used.

mokak karanavaada? mokakda karanne?	what are (you) doing?

With **koo** (where), when used as in lesson 2 above, the particle **da** is not required.

pota koheda? / pota koo?	where is the book?[1]

koo is also used as an initial exclamation, 'what?' or 'oh!'

koo, pota otanada?	oh, is the book over there?

The word to which **-da** is added receives a certain emphasis thereby.

ee gollo heṭa enavaada?	are they coming tomorrow?
ee gollo enne heṭada?	is it tomorrow that they are coming?
heṭa enne ee golloda?	is it they who are coming tomorrow?
meeka eyaageda?	is this his?
meekada eyaage?	is it this which is his?

In the case of the interrogative words **kavda** and **mokada** (who, why) the **-da** cannot be separated from the first part of the word, and they are therefore printed without a hyphen. However **mokak-da** (what) can sometimes be separated into **mokak** (or **mak**) and **-da**, as in the example given above; and so can case-forms such as **kaava-da** (lesson 3 (f)), **kaaṭa-da, mokaṭa-da**.

monavaa is sometimes used without **-da** as a one-word sentence, 'what?'.

Normal usage with the interrogative words listed above is to keep **-da** with the interrogative word and use the verb in the incomplete form, since if **da** is added directly to the verb the sentence often becomes a kind of complaint.[2] For instance, eyaa ada kohe yanavaada? where will he go today? often implies 'he won't go anywhere to-day'.

(b) The incomplete form of the present tense is arrived at by changing **-navaa** to **-nne**, and of the past tense by changing final **-aa** to **-e**.

balanavaa	balanne
bæluvaa	bæluve

The incomplete form of **nææ** is **nætte**.

(c) Whereas **mokakda** (what) is grammatically singular and indefinite ('a which thing?'), **monavaa** is plural, 'which things?' Thus mee mokakda? What is this? mee monavaada? What are these? Similarly the plural forms of **meeka, eeka, ooka,**

---

1. There is however a certain difference between these two, namely that **pota koo**? is a kind of command, and the person addressed will be expected to **fetch** the book. This is not so where **koheda** is used.

2. Unless it is part of reported speech; see lesson 27.

araka are **meevaa, eevaa, oovaa, aravaa.**[1]

Most of the interrogative words listed in this lesson can also be used with the dative case-ending **-ṭa**. Thus **kavadaa-da** and **kavadaaṭa-da** both mean 'on which day' (**daa** = day): **kavadaaṭada** usually refers to the future, **kavadaada** either to the past or to the future. Where 'when' means 'at what time of day', it must be translated differently.[2]

The dative forms of **kohe-da, kotana-da** are **kohaaṭa-da** (**koheṭa** is less common), **kotanaṭa-da**, which specifically mean 'whither?', but the form **koheda** is also used in this sense (cf. note on lesson 2 (b)).

koheda mee yanne? where are (you) going now?

Similarly, eyaa mehe enavaa, he is coming here. **atana, otana, etana, metana** may all take a **-ṭa** suffix in the meaning 'thither', 'hither' (all these contain the word **tæna**, place, with various prefixes). **aharaṭa** (or **arahaṭa**), **ohaaṭa, ehaaṭa, mehaaṭa** (from **ahare, ohe, ehe, mehe**) give the same meanings. In some contexts **metana** and **mehe** are not interchangeable; e.g.

mehe balanavaa means 'looks in this direction' (lesson 2 B 13).

but

metana balanavaa would mean 'looks for something here'.

The dative form **mokaṭa-da** 'why?' (also **mokakaṭa-da, monavaaṭa-da**) means 'for what purpose?', and not 'as a result of what?' **æyi** is best placed at the end of a sentence, when asking a question; at the beginning of a sentence it is usually inferential; cf. the difference in English between 'why didn't you want it?' and 'Why, didn't you want it?' 'What, didn't you want it?' **æyi** is also used in answer to a call or summons, 'Yes?'

(d) Notes on pronunciation:

(i) In the word **nama** (name), the **-m-** is often inaudible, and the word sounds like **nava**, with nasalized vowels.

(ii) **kotanaṭada** is usually pronounced in rapid speech **[kotenṭədə]**; so also **[metenṭə]**, etc.

(iii) In **kohaaṭada** and similar words (including **monavaada**), the **-aa-** is shortened in rapid speech to **-a-** (see Introduction). Some speakers also double the **ṭ** and say **[kohaṭṭə]** or **[koheṭṭə]**. Similarly **mehaaṭa** may become **[meheṭṭə], aharaṭa**

---

1. **mevvaa, ovvaa** are sometimes used for **meevaa, oovaa**.

2. See lesson 8.

may become [**ahaṭṭə**],[1] **ehaaṭa** and **ohaaṭa** may become [**eheṭṭə, oheṭṭə**]. **mokakaṭa** becomes [**mokeṭṭə**] or [**mohokəṭə**]. In **kavadaada**, **-aa-** is shortened, or may be omitted: [**kavədadə, kavaddə**]. (But in **hæmadaama**, every day, which contains the same word **daa**, the full vowel length is preserved).

(iv) **-da** is not spoken with a high pitch, even if the pitch rises on the verb preceding it

↗   ↘
yanavaada?

It is important to remember, however, not to lengthen or stress the syllable written **vaa** in such cases. **-vaa** is pronounced [**-va**], and the stress, if any, will appear to be on the first syllable of the verb.

A.   væḍakaarayaa væḍa karanavaa.

oya kavda?

nama mokakda?

ee kavda ee?

5   mee kavda mee lamayaa?

taattaa kavadaada enne?   *when.*

mahattayaa kohaaṭada?

mee aliyaa kaageda?

kotanaṭada yanne?   *– don't use. – koheda / kohaaṭada instead.*

10   taattaaṭa dæn kohomada?

tee kaaṭada? tee maṭa.

• salli mokakaṭada?   *for what is this money?*

taattaa ee minihaaṭa salli dunne æyi?

taattaa ara dæn gedara enne mokada?   *– why is he coming now*

15   ee minihaa iiyet væḍa keruvaada?

eyaa ada yanne koheda?

lamayaa iskooleeda yanne?

ammaa monavaada bonne?

ee kavda dæn aave?

20   ee gollo iiyeṭa gamaṭa giyaa.

gama koheda?

eevaaṭa koheda apiṭa salli?

lamayaa hæmadaama ehe yanavaa.

mee loku puṭuva otanaṭa.

---

1. [**ahaṭṭə**] also represents a different word, **ahakaṭa** (lesson 28).

mee mokada mee puṭuva metana?
ape ballaa ohaaṭa aavaada?
lamayaa ehaaṭa mehaaṭa yanavaa.

B. Who (is it)?
What is (all) this? That is money.
Where is that?
What's his name?
Where is the letter? liyuma koo?
Will father write that letter today?
Does the boy go to school every day?
Is that our father coming?
Is that book mine?
Is the red book mine?
Where did father go yesterday?
Who's drunk my tea?
What is the child doing?
Why did the child go home?
What did that man come to our house for?
That is a book.
Is **that** my book?
Whose is this book?
These are mine, those are yours.
I looked at a big book today.
What did that man do to our dog?
Is this letter for me?
Who wrote this book?
I haven't (any) money now either.
Your chair is over there.
Why is that? æyi ee?
Your (pl.) dog is here.

Notes

A. 2 'Who is that?' But **oyaa kavda**? means 'Who are you?'

3 Personal pronouns are very often omitted in Sinhalese, as being evident from the context. In short sentences the context may be in doubt, but in

this instance we can confidently translate 'What is your name?' So also 9 below.

4 & 5 The words **ee** and **mee** are often repeated in this way: ee koheda ee? where is that?

6 **taattaa** may, according to the context, mean either 'my father' or 'your father'. Sentences such as this may also be actually addressed to the father, since it is a normal politeness to speak in the 3rd person (lesson 1 (c)). So also 10 and 13 below; in 14 however the word **ara** shows that the father is far off and cannot therefore be being spoken to.

7 i.e. kohaaṭada yanne.

9 See n. on 3 above. **-da yanne** tends to sound as [**-deyænne**].

10 'How is father?' or 'how are you, father?' No verbal form is required. The dative case here shows that the enquiry concerns the father's health, and is more than a mere politeness such as kohomada mahattayaa? or loku unnæhe kohomada?, how are you sir? (i.e. how are things with you). (**loku unnæhe**, 'big he', is a term of address sometimes used to elderly people of moderate status).

11 tee maṭa, 'it is for me'. It is best to repeat **tee** here, and not to use **eeka**.

12 May be either a general or a particular question.

16 The word **ada**, beginning and ending with a vowel, is obviously likely to be difficult to distinguish in certain phonetic environments, as here (and, you may find, in B 6 below).

18 Food and drink are generally referred to in the plural.

20 iiyeṭa, 'for (the day) yesterday'.

21 'What is (your) village?' 'where are you from?' **koheda** is preferable to **mokakda** here. Ceylon is a rural civilization, and most of the inhabitants of Colombo (the only large town) still feel they belong to some country village.

22 i.e. we can't find the money for that. Be careful to pronounce eevaaṭa correctly ([eevaṭə]).

24 otanaṭa, '(is) for there', i.e. belongs over there.

25 'Why is this chair here?' The first **mee** can be omitted.

27 ehaaṭa mehaaṭa (always in this order), 'hither and thither', i.e. he is just wandering about.

B. 2   'All this' – use the plural of the interrogative word.

   3   cf. A 4 above.

9,10   The **-e** of **mage** is usually lengthened before da.

 21   To our dog: dative case.

 24   I haven't: say 'There is not for me'.

 25   If **-yi** is added to **atana** it gives particular emphasis, '**there**'.

Script

ය (ය)   ර (ර)   ව (ව)

  ya   ra   va

ය්   ර්   ව්

y   r   v

To represent the vowels **æ** and **ææ**, the signs ැ and ෑ are placed after the consonantal sign: කැ ගැ තැ etc. **dæ, dææ** have the special forms දැ දෑ; **ræ, rææ** have the special forms රැ රෑ.

To represent the vowel **i**, a semi-circular stroke .⌒. (called **ispilla**, head-mark) is added above the consonantal sign. කි ගිති දි නි පි සි රි.

Letters which end by curving upwards to the left (which use .⌒. for the **al-kiriima** sign) join the i-sign to the letter in a single stroke. ටි ඩි මි බි ටි චි. For the long vowel **ii**, the sign is .⌒. කී තී etc.

ose kakula-leg (පය paya)	නෑනා naenaa sister-in-law	යනවා yanawa	වචනයක් wachanayak – a word
? බව bawa	බෑනා baenaa – brother-in-law	ටකරම් takaram corrugated	කරනවා keranwaa
rata wata – around the country. around වට wata	කිව්වා kiwwa	දෙනට denete deenete	වැඩකාරයා vædkarya = servant
left. වම wama	බිව්වා biwwa	වචන wachana words	මීරිගම Mirigama
Scared බය baya	කව්ද kawde?	ගින්දර gindara fire	දිනමින Dinamina = newspaper
use égere about ? වග wage	දැක්කා deka-saw	ටිකිරි Tikiri	පිරනවා pirenvaa = comb/brush hair
(යම yama)	තෑගි tæægi=gift	පිරිමි pirimi	තිරනය teerenaya = decision.
shoulder කර kara	තෑග්ගක් tæægak = gift	නරියා narya jackal	රාජපතිරන =name
down. under යට yata	තරම් tharam	වජිරා Wajira.	කරගත්තට

මව	කිරි	බිත්තර	චක්කරනවා
රට	ටිකයි[1]	මයිනා	පීනනවා
තර	පිරි	කියන	රාජකීය
නව	චික්කා	කීයද	බන්ඩාරනායක
ජය	නිච්චි	කීයක්ද	රත්නායක
යන	කිචි	නානවා	දැදිගම
රජ	පඩි	රාගම	මැදිරිගිරිය
නය	නැද්ද	රත්රන්	පියරතන
පව්	දිදී	මාතර	පියවර
වප්	ටීකා	නිතරම	මරදන
නයා	මීයා	රබර්	කියවනවා
බෑ	බීඩි	කවද්ද	වටිනාකම
නෑ	රිදී	කනවා	තාරකාවක්
දැන්	චීන		බාදවකට
ගියා	වීනා		කතරගම
වැඩ	රීප්ප		තරමටම
යෑම	පැනක්		මන්නාරම
බැද	නැවා		
ජෑම්	නැර		
මැව්	ගීතා		
ගී	කරයි[2]		
රැට	පැටව්		
තව	ගිනි		
	නීති		

1. Pronounced ටිකය්.
2. Pronounced [kəray].

LESSON 5

innavaa	be, live, remain
hiṭiyaa	was, etc.
tiyenavaa[1]	be
tiyunaa, tibunaa[2]	was
ov	yes
game	in the village
pote	in the book
liyume	in the letter
puṭuve	in the chair
gedara	at home
paaṭa	colour
meesee	table
pææna	pen
pænsalee, pænsala	pencil
nil	blue
keṭṭu	thin (of animates)
mahata (in some areas, **tara**)	fat, thick
usa	high, tall
koṭa (in some areas, **miṭi**)	short, low

(a) When adding the suffix **-k** to nouns ending in **-ee**, **ee** is changed to **aya**. This change does not always occur, however, if a further termination follows.

meesee	table
meesayak	table
meesayakaṭa / meeseekaṭa[3]	for a table

'A piece of work', however, is always væḍak, not væḍayak.

1. In books, this word is written **tibenavaa**.
2. **tibbaa** is used in Kandyan districts.
3. Pronounced [meesekəṭə].

(b) To form a negative sentence, the incomplete verb-form is used with the word **nææ**. maŋ yanne nææ, I will not go. When **nææ** immediately follows this verbal form, the **-ne** ending is hardly pronounced (**maŋ yan-nææ**). **nææ** here is usually spoken at a **lower** pitch than the word preceding it, unless special emphasis is required. Quite often, however, **nææ** is put earlier in the sentence: **nææ eyaa aave**, he has not come. In a negative question, **nææ** and **da** can combine in the form **nædda**. Where a further interrogative word (such as why, what) is used in a negative question, the incomplete form of the verb may either 1) be followed by the incomplete form **nætte,** or 2) be preceded by **no-**.

aave nædda?	didn't (he) come?
keruve nætte / nokeruve] æyi?	why didn't (you) do (it)?

If the verb begins with a vowel, **no-** is often altered to correspond:

no + enne = neenne,

no + aave = naave.

(c) **innavaa**, to be, is used only of animates. A past tense form **unnaa** is heard in places, but more generally **hiʈiyaa** is used; this is in fact the past tense of the verb **hiʈinavaa**, to stand, stop, but **hiʈinavaa** in the present tense is not so much used.[1] The incomplete form of **innavaa** is **inne** (not innne).

tiyenavaa, to be, is used of inanimates.[2] There is no Sinhalese verb corresponding to Eng. 'have'; the normal way of expressing a sentence such as 'I have a pen' is **maʈa pææenak tiyenavaa**, 'there is a pen to me'. 'I have not' is simply **maʈa nææ**; here, the present-tense verb is omitted.

These verbs can be omitted in short sentences such as eyaa gedara, he is at home; liyuma pote, the letter is in the book. They are **not** used in place of the copular **-yi**, or with the corresponding negative **nææ**, i.e. we cannot say 'pota loku tiyenne', 'pota loku tiyenne nææ'. **inne nææ** means 'does not wait.'

(d) **ov** and **nææ** correspond to 'yes' and 'no', but in certain cases where we usually say 'yes' in English, Sinhalese may say 'no', and vice versa.

eyaa aave nædda?	ov, eyaa aave nææ.
hasn't he come?	no, he hasn't.

---

1. Intervocalic **-ʈin-** (as in **hiʈinavaa**) is usually pronounced -ʈn- **[hiʈnəva]**). In certain phrases **hiʈinavaa** (though not **innavaa**) is used of inanimates.

2. **tiyenavaa** is also used as an auxiliary verb, both of animates and inanimates. See lesson 19.

A second-person question is often expressed negatively, without the uncomfortable implications which this mode of utterance may involve in English.

giye nædda?	haven't (you) been?

(but without any implication that you **ought** to have been).

In answering a question containing a verb, it is usual to repeat the verb (preceded optionally by **ov** or **nææ**), rather than to answer by **ov** or **nææ** alone.

keruvaada? keruvaa	did (you) do (it)? Yes (I did).

ov is often doubled; ov ov (pron. [**ovvov**]), oh yes.

(e) Inanimate nouns have a locative case-form, formed by changing **-a** to **-e**,[1] except in a few words such as gedara, metana, Kolam̆ba, Nuvara, havasa where it ends in **-a** (at home, in this place, in Colombo, in Kandy, in the afternoon). Nouns ending in **-ee** usually remain unchanged in the locative, e.g. **meesee**, on the table, though **meesaye** (cf. **a** above) may sometimes also be heard.

eyaa ape game innavaa	he lives in our village.

Where two nouns are closely connected in sense, and one of them is in the locative case, this case will be translated with the word 'of', i.e. like a genitive case. (Inanimate nouns do not take the suffix **-ge**.)

ape game minihek eyaa	he is a man of our village.

In such cases, the noun in the locative case must precede the other noun. There are also cases, however, where this case-form cannot be used to translate English 'of', e.g. 'a glass of water'.[2]

Sometimes the locative case is used with verbs implying motion.

game / gamaṭa } yanavaa	go to the village

game enavaa, however, is not said.

After the indefinite suffix **-k**, the locative case suffix is **-a**.

gamaka	in (of) a village.

(f) loku when used of people means either 'fully grown' or 'important'. It is not normally used to mean 'tall' or 'fat'. **koṭa** often connotes 'deformed'.

---

1. In books, often written **-ee**, and lengthened in speech also in disyllables where the first syllable is short, when these are followed by **-ma**, **-da**, **-di**: see 4 B 9, 12 A 1, 18 A 17 (and 30 B 45).

2. Lesson 20d.

A.

mama heṭa iskoolee yanne næ. *I'm not going to school tomorrow.*

ee minihaa dæn mehe enne næ. *this person is not coming here now.*

koṭa mahata lamayek mehe aave næ. *the short fat boy has not come here.*

mee lamayaa iiye pota bæluve næ. *this boy didn't look at the book yesterday.*

5 taattaa gedara nædda? *isn't father at home?*

liyuma ratu pote. *the letter is in the red book.*

ee lamayaa keṭṭu næ. *this boy is not thin.*

gedara kavda inné? *who's at home?*

puṭuve mokakda tiyenne? *what's on the chair?*

10 sudu aliyek koheda inne? *where does the white elephant live? (where is there a...?)*

puṇci mahattayaa gedara næ. *the small sir is not at home.*

loku ammaa mee gedara næ. *aunt is not at this house.*

ara ratu paaṭa pota koo? *where is that red coloured book?*

mahattayaa game yanne nædda? *the man is not going to the village?*

15 pæna nil paaṭa pote bæluve nædda? *have you seen the pen in the blue coloured book?*

mahattayaa koheda inne? *where does this man live?*

lamayaaṭa taattek ammek næ. *the boy doesn't have a father or mother.*

taattaa kenek apiṭa dæn næ. *we don't have a father now.*

taattaa vædak. — *father is working (is busy)*

20 oya pota koheda tiyune?

kavda mee pote tee vækkeruve? *who spilt tea on this book?*

ee minihaa ada vædak keruve næ. *this person didn't working today.*

B.

Why doesn't he go to school now? *æyi eyaa dæn iskollee yanne nætte?* after verb

I have no home. *mate gedarak næe.*

Didn't our child come to school today? *apé lamayaa ada iskolee aave næedde?*

I have a red pen. *mate ratu pæsene etak tiyevaa.*

5 I have no chair. *mate puṭuvak næe.*

I have a big dog. *mate loku bullek.*

Yes, I shall be at home tomorrow. *Ou, mama heṭa gedara mevaa.*

Mother isn't at home either. *Ammaat gedara me-næe.*

The book is at home, *Potak gedara tievena.*

10 Won't you give us tea, mother? *ammaa, apiṭe tee denné næedde?*

Hasn't that man mended the chair? *oya mahattaya poṭuvak hæduve næedde?*

(You) haven't written that letter to that gentleman, have you? No, I haven't written it. *Ara liyanak oyak mahattayak liuve næede? ou, liuwe næe.*

Father is at home today. *Tauttaa ada gedara mevaa.*

What is the colour of the boy's pen?
15 The cat is on the chair.
Where is the big table?
Father isn't going to work tomorrow.
What is in that letter?
What is the pencil in?
20 What is that over there?
Where is (there) a chair for this table?
Why, is there an elephant (there)?

Notes

A. 3 We would say 'No short fat boy has been here'. There is no word in Sinhalese corresponding to 'no' as an adjective.

4 Probably refers to a student, 'didn't look at his book(s) yesterday'.

10 Where is, i.e. where is there?

11 puŋci (or poḍi) mahattayaa, 'the young gentleman'; loku mahattayaa, 'the master'. Here, as in 17 below, **nææ** may be spoken with a falling intonation, i.e. appear quite unstressed.

13 paaṭa, 'colour', is also used, as here, adjectivally; translate 'coloured'. So in 15 below. When **nil** is used predicatively, it is usually followed by **paaṭa**; meevaa nil paaṭayi, these are blue, is commoner than meevaa nil.

15 balanavaa here = 'to look for'. In 4 above it might have this meaning instead of the meaning 'look at'. **nil** is also used of the colour of grass, leaves, growing rice etc., i.e. green.

16 'Where do you live?', not 'where are you?', which is **mahattayaa koheda**?

18 taattaa kenek, ammaa kenek are more respectful than taattek, ammek (lesson 2b).

19 This means 'Father is busy'.

20 This sentence implies that you have been searching for the book.

21 vækkeruve, past tense incomplete of **vakkaranavaa**, 'pour' (see lesson 1 d), means 'spilt' here. The locative case **pote** is used in preference to the dative **potaṭa**.

22 Did not do a job of work, i.e. didn't do anything.

B. 2 See A 3 above.

12   Say 'Haven't you written'.

14   Can be translated literally.

19   The locative case of **mokak** is **mokaka** (sometimes pronounced [**mohokə**]).

Script

ස (**ඓ**)   හ (**ඖ**)   ල (**ළ**)

sa   ha   la

To represent the **e** vowel, a sign ෙ (called **kombuva**, horn) is placed **in front of** the consonant sign. The resulting pair of signs count as a single letter, and should not be divided between lines.

ජෙ ගෙ තෙ දෙ නෙ පෙ වෙ. සෙ හෙ

Where the vowel is long, the al-kiriima sign is added to the consonant sign.

කේ යේ රේ ටේ ඩේ මේ බේ වේ ලේ

සල්	sal - type of tree	කෙහෙල්	kehel	බලනවා	balanavaa.
හාල්	haal - rice	සාලා	(saalaa.)	ලියනවා	liyanawa
සහ	saha - and	දේවල්	deewal - things	තියෙනවා	tiyenena
හය	haya - 6	සල්ලි	salli	බෙරෙනවා	beerenaa - drain (water)
සර්	sar - sir	පීරිස්	piiris Peiris.	හදනවා	hadenena.
කල	kala - water pots	සිල්වා	silwa.	නමයකට	namayakate - to me.
පහ	paha - 5	ජේම්ස්	james.	වේදනාව	weedenava - pain.
හත	hatha - 7	හාවා	hawa - hare	පේරාදෙනිය	Peradinya.
ගේ	gee - house	හේරත්	Heerath.	පිච්චෙනවා	pichchenevaa - burn.
නිල්	nil - blue.	ලිව්වා	liiwa	බන්ඩරවෙල	Bandarwela.
තේ	thee - tea	බල්ලා	balla.	වැල්ලවත්ත	Wellawatte.
මේ	mee - this	කේලාම්	keelam rumour	දෙහිවල	Dehiwala.
බැරි	beri - can't	ගාල්ල	galle.	හලාවත	Halawatte = Chilaw.

කටේ	ලැයිසා	හැමදම
මෙහෙ	හිටියා	වෙනවාට
නැහැ	ළමයා	සෙල්ලමට
බැහැ	මිනිහා	ගඩලාදෙනිය
මගෙ	ගෙදර	පලච්චා
මිටි	දෙනවා	හිටිනවා
කඩේ	හෙටට	කච්චේරිය
වැඩේ	දහයෙ	හැත්තැපස්වෙනියා
ගමේ	හැටට	සිරීපාදේ
පේර	වටේට	සෙනෙවිරත්න
නේද	කාගෙද	මහත්තයා
මඩෙ	බලලා	රැවටෙයි
දෙකක්	මහත	රේල්පාර
පල්	පෙරෙරා	ගල්කිස්ස
පස්	නෙමෙයි	තෙපානිස්
කල්	මීටිමක්	තිරියායි
තල්	ලෙහෙනෙක්	කැගල්ල
ගස්	බෙදන්න	හතරයි
ගහ	විස්සට	සේනානායක
තල	පැන්සලේ	මල්වත්ත
හීල්	කැමති	විහාරයක්

හිල්
හීන්
ගල්
ගාල
ලිප
හරි
මිල
වගෙ
මේසේ

සැරේට
පල්ලිය
පලිය
පහන
සිරිමා
ඩඩ්ලි

මාතලේ
මිහින්තලේ
දියතලාව
ගිතිමැලයක්

LESSON 6

puluvan	is possible
oonæ[1]	is required
bææ, bæhæ, bæri	is impossible
epaa	is not wished
kæmati	wish, like (verb)
tava, tavama	yet
poḍḍak / **ṭikak**	a little
kiyanavaa	say
kivvaa	said
kanavaa	eat
kæævaa	ate
dannavaa	know
bat (pl.)	cooked rice
kææma	food, meal
kaḍee	village shop (called 'boutique' in Lanka)
kaḍakaarayaa	shopkeeper

(a) The infinitive verb-form is made by changing **-navaa** to **-nna** (**-na** if there is already an **n** before -navaa); karanna, inna, balanna etc. In certain districts forms such as **karanṭa**, **inṭa**, **balanṭa** and **karanḍa**, **inḍa**, **balanḍa** are also used.

These words can be used as commands; enna, come (here)! **ko** after such a command adds extra politeness, and is approximately equivalent to 'please do' in English.

(b) puluvan, oonæ, bææ, kæmati, epaa are often used with the infinitive verb-forms.

---

1. Also pronounced **oone**.

puluvan[2] and **bææ** with a dative case of the person concerned indicate physical capacity or incapacity.

maṭa meeka karanna puluvan	I can do this
maṭa meeka karanna bææ	I can't do this
maṭa meeka puluvan	this is possible for me
maṭa meeka bææ	this is impossible for me

With the direct case of the person or thing concerned, puluvan and bææ indicate possibility, not actual ability. Here the infinitive verb-form is essential.

eyaa meeka karanna puluvan	he may do this
liyumak enna puluvan	a letter may come

oonæ with a dative case of the person of thing concerned represents need or desire.

maṭa gedara yanna oonæ	I want to go home
meeka maṭa oonæ	I want this
gedaraṭa puṭuvak oonæ	a chair is needed for the house

With a direct case of the person or thing concerned, and an infinitive verb-form, it represents obligation, moral or physical respectively.

maŋ gedara yanna oonæ	I ought to go home
liyumak enna oonæ	a letter ought to come

kæmati (sometimes written **kæmatiyi**) is associated with the direct case of the person concerned.

maŋ yanna kæmati	I wish (should like) to go
	or also
	I like going

Where kæmati is used without an infinitive verb-form, the object of the liking is in the dative case.

maŋ eyaaṭa kæmati	I like him
maŋ eekaṭa kæmati	I like that
	or
	I want (should like) that

epaa, with an infinitive verb-form, is used in prohibitions or negative commands.

(oyaa) meeka karanna epaa	don't (you) do this!

When epaa is used without an infinitive, the person or thing not wanted is in the

---

2. Or sometimes **puluvani**. **bæriya** is used as a written form of **bææ**. The suffixes **-i** and **-ya** here are variants of the copular **-yi**.

direct case, and the person or thing who does not want or require is in the dative. This is the opposite usage from that with **kæmati** given above.

maṭa eeka epaa	I don't want that
Joon[1] apiṭa epaa	we don't want John
gedaraṭa puṭuvak epaa	a chair is not needed for the house

puluvan, **oonæ**, **epaa** and **kæmati** all serve as incomplete verb-forms without further change.

kaaṭada puluvan?	who can?
kaaṭada oonæ?	who needs (it)?
kavda kæmati?	who wants (it)?
maŋ kæmati nææ	I don't like (it)
oonæ nææ	(it) is not required

(**oonæ nææ** is often pronounced **oon nææ**).

bææ uses **bæ**ri as the incomplete verb.

kaaṭada bæri?	who can't?
bæri nææ	it is not possible

puluvan nææ and **epaa nææ** are not used, but **bæri nææ** is not uncommon.

(c) **denavaa**, when used with an infinitive (and the dative case of the person concerned), can be translated 'let (someone do something)'. (In such cases the word **iḍa**, space, is sometimes added before denavaa.)

(eyaaṭa) yanna denna epaa	don't let (him) go.

(d) **dannavaa** has no past tense form in modern use. It can be used with the past tense form of an auxiliary verb (as explained in a later lesson), but the present tense form is often used of past time. The incomplete form is **danne**.

maŋ danne nææ	I don't know **or** I didn't know

(e) **tava** and **tavama** (to which **-t** is often added), when used with verbs, have in English two different meanings. When the verb is negative, **tavama** can usually be translated 'yet' and **tavat** 'any more'. **tava** (without **-t**) is sometimes used for **tavama**; the meaning will usually be clear in the context.

When the verb is positive, present tense, these words can be translated 'still'. (Before a positive verb in the past tense these words only occur in restricted contexts.)

1. This form, with lengthened vowel, is always used for 'John' (which is therefore indistinguishable from Joan).

eyaa tavama aave nææ	he hasn't come yet (still hasn't come)
eyaa tavama nææ iskoolee yanne	he doesn't go to school yet
eyaa tava mehe enne nææ	he does not come here any more
eyaa tavat aave nææ	he didn't come any more
eyaa tavama iskoolee yanavaa	he still goes to school

Before nouns or adjectives, **tava** usually represents 'yet another' or 'still more' respectively. Before adjectival words, the form **tavat** is common. **tavama** here can only represent 'still' (in time).

tava potak	(yet) another book
eyaage pota tava(t) puŋci	his book is even smaller
eyaa tavama puŋci	he is still little

tavama is often realized as **[taamə]**.

(f) **poɖɖak** and **ʈikak** can, like Eng. 'a little', mean either 'a little time' (poɖɖak inna, wait a bit), or 'a little quantity' (poɖɖak denna, give (me) a little). When used with a noun ('a little rice'), the noun usually stands first (bat ʈikak). ʈikak sometimes corresponds to 'fairly'; ʈikak usa, fairly tall: ʈikak lañga, fairly near.

A.
minihaa mee dæn yanna giyaa.
taattaaʈa poɖɖakaʈa enna kiyanna.
lamayaa ballaaʈa kanna denavaa.
liyumak liyanna lamayaa dannavaa.
iskoolee yanna lamayaa kæmati nææ.
taattaa dæn enna oonæ.
maŋ bat kanna yanna oonæ dæn.
maʈa hæmadaama bat kanna oonæ.
maʈa heʈa gedara yanna puluvan.
maʈa tava tee poɖɖak denna.
kææma kanna enna.
heʈa iskoolee yanna epaa.
api dæn game yanavaa, mahattayat enna ko.
ee minihaa maʈa kæmati nææ.
maʈa dæn tee epaa.
heʈa enna puluvan kaaʈada?
kavadaaʈada meeka oonæ?
kavda kæmati sudu aliyek balanna?

ee minihaa ada gedara enna bæri nææ.
20 lamayaaṭa iskoolee enna bæri æyi?
tavama nææ eyaa aave.
tavat eyaaṭa maŋ potak denne nææ.
oya pota maṭa adaṭa denna.
tava tiyenavaada?
25 minihaa vædee kææyaa.
ee mahattayaava maŋ tavama danne nææ.

Words in square brackets in B sentences are needed in Sinhalese though not necessary in English.

B. We will be off.
We must give the bullock (something) to eat.
Mother told me to come home tomorrow.
Come here, boy.
5 Write [a letter] to father today.
Please lend me that red pencil for a bit.
We should like to have tea now.
The boy doesn't want to work.
That boy doesn't like work.
10 I don't want that chair.
The cat won't drink tea.
I don't want the pen now.
I don't know (how) to mend that chair.
I can't drink (any) more tea.
15 Does your elder boy still go to school?
I won't be going to school any more.
That man is still working.
I had (yet) another dog.
Another book came for me yesterday.
20 Mother wrote another letter today.
Why, hasn't he given (you) the money for that book yet?
Is the boy still at school?
Who is coming to the meal today?

Eat a little more rice.

25 Father may come today (or) tomorrow.

Please let me come tomorrow too.

Notes:

A. 1 yanavaa yanna, 'go to go', i.e. depart (rather than just 'move about'). yanna enavaa, 'come to go', is used of going to a place at which the speaker has not yet arrived: Nuvaraṭa yanna enna, 'come (with me) to Kandy.'

2 'Ask father to come here a moment.' 'Say to come' can, according to context, represent either 'ask (him) to come' or 'tell (him) to come'. poḍḍakaṭa (or ṭikakaṭa), 'for a little (time)', sometimes has almost the effect of Eng. 'please'.

3 'Gives to eat', i.e. gives something to eat. In suitable contexts such a sentence may also mean 'allows (him) to eat.' Here, the latter meaning would be given by **(ballaaṭa) kanna iḍa denavaa**.

4 dannavaa with infinitive = know how to.

6 The obligation here is not likely to be moral; 'father will be home soon'.

23 denna = lend.

24 'Is there (any) more?'

25 This means 'He made a mess of the whole thing'.

B. 7 'To have' – say 'to drink'.

8 To work = to do work.

11 Here 'won't' = doesn't like to.

14 This is (in Sinhalese) quite a polite way of saying 'I don't want any more thank you'. Perhaps it should rather be put in English as 'I couldn't drink …'

15 Elder = loku.

16 Use **tavat**. Compare this with: dæn maŋ iskoolee yanne nææ, I don't go to school (**any more**) now.

25 See lesson 2 note.

Script

ළ  ණ 

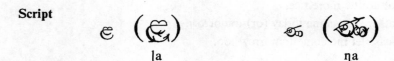

ḷa ṇa

These letters historically speaking represent a retroflex (**muurdhaja**) lateral and nasal. The distinction between the sounds l and ḷ, and between **n** and ṇ, is no longer significant in Sinhalese (though it still is in Tamil), and the correct use of ණ and ළ is thus a matter of spelling rules only. These rules are not generally known at the present time, and therefore the learner must be prepared to find these two characters used for න and ල in almost any word. He need not use them himself at all (unless he has a knowledge of Sanskrit).

ṇaa, ṇi, ṇee are written ණා, ණි and ණේ.

The **o** vowel is represented by a kombuva before the consonantal sign and an ælapilla after it. ළො ḷo ණො ṇo.

If the **o** vowel is long, the al-kiriima sign is added **to the ælapilla**.

දෝ doo ලෝ loo

කෙළ	කළගෙඩිය	බෝගහ	රත්මලාන
මළා	තණකොළ	මොකද	හම්බන්තොට
කෙළි	සැළලිහිණි	යෝදයා	ගම්පොල
කෙළෙ	කළේකට	ලොරිය	සෝමපාල
කණා	තැළීම	දෙළහක්	මෝරනවා
කොට	ගැණෙයි	වෙලාව	තෝරනවා
ගොඩ	කාරණේ	කාර්වල	මොකකටද
පොත	මරණේ	බස්වල	කොතනටද
පොඩි	බරණෑස්	බොනවා	මොනවාද
දෙර	නෝනා	කොහෙද	කොහොමද
රොටි	නොනා	යොදන්න	ගිරිගෝරිස්
කෝ	නොනෑ	දෙඩන්ත	පවෝරිස්

සියම්	නේන්නෙ	මැණිකෙ	සියදේරිස්
පොරෝ	සොහොන්	හාමිනෙ	මහරජ
ගොනා	ගොල්ලො	සීදේවි	හොයනවා
පෝර	පොඩ්ඩක්	ලීලාවතී	කොතලාවල
ලෝකේ	ටොක්ක	පරණ	විජහට
පෝය	හෝරාව	කන්නාඩි	කබරගොයා
පැණි	ලොක්කා	තක්කාලි	මොලවනවා
පොල්	තාප්පේ	පැපොල්	පිළිවෙළ
පැයක්	බොහොම	බොරැල්ල	කැලණිය
කොස්	කෝට්ටේ	බෝතික්කා	
නාකි			
ජෝන්			

LESSON 7

anee	ah, alas
aayu boo van	how do you do, good-bye
karunaa-karalaa	please
sæpa-saniipa	health
pin	merit

(a) aayu boo van (**van** always with a falling intonation) means literally 'may your life be long'. It is often pronounced **aayi booŋ**. Karunaa-karalaa means literally 'having shown compassion'; it is not used as frequently as 'please' in English. The effect of 'please' in commands may often be given by **ţikak**; denna ţikak, please give. See also Lesson 6 **a** above, and note on 6 A2. sæpa-saniipa means literally 'prosperity (and) health'.

(b) The formal equivalent of 'thank you' is **istuti** (lit. 'praise'), but this is seldom used in practice. For real thanks, some such phrase is **anee pin**[1] ('ah merit') is often heard. The acquiring of merit is an important part of practical Buddhism. As a mere formality of acknowledgement, nothing is necessary, except perhaps a wag of the head (just as for example in many countries of Europe a formal answer to 'thank you' is necessary, but not in England).

A. lamayaa bat kanavaa.
ara puŋci ratu pota kaageda? eeka mageyi.
mama heţa gedara yanna balanavaa.
ee mahattayaaţa tee hadanna puluvanda? puluvan.
5 mahattayaa iiye koheda giye?
ee gollange balalaa keţţu sudu paaţa ekek.
mahattayaa game yanne kavadaada?
ee minihaage nama mokakda?
væḑakaarayaa gonaaţa kanna denavaa.
10 mahattaya kohomada? ohe innavaa.

1. Usually pronounced **piŋ**; see Introduction.

maŋ kæmati tee bonna.
maŋ dæn kaɖeeʈa poɖɖak yanna oonæ.
taattaa væɖaʈa yanne kohaaʈada?
taattaa væɖa karanne koheda?
15 ee gollanʈa maŋ kæmati nææ.
maʈa paaʈa pænsalayak denna.
mee meesee maʈa ʈikak lokuyi.
ee gollanut heʈa ape gedara enavaa.
inna ʈikak, mage puʈuvaʈa yanna.
20 mee balanna, mee lamayaa.
mee... mahattayaage pææna maʈa ʈikakaʈa denavaada?
taattaaʈa tavama bærida væɖaʈa yanna?
mage nil paaʈa pænsalee iskoolee.
ee minihaage usa!
25 poɖɖak inna maʈat balanna.
minihaage puʈuve puŋci!
gonaa ohe yanavaa.

B. The servant will come tomorrow.
Father is mending the chair.
Where is the boy? At school.
We have no cat; we have a dog.
5 We gave that elephant to the young gentleman.
Whose is that blue pen? It's mine.
The table is not high.
The man is not at home.
You are thin now, sir.
10 Who is that coming?
What are you (all) doing tomorrow?
There is a big elephant in our village.
I too went to (my) village yesterday.
Father stayed at home yesterday.
15 Hasn't the child a pen?
They don't know how to bring up a child.
There is no book of yours here.
Where are you going now?

I will write a letter to mother today.
Sir, are you going to the village one of these days?
Our elder boy is coming home tomorrow.
Where is (there) a chair for father too?
How small this book is!
Why is this child at home today?
Why, isn't he paying for that book?
Good day sir, how are you?
I don't know (how) to get to their house.

Notes:

A. 3 balanavaa = try, see about.

4 The answer is not 'Yes' or 'No', but 'puluvan' or 'bææ'. These may be preceded by **ov** or **nææ,** but those words by themselves are insufficient.

6 ekek – see n. on 3 A9. **paaṭa** can be omitted.

9 See n. on 6 A3.

10 See n. on 4 A10. ohe innavaa, 'all right': lit. 'I just am'. **ohe** is often used without literal significance.

12 poḍḍak or poḍḍakaṭa: 'for a little (while)'.

16 paaṭa pænsalayak = a coloured pencil. paaṭapaaṭa = multicoloured.

19 **inna** here and in 25 below does not mean 'wait', but 'make way' (for me to get to my chair). **maṭa** may be used here instead of **mage**; see note on 21 below. (But note that **inna maṭa** cannot mean 'wait for me').

20 Look here, (at) this child! i.e. see what he's doing! **mee** etc. (rather than **mehe** etc.) are much used with infinitive command forms: ara balanna ara! look there! (cf. meeka balanna, look at this). If this sentence were written 'mee balanna mee, lamayaa!' we would translate differently: 'look here, child!'

21 **mee** is commonly used to attract a person's attention: 'I say!' (**ayise**, which represents Eng. 'I say', is also much used, but only as part of a phrase and not by itself).[1] **mee** also occurs in the middle of utterances, rather like Eng. 'er' (mark of hesitation). Similarly **ara**! (by itself) may mean 'Look there!'

---

1. It is in fact often felt to mean 'you'.

Notice the case-form **mahattayaage**, which is more natural in Sinhalese than **mahattayaa** here, although it leaves the sentence without a grammatical subject. Compare the use of **mage** in 19 above.

22 **bærida** is the form normally used for 'is it impossible?', though **bæhæda** is heard in some districts.

24 An exclamation, 'How tall that man is!' (cf. ee minihaa usayi, that man is tall). Similarly, ee lamayaage sudu! how fair that boy is! Here **usa**, **sudu** and similar words function as nouns (this is discussed further in lessons 17 and 23). Notice the intonation of such sentences, where the absence of a final drop in tone may make the sentence sound unfinished.

sudu, 'white', need not refer to a European; distinctions between different shades of complexion are much noticed in Ceylon, as in India generally. **ratu** when used of people also means 'fair' (red-headed men being virtually unknown in Lanka).

25 See 19 above. **koo balanna** is much used in similar contexts, 'Let me see' (lit., where [is there] to see).

27 ohe yanavaa, 'is just wandering about'; see 10 above.

B. 3 Repeat 'boy'.
13 Omit 'my' in translation.
16 How to – see 6 A4n.
20 One of these days: see lesson 2A, note.
25 Pay: say 'give money'.
26 Say 'How is (your) health?'
27 Get: say 'go'. 'How' need not be translated.

Script

ං This sign, called **binduva**, represents the nasal ŋ, but unlike other consonantal signs it contains no inherent vowel. In practice it may be found used for න් or ම්, where the difference in pronounciation is not significant (see Introduction).

The **u** vowel is represented by the sign called **paapilla** (foot-mark). This has normally the form ු (ු in handwriting) for the short vowel; ූ for the long vowel.

දු නු පු වු ෂු හු ඥු ලු ශු යු ධු ඛු මු ඩු චු

The following letters however use signs like those for **ae**, **aeae**, but joined to the consonantal sign.

කු ගු තු කූ ගූ තූ (cf. කැ ගැ තැ)

ku gu tu kuu guu tuu

ru, ruu have the forms රු, රූ (whereas **rae, raeae** are written රැ, රෑ, see lesson 4 above). **ḷu, ḷuu** have special forms ළු, ළූ.

බං	වුනා	මුහුණ	කළුතර
ගං	වුට්ටි	මුදු	නුවර
මං	පොදු	බූරුවා	මඩකලපුව
ළං	කුඩා	මයූර	කුරුණෑගල
ඩිංගක්	කුළු	පූජාව	රත්නපුර
හුලං	කුණු	බුලු	මීගමුව
පංගු	ලුනු	බුරුම	පානදුරේ
වූ	චූටි	සත්තු	තංගල්ල
නූල්	ලූනු	කෙටූ	බදුල්ල
දූ	කුඩේ	පැතූ	පුත්තලම
සුදු	කූරු	කැඩූ	තිරිකුණාමලේ
ලොකු	කුඩු	කොටුව	යාපනේ
පුංචි	රූප	ජෝඩුව	කොල්ලුපිටිය
රතු	යුතු	මිනිස්සු	පිටකොටුව
කෙට්ටු	ජූසේ	පුලුවන්	ගුරුවරයා
කිට්ටුව	පටු	පුටුව	හූරනවා
දුන්නා	ජූනි	ලියුමෙ	හූනියම්
නැංගු	සූර	හදපුවා	සූකිරි
හැදුවා			හංගනවා
බැලුවා			තියුනා
			කෙරුවා

LESSON 8

nemeyi, neveyi	is not
vaḍaa, væḍiya	more
uḍa	above
yaṭa	below
dihaava	direction; towards
vijahaṭa, vigahaṭa	soon, quickly
dænaṭama	now already
velaava	time (when measurable in hours)
kiiyada, kiiyak-da	how much? how many?
kaala	quarter
baala	younger (and inferior)
na(ñ)ginavaa	climb; get into (vehicle)
næggaa / **næŋgaa**	climbed
Gaalla	Galle
Kolam̆ba	Colombo
Nuvara	Kandy
deka	two
tuna	three
hatara	four
paha	five
gaha	tree, bush

(a) **nemeyi** or **neveyi**[1] (**nevi** in some areas) is used for the copular 'is not' when the complementary word – which must immediately precede it – is a noun-form. **nææ** is used only when the complement is an adjectival word.

---

1. **noveyi** in literary language.

gaha loku nææ	the tree is not big

but

gaha loku ekak nemeyi	the tree is not a big one
mee pææna mage nemeyi	this pen is not mine
mee ape pota nemeyi	this is not our book

Where **nemeyi** is found after adjectival words, the sentence is incomplete. pota loku nemeyi poḍi, the book is not big but small (note that in such a sentence no word corresponding to 'but' is required; cf. Lesson 3 A 12).

In the sense 'does not exist, is not here', **nææ** must be used, not **nemeyi**.

meesee uḍa potak nææ	there is no book on the table

nemeyi can also be used to negate a single word in a sentence.

minihaa yanavaa nemeyi enavaa
  the man is not going but coming.
meesee uḍa potak nemeyi pæænak tiyenavaa
  there is not a book but a pen on the table.

This last can also be expressed by two consecutive sentences;

meesee uḍa potak nææ;   pæænak nam[1] tiyenavaa

(b) Adjectives have no separate comparative and superlative forms. In comparisons, **vaḍaa** or **væḍiya**[2] is used (or sometimes **vaḍaa væḍiya**) before the adjective with a dative case of the object of comparison.

	vaḍaa	
mee pota arakaṭa	væḍiya	lokuyi
	vaḍaa væḍiya	

  this book is bigger than that.

In positive sentences, the dative case alone – especially when followed by **-t** – is often sufficient to indicate comparison, provided the adjectival word immediately follows. In negative sentences **vaḍaa** is usually added.

maŋ eyaaṭa baalayi	I am younger than he is
meeka iiṭa vaḍaa loku nææ	this is not bigger than that
meeka iiṭat lokuyi	this is (even) bigger than that

Notice the position of -t in **iiṭat lokuyi**; **iiṭa lokut** is not possible. Similarly **iiṭat vaḍaa**, and not **iiṭa vaḍat**. (However, **væḍiyat hon̆dayi**, by itself, means 'even better'.)

---

1. **nam** is an emphasizing particle. In Lesson 7 above, B 4 is a similar sentence when **nam** could also be used.

2. Some speakers prefer the form **væḍiye**.

tavat or **tava ṭikak** may also be used (but if the object of comparison is mentioned, **vaḍaa** is required too).

tava ṭikak / væḍiya	loku potak oonæ	a (rather) bigger book is needed
meeka tavat / vaḍat	lokuyi	this one is still bigger.

In negative sentences **væḍiya** sometimes gives a different English sense, see Lesson 16.

væḍiya (or vaḍaa if an object of comparison is mentioned) can also be used with verbs.

eyaa taattaaṭa vaḍaa bonavaa	he drinks more than (his) father (does)
eyaa væḍiya kæmati meekaṭa	he prefers this one

(c) **iiṭa**, **oyiṭa**, **miiṭa** are alternatives to **eekaṭa**, **ookaṭa**, **meekaṭa**.

(d) **uḍa**, **yaṭa** and other similar words function as post-positions, i.e. they are closely connected with the word which precedes them. The preceding noun is generally in the direct case, but other case-endings can be added to the post-positional words, which are also formally nouns. The interrogative particle **-da** is added (where necessary) to the postpositional word, not to the preceding noun.

meesee uḍa	on the table
meesee yaṭa	under the table
gaha uḍaṭa / gahaṭa[1] naňginna	to climb up the tree

When these words are used predicatively, **-yi** is not normally added.

pota meesee yaṭa	the book is under the table
pota meesee yaṭa nææ	the book is not under the table

(e) When counting, each numeral is usually followed by **-yi**; ekayi, dekayi, tunayi, etc.

Remember to pronounce the second **a** of **paha** like the first.

In telling the time, the numerals alone are used, no word for 'hour' being necessary.

velaava dæn tunayi	it is 3.00 now (**-yi** is needed here)
pahaṭa enna	come at 5.0

Notice the use of the dative case to represent Eng. 'at (such and such a time)'. This case also represents Eng. 'to' in phrases such as tunaṭa kaalayi, it is a quarter to three. **-k** is not used after **kaala** here.

1. [gahaṭə], not [gahəṭə].

(f) In the word **kiiyada**, as in **kavda** and **mokada** (Lesson 4), **-da** cannot be separated from the first part of the word. **kiiyak-da**, however (with the indefinite suffix – usually pronounced **[kiiyaddə]** – can be separated into **kiiyak** and **-da**, and so can case-forms such as **kiiye-da** (9 A 25 below). If the indefinite form is used, a verb is needed in the sentence.

pot kiiyak tiyenavaada?	how many books are there?
tava pot kiiya(k)da tiyenne?	how many more books are there?

Notice that the noun **pot**[1] must come **before** kiiyada. This word is used in asking the time, velaava kiiyada? what is the time? kiiyaṭada? at what time?

(g) Remember to pronounce correctly the **-aha-** in **vijahaṭa**, **vigahaṭa**. (On the other hand, the literary form of this word, **vigasaṭa**, is pronounced [vigəsəṭə]).

(h) Nuvara means 'city'; in the locative case, **Nuvara** means 'in the City', i.e. in Kandy (which was the Sinhalese capital for about three centuries up till 1815). Its full title is **Mahanuvara**, 'the Great City'; the name Kandy is connected with the Sinhalese word **kanda**, hill (Kandy being up in the hills). The original proper name of the Great City was **Senkaḍagala**, which has now been revived as the name of a parliamentary constituency. Kandy is not really a large city nowadays. **Kolam̆ba** also remains unchanged in the locative; remember not to stress the second syllable ([Kolə̆bə]). Galle (the English name rhymes with 'call') is a port to the south of Colombo; one of the principal hotels in Colombo is called the Galle Face Hotel.

When these place-names are used with verbs implying motion such as **yanavaa**, **enavaa**, the forms **Kolam̆ba, Nuvara, Gaalu**[2] are more frequently used than **Kolam̆baṭa, Nuvaraṭa, Gaallaṭa**; api Gaalu yanavaa, we are going to Galle.

A.
dæn velaava ekayi
ee pota mage nemeyi
pææna meesee uḍa nææ; yaṭa
nil eka nemeyi, ara poḍi ratu eka(yi) mage pota
ee lamayaa dæn maṭat vaḍaa usayi
eyaa maṭa baalayi
meesee uḍa mokakda ara tiyenne?

---

1. **pot** is the plural of **pota** (see lesson 9).
2. This is a stem-form; see lesson 17**b**.

pææna pota yaṭa
meesee uḍa pææna k tiyenavaada?
poḍi lamayaa puṭuva uḍaṭa naginavaa
mama ada Nuvara dihaave yanavaa
aliyaa maŋ dihaa bæluvaa
puṭuva meesee dihaavaṭa karanna
heṭa ekaṭa ee gollo enavaa
pahaṭa tava ṭikak tiyenavaa
meeka baala pææ nak
ee minihaa ara gahaṭa nægge nætte æyi?
mahattayaa bat kanna kæmati nætte æyi?
aayu boo van, mahattayaa; koheda mee yanne?
ape loku lamayaa dæn pahe
ape baala lamayaaṭa dæn pahayi
vijahaṭa enna yanna, dænaṭama pahayi
tava(ma) hataraṭa nææ
tavama hatarayi
oyaage velaava kiiyada?
lamayaa velaavaṭa iskoolee aavaa
mokada anee mee?
ohoma ṭikak!
taattaaṭa vigahaṭa naginavaa
pota meesee uḍada tiyune?

B. Father is even taller than mother.
The letter is on the table.
There is a book on the table.
The dog is under the chair.
Are you (all) coming our way to-morrow?
That gentleman is even younger than I (am).
Our younger boy is not at home today.
Colombo is even bigger than Galle.
It is a quarter to one now.
There is a bull under the tree.
Whose is this pen?

There is a cat on the chair.
Look there, there's a letter for father on that table.
What is (there) under that book?
15 Tell father to come soon.
The book is not on the table.
Is my pen on your table?
Who did this?
That man comes to work on time every day.
20 I need a rather higher chair than this.
That dog is bigger even than this boy.
Who wants (some) more tea?
Haven't you a **chair**?
Why doesn't this child come to school every day?
25 Father comes home tomorrow.
Write (your) name here.
Who did this job?
How tall that elephant is!
Father won't let that child come our way (=near here).
30 I'm going towards the shop for a while.

Notes:

A. 10 uḍaṭa or uḍa.

11 dihaave or dihaavaṭa or dihaa, 'in the Kandy direction'. **dihaa**, the plural or 'stem-form' of this word,[1] is used as a postposition meaning 'towards'.

12 **dihaa** (also sometimes **dihaava** here) used postpositionally; the preceding noun is usually in the direct case, but sometimes, especially where it is a pronominal word (maŋ, eyaa etc.), it may be in the genitive case. Thus **mage** is alternative to **maŋ** here (but not **maava**). Before case-forms such as **dihaave** or **dihaavaṭa** a preceding animate noun cannot be in the direct case-form but **must** be in the genitive, cf. B.5 below. Notice how to say 'looked at a person' (as v. 'looked at a book'). balanavaa, however, is not felt to imply motion so that we say maŋ dihaa bæluvaa, mehe bæluvaa, and not dihaavaṭa, mehaaṭa.

13 'Push the chair in'. Notice this use of **karanavaa**.

---

1. See Lesson 17.

15 pahaṭa = till five.
16 baala = inferior, cheap.
17 **naginavaa** is associated with a dative case (A 10 above) or a locative case (cf. also 9 A 20 below).
20 pahe = in the fifth standard (from the bottom – at school).
21 lamayaaṭa pahayi = the child is (lit. has) five (years old). This normally means that the child is in his fifth year, i.e. is what we call four.
22 'Come to go', i.e. come (and go) with me.
23 'It is not yet (at) four o'clock'. The direct case alone is insufficient here.
24 'It is still only 4.0'. Note this idiom – 'only' does not have to be expressed in Sinhalese.
25 'What is the time by you?', 'What do you make the time?' This gets put into English in the attractive form 'What's your time?' **kiiyada** (without **-k** suffix), not **mokakda**, must be used here.
26 velaavaṭa = in time.
27 'Here, what's this?', i.e. what's going on? cf. mee mokakda, what is this object?
28 This can mean 'Keep it like that!', or 'Just a moment!' ohoma = 'thus' (lesson 17).
29 This means 'Father easily loses his temper'.

B. 5 See notes on A11 and 12 above.
19 See note on A26 above.
22 More: lesson 6e. væḍiya cannot be used here. Wants: oonæ is more usual than kæmati here.
26 Here: use metana, not mehe (lesson 4c).
29 Let: see Lesson 6c. Won't let = doesn't let.

Script

ඤ (ඥ)[1] ඃ

ña ḥ

ඤ is not very common. It occurs doubled in certain Sinhalese words, usually written as ඤ්ඤ; කරඤ්ඤම් (karaññam), I will do; but these words are not often

1. In form, this is **k** followed by **d**.

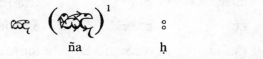

seen written. While in theory any nasal immediately followed by ච or ජ should be written ඤ, in practice ං is usually substituted.

ඃ only occurs in a few interjections;[1] චඃ (cah). Like ං, it contains no inherent vowel.

ග  ඩ 

ňga ňda

ද  බ 

ňda m̆ba

These signs (called **saňñaka g-**, **saňñaka d-** etc.; ඹ is called **am̆ba bayanna**, 'mango-B') can be modified like other consonantal signs.

ඟු	ඬු	ඳු	ඹු	ඟි	ඬි	ඳි	ඹි
ňgu	**ňdu**	**ňdu**	**m̆bu**	**ňgi**	**ňdi**	**ňdi**	**m̆bi**

ඦ (ňja) occurs very occasionally; ඉඦු (iňju!) - exclamation used in calling to dogs.

There is a special conjunct character ඤ for **nda**, which can also of course be written න්ද. **nga** is normally written ංග.

The names of the Sinhalese letters consist of their sounds followed by **yanna**; thus **ga** is called **gayanna** (tends to be realised as **gæænna**), **pi** is called **piyanna**, etc. **g** (without vowel) is called **hal gayanna**.

කඳ	නැංගා	කඤුන
කඳු	බැඳ	රඹුක්කන
කනඳ	බංග	කොම්පඤඤ වීදිය
දඬු	හම්බ	හිඟුරක්ගොඩ
දණ්ඩ	කොන්ඩේ	හඟුරන්කෙත
හැඳි	බිඳ	කන්තෝරුව
හැඳක්	ගෙම්බා	හපුතලේ
හන්ද	කොහු	හික්කඩුව
දඟ	මචං	කුහුඹියෝ
ගඳයි	නහාලා	කටහඬ

1. Or in Sanskrit words.

ළඟින්
ගහෙ
ලිඳෙ
තඹ
කළු
කෝටු
කඹේ
මෙයා
ඤවි

පිංචක්
කරෝලිස්
කඳුලු
කොළඹ
පඤ්ච
කොම්බුව
කරන්ඩ
චණ්ඩියා
හුලඟ
මජං
කුරුම්බා
මහින්ද

නහිනවා
තැම්බෙනවා
බඳිනවා
ජෝග්ගුව
බිඳිනවා
නැඹිලි
නුගේගොඩ
කොටහේන
පැලියගොඩ
කැඳැත්තා
කපිරිඤ්ඤ

LESSON 9

hoňda	good
-lu	it is said
ekko / **hari**	or
kælææva / **kælee**	forest, jungle
paara	way (route); time (fois); blow (coup)
-hamaara	and a half
rupiyala	rupee
satee	cent
haya	six
hata	seven
aṭa	eight
namaya	nine
dahaya	ten
Yaapanee / **Jaapanee**	Jaffna
Tirikunaamalee	Trincomalee
Maḍakalapuva	Batticaloa

(a) **Plural**. The plural of an inanimate noun may normally be formed by cutting off final **-a** (except where this is preceded by a double consonant), **-va** or **-ya**.

pota	pot
puṭuva	puṭu
nama	nam
gama	gam
liyuma	liyum
pææna	pææn

Where such a noun ends in **-ha**, the plural ends in **-s**.

gaha gas

Nouns which end in **-ee** may also be writen to end **-aya**,[1] and the plural form consequently ends in **-a**.

meesee (meesaya) meesa

Some nouns in **-lee**, however, usually have plural forms in **-l**. These are words which have been borrowed from European languages.

pænsalee pænsal

Where removal of final **-a** would leave consonants such as **-r**, **-ḍ**, **-ṭ**, which cannot stand at the end of a genuine Sinhalese word,[2] a termination **-val** can be added instead. This termination is sometimes added where not strictly necessary.

paara	paaraval
kaḍee	kaḍa, kaḍaval.

(Further rules are given in lesson 24.)

(b) Numerals normally stand **after** the noun enumerated (except **eka**, which stands first), and if not preceded by 'the' or a similar deictic word in English, will then be followed by the indefinite suffix **-k**. (In other words, whereas in English we say 'a hundred', 'a thousand', in Sinhalese you also say 'a five', 'a ten'.)

pot paha	the five books
mee pot paha	these five books
pot pahak	five books
eka potak	one book, a certain book
ekak tiyenavaa	there is one (thing)

The last phrase often means 'There is a (noteworthy) thing, however'; cf. Eng. 'there's one thing anyway'.

ekakaṭa, **dekakaṭa** are often pronounced **[ehekəṭə, dehekəṭə]**.

(c) Where 'and' directly connects two or more nouns (in any case-form) it can be translated by adding **-yi** to each noun in Sinhalese. Two verbs, however, are not often connected in this fashion, nor are two qualifying adjectives (which need no connector). A final long vowel is shortened before **-yi** (except in monosyllables); where **-yi** is added to a word ending in a consonant, **-u-** is inserted.

mamayi eyayi	him and me, he and I
ammayi taattayi	mother and father (this is the usual order here)

---

1. See Introduction and lesson 5**a**.

2. See Introduction.

eyaaṭayi maṭayi	to him and me
potakuyi pææenakuyi	a book and a pen

This suffix is used in telling the time.

tunayi kaalayi	it is 3.15
hatarayi kaalaṭa enna	come at 4.15

Note that only one **-yi** is required in the second case. 'At a quarter to four'. however, cannot be expressed by **hataraṭa kaalaṭa**, and has to be stated in a longer way (see lesson 26); and similarly with 'at five to four' etc.

hamaara is always joined to a numeral without intervening **-yi**, and (of time) without **-k**.

tunahamaarayi	it is 3.30

but

ekahamaarak	1 ½

Notice the contracted forms **pahamaarayi**, **dahayamaarayi**, it is 5.30, 10.30.[1]

(d) Where 'or' connects two nouns, this can be translated by adding **hari** after each noun, or by **ekko** before each noun, or **ekko** between the two.

eyaa hari maŋ hari heṭa iskoolee inna oonæ
ekko eyaa ekko maŋ heṭa iskoolee inna oonæ
maŋ ekko eyaa heṭa iskoolee inna oonæ
either he or I must be at school tomorrow

Where 'or' occurs in an alternative question ('do you want this or that?'), **ekko** and **hari** are not usually used, but the interrogative particle **-da** is repeated. Two verbs may also be connected in this matter with **-da**.

pææenada puṭuvada oonæ?
do (you) want the pen, or the chair?
yanavaada enavaada?
are (you) going or coming?
yanavaada nædda?
are (you) going or not?

Where 'or' (or 'nor') occurs in a negative sentence, **vat** is usually used after each alternative (though **hari** is also possible here). This includes sentences containing **bææ** or **epaa**.

pææena vat puṭuva vat maṭa oonæ nææ
I don't want the pen or the chair

1. See also lesson 20**d**.

maŋ yanne vat (nææ) enne vat nææ

I am neither going nor coming

A single **vat** in a negative or interrogative sentence can be translated 'even'.

maṭa satayak vat nææ

I haven't even a cent

Compare this with

maṭa satayakut nææ

I haven't got a cent either

(e) **-lu** is a particle added to any word to represent reported tidings. As in the case of the interrogative particle **da** (lesson 4), the verb of the sentence must be in the incomplete form, unless **-lu** is added directly to it.

eyaa heṭa yanavaalu / eyaa yanne heṭalu	he says / I hear] he's going tomorrow
eeka hoñdalu / hoñdayilu	it's good, I hear

Where **nææ** is followed by **-lu**, the **l** is often doubled (**næ(h)ællu**), or the form **nætilu** may be used. **bærilu** is more common than **bæhælu** (cf. note on 7 A 22).

(f) The Sri Lanka currency is the rupee (about 32 to the £ in 1979), divided into 100 cents. Notice the use of the locative case in expressions such as

sata dahaye / dahayaka] pææenak, a 10-cent pen.

'One rupee' is **rupiyalak, rupiyalayi; eka** is only used here for special emphasis ('one single rupee'). Note that in enumerating sums of money, etc., **-k** at the end of a sentence is replaced by **-yi**. So also in **tunayi kaalayi**, above.

mee pota rupiyal hayayi

this book is (= costs) Rs. 6/-.

(g) Jaffna is a large town in the extreme north of Ceylon, mostly inhabited by Tamils. Trincomalee (often called Trinco) and Batticaloa (often pronounced Batticalo) are on the east coast. The Sinhalese name for Batticaloa is pronounced [**Maḍəkaləpuva**] (not [**Maḍəkəlapuvə**]), and means 'muddy marsh'.

Though 'jungle' and 'forest' seem to convey different impressions at first to the westerner, in Ceylon they are synonymous. Any waste and overgrown land in Lanka may be called jungle. Similarly, there is sometimes no difference there between 'earth' and 'sand', since nearly all the earth is sandy.

A.

Tirikunaamalee mehe nemeyi
sata dahayaṭat dæn pænsal tiyenavaa
Kolam̆ba dæn hon̆da hon̆da paaraval tiyenavaa
iiyeṭa lamayaa pot pahak bæluvaalu
ara puṭu kaaṭada?
paaṭa pænsal kiiyak tiyenavaada?
pot tunaṭa rupiyal dahayak giyaa
lamayaa puṭuvaṭa naginavaa
vijahaṭa gedara enna
vigavigahaṭa ara lamayaa yanne koheda?
maṭa pææṇakaṭa vaḍaa pænsalayak oonæ
taattaa ada Nuvara yanna bæri nææ
mama ekak dannavaa, mee lamayaa væḍa karanne nææ
Kolam̆ba kavda?
pææna meesee uḍa hari puṭuva yaṭa hari balanna
taattaaṭada ammaaṭada væḍiya kæmati?
ee pota rupiyal hayayilu
pææna pota yaṭalu
velaava dæn tunalu
mahattayaaṭa gas naginna puluvanda?
pahayi pahayi kiiyada? dahayayi
taattaa ee minihaaṭa puṭuvakaṭayi meeseekaṭayi salli dunnaa
ada heṭa mama game yanna oonæ
kavda mage pot ehaaṭa mehaaṭa karanne?
mee pææna kiiye ekakda?
ee lamayaa eka væḍak vat danne nææ
taattaa ekat ekaṭa dæn enavaa
mahattayaa Jaapanee yanna paara dannavaada?

B.

Give me the table or the chair.
Lend me five rupees.
Father is coming home at 1.0 today.
Don't let either that boy or his father come here.
This boy is well-behaved today.
Father is either going to Galle tomorrow or to Jaffna.

Is that gentleman tall or short?
Is it a stout gentleman or a thin one that's come?
Who is this tea for, me or father?
10 I can't go to Colombo or Kandy tomorrow.
They say that boy's father went to Colombo yesterday.
Why can't you go to either Colombo or Kandy tomorrow?
How many cents in a rupee?
I go home at 5.30.
15 Come here at a quarter past two.
There is one consolation, this boy works.
One book is mine.
Those two books are mine.
One more chair is needed.
20 These cost one rupee.
How much is this pen?
Give me one rupee, or two.
That boy still doesn't know the way home.
They will come our way at 4.30 tomorrow.
25 How many chairs are there for that table?
Father is there, I am here.
What is this called?
There is (enough) money for one pen here.

Notes:

A. 1 Or mee Tirikunaamalee nemeyi; 'this is not Trinco' (but somewhere else). **næææ** here would give a different impression, rather like 'there is no Trinco here' – which is not a thing one would normally say.

2 dahayaṭat or dahayakaṭat; dative case used of the price of an article. Compare 17 below, where the direct case is used in this sense. Similarly in English we can say either 'cabbages sell at 6p.' or 'cabbages are 6p.'

3 hon̆da hon̆da paaraval = many good roads. Sometimes **hon̆da hon̆da** may mean 'very good'. Kolam̆ba is locative here, cf. note on 28 below.

4 iiyeṭa: either 'yesterday' or 'up to yesterday' (cf. lessson 4 A 20).

6 Notice the difference between this and **paaṭa pænsal kiiyada**?

7 giyaa = were spent.

8 See note on 8 A 17.

10 Intensificatory doubling: 'so quickly'. (This word is not used to mean 'very soon'.)

12 bæri nææ = it is not unlikely.

13 **mee lamayaa** sometimes also means 'you' (lesson 1 c).

14 'Who is for Colombo?' May be said e.g. in a bus in this sense.

15 balanna; see 5 A 15.

16 'Do (you) like father or mother best?' **vædiya** is preferable to **vaḍaa** here.

17 hayayilu or hayalu or hayaklu.

20 gas naginavaa, 'climb trees', is a general expression; gasvalaṭa naginavaa is rather 'climb the trees'.

21 **kiiyada**, not **monavaada**, must be used here (cf. also 5 A 25).

23 ada heṭa, see lesson 2, note. game, see lesson 5 e.

24 karanne, is putting (see note on 8 A 13): 'who is moving my books around?' ehaaṭa mehaaṭa, see note on 4 A 27.

26 Doesn't know how to do anything.

27 ekat ekaṭa (pr. ekattekəṭə]) = surely. 'I expect father is now on his way.'

28 'The way (to go) to Jaffna'. **Jaapaneeṭa paara** is insufficient here. **Jaapanee** is used like **Kolam̆ba** (lesson 8 h).

B. 5 Well-behaved = good.

8 **ekek** is not generally used of persons, but only of animals. Say 'a thin gentleman'.

13 In a rupee: rupiyalakaṭa, rupiyalaka, rupiyalaṭa, rupiyale are all possible here.

16 See **b** above.

23 See note on A 28 above.

27 Say 'What is the name of this?'

Script

අ  ආ 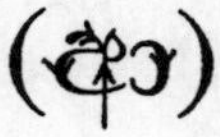 ඉ  ඊ 

a aa i ii

උ  ඌ 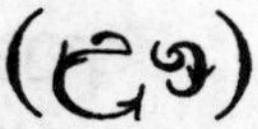

u uu

Since Sinhalese words can begin with vowels, there are separate vowel symbols, although as previously explained these are not used where a consonant precedes the vowel-sound in the same word. Where two dissimilar vowel-sounds might seem to come together in a Sinhalese word, it is usual to write an intervocalic glide v or y between, e.g. not තිඋනා (tiunaa) but තිවුනා (tivunaa) or තියුනා (tiyunaa). Vowel symbols are therefore almost always initial in a word.

අද	අතන	ඊරියගොල්ල
අපි	අරහෙ	ඉලංගකෝන්
ආවා	අටට	උබේසේකර
අර	උසට	අඹේපුස්ය
ඉදි	උන්නැහෙ	අම්බලන්ගොඩ
ආඳ	ඉන්නවා	ඉදිනවා
අඃ	ආදරේ	අවලංගු
උඩ	අලියා	විල්පත්තු
අපෙ	ඉස්කෝලේ	අවිස්සාවේල්ල
ඌට	අච්චාරු	අතරමං
ඊයෙ	උඹලා	අඟහරුවාද
උන්නා	ඉරිද	ඉඹිනවා
ආයු	සඳුද	වෙස්සන්තර
අතේ	අන්දරේ	ඉරනවා

උන්	ඉබ්බෙකුට	ඉගිල්ලෙනවා
අම්මා	ඉබේම	උරනවා
අච්චු	උදැල්ල	අහනවා
ආප්ප	උනුසුම්	තමන්කසුව
යාල	ඉත්තැවෝ	අඬනවා
ඊට	ඉස්තුති	උගුල්ලනවා
ඌරා	ඊයම්	ඉදිකටුපාන
අං	ඌව	උසුලන්ට
ආච්චි	ආඩියා	ඉන්දනවා
ආන්න	ආනන්ද	ඉන්දියාව
අණු		

LESSON 10

ahanavaa	listen: ask
æhuvaa	listened, asked
paninavaa	jump
pænnaa	jumped
gannavaa	take: buy
gattaa	took, bought
guruvarayaa	teacher
vatura	water
am̆ba	mangoes
naraka	bad
koyi / **mona**] + **da**	which?
koccara-da	how much? (in quantity)
ekolaha	eleven
dolaha	twelve
dahatuna	thirteen
dahahatara	fourteen
pahalova	fifteen
hun̆gak(ma)	much, many; very
hari	correct; very
hæbæyi	but
okkoma	all (i.e. every); everything, everybody
eccara / **occara** / **accara**	that much/many
meccara	this much/many
ivara	completed

(a) Animate nouns form an ablative case by adding the suffix **-gen**. After the indefinite suffix, a connecting vowel **u** is required.[1] This case-form will usually be translated into English with the word 'from'.

maŋ eeka minihaagen gattaa

I got it from the man

maŋ minihekugen æhuvaa

I asked a man (a question).

Notice this use of the case with the verb **ahanavaa**, of the person of whom a question is asked. The ablative case of **api** is **apen**, and of **mama, magen.**[2]

Inanimate nouns form an instrumental case by changing **-a** to **-en**, or sometimes **-in**; when used after an indefinite suffix, the ending is always **-in**. Nouns ending in **-ee** usually change **-ee** into **-en**, e.g. **meesee**, instr. **meesen,** although **meesayen** may sometimes also be heard (cf. lesson 5 **e**). This case-form will often be translated into English with the word 'with'.

api pæænen liyanavaa

we write with the pen, in pen.

It is also used in ablative contexts, i.e. where it may be translated 'from'. In this sense, these case-endings are used with words like **ada, yaṭa, ehe**.

pota meesee uḍin ganna

take the book from off the table.

This case is also used in a partitive sense.

hoňda vaturen bonna

drink (some) of the good (i.e. clean) water

Sometimes this case-form indicates position in space.

ballaa mehen aavaa

the dog came this way

When **uḍin** and **yaṭin** are used in this way, the noun which precedes them can be put in the dative case, which avoids ambiguity.

ballaa puṭuva uḍin pænnaa

the dog leapt over the chair (position in space)

or the dog jumped down off the chair (ablative)

but

ballaa puṭuvaṭa uḍin pænnaa

the dog leapt over the chair (**only**)

---

1. This **-u-** however is sometimes inaudible.

2. The gen. and abl. of **umba**, you (lesson 1 c) are **umbe, umben**.

(b) Inanimate nouns in the plural use the following suffixes in the various cases:

-valaţa (dative)
-valin (instrumental)
-vala (locative).

puţu – puţuvalaţa –puţuvalin – puţuvala
paaraval – paaravalvalaţa – paaravalvalin – paaravalvala

Be careful to pronounce [-vələţə] etc. – not [valəţə].

(c) 'Very', in positive or interrogative sentences, can be represented by **huňgak** or **huňgakma**,[1] or by **hari, harima, hari huňgak** or **hariyaţa**[2] (the last usually with verbs).

eyaa huňgak(ma)	usayi	he is	very tall
	usa minihek		a very tall man
eyaa hari(ma) lokuyi		he is very big	

The emphasizing enclitic particle **-ma** after an adjectival word usually gives the sense of 'the most'.

hoňdama lamayaa eyayi — he is the best boy

In this connection the plural ablative or instrumental case-forms are used where we say in English 'of'.

potvalin hoňdama eka — the best of the books

Notice also that sentences of the type 'he/this is the best' are usually expressed in Sinhalese in the reverse order, 'the best is he/this'. In such sentences, he/it is usually followed by the copular **-yi** or the emphasizing word **tamayi**, self.

eyaa / eyayi / eyaa tamayi	iskoolee hoňdama lamayaa	he is the best boy in the school
or iskoolee hoňdama lamayaa	eyaa / eyayi / eyaa tamayi	

'eyaa iskoolee hoňdama lamayayi' is unidiomatic.

An adjective is sometimes repeated after **ma**: lokuma loku lamayaa, the very biggest boy.

huňgak meaning 'much' or 'many' may either precede or follow a plural noun.

tee huňgak / huňgak tee	tiyenavaa,	there is plenty of tea

1. Sometimes realized as **huňgaak(ma)**.
2. For the adverbial case-form, see lesson 17 **a**.

minissu huňgak / huňgak minissu	aavaa,	many men (lesson 11) came.

It is not normally used predicatively. **huňgak** is also used with verbs:

eyaa huňgak mehe yanavaa enavaa — he is always around here.

(d) We have seen that in questions where the incomplete verb-form is used, emphasis may be thrown upon the word to which **-da** is added (api yanne heṭada? is it tomorrow that we go?). The same emphasis may be given in affirmative sentences by **-yi**, the verb being in the incomplete form.

heṭayi api yanne — it is tomorrow that we go, we are going **tomorrow**.

In such sentences **-yi** is often omitted, especially where the emphasized word stands last.

api yanne heṭa — we are going **tomorrow**

or after words ending in **-n**

api pææṇvalin liyanne — we write with **pens**.

To give strong emphasis, **-yi** can be replaced by **tamayi**.[1]

minihaa aave iiye tamayi — it was yesterday that he came.

Where such sentences are negative, the emphasized word is usually negated by **nemeyi**, though sometimes an incomplete verb-form may be used preceded by **no-**, especially in generalized statements (instead of being followed by **nætte**).

(e) **koyi** and **mona** are adjectival words; the **-da** is usually attached to the noun they precede. 'Which one?' (noun) is **kooka-da** (koyi + eka), pl. **koyivaa-da**.[2] **mona** means rather 'which kind', and the noun then often has the **-k** suffix.

mee mona potakda? — what kind of book is this? (usually sarcastic)

koccara, etc., unlike **kiiyada**, may stand either before or after a noun:

pot koccarada? / koccara potda? — how many books?

meccara pot (**or** pot meccarak), — this number of books.

It is also used before adjectival words: koccara hoňdada! how good!

(f) Exclamatory sentences such as 'How much he eats!' have in Sinhalese exactly the same form as questions of the type 'How much does he eat?' The difference is one of intonation only, a question normally having arising intonation (except for

1. When final in a sentence, **tamayi** is often realized as **tamaa**.
2. Or **kovvaa, koovaa**.

the final **-da**), and an exclamation a falling intonation on the verb.

koccara kanavaada?	koccara kanavaada!
kiiyak keruvaada eyaa?	how much has he done?
kiiyak / koccarak — keruvaada eyaa!	what a lot he has done!

(g) **okkoma**, when used adjectively, may either precede or follow a noun. If used with a pronoun, the pronoun must stand first.

tee okkoma / okkoma tee	all the tea
api okkoma	all of us
mee okkoma / meevaa okkoma	all this, all these

(but not meeka okkoma).

In the meaning 'everything', it has a dative case-form **okkoṭama**. Where it means 'everybody' it also has further case-forms **okkogema** and **okkogenma**,[1] and in the direct case **okkomalaa** can also be used (optionally followed by a further **ma**).[2]

ee gollo / ee — okkoṭama	to all of them

okkoma is not normally used for 'all' in the sense of 'whole' (as in 'all the week'),[3] nor predicatively (see A 35 below).

hari! or **hari hari**! is often used as an exclamation, 'right!' ee hari/eeka hari (not written 'hariyi') means 'that is correct.'

A. mama ee lamayaagen okkoma dannavaa.
am̆ba kiiyada?
koyi potada onnæ?

---

1. Also **okkomaŋgema, okkomaŋgenma**.

2. **okkomalaama** is pronounced [ookoməlamə] – but has nothing to do with the word **lamayaa**. -laa is a plural personal ending, see Lesson 11.

3. See also lesson 14 **e**.

baalama lamayaa suduma suduyi.
hun̆gakma hon̆da lamayaa kavda?
maŋ sallivalaṭa minihaaṭa potak denavaa.
uḍama pota taattaage.
ee lamayaa dæn usaṭa usayi.
eyaa ee poten dæn væḍa karanavaa.
taattaagen kiiyada?
eyaa inne hari kælææve.
maṭa ekak nææ eeken.
ee lamayaa heṭa iskoolee enavaada?
mama nemeyi ee liyum livve.
minihaa puṭuva gedarayi hadanne.
Kolam̆ba nemeyilu eyaa yanne.
ee gollanuyi heṭa enne.
taattaa dæn gedara nemeyi inne, Gaalle.
maŋ kæmati poḍi puṭuvakaṭayi.
pææna meesee uḍa nemeyi tiyenne.
tunen dekak ekayi.
koyivaada mahattayaaṭa oonæ?
mahattayaage teevatura-eken maṭat ṭikak denna.
lamayaa karanne hari væḍee.
ṭikakaṭa mehen inna.
apiṭa oya puṭu ekak vat epaa.
ada hæbæyi maṭa enna bææ.
api heṭa mehen yanavaa.
maṭa adin væḍa ivarayi.
ee væḍee adin karanna puluvanda?
mee pææn tava ekayi ee kaḍee tiyune.
maŋ dænuyi bat kææve.
meevaa kohenda gatte?
velaava dæn ekolahamaarayi.
eccarayi.
Kolam̆baṭa yanna kiiyak gannavaada?

B. I will come today but I won't stay for tea.

Whose is the snow-white cat?
Where is the smallest boy?
What did the teacher ask the child today?
Yesterday I bought a book from that man.
The biggest chair is mine.
Who is the tallest man in the village?
The boy is writing in pen.
I asked you to come for a small job.
How much for these books?
Who took the pen from my table?
How many cents is two rupees?
It is tea that we are drinking here.
It is (his) father that the boy is writing the letter to.
It is not me that is going home tomorrow.
That boy is going **home**.
I have (only) one pen.
That elephant is looking (over) **here**.
We are now writing with **pens**.
How much is four rupees in cents?
Father is drinking out of my tea(-cup).
The man didn't come this way.
This child is very good.
That man is very nice, they say.
They say that gentleman is very good at (his) books.
Where did (you) get this book from?
I wrote that letter not to father (but) to mother.
It's not mother (but) father that gave me this book.
Everyone came punctually at 5.0.
This dog doesn't want to jump into the water.
He wasn't **there** either.
We had (our) meal (only) just now.
We don't want such a bad one (as this).
The cat jumped on to the chair.
Yesterday I wrote eight letters.
They say it's tomorrow (they) go.

Notes:

A. 2 'How much are the mangoes?' In certain contexts this might also mean 'how many mangoes?', but that would more usually be am̆ba kiiyakda? or am̆ba kiiyada tiyenne?

3 Cf. mona potakda, which kind of book?

5 Here, huṅgakma hon̆da is the same as **hon̆dama**.

7 uḍama = uppermost, top.

8 usaṭa usayi = harima usayi.

10 'How much from father?', i.e. 'What will you contribute, father?'

11 'Real jungle'.

12 'There is not one thing for me from that', i.e. it doesn't matter to me.

17 For the -u-, cf. lesson 9 **c**.

18 See note on 3 A 12.

19 Note that -yi is added to puṭuvakaṭa, not to poḍi. Noun and qualifying adjective are inseparable. The same applies with genitive case-forms, e.g. 'mee pot kaageda?' may be expressed as 'mee kaage potda?' but not as 'mee kaageda pot?' (though 'mee kaageda mee pot?' is possible, see Lesson 4 A4).

21 'Two from three is one'.

23 Strictly speaking, **teevatura** ('tea-water') is the drink, while **tee** is the bush or leaf; but tee-ekak is used as well as teevatura-ekak for a cup of (brewed) tea.

24 Besides meaning 'the boy is doing the **right** work', this can also mean 'the boy is doing the unexpected thing' (cf. dialectical English expressions such as 'a right mess'). **hari væḍak** would have the first meaning, **hari væḍa** (pl.) the second.

25 Cf. 7 A 19 (mehen = hence). Or 'stay here' (mehen = mehe).

26 puṭu or puṭuvalin.

27 Where **hæbæyi** does not stand initially, we can translate 'however'.

28 **mehen** may mean either 'from here' or 'this way', according to context.

29 adin = after today. **heṭin** (from heṭa) is also used, but not **iiyen**.

30 adin = by today ('time within which').

31 Cf. 26 above. 'Still one of this sort of pen.' With incomplete verb, the -yi suffix is necessary here after eka (cf. B17 below).

32 dænuyi = (only just) now.

33 kohen = whence?
34 Notice the contracted forms ekolahamaara, dolahamaara, pahalovamaara.
35 This means 'That's all'. Similarly, **pot meccarayi**, this is all the books there are. okkoma cannot be used here.
36 gannavaada, 'do (they) take', i.e. charge (subject indefinite).

B. 1 Say 'to drink tea' (infinitive).
7 Locative case can be used here.
9 vædakaṭa: see lesson 5 **a**.
10 'For these books', dative case; but also **mee pot kiiyada**? how much are these books? Compare the corresponding uses of the dative and direct cases of the price, 9 A 2 note.
12 dekak or dekakaṭa; cf. preceding note, and also 9 B 13.
13 'Here': see lesson 3 **e**.
15 See lessons 8 **a** and 10 **d**. The verb-form must be incomplete here.
17 The effect of 'only' can be given here by inverting the sentence and using the incomplete verb-form (so also 32 below). Here **pææṇayi** is preferable to **pææṇak**, cf. A 31 above.
18 Here: see lesson 4 **c**.
20 'In cents' – satavalin.
25 'At his books' – potvalaṭa.
27 Invert this sentence.
29 Punctually – hariyaṭa.
34 On to – uḍaṭa. **puṭuvaṭa** alone would give the idea '**down** on to the chair'. With the verb **naginavaa**, however, puṭuvaṭa alone would be insufficient.

Script

æ ææ e ee

o oo

ඇඟ	ඕකට	ඇඳනවා
ඇන්ටි	ඔතන	එඬේරමුල්ල
එයා	එනවා	එකොළහමාරට
එක	ඇහුවා	ඇපිල්ලුවා
ඒක	එච්චර	ජාඇල
ඔය	ඔක්කොම	ඇත්තටම
එහෙන්	ඕකාට	පොලොන්නරුව
ඔව්	ඒකිගෙ	ඇරපිය
ඕනැ	ඇරියා	ඇහින්ද
එපා	ඇල්ලුවා	අන්තරාවයි
එක්කො	ඔතැනි	ඒ ගොල්ලො
ඒ	ඔමරි	
ඇපල්	ඇල්ල	
ඇත	අංගොඩ	
ඇද්ද		
ඕලු		

LESSON 11

kapanavaa	cut (present)
kæpuvaa	cut (past)
kaḍanavaa	break (off), pick
kæḍuvaa	broke
bahinavaa	go down, get out (of vehicle)
bæssaa	went down
duvanavaa	run, run away
divuvaa	ran
vahinavaa	rain
væssaa	rained
naanavaa	bathe, have bath
næævaa	bathed
un	they (of animals)[1]
mokaa-da, **kookaa-da**	which one? (of animals)
uu, **eekaa**	it (of animals)[1]
duu	daughter
putaa	son
koocciya	train
bas-eka	bus
kaar-eka	car
kiidenaada, kiidenek-da	how many people?
ekkenaa	one person
dennaa	two people
tundenaa	three people
hataradenaa	four people

---

1. Impolite if used of people.

pasdenaa	five people
hayadenaa	six people
hatdenaa (pron. **haddenaa**)	seven people
aṭadenaa	eight people
namadenaa	nine people
dahadenaa	ten people
ekolosdenaa	eleven people
dolosdenaa	twelve people

(a) Plural. The plural of animate nouns usually ends in **-o**, variant **-an** (sometimes **-in** if preceded by **-y-**), or else in **-u**, variant **-un**. -u is usually preceded by a doubled consonant.

ballaa	ballo, ballan
balalaa	balallu, balallun
minihaa	minissu, minissun (for the alternation h/s, cf. lesson 9 **a**, and Introduction 4).
gonaa	gonnu, gonnun
væḍakaarayaa	væḍakaarayo, væḍakaarayan, væḍakaarayin
guruvarayaa	guruvarayo, guruvarayan, guruvarayin

but notice the following –

aliyaa	ali, alin, aliyo, aliyan
lamayaa	lamayi (pron. [lamay]), lamayin

-va can be added, where applicable (lesson 3 **f**), after the forms in **-n**: ballanva.

In the case of persons, however, the suffixes **-laa** or **varu**, **varun** are often employed. **-laa** is sometimes used respectfully of a single person. It can be followed by **-va**. Notice the following –

(guruvarayaa)	guruvaru, guruvarun (alternative to guruvarayo)
(mahattayaa)	mahatturu (=mahat+varu), mahatturun, mahattayaalaa (as well as mahattayan)
duu	duuru (duu+varu), duurun, duulaa
putaa	puttu, puttun, putaalaa

In the remaining case-forms, the endings **-ṭa**, **-ge**, **-gen** are added after the plural form ending in **-n**, or directly after **-laa**.

ballanṭa	duulaaṭa
ballange	duulaage
ballangen	duulaagen

The four noun case-forms can therefore be tabulated as follows:

SINGULAR

	Animate	*Inanimate*	
Direct	aliyaa		pota
Genitive	aliyaage	Locative	pote
Ablative	aliyaagen	Instrumental	poten
Dative	aliyaaṭa		potaṭa

PLURAL

aliyo	pot
aliyange	potvala
aliyangen	potvalin
aliyanṭa	potvalaṭa

When a noun has the indefinite suffix **-k**, the case-endings are added to it as follows:

aliyek	potak
aliyekuge	potaka
aliyekugen	potakin
aliyekuṭa	potakaṭa

(b) When enumerating animates, the numeral (sometimes in a slightly altered form) is followed by a noun **denaa** ('person(s)'). **dedenaa** is usually shortened to **dennaa**; with **eka**, a similar word **kenaa** is used of people, but **ekaa** is used of animals (see lesson 7 A 6).

sudu ballaa ape ekaa

the white dog is our one (ours)

ara minihaa ape ekkenaa

that man is 'our one', i.e. my husband (see 3 B 13 note).

The indefinite suffix **-k** is added where necessary, as explained in lesson 9 **b** above.

ballan dennek innavaa

there are two dogs (there)

minissu tundenek aavaa
three men came[1]

In the word **kiidenaada**, the **-da** is inseparable (cf. 8 **f** above), so that kiidenek should be used, not kiidenaa, in questions where **-da** is attached to the verb.

kiidenek aavaada? how many (people) came?

or kiidenaada] aave?
kiidenekda]

denaa is only used when compounded with a numeral or similar word (e.g. huṅgadenek, many people), but **kenek** is found by itself.

eyat ape kenek he also is one of us

'Which one?', when referring to people, is koyi ekkenaada? The forms **kookaa** and **mokaa** are usually confined to animals. Similarly **eekaa, ookaa**, **arakaa, meekaa** are used of animals, but **eyaa**, **arayaa** and (usually) **meyaa** (3rd person), **oyaa** (2nd person) of people (cf. lesson 1).

(c) Note the words bas-eka, kaar-eka (pron. [**bassekə**, **kaarrekə**], see Introduction). Any foreign word can be adapted into Sinhalese in this way. Modern official policy often tries to replace such words by more learned official alternatives. The plural forms of these words are **bas**, **kaar**, etc.

(d) **kaḍanavaa**, to break off, is used of picking flowers or fruit, and of breaking things (e.g. furniture) so that they are no longer serviceable; but not of crushing or dissolving into small bits, as in breaking glass or china, for which a different verb is required (lesson 20).

duvanavaa is used not only of human beings, but also of e.g. buses, trains, horses. **naanavaa** indicates the process of washing oneself; this is normally done daily at a well or pond, and involves pouring cold water over the whole body, including the head, but not getting into the water. A bathe in the modern English sense is normally referred to (in English) as a 'sea bath', and is by no means a common practice; for women it is almost unknown.

A. ara minissu monavaada ara karanne?
lamayin aṁba kaḍanavaa
mee lamayin hataradenaagen usama ekkenaa kavda?
Kolaṁbaṭa vahinavaa

1. There is also a somewhat ungrammatical phrase **eka minissuyi**, [we are all] one people.

taattaa væḍaṭa yanne koocciyen
maŋ Gaalle
ee lamayaa dæn huñgak paaṭayi
taattaa Gaalu koocciyaṭayi nægge
ara kavda ara dæn kaar-eken bæsse?
eka kaar-eke minissu aṭadenek hiṭiyaa
ee minihaaṭa puttuma dahadenek hiṭiyaa
mage putaalaa aṭadenaama heṭa mehe enavaa
api tundenaagen taattaa væḍiya kæmati kaaṭada?
mee paara hari nææ
Kaṭugastoṭa hæmadaama ali naanavaa
ee minihaa dæn mehe nemeyi væḍa karanne
mahattayaa mokakada aave?
kavda hæmadaama ape liyum kaḍanne?
lamayaaṭa puṭuven bahinna kiyanna
loku putaa iiye Yaapaneeṭa giyaa
ee minihaage duuṭa ee minihaa dæn gedara enna denne nææ
iiye ape dihaavaṭa huñgak væssaa
lamayi hataradenaaṭama koocciyaṭa giye loku minissu dennekuge salli

B. Two men are going along the road.
The two boys are eating rice.
(Our) son is cutting (down) the jungle.
Wait a little – mother is bathing now.
Whose is that big red car?
One of their boys came here.
There are elephants in this jungle.
How many teachers are there in this school?
Tomorrow ten gentlemen are coming to tea with us.
Does it rain every day in Kandy?
I'm going to Galle by train tomorrow.
The good boy is working, the bad boy is not [working].
Either he or I must go to Colombo today.
Here is Jaffna.
He is from Kandy.
Do buses run on this road?

I have two dogs.

How many boys came to school today?

There were two or three elephants on the road.

20 How many others came in your car?

Did everyone get into the bus?

That man is running to get into the bus.

Is this car still [running] on the road?

Notes:

A. 2 See n. on 15 **B** 17, below.

3 For the case-form, see Lesson 10 **c**.

4 The dative case is more usual than the locative here.

6 I am of Galle, from Galle. **Gaallen** is also possible here. Or the phrase could be spoken on a telephone, 'I am at Galle'.

7 paaṭa = fair, handsome (see note on 7 A 24).

8 Gaalu koocciya (lesson 8 **h**) 'the Galle train'. Remember that **koocciya,** although derived from 'coach', does not mean a motor-bus.

10 **The** one car (as v. eka kaar-ekaka).

11 puttuma dahadenek = ten children, all sons.

12 aṭadenaama = all eight. As **denaa** is a dissyllable with an initial light syllable, the final **-aa** is not shortened before terminations (see Introduction). Similarly putaalaa; but **ammaalaa** is pronounced [ammalaa].

13 See note on 9 A 16.

14 'This road is not right', or 'Not right this time'. The second sense is given unambiguously by: mee paara hari giye nææ, 'it didn't work this time'. hari yanavaa = go right, suit.

15 Kaṭugastoṭa (unchanged in the loc. case) is a place near Kandy where elephants bathe in the river.

17 mokakda or mokakinda, 'in what vehicle?' In these case-forms of the interrogative, the indefinite suffix can also be omitted: mokenda or mokeeda (the **-e** of **moke** being lengthened before **-da**). See also note on 5 B 19.

18 kaḍanavaa here = to open.

19 This implies that the child is **standing** on the chair.

23 loku minissu dennekuge salli = the cost (fare) of two adults. giye, 'went', i.e. was spent (as in 9 A 7).

B. 1 Along; locative case.
5 Adjectival order should be the same as it is in English.
9 Say 'to drink tea at our house'.
10 See note on A 4 above.
14 In this sentence, **menna** or **mee tiyenne** ('here it is') can be used if pointing to a map (but not when actually on the spot. When actually on the spot, one may say **mee Yaapanee**, this is Jaffna; cf. note on 9 A 1.)
16 Run – tr. literally.
19 Two or three – **detundenek**. (But **detunak** is not used.)
20 Others – use **tava**.
23 See 16 above.

Script

Sanskrit and Pali, the classical languages of India, have a separate set of aspirated consonants, **kh**, **gh**, etc. Although the distinction between aspirated (**mahapraana**) and unaspirated consonants is not significant in Sinhalese, the script contains the full set, and the aspirated letters are frequently used in writing Sanskrit and Pali loan-words, though they may always be replaced by the corresponding unaspirated forms. One must also be prepared to find aspirated letters used where there is no historical justification for them (e.g. **viʃiʂʈa**, **stambha** are often written viʃiʂʈha, sthambha).

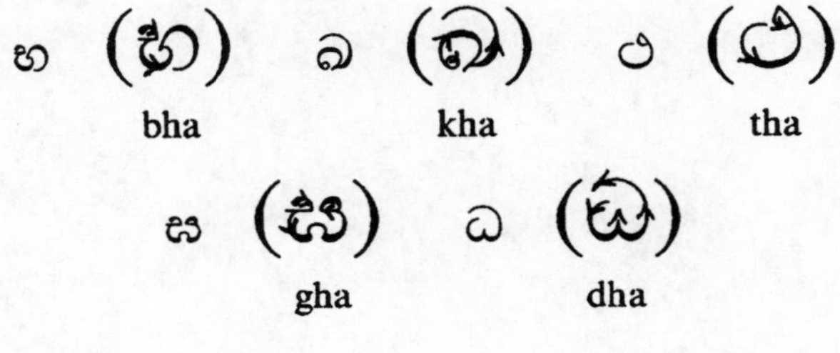

භු	ඛු	ථු	ඝු	ධු
bhu	khu	thu	ghu	dhu

කථා	සාධු	ථූපවංසය
භීතිය	මාගධි	ඛුද්දක නිකාය
තිඵීය	ධාවනය	ආධුනිකයන්
මුඛය	ධෝවනය	මඛාදේව
සුඛිත	ආඝාත	අභිධාන
ඝෝර	ආභාස	අභයසිංහ
ඵුල්ල	භුවන	පඤඤසේඛර
ධූපයන්	ඵීන	තථාගතයා
භූමිතලය	ථෝක	නභෝතලය
	භික්ඛු	මහාභාරත
	මේඛලා	

LESSON 12

piinanavaa	swim
uyanavaa	cook
haaranavaa	dig (up)
huuranavaa	scratch (so as to leave a mark)
hoodanavaa (**soodanavaa**)	wash (tr.)
otanavaa	wrap up
makanava	rub out
venavaa	become, happen, be
arinavaa	send (away); open; (with dative case of the person) allow
udee	(in the) morning
havasa	(in the) afternoon
paarsalee (pl. **paarsal**)	parcel, packet
ganana, gaana	price; sum (calculation)
kantooruva	office
kohetma	(with negative) at all
ata	hand, arm; direction

(a) Past tense. Sinhalese verbs can be divided into two conjugational types: those which, in their present tense-form, end in **-anavaa** (Type I), and those which end in **-inavaa** (Type II). There are also a few special cases, such as **enavaa, denavaa, venavaa, bonavaa, gannavaa.**[1]

1. The past tense of verbs in **-anavaa** is regularly formed by changing **-anavaa** to **-uvaa**, and also modifying the vowel of the root in the following ways:

---

1. For involitive forms, see Lesson 13.

a ⟶	æ
aa	ææ
u	i
uu	ii
o	e
oo	ee

If the vowel in the root is æ, ææ, e, ee, i or ii, it does not change. Thus

balanavaa	bæluvaa
haaranavaa	hææruvaa
uyanavaa	ivvaa
huuranavaa	hiiruvaa
otanavaa	etuvaa
hoodanavaa	heeduvaa
piinanavaa	piinuvaa

Note that in the case of **uyanavaa**, the resulting past tense-form **iyuvaa** is normally spelt **ivvaa**. Similarly with **kiyanavaa, liyanavaa** the past tense-forms **kiyuvaa, liyuvaa** are usually written **kivvaa, livvaa**[1] (and in some districts contracted to **kiivaa, liivaa**).

2. The past tense of verbs in **-inavaa** can be formed by changing **-inavaa** to **-iyaa**, and modifying the root vowel where necessary in the same manner as explained above.

hiṭinavaa	hiṭiyaa
arinavaa	æriyaa

More usually however the ending consonant + **-iyaa** in this position is contracted to double consonant + **-aa**.

naginavaa	næggaa (contracted from nægiyaa)
bahinavaa	bæssaa (alternation h/s, lesson 9 **a**).

3. The following common verbs use irregularly formed past tenses:

enavaa	aavaa
yanavaa	giyaa
denavaa	dunnaa
bonavaa	bivvaa[2]
gannavaa	gattaa

---

1. Or **kivuvaa, livuvaa.**
2. Or **biivaa**; in some districts **bunnaa**.

venavaa	vunaa, unaa
karanavaa	keruvaa; sometimes kalaa, karaa (pron. [kəla, kəra])[1]
kanavaa	kæævaa
naanavaa	næævaa

(For innavaa and dannavaa, see lessons 5 **c** and 6 **d**).

(b) **havasa** means any time after mid-day; it it usually translated 'evening' (the English word 'afternoon' being little used), but normally refers to times before it gets dark (which happens soon after 6.00 all the year round). It remains unaltered in the locative case.

(c) The initial **v-** of venavaa is often hardly audible (especially where the previous word ends in **-k**). In the past tense it is often omitted in writing also. Unlike tiyenavaa and innavaa (lesson 5 c), this verb can be used with a complement, i.e. we can say **meevaa mage venavaa**, these will be mine (notice the meaning).

A.

udee havasa dekeema ammaa bat uyanavaa
balalaa maava hiiruvaa
taattaa udeeṭa kantooru yanavaa, havasa gedara enavaa
ee minihaa udee namayaṭa kantooru yanavaa, havasa pahaṭa gedara enavaa
5 mama heṭa uden yanavaa Gaalu yanna
taattaa kantooruven gedara enne havasaṭayi
kavda ara vature piinanne?
api kæmati tee bonna
taattaa ada væḍaṭa giye bas-eken
10 lamayaa pæænen liyanavaa makanavaa, liyanavaa makanavaa
apiṭa udeeṭa tee hæduve kavda ada?
ee lamaya ada hariyaṭa velaavaṭa iskoolee aave
taattaa vigahaṭa enna kivvaa
potakaṭa paha gaane denavaa
15 mee pote gaana kiiyada?
mahattayaa gonaa venna epaa
ballaa monavaada oya haaranne?

---

1. Also **koranavaa, kolaa, koraa** in some areas.

mee pææna Nuvara rupiyal tunak venavaa ehaaṭa venna!
20 eyaa apiṭa ganan arinna aavaa
ee gollo apiva dæn ganan ganne nææ
oovaayin kiiyen kiiyakda hari yanne?
api bat kanne atin
putaa ada monavaada iskoolee keruve?
25 ekak sata dolaha ganane am̆ba dahayakaṭa kiiyada?

B. The dog can swim [in water].
That gentleman works the whole day.
I swam a lot yesterday.
Who opened my letters?
5 Did (you) wash the car today?
Did the gentleman go to the office today?
Did mother cook rice for them too?
What a lot of books that boy has looked at today!
This dog didn't eat yesterday.
10 Did that man wash the car yesterday too?
Did (you) send my letter to that gentleman yesterday?
I came by **bus**.
This book will be one rupee.
This boy's work is not good at all.
15 That man cannot wrap up a parcel at all.
Father goes to the office at **nine**.
Where did you go yesterday morning?
How many more parcels are there on that table?
When do (they) open this office?
20 Give me all that.
Please move over there.
What happened to you yesterday?
My work is finished from tomorrow.
He is at home for (the day) today.
25 It is 12.10 now.

Notes:

A. 1 Notice how 'both' can be expressed by **deka-ma** (**dennaa-ma** for animates) following two nouns, with or without -yi suffixes: 'in both morning and afternoon (evening)'. Here **dekeema** is not essential; **udee havasa** alone gives the same meaning. The final **-e** of **deke** is lengthened before **-ma** (cf. 11 A 17 note): **dekama** is also possible here.

2 maava: lesson 3 **f**.

3 kantooru: 'stem-form', see lesson 8 **h**. **udeeṭa** and **havasaṭa** (6 below) usually mean 'in the morning', 'in the afternoon', and are interchangeable in this sense with **udee** and **havasa** – except where, as in sentence 4, a further specifying word of time is added (cf. note on 4 A 20).

5 uden, udee = in the morning. **udeema**, **udenma** mean 'early in the morning'. Gaalu, see lesson 8 **h**. yanavaa yanna, see 6 A 1.

8 This is an inverted sentence (lesson 10 **d**).

10 'Keeps scratching things out'. For the repeated verbs, cf. yanavaa enavaa, lesson 2 note.

11 'Who made our breakfast?' Breakfast in Ceylon is still often referred to as 'morning tea' (tea in bed not being a general custom), and some people used to refer to the mid-day meal as 'breakfast'.

12 hariyaṭa velaavaṭa = exactly on time. Cf. hari velaavaṭa, which means 'at the right time', or 'at an unsuitable time' (**hari** used sarcastically).

14 potakaṭa or potaṭa. '(I) will give (you) (Rs.) 5/- for each book', lit. at the rate of five for a book. This refers to an offer to purchase, but cf. **potak** paha gaane denavaa, sell the books at Rs. 5/- each. **gaane** following a numeral (without **-k**) is equivalent to 'at the rate of'.

15 pote or potaṭa. Cf. ape gaana kiiyada? 'what's our bill, please?' (**mokakda** would not be used here.)

16 'Don't be an ass' (lit. 'the bull'). See lesson 3 **g**.

18 venavaa = will be, would be, i.e. would cost. **tunayi** can be substituted for **tunak venavaa**, see lesson 9 **f**.

19 'Be thither!' i.e. 'stand back!'

20 **apiṭa ganan arinna** means 'to get round us'. 'Came to' means 'tried to'.

21 **apiva ganan ganna** means 'to take account of us, bother about us'.[1]

22 oovaayin, instr. case of **oovaa**, pl. of **ooka**. The -y- is a glide sound

1. See lesson 14 **d**. Cf. oovaa ganan ganna epaa, never mind that.

inserted before case-endings that begin with a vowel after noun-forms which end in **-aa**; similarly **oovaaye**, loc. kiiyen kiiyakda = what percentage (how many out of how many)? – i.e. how few! hari yanavaa, see 11 A 14 note.

23 Food in Ceylon is normally eaten (except in highly westernized contexts) with the right hand, but a spoon is always used to serve out the food.

24 This is addressed to the son. Proper names are not generally used between parent and child, or between brothers and sisters. Daughters are sometimes addressed as **putaa** also.

25 At (the rate of) 12 cents each. dahayakaṭa or dahayak; with dahayakaṭa, **ekakaṭa** can also be used instead of **ekak**.

B. 1 Dogs can also be said to 'swim', i.e. wallow, in mud. **vature** may optionally be added here.

2 The whole day: say 'both morning and afternoon'. See A 1 above.

4 **arinavaa** can mean to open a letter, as well as to send one (B 11 below). **kaḍanavaa** can also be used of opening letters (11 A 18).

6 Cf. A 3 above.

13 Cf. A 18 above.

21 Cf. A 19 above, and lesson 7 **a**.

22 Happened to you, tr. literally.

23 From tomorrow: cf. 10 A 29.

Script

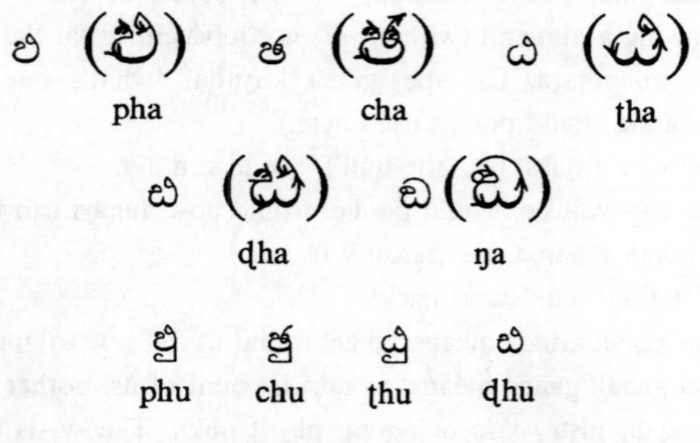
ඵ pha
ඡ cha
ඨ ṭha
ඪ ḍha
ඞ ŋa
ඵු phu
ඡු chu
ඨු ṭhu
ඪු ḍhu

ŋ (ඞ) only occurs immediately before velar consonants in loan-words from Pali or Sanskrit (as in anka, sangha), and is often replaced by ං, from which it does not differ in pronounciation.

When a consonant (with inherent a-vowel) is joined in the script to a following consonant, the two signs become a single Sinhalese letter, and the inherent vowel of the first consonant is lost. This method of **al-kiriima** is conventionally employed in writing Sanskrit and Pali loan-words.

ndha is usually written න්‍ධ.

අඞ්ක	සාංඝික	කඞ්ඛාවිතරණී
අන්ත	මිථ්‍යාචාර	දුට්ඨගාමණී
ස්ඵුට	උච්ඡේද	මිලින්දපඤ්හ
අන්‍ධ	ඡායාව	ඤාණිස්සර
ඵාසු	ස්තම්භ	පිණ්ඩපාතික
අස්තු	කුණ්ඩලි	දාඨාවංසය
ඨිති	සම්බන්‍ධ	සමන්තකූට
අඞ්ග	පාඨකයා	සරණඞ්කර
ගූඪ	ඡද්දන්ත	රත්නාකර
ආස්මි	දුට්ඨුල්ල	අට්ඨකථා
දුක්ඛ	නිගණ්ඨ	සුමඞ්ගල
දුඃඛ[1]	උපතිස්ස	ධම්මරක්ඛිත
ශ්‍යේනය	ඵලය	සඞ්ඝබෝධි
ජීත	ඡුරිකා	විමලබුද්ධි
	මණ්ඩපය	
	ජ්වර	
	තණ්හා	

1. **duḥkha** is normally pronounced the same as **dukkha**.

LESSON 13

vikunanavaa (alternative irregular past tense, **vikkaa**)	sell
vahanavaa	shut, cover (up)
maranavaa	kill
læbenavaa	be got
ganan karanavaa	count; do sums
dækkaa	saw (vb.)
dænenavaa	be known (felt, heard)
penenavaa, peenavaa	appear, be seen
ibeema / **ibeeṭama**	automatically
bæri velaa	accidentally, forgetfully
hoňdaṭa / **hoňdin**	well (adverb)
-kaarayaa	'doer'; used in compound words (following a 'stem-form'),[1] e.g. katkaarayaa, 'pingo'-carrier, elavalukaarayaa, vegetable-seller (cf. væḍakaarayaa, lesson 4)
kuḍee	umbrella
dora	door
almaariya	cupboard, wardrobe
kada	'pingo' yoke
elavalu (pl.)	vegetables
geḍiya	fruit
baḍuva	object, thing

1. Lesson 17 **b**.

pihiya (pl. **pihi** or **pihiyaa**)	knife
tææga (pl. **tæægi**)	present, prize
væssa	rain
aḍiya	foot (length)
kalu	black, dark
diga	long, length
palala	broad, width
aňgala	inch

(a) Involitive verbs. Besides **arinavaa**, to open (tr.), there is also a verbal form **ærenavaa**, get (itself to) open, be opened. Such verbal forms always end in **-enavaa**, and the root vowel is modified where applicable, just as in the past tense. In theory, every verb, whether in **-anavaa** or in **-inavaa**, can have an involitive counterpart in **-enavaa**, though in some cases this form will hardly be used. Some verbs, such as **penenavaa**, are found only in an involitive form. In some cases, the involitive is formed from a causative (Lesson 18). The past tense-form of verbs in **-enavaa** ends in **-unaa**: læbenavaa, læbunaa.

An animate **subject** of an involitive verb often adds the ending **-va**.

mee ballaava læbune kohenda?
where did (you) get this dog from?
(where was this dog got from?)

The English equivalent of an involitive verb may take several forms. For instance –

maŋ dora æriyaa	dora ærunaa
I opened the door	the door opened
maŋ eeka pihiyen kapanavaa	mage pihiya hoňdaṭa kæpenavaa
I cut it with the knife	my knife cuts well

Here the same words 'cut' and 'open' are used in both cases in English. Compare on the other hand –

maŋ eyaava mæruvaa	I killed him
eyaa mærunaa	he died

Sometimes the English equivalent will be expressed passively.

maŋ eevaa karanavaa	I will do that
eevaa kerenne nææ	that will not get (be) done

Note that in this verb the root vowel is modified to **e** instead of **æ**. In practice,

venavaa often serves as an involitive equivalent of **karanavaa** (cf. A 13 below).

eeka mage pihiyaṭa kæpunaa

it got (accidentally) cut by (lit. 'to') my knife

mee pænsalee hoňdaṭa kæpenavaa

this pencil gets well cut, i.e. is easy to sharpen

Many involitives are associated with a dative case of the person: maṭa bælunaa, I happened to look.

læbenavaa is in form the involitive counterpart of **labanavaa**, obtain, which is however only used in restricted contexts. læbenavaa can be used with a dative case of the person in translating the Eng. verb 'get'.

maṭa tææggak læbunaa	I got a present

dænenavaa (involitive counterpart of **dannavaa**) is used similarly.

eeka maṭa dænunaa	I realized that, I felt that

atin, the instrumental case of **ata**, hand, is often used as a postposition (lesson 8 **d**) following an animate noun, meaning 'at the hands of' or 'by', especially in connection with involitive verbs. The preceding noun may be in either the direct case or the genitive case.

mage / maŋ] atin eyaage pææna kæḍunaa	I (accidentally) broke his pen

mage atin can also simply mean 'from my hands, from me'.

(b) **dækkaa** is the past tense of **dakinavaa**, see, which is however not very frequently used in the present tense. 'I can see ...' is more usually expressed by ... maṭa peenavaa, 'appears to me'. In sentences such as 'I saw the dog **in the forest**', a further verb is usually added: ballaa kælææve innavaa maŋ dækkaa, 'I saw the dog being in the forest'.[1]

(c) **diga, palala** can be used adjectively like **sudu** etc. A measurement is put in the direct case.

meeka hari digayi	this is very long
meeka aḍi hatak digayi	this is 7 feet long

Alternatively, these words can be used as nouns, 'length', 'breadth' (cf. note on 7 A 24). The same applies with the words **usa, mahata**.

meeke diga aḍi hatayi	the length of this is 7 ft.

---

1. See also lesson 25 **d**.

In a more learned way, this last can also be expressed:

meeka digin aḍi hatayi — this is 7 feet in length

Notice the use of the instrumental case here.

mage usa aḍi pahayi aňgal hatayi — my height is 5ft. 7 ins.

Notice here that where a numeral stands last in the predicative portion of a sentence of this kind, the indefinite suffix **-k** is either replaced by **-yi** or followed by **venavaa**. This applies also when speaking of sums of money (lesson 9 **f**; see also note on 12 A 18).

eeke palala aňgal tunak venavaa
its breadth will be 3 inches

mee am̆bageḍiya sata [dekak venavaa / dekayi]
this mango will cost two cents

(Notice the word for a single mango. **am̆bee** is less usual). In numerical expressions which contain two units of measurement, such as 7ft.6ins., Rs.12/50, the first numeral can either end in **-ayi** or in **-akut** (not **-akuyi**).

aḍi [hatayi / hatakut] aňgal hayayi — 7ft.6ins

rupiyal [dolahayi / dolahakut] sata pahalovayi — Rs.12/15

(this last is more usually expressed simply by saying **dolahayi pahalovayi**, 'twelve fifteen').

(d) **kada** is a shoulder-yoke with two hanging baskets, carried by itinerant sellers of vegetables, etc. In English it is called a 'pingo'. The man who carries it is called **katkaarayaa**.

almaariya comes from a Portuguese word; in English the term 'almirah' (rhymes with palmyra) is frequently used.

A.

kade elavalu vigahaṭa vikununaalu
lamayaa almaariya arinavaa
maṭa loku tææggak læbunaa
ee gollange ballaa iiye ape balalaava mæruvaa
mee pota digin aňgal namayayi palalin aňgal hayayi
ape ballaa iiye havasa mærunaa/(malaa)

katkaarayaa kaden elavalu vikunanavaa
ee pihiyaṭa mage ata kæpenna giyaa
kuḍee vaturaṭa heedunaa
dora ibeema væhunaa
mee pihiyen hon̆daṭa kæpenavaa
mehe am̆ba hon̆daṭa hædenavaada?
meeka vune ara lamayaa atin
ada udee mage atin kaar-eka hiirunaa
kaar-eka væssaṭa heedunaa
kaar-eka ibeema hari giyaa
maŋ rupiyal dekaka elavalu gattaa
ape lamayaa hon̆din hiṭiyaada?
ara meesee digaṭa vaḍaa palalayi
æhunaada?

B. I will send that letter tomorrow.
The teacher gave (me) a nice prize for my labours.
Yesterday our white cat died.
The umbrella is black-coloured.
I have a long name.
This road is very broad (and) long.
Good boys get prizes at school.
Did (you) wrap up my parcel properly?
There was a good knife (lying) on the road, (and) I took it.
This child is not at all good.
This child works well.
I let the door shut.
This boy knows (how) to count (quite) well.
Father is eating (some) of my mango.
Hasn't the umbrella man mended our umbrella yet?
The teacher took that book from me.
I accidentally broke your pen.
Yesterday there was an inch and a half of rain at Batticaloa, I hear.
This book is ten inches thick.
We want a table six feet long.

Notes:

A. 1 elavalu is usually pronounced **eloolu**. vikununaa is the past tense of **vikinenavaa.**

6 **malaa** is an alternative form for **mærunaa.**

8 Notice this use of the dative case-form, which is preferable to the instrumental in such contexts: to get cut by ('to') that knife. Similarly **væssaṭa** in 15 below. **-nna yanavaa,** to be on the point of doing something.

9 'Was washed', i.e. lost its colour, faded.

11 pihiyen or pihiya.

12 hædenavaa, 'get made', = to grow. This word is also used of illnesses, to arise, occur.

13 lamayaa or lamayaage.

14 As in English 'I scratched the car', this means while driving it.

16 hari giyaa, i.e. (probably) 'started'.

17 Two rupees' worth of vegetables; see lesson 9 **f.**

18 Was he good, did he behave well? (**hon̆da hiṭiyaada** is not possible, see lesson 5 **c**). This does not refer to health.

19 Is broader than (it is) long.

20 'Do (lit. did) you hear?'

B. 2 Labours – use the plural form **væḍa**. For the omission of **maṭa** after **mage**, see notes on 7 A 19 and 21.

5 This probably means 'I have **a lot of** names.'

7 iskoolee **or** iskoolen.

8 Properly = well; the form **hon̆daṭa** is preferable here.

9 There was a knife = a knife was. On the road: loc. case (**not** uḍa).

12 Say 'the door shut itself at my hands.' This implies that the shutting was accidental.

13 Cf. 7 B 27.

14 Some, see lesson 10 **a**. Mango, see under **c** above.

15 Mend, hadanavaa. Umbrella man, see **kaarayaa** in vocabulary above. In Ceylon, umbrellas are very common and necessary (they are also used as parasols), black ones being carried even by Buddhist monks; umbrella repairers are also common, often carrying on their work on

the street pavement.

16 With a simple case-form, gattaa would mean 'bought'; use a post-position.

18 Say 'it rained one and a half inches' (direct case; plural noun-form).

Script

ශ (ශ) ෂ (ෂ) ඥ (ඥ)

ʃa ʂa jña

ශු ෂු ඥා

ʃu ʂu jñaa

ශ (called **kada sayanna**, 'broken s') represents a Sanskrit palatal sibilant ( ); ෂ (called **golu sayanna**, 'broken s') represents a Sanskrit retroflex sibilant (s). In normal Sinhalese speech however they are both read as s. The beginner should not generally use them in writing unless he knows Sanskrit. As in the case of the aspirated stops, these sibilants are often written by Sinhalese people where there is no historical justification for them. ks is written ක්ෂ.

ඥ represents a symbol which occurs in Sanskrit and is there usually transliterated **jña**; it is however normally pronounced **gña**. In Pali this letter is replaced by **ña** (ඤ), and in reading Sinhalese, the symbol ඥ, when initial, is usually pronounced ඤ.

ආඥා	සන්දේශය
ක්ෂමා	භාෂාව
ශික්ෂා	සංඥිත
ශාන්ති	පක්ෂවශීල
භික්ෂුවක්	ශිලාලේඛන
අශුභ	ශබ්දකෝෂය
අශෝක	ශකුන්තලා
ශෝභාව	රඝුවංශය

ශ්ලෝක	මහාවංසය
ශ්ලේෂ	දේවරක්ෂිත
ධෛර්ය	ශාසන මණ්ඩලය
අක්ෂර	සුභාෂිතය
විශේෂයෙන්	අඥජන
අඝෝෂ	ස්වාමින්වහන්සෙ
ඊශ්වර	අශිෂ්ට
විශිෂ්ට	මහාස්ථවිර
ස්කන්ද	ස්වභාෂා
ස්කන්ධ	

LESSON 14

kanda (pl., **kaňdu**)	mountain, hill
æňda (pl., **æňdan**)	bed
rææ (pl., **rææ**)	night
janeelee (pl., **janeel, janeela**)	window
bootalee (pl., **bootal**)	bottle
gala	stone, rock
kiri (pl.)	milk
paan (pl.)	bread
lææsti	ready
særa	strict, strong, fierce, rude
mooḍa	foolish
hapan	clever
ehenam	if so; then (inferential)
nætinam / **nættam**[1]	if not
lææsti karanavaa	prepare
horakam karanavaa	steal
særa karanavaa (with dative case)	scold
maṭṭu karanavaa (with either direct or dative case)	punish
paaṭa karanavaa	colour (tr.), paint
yaṭa karanavaa	run over (tr.)
loku karanavaa	make bigger
puŋci karanavaa	make smaller
nam karanavaa	name

1. Usually written **nætnam**.

tæægi karanavaa	present
poḍi karanavaa	crush, smash; make smaller

(a) **-da** can be added to an infinitive verb-form to make a question of the type 'Shall I ...?'

apit ennada? shall we come too?

This form is also used of the 2nd and 3rd persons, but here there are two possible translations: Are you/they to ...? or Do you/they want to ...?

(b) **Indefinite future**. Certain verbal forms convey the idea of possibility in the future. The endings used are **-yi** and **-vi**, in place of **-navaa**. **-yi** is pronounced **-y** (see Introduction): karayi, pron. [kəray]. **-iyi** is usually written **-ii**. Before **-vi** the preceding vowel is lengthened: karaavi, eevi (from enavaa). The indefinite future forms of gannavaa and innavaa are **ganii**(**vi**) and **iňdii**(**vi**) respectively. (The latter is derived from **iňdinavaa**, an older form of innavaa).

These forms are mostly used of the 3rd person.

eyaa mee væḍa ṭika heṭa karayi

he may do this job tomorrow

They can be used in questions, followed by **-da**.

eyat etana iňdiivida?

will he be there too?

Where these forms in **-vi** are followed by **ehenam** (always spoken with a falling intonation here) – and sometimes even if they are not – the sense implied **is often the reverse of that expressed.**

ee gollo eevi ehenam

so you think they'll come then? (they won't)

In this idiomatic usage, these forms appear also in the first person, and also in a negative form preceded by **no-** – but usually not with **da**.

maŋ yayi[1] ehenam

you think I'll go then? (I won't)

maŋ noyayi ehenam

you think I won't go? (I will)

These forms are also used in the first person with intransitive involitive verbs.

---

1. The form **yaavi** is less common.

maŋ mæreyi

I may die.

(c) **Exclamatory form**. The verbal ending **-ññam** (or **-nnam**; sometimes also **-nnãã** with nasalized vowel) is used in two ways.

Firstly, where approval of a future action is expected. Such cases are always found in the first person; the particle **ko** often follows. This particle being unstressed, the preceding syllable **–nnam** usually bears a high pitch.

maŋ yannam	I'll go then?
api heṭa ennam ko	I'll come tomorrow then?
api oyaage dihaave ennam ko ehenam	I'll be coming your way, then.

Note that ehenam here does **not** reverse the sense.

Secondly, when used of the 3rd person this form expresses surprise and often disappointment (especially when preceded by **ee paara**, lit. 'that time'); here it does not refer to future time, but to the time when the action in question is first evident to the speaker.

aaŋ, ee paara eyat ennam

ah, so he's coming too

ee paara vahinnam

look, it's raining now

ee gollat dæn ennam

at last they're coming.

This, however, is a rare usage and should not be imitated.

(d) **Conjunct verbs**. Many nouns and adjectives can be combined with the verb **karanavaa** (do) or its involitive counterpart **venavaa** (become) – or occasionally also with other verbs – to make a 'conjunct verb' which functions as a single verbal unit. A number of these verbs are listed above.

kææma lææsti karanna

prepare the meal

taattaa lamayaa maṭṭu keruvaa

the father punished the child.

eyaa ape baḍu ṭika horakam keruvaa

he stole our things

ganan gannavaa (see lesson 12 A 21 above) is a verb of this type. **vakkaranavaa**, though in appearance a conjunct verb of this type, is treated as a single word and forms a past tense vækkeruvaa or vækkaruvaa.

(e) **ţika(k)** is often found after a plural noun, animate or inanimate, where in English 'a little' is out of place. It is approximately equivalent to 'some' (cf. French **du pain**).

paan ţikak denna
    give (me) some bread (a little bread)
minissu ţikak aavaa
    some men came

(where **minissu ţikadenek** means 'a few men').

It can also be combined with demonstratives such as **mee**, or with **okkoma**; here no English equivalent is possible, but the meaning is made specific instead of general.

mee minissu ţika væḑa karanne nææ
    these men are not working
(mee) tee okkoma ţika bonna oonæ
    (you) must drink up all the/this tea

'all this/that (these/those) ...' is regularly represented by (m)ee ... okkoma ţika, or ţika okkoma.

The use of **ţikak** before adjectival and adverbial words is not always the same as in English, e.g. meeva ţikak hoňdayi, these are fairly good; ţikak hayiyen yanna, go a little faster (**væḑiya** is not required here); ţikak hoňda nææ, not very good.

(f) Milk, until recently, was not often drunk by itself in Lanka, even by children. Buffalo-milk is eaten, however, in the form of curd; this is called **kiri kanavaa** 'eating milk'. For tea, tinned condensed milk (always sweetened) is used more often than real milk, and is often preferred by the Ceylonese to the indifferent quality cow's milk which is the normal alternative. The climate in Ceylon is unfavourable for milch-cows. Tea is often drunk without milk, but never without sugar. It is usually drunk luke-warm.

A.
mama ee væḑee heţa karannam
taattaa tava ţikakin gedara eyi
taattaa dæn eyi
mama heţa gedara ennam
mee tee eka maŋ bonnam æ
ammat heţa iskoolee eyi
taattaa heţa iskoolee eevida?
taattaa Kolaňba yanne næælu; gedara iňdiivida ehenam?

balanna ko ara kande usa!
10 maţa hoňda pihiyak tææegi læbunaa
ara lamayaa kaarvala væḑaţa huňgak hapan
lamayi ţika bas-ekaţa næggaa
ee lamayaa maţa ŋam hadanavaa
bat ţika vijahaţa kanna
15 mama heţa gedara enna bæri nææ
Tirikunaamaleeţa tava(t) koţa paarak tiyenaava
taattaa tava ţikakin enna puluvan
lamayaa nam karanne kohomada?
ee minihaa ape ballaava kaar-ekaţa yaţa keruvaa
20 mage pææna oya meesee uḑat nædda? ov, nææ, mama yaţat bæluvaa
ganan ţika okkoma hæduvaada?
balalaa janeelen æňdaţa pænnaa
æyi ehenam mahattayaa maţa enna kivve?
ada rææţa mehe inna
25 mage bat ţika kææve balalaa nemeyi

B. There is still (some) milk in the bottle.
Father will be coming soon now.
That boy does many silly things.
Father presented me with a good pen.
5 The mango was crushed by the car.
The father scolded the child.
The boy smashed the milk bottle.
The child is painting the book.
That gentleman smashed my car.
10 Make that table a bit bigger.
(You) must make this book a bit smaller.
The boy is smashing a (piece of) black rock [=road metal].
When will (you) name the child? [i.e. register the birth]
My teacher presented me with a pen.
15 The cat was run over by the car.
Shall I go then?
How rude that child is!
I was presented with a small book.

Who stole this child's pen?
20 (We) must punish bad children.
It is all prepared.
It gets dark very early now.
It is 5 o'clock already, (and) he's still not ready.
We ate all those fruits.
25 Oh dear, what is to be done?

Notes:

A. 2 tava ţikakin = within a short (future) time.

5 **æ** or **aa(ŋ)** is a particle which adds politeness, 'shall I?' Similarly after a command: maţa denna aaŋ, please give me.

10 **tæægi læbenavaa** here serves as a conjunct verb. Conversely **tæægi denavaa** can also be used as a conjunct verb, with the same meaning as **tæægi karanavaa**, where it is necessary to indicate that a gift, not a loan, is in question.

13 maţa nam hadanavaa, 'is calling me names',

14 bat ţika = 'your rice'.

16 Either 'another short route' or 'a still shorter route' (in the second case **tavat** will be more emphatically pronounced).

18 'What will you call the child?' (not **mokakda** here).

19 This implies that the man did it on purpose. More normal would be: ape ballaa ee minihaage kaar-ekaţa yaţa vunaa. Notice the use of the dative case here (kaar-ekaţa) in both instances.

20 Ov, nææ = no it isn't.

22 janeelen = through (by way of) the window.

23 This may be a real question, but more probably means 'Well, but you did tell me to come'. It is spoken in both senses with a rising (questioning) intonation.

24 ada rææţa (cf. 12 A 3 note) = (for) tonight. **rææţa** also means 'by night'.

B. 3 Say 'much stupid work'.

4 and 14. Say 'presented a pen to me'.

7 **kiri bootalee** is a milk bottle, whether full or empty. The Eng. distinction between 'a bottle of milk' and 'a milk-bottle' cannot easily be made in Sinhalese. The locative case-form is not used in such

expressions in Sinhalese (see lesson 5 **e**).

11 This might be said to a book-binder.

15 See note on A 19 above.

17 Use **særa**, as a noun: cf. note on 7 A 24.

21 See Lesson 10 g.

22 Gets dark, **rææ venavaa**. Early: say 'quickly (soon)'. The difference between the shortest and the longest days in Ceylon is only about an hour.

25 monavaada karanne? **or** monavaa karannada?

Script

ඓ (ඓ) ඖ (ඖ)
ai au

ඣ (ඣ) ද්ධ (ද්ධ)
jha ddha

ඓ, ඖ. These symbols represent Sanskrit diphthongs **ai** and **au**. When these sounds occur in normal Sinhalese words they should be written as අයි, අව්, අවු, (ayi, av, avu). In Sanskrit loanwords however these sounds are represented by the special symbols.

ඓතිහාසික ඖෂධ
aitihaasika ausadha

In connection with a consonant symbol, **ai** is represented by two kombuvas before the symbol. කෛලාස, Kailaasa. **au** is represented by a kombuva before the consonant and the **gayanukitta** (ෟ) after it. බෞද්ධ, Bauddha.

The English sound **f** may occur in loanwords but will usually be replaced by **p**, and written either with plain ප or as f ප . The symbol ෆ is also sometimes used. Care is needed in identifying such foreign words as පැෂන් (fashion, not passion), පැනල් (flannel, not panel).

ද්ධ is a compound symbol (**baeňdi akura**) representing ද් + ධ and occurring in Sanskrit or Pali loanwords such as බුද්ධ, Buddha.

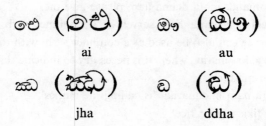

ඣංකාරය	අනුරුද්ධ
අජ්ඣත්තික	විමලබුද්ධි
ඖදරික	වෛවස්වත
ඓරාවණයා	සද්ධම්මසංගහ
කෛරාටික	අජ්ඣාසය
කෞරව	සද්ධම්මෝපායන
තද්ධිත	ටැලිපෝන්
බද්ධසීමා	සෞඛ්‍ය
ගෞතම	මෞලි
ඣාන	ජෛන
	ගෞරවාදරයෙන්

LESSON 15

tiyanavaa[1] (past tense, **tivvaa** or **tibbaa**)	place, leave
geenavaa	bring
geniyanavaa	take (away)
hærenavaa	turn (intr.)
gahanavaa (with dative case of the animate who is struck)	strike
ek venavaa	unite (intr.)
ek velaa, ekkalaa	together
hamaara karanavaa	finish (tr.)
narak karanavaa	spoil (tr.)
narak venavaa	go bad
raa (pl.)	toddy
pætta (pl. **pæti**)	side, direction
arakku (pl.)	arrack
orloosuva	watch, clock
karattee	cart
pattaree	newspaper
enjima, ænjima	engine
Laŋkaava	Ceylon
utura	the north
dakuna	the south, the right
vama	the left

(a) **Absolutives**. In Sinhalese, two finite verbs are not normally used in one sentence connected by 'and', as in English. Instead of saying 'I go and come back', Sinhalese will say 'Having gone, I come'. The form which represents 'having gone' is here called 'absolutive', and normally – though not invariably – the person who

1. In literary language, **tabanavaa, tæbuvaa**. In ordinary speech, it is difficult to distinguish between **tiyanavaa** and **tiyenavaa**.

'goes' (in this sentence) will also be the subject of the main verb which stands later in the sentence.

To form the absolutive, verbs in **-anavaa** change **-anavaa** to **-alaa**[1] or sometimes **-aa**; verbs in **-inavaa** change to **-alaa** or sometimes **-a** and also modify the root vowel where applicable, as explained in lesson 12 **a** above. The involitive verb-forms in **-enavaa** form their absolutives in **-ilaa** or sometimes **-ii**.

balanavaa	balalaa, balaa
arinavaa	æralaa, æra
hærenavaa	hærilaa, hærii

The following verbs have an irregularly formed absolutive:

enavaa	ævillaa,[2] ævit (negative nææyit – see below)
yanavaa	gihillaa, gihin[3]
denavaa	diilaa
bonavaa	biilaa
venavaa	velaa (in certain contexts, -va. Negative, novii)
gannavaa	gena (only used in compound verbs, see below)
karanavaa	karalaa, kara (pr. [kərə])[4]
kanavaa	kaalaa

'To bring' is gena + enavaa (to come having taken), which takes the form **genenavaa** or **geenavaa**, past tense **genaavaa**, of which the absolutive (gena + ævillaa) is **genællaa**, **genallaa**, or **genæt**, **genat**. 'To take away', gena + yanavaa, takes the form **geniyanavaa**, past tense (irregular) **geniccaa**,[5] absolutive **genihin**, **genihillaa**. **gannavaa** itself for its absolutive usually uses the word **araŋ** or **aragana**, which is in fact the absolutive of aragannavaa, to take. In English, this word may often be translated 'with': potak araŋ aavaa, (he) came with a book. These words imply 'carrying' and are therefore seldom used of bringing or taking people.[6]

---

1. In some districts, **-aalaa**.

2. Often pronounced æyillaa. **ævidin**, **ævidillaa** are also found. In some colloquial styles, these words are used without any meaning: eyaa ævidin kavda? who is he?

3. Sometimes **gohin**. In books, **gos**.

4. In books, **koṭa**.

5. In books, **genagiyaa**.

6. See lesson 17c, **ekka-yanavaa.**

The opposite of araŋ is **nætuva** (or **nætiva**), a special form of the absolutive of næti venavaa (lesson 21), which may often be translated 'without'.

innavaa uses as absolutive **iňdaŋ** (shortened form of **iňdagana**,[1] the absolutive of iňdagannavaa, sit), or **iňdalaa, iňda** (absolutives from iňdinavaa), or **hiṭa** (absolutive of hiṭinavaa). These words frequently correspond to Eng. 'from', the preceding noun being normally in the locative case. api Kolaňba iňdaŋ aavaa, we came from (lit. 'having been in') Colombo; api Laŋkaave iňdalaa aavaa, we came from Ceylon.

hiṭalaa is used in the sense 'having stopped', and **hiṭagana** (absolutive of hiṭagannavaa) means 'having stood up', i.e. 'standing'.[2]

When two actions occur simultaneously, the absolutive can be doubled; here the termination **-laa** is omitted, and the first of two long **-aa** or **-ii** vowels is shortened.[3]

kaalaa	having eaten
kakaa	while eating

In speech, the final -aa is usually also reduced to -ə (e.g. balabalaa, but pron. [baləbalə]), except with monosyllabic roots. The repetition of the full absolutive gives a different meaning.

kaalaa kaalaa	(by) constantly eating

-t, 'even', (lesson 2) can be added after **-laa**: kaalat, even after eating.

The absolutive of dannavaa is **dæna**; this is only used when doubled (**dænadæna**) or compounded with -gena (**dænagana**, see lesson 23 **a**).

There are three ways of negating an absolutive:

(i) by putting **no-** (assimilated before vowels, cf. lesson 5 **b**) before the shortened form (nobalaa:[4] nææra (no + æra));

(ii) by using the incomplete verbal form followed by **nætuva** (balanne nætuva);

(iii) with **nemeyi** after the absolutive, and the main verb in incomplete form. Here special special emphasis is thrown on the negated absolutive.

mehe bææ væḍa nokara inna
you can't stay here without working

pot balanne nætuva lamayaa ehaaṭa mehaaṭa yanavaa
the boy wanders around and doesn't look at his books

---

1. Lesson 23, below.
2. For the form **hiṭaŋ**, see Lesson 33 **f**.
3. The verb venavaa uses the form **vevii** here.
4. The final -aa is usually shortened in speech.

maŋ liyalaa balalaa nemeyi mee pææna gatte

I bought this pen without trying to write with it first (lit. 'not having written and seen' – **nemeyi** negates both absolutives)

(b) **Imperative**. As mentioned earlier (lesson 6), verbal forms in **-nna** are often used in an imperative sense. Sometimes forms in **-navaa** are also used in this way.

yanavaa / yanavaada	yanna metanin!	(will you) get away (lit. 'go to go') from here!

And in prohibitions –

yanne nææ metanin!	you are not to leave here!

There are also imperative verb-forms ending in **-pan** or **-an** in the 2nd person (singular). Such forms are often followed by **baŋ** as a 2nd personal pronoun. These forms are not polite (though in common use), and should be generally avoided by the foreigner. Among forms of this type, the irregular **palayan**! (go!) and **varen**! (come!), which are very common, should be noted. A 1st person plural imperative form ending in **-mu** is in common use. The interrogative **-da** can be added to it.

yamu ko dæn	let's go now
yamuda?	shall we go?

yamu is often shortened to **yaŋ**. **yamaŋ** is a more intimate form. Other common short forms are **immu**! (innavaa), **gammu**! (gannavaa).

ko may be added after imperative verb-forms, to give additional politeness; women and children also tend to add **anee** (cf. lesson 7).

denna ko anee, do give it to me.

(c) epaa, puluvan, oonæ, bæri, kæmati. When it is necessary to give these words a past or future time significance, they are followed by **vunaa** or **venavaa (veyi)** respectively. (The form **bæri** – not **bææ** – is always used before venavaa).

puluvan vunaa	was possible (able)
oonæ venavaa	will be necessary

'Could not' is often used in the sense 'forgot to' (cf. bærivelaa, lesson 13).

(d) Toddy is an alcoholic drink made from palm-flower, usually of the **kitul**, of the coconut **(pol)** or of the palmyra **(tal)**. Since palmyra palms are mostly found in the Jaffna area, palmyra toddy is mostly made there. Arrack is a spirit distilled from toddy.

karattee means any kind of cart. There are several different kinds in common use in Ceylon, usually drawn by small bulls.

(e) When used adjectively, utura, dakuna and vama appear in their stem-forms

uturu, dakunu, vam: vam pætta, the left-hand side.

A.

mahattayaaṭa mama hoňda orloosuvak genallaa dennam
kavda mage pota araŋ giye?
iňda-hiṭa api Yaapanet yanavaa
maŋ arakku bonne iňdalaa-hiṭalayi
ee lamayaa maṭa loku galakin gahalaa divuvaa
ee minihaa magen salli araŋ, denne nææ
oya væḍee tiyalaa poḍḍakaṭa mehe enna
maŋ dæn gedara gihin naalaa bat kaalaa ennam
karattayak genallaa mee puṭu ṭika araŋ yannam
tee-eka oya puŋci meesee uḍin tiyalaa yanna
lamayaa bat koccara kanavaada!
mahata mahattayek mee dæn ara paaren vamaṭa hærilaa giyaa
bæri velaa mage atin dora væhunaa
lamayaage væḍa balanne kavda?
havasaṭa tee bonna api gedara yanavaa
kaar-eke enjima tavama væḍa karanavaa
maṭa iiye Gaallaṭat yanna puluvan vunaa
maṭa oya pææna tava ṭikakin oonæ venavaa
taattaaṭa iiye Yaapanee yanna bæri vunaa
eekaṭa maat kæmati vunaa
maṭat vatura ṭikak denna ko anee
lamayaa duvalaa enna!
kaḍee gihin ada kiiyaka baḍu genaavaada!
mee gaana maṭa kiyaa denna
enavaa, bonavaa lamayaa tee!
api detundenaa ek velaa mee pota livve
paarsalee geenna kaavada æriye?
Yaapanee tiyenne Kolam̌baṭa uturen
oya pattaree pættakin tiyalaa mehaaṭa enna
denna ko anee oya pota maṭat ṭikak balanna

B.

They are in Kandy.
Where does this road go to?

Where do you (pl.) get water for (your) house from?
Two and three is five.
Three for a rupee.
It is ten to three now.
Two to Colombo please.
Do (you) want some more?
I got to the office very early today.
Tell the servant to bring the food to the table.
Open the door for me to come (in).
How much is it from Colombo to Galle by bus?
They didn't even give us a cup of tea.
The boy doesn't even eat **rice**.
Ask that gentleman to come here when he's finished work.
The men of Jaffna are very good at work(ing).
Those boys are throwing stones to pick mangoes.
That gentleman's left arm is shorter than (his) right [arm].
When did you come to Ceylon?
One side of this table is high, (and) one side is low.
Put the loaf of bread on the table, or else the dog will eat (it).
I have come from home (just) now.
Keep the milk bottle covered, or it'll go bad.
Don't sell toddy so that[1] small children can see.
Take these [few] things away and put them in the cupboard.
Put the letter under that book.
Cover up my cup of tea and leave it on the table.
Leave those [few] books on this bed for now.
Father reads Dinamina every morning.
We don't take the Silumina.

Notes:

A. 1 denavaa after an absolutive can usually be translated 'for (somebody)', e.g. taattaa maṭa mee puṭuva hadaa denna, please father mend this chair **for me**. **-laa** is often omitted here. When speaking English, this type of verbal unit is often translated as 'mend it **and give**'. See also 24 below.

1. i.e. in such a way that.

2 araŋ giye = taken away.

3, 4 iňda-hiṭa, iňdalaa-hiṭalaa = from time to time. Yaapanee(t): see lesson 8 **h** (so also in 19 below).

6 denne = give **back**.

7 poḍḍakaṭa, see note on 6 A 2.

8 Notice how several absolutives may be used one after another.

10 uḍin or uḍa. yanna, 'and then go away'. The addition of **yanavaa** or **enavaa** to the end of a sentence where they would normally be omitted altogether in English is particularly characteristic of Sinhalese. It is often felt to be somewhat abrupt to use a verb indicating an action alone when motion is also involved. For example, rather than say 'to go **to do** something', Sinhalese will frequently prefer 'having gone to do something, to come (back again).' In English, one will often hear such sentences as 'I'll just speak to him for a moment **and come**'. **maŋ gihin ennam ko ehenam** is a normal way of saying, 'I must go, then' (I'll be going and coming back again (another time), au revoir), and it is in fact impolite to leave somebody you have been talking to without some remark of this kind, which replaces Eng. 'good-bye'.

12 '. . . has just taken that turning to the left.'

16 væḍa karanavaa = is running ('is working' would be just 'hoňdayi').

17 I was able to go (**not** 'I could have gone'). Similarly in 19 below.

18 See 14 A 2.

20 kæmati vunaa = consented.

22 Here the two verbal actions are simultaneous, lit. 'run and come', i.e. come running, run over here (compare English phrases like 'try and do it').

23 kiiyaka, i.e. rupiyal kiiyaka. The subject of the verb (understood) is probably 'you'.

24 gaana = sum (to work out). kiyaa denna = explain, see note on A 1 above.

25 Imperatives.

26 api detundenaa = several of us (cf. 11 B 19). But apen tundenaa = three of us.

28 Kolaňbaṭa uturen = (to the) north of Colombo (alternatively, Kolaňbin uture).

29 pættakin tiyalaa, having left on one side (lit. a side) – having put aside.

The locative case (pættaka) is unidiomatic here. Notice also that the dative case (with -ṭa ending) is not used with **tiyanavaa** in such contexts, but is used with **daanavaa**, which also means 'to put' (lesson 20): pættakaṭa daalaa.

30 balanna = 'to look at', so that I can look at it.

B. 2 **kohaaṭada** is preferable to **koheda** here. Go: translate literally. The same Sinhalese sentence could also mean 'Where are (you) going to this time?' (Or **paare**, **paaren** could be used.)

3 Cf. 10 A 33.

4 Translate literally.

5 Say 'for the rupee' (cf. 9 B 13).

6 Lesson 8 **e**.

7 'Please' is not necessary in Sinhalese here (see lesson 7 **a**). **maṭa** is sometimes used in these contexts ('two to Colombo for me').

9 'Got' = came. Very early: see 12 A 5 note.

10 'Bring' – in this context **kææma arinna** is the normal 'technical' term.

11 To come: infinitive.

12 bas-eken or bas-eke. 'Is it' needs no equivalent in Sinhalese (cf. 9 A 17 and note on 9 A 2). From: see under **a** above.

15 Say 'having finished'.

16 'Of Jaffna' – loc. case (which is the same in form as the direct case).

17 Throw stones: gal gahanavaa. Mango-trees are big, and the mangoes are often brought down (for immediate consumption) by throwing stones or sticks at them.

21 See note on A 29 above. Loaf of bread: paan geḍiya.

22 From home: either the case-form or the postpositional **iňdalaa**.

23 'Keep covered' – say 'cover and leave'.

24 Say 'to appear to small children'; cf. A 30 above.

25,26,27,28 The instr. or loc. cases can be used, but not the dative: see note on A 29 above.

29, 30 **Dinamina** is a well-known Sinhalese newspaper, **Silumina** is its counterpart on Sundays. 'Take', tr. literally. Reads: say 'looks at'. **eka** or **pattaree** are sometimes added after the names of newspapers. Every morning: say 'every day in the morning'.

Script

The Sanskrit alphabet contains two vowels r and rr. The second of these, in Sanskrit, only occurs in declensional inflections. The Sinhalese equivalent of r is ඍ, used in loanwords such as ඍතුව rtuva, season. This is generally realized, in initial position, as **ir-** or **iru-**; in other positions as **ru**.

It is advisable to distinguish the first portion of this character from ස, by omitting the side-stroke ෘ , since Sanskrit words may also begin with sr-. However, many Sinhalese printed books do not make this distinction.

After a consonant, the sign ෘ is added to represent this vowel: කෘ kr තෘ tr etc. Thus හෘදය (usually realised **hərdəyə** or **hərudəyə**). Frequently however a word written in Sanskrit form will be read in a Sinhalese adaptation, e.g. කර්තෘ (kartr), editor, read as **kattru. dr** is written දෘ.

The equivalent long vowel is written කෲ, තෲ, etc. This should not occur in Sanskrit loanwords, but in fact combinations such as **krr** are sometimes written for **kruu,** e.g. කෲර for **kruura**, cruel, and even ඇන්ඩෲ (Andrew), බෲක් බොන්ඩ් (for Brooke Bond).

When r is followed directly by another consonant, in a classical loanword , it is represented by the sign . ර්‍ . (called **reepha**), written above the second consonant, which is frequently doubled in this position.

ධර්ම, ධර්ම්ම	dharma, dharmma
ධාර්මික	dhaarmika

Where r directly follows another consonant, it is represented by the sign ්‍ර. written below the first consonant.

ක්‍රමය	kramaya, method (pron. [**krəməyə**])

(In handwriting, confusion may arise between e.g. **pra** and **pu**).
Combinations of this sort also occur in English loanwords ට්‍රෑම් (tram).

Where the **u** vowel has to be added after such a combination, it is usually written ෑ (ක්‍රෑර, kruura). This is potentially ambiguous, since the same symbol would be used for the **ae** vowel; but the **ae** vowel does not in fact occur in Sanskrit or Pali. However, as stated above, ෲ is sometimes used for **ruu** (කෲර).

ගෝත්‍ර	නක්ෂත්‍ර	ශකවර්ෂ
තර්ක	සර්පයා	ශීඝ්‍රයෙන්
තෘෂ්ණා	මෘදඞ්ග	චක්‍රවර්ති
වර්ණ	අමෘත	හර්තෘහරි
ආර්ද්‍ර	කෘතඥ	ඉන්ද්‍රඛීල
අර්ධ	කෘත්‍රිම	වෘත්තිසංගම්
ස්වර්ග	බ්‍රාහ්මණ	බෘහත් කථා
සෘෂි	ශෘඞ්ගාර	ක්ෂුද්‍ර ප්‍රාණීන්
ගර්භ	ශක්‍රයා	අතන්ද්‍රිත
සෘත	දෘෂ්ටි	ස්‍රෝතාපන්න
සෘෂට	සිද්ධාර්ථ	උදහෘත
අග්‍ර	ප්‍රශස්ති	උද්ධෘත
ධ්‍රැව	නෘපති	විස්තෘත
ව්‍රණ	මහේන්ද්‍ර	ටැලිග්‍රෑම්
ශ්‍රේණි	ගෘහස්ථ	ම්‍රමමවංශ විනිශ්චය
සර්ප	පෘථුල	මහාර්ඝස
කෘෂ්ණ	කර්පූර	ශ්‍රී කානහාව
විෂ්ණු	භ්‍රාන්ත	ධර්මකීර්ති
රෞද්‍ර	හ්‍රී	ප්‍රාඥයෝ
ශ්‍රෝත්‍ර	නිර්භීත	
	ශ්‍රාවක	

LESSON 16

aňdinavaa[1]	draw (pictures); put on (clothes); wear
baninavaa	insult, swear at, scold (with dative case)
kiyavanavaa[1]	read
aňḍanavaa	weep
redda (pl. **redi**)	cloth
saroma	sarong
hæṭṭee	woman's 'jacket'
noonaa, noonaa mahattayaa	lady (pl. noonaalaa, noonaavaru)
duppat	poor
pohosat	rich
taruna	young
naaki	old (=not young)
parana	old (=not new)
alut	new
nitara(ma)	often, regularly (always)
gææni (pl. **gæænu**)[2]	woman
vayasa	age; old

(a) A sarong is a kind of long skirt, which is the normal garment of the non-westernized male Sinhalese, and is worn by the westernized at night. It is usually made of coloured cotton. A plain-white man's skirt of a different design is called a 'cloth' (though the word **redda** also means cloth in general), and forms part of what is now called 'national dress' (a term usually applied to male dress only). When worn by women, **redda** is a skirt of any colour. The **hæṭṭee** is a small tight-

1. For past tenses, see lessons 18 and 20.
2. Indefinite form **gææniyek** (or **gææniyak**).

fitting upper garment with short sleeves, worn by women with a cloth, or with a sari by the better-off. **redi** also means 'clothes' in general.

(b) **taruna** is the general word for 'young'; **baala**, which denotes inferiority as well as youth (lesson 8), is used where a comparison is involved.

maŋ eyaaṭa baalayi	I am younger than he is
mage baala putaa	my younger son

It is also used with **vayasa**: baala vayase ekkenek, a youth ('one of young age'). **taruna vayasa** is less common. The word **naaki** is not polite; **vayasa** can be used predicatively instead in 3rd personal sentences; ee gææni vayasayi, she is old. When used attributively, i.e. as a qualifier, we must say **vayasaka** (lit. 'of an age'): vayasaka gææniyek, an old woman, ara vayasaka minihaa, that old man.

(c) We have seen that **væḍiya** means 'more' (lesson 8). In negative sentences (including those containing bææ or epaa) it can also be translated 'too' or 'too much/many', 'rather much', or sometimes just 'very' or 'much'.

væḍiya loku potak geenna epaa

don't bring too big a book

eekaṭa maŋ væḍiya kæmati nææ

I'm not too (very) keen on that

maṭa tee væḍiya / væḍiya tee epaa

I don't want (too) much tea

Compare this last example with

maṭa tavat tee epaa

I don't want (any) **more** tea

Note that **væḍiya** must precede an adjectival word (such as **loku**), but may stand either before or after a noun (such as **tee**).

In positive sentences, when 'too big' or a similar adjectival phrase is used predicatively, the form **væḍi** is used **after** the adjectival word. Here **-yi** is not required after the adjective, but **væḍi** is usually written as **væḍiyi** (lesson 3 **c**).

pota loku væḍi(yi)

the book is too big

væḍi(yi) is also used without a further adjectival word:

mee tee maṭa (ṭikak) væḍi

this tea is (rather) too much for me

atana kaḍa væḍi

the shops there are (too) numerous; there are too many shops there

In positive sentences of this type, no verbal form other than **væḍi(yi)** is possible. You cannot say atana væḍiya kaḍa tiyenavaa, unless væḍiya is preceded by an object of comparison[1] (Kolaṁba Gaallaṭa væḍiya kaḍa tiyenavaa, there are more shops in Colombo than in Galle). **væḍi(yi)** is also used after a present or past tense verb:

> eyaa bonavaa væḍi
>> he drinks too much
> maŋ ada bat kæævaa væḍi
>> I ate too much rice today

A.   ape lamayaaṭa tavama hoňda nææ

maŋ heṭa kaar-eken Nuvaraṭa duvalaa enna oonæ

mee paare nitara koocci yanne enne nææ

lamayaaṭa kohenda oya orloosuva læbune?

5   ara vayasaka noonaa kaaṭada ara baninne?

ape taattaa nitara Gaalu yanavaa

væḍa atin mee lamayaa huňgak hoňdayi

hoňda velaavaṭa maŋ ada aave

oya aavaamada mahattayaa, ævillaa huňgak velaa vunaada?

10   maŋ giyaa, aavaa

Laŋkaave minissu nitarama rææṭa sarom aňdinavaa

mama iiye parana kaar-eka diilaa alut kaar-ekak gattaa

gonaaṭa paare yanna arinna epaa

hæmadaama bootal vikunavikunaa iňdalaa pohosat venna bææ

15   mee paara kælæævaṭa yanna arinna epaa

aanna hari; oovaayin ṭikak maṭat denna

kiiyak karannada!

metanin væḍiya yanna enna epaa

batvalaṭa mama væḍiya kæmati nææ

20   Kolaṁba dihaave kaḍa væḍi

ee meeseeṭa mee puṭuva ṭikak loku væḍi

mehaaṭa væḍiya vahinne nææ

tava ṭika velaavak inna

ekat ekaṭa apiṭa dekak oonæ veyi

---

1. Or unless the verb tiyenavaa is followed by **nam** (lesson 29).

25 velaava yanavaa maṭa dænunema nææ
bootalen kiri yanavaa
api rææ velaa gedara aavaa
oya gahe væḍiya uḍaṭa naginna epaa

B Do buses still run on this road?
This child is a great one for drinking milk, but he doesn't like eating rice.
Don't swear at that poor old man.
Small children are always crying.
5 I've broken father's watch.
In Ceylon, women wear cloth and jacket.
The lady is not at home.
That old man has just gone off in that bus.
Who is that old man swearing at?
10 That man is always hanging round here.
She is rather old but still very handsome.
I sold him my old pen at a good price.
Father doesn't like that man much.
I can't work much today.
15 The boy drinks a lot of water.
We are too good to them.
I don't want much tea.
There are lots of shops by the road.
The men are too many for the bus.
20 This table is a little too big for that child.
I simply didn't know the dog had eaten the pencil.
The boy is still too thin.
This boy is still too young to send to work.
How is toddy changed into arrack?
25 I like money.
(I) don't want too big a one.
The shopkeeper charged you too much for the mangoes.
This boy won't let me read the book.

Notes:

A. 1 Refers to health, 'our child is not yet well'. Cf. ape lamayaa hoňda nææ, which refers to character, 'our child is not good'. See 4 A 10 note.

2 kaar-eken or kaar-eke. duvalaa, 'hurry'. For enna, see note on 15 A 10.

3 'Do not run frequently', not 'do not ever run'. paare or paaren, 'on this line'.

6 **ape** is more usual than **mage** here (see lesson 1).

7 væḍa atin, 'in respect of his work'. Cf. **ee atin**, in that respect.

8 hoňda velaavaṭa, 'at the good time', i.e. at a lucky moment. Inverted sentence.

9 For the double question, see lesson 9 **d**. oya aavaa-ma-da, 'have you **just** arrived?' Notice the position of **ma**, and its effect with this verb; cf. **maŋ mee aavaamayi**, I have just arrived. ævillaa, 'since (you) came'. Here the absolutive is grammatically detached from the rest of the sentence. This is normal in patterns of this kind, where Eng. uses 'since'; 'it is five years since father died', taattaa mærilaa dæn avurudu pahak venavaa (or vunaa). The final verb is **venavaa** (not **tiyenavaa**); **-yi** is less often used as an alternative here. In the sentence in the lesson, **venavaada** is an alternative to **vunaada**. **huňga velaavak** is alternative to **huňgak velaa;** similarly huňga særayak, many times, huňgadenek, many people, may alternate with huňgak særa, huňgak denaa. velaa, pl. of velaava; in English, the meaning cannot easily be distinguished from that of the singular, but velaava (sing.) usually corresponds to '**the** time'.

10 This means 'I returned immediately'. So **tiyanavaa yanavaa**: maŋ eeka tibbaa, giyaa, I put it down (and) hurried off. This type of statement is, however, exceptional.

11 Final **-m** will normally be realized as ŋ (see Introduction). Separate kinds of sleeping garment are not normally worn in Ceylon, any more than separate kinds of bathing garments (see lesson 11 **d**); the everyday sarong serves for all purposes.

12 diilaa = sold, gattaa = bought.

13 arinna: lesson 12.

14 bootal vikunavikunaa iňdalaa, 'by selling bottles'. **bootal vikunavikunaa** just = selling bottles; **iňdalaa** ('having been') adds the same effect as Eng. 'by' in this case.[1] The **bootalkaarayaa** or secondhand bottle dealer is a well-known character of the Ceylonese scene.

---

1. Further explained in lesson 22 **b**.

15 kælææva{ta} yanna, 'to revert to jungle, get overgrown.' Compare 13 above; paara, being inanimate, does not have a **-ṭa** ending here.

16 See note on 12 A 22. aanna hari = 'O.K. then.'

17 'What a lot there is to do!'

18 yanna enna, see lesson 2 notes. metanin, see lesson 10 **a**; cf. the different use in lesson 15 **b**.

23 ṭika velaavak or ṭikak velaa; cf. note on 9 above. Likewise ṭikadenek, a few people.

24 See 9 A 27.

25 dænunema nææ or **dænune nææmayi**, depending upon whether the stress is laid on the noticing or on the 'not'. (For the final -yi, cf. **aavaamayi** in note to A 9 above).

26 yanavaa, i.e. leaks. (The Eng. borrowing **liik venavaa** is sometimes used for 'leak').

27 rææ velaa (14 B 22) = after dark, late.

28 vædiya uḍaṭa, 'too high up'. Compare this with oya gaha uḍaṭa vædiya naginna epaa, which means 'Don't climb up that tree so much (i.e. so often)', and with oyiṭa vaḍaa uḍaṭa, 'any higher.'

B. 2 Great one for – say 'very clever to'.

3 Here the order of adjectives is immaterial; cf. note on 11 B 5.

5 Not deliberately (see 14 A 19).

8 Say 'has just (**mee dæn**) climbed (in) and gone in that bus'.

10 See A 18 above.

11 She; say 'that woman' (lesson 2 notes). Handsome: see 11 A 7.

12 'At a good price' can be translated literally.

16 Translate literally.

18 By the road: paara dihaave.

21 'Simply': cf. A 25 above.

23 To send – use infinitive.

24 Changed = turned.

27 Charged you: say 'took from you'.

Script

Where ya occurs immediately after another consonant, it is represented by the sign ්‍ය (called yansee) written after the first consonant. (This is only found in learned words.)

ක්‍ය	ක්‍යා	ක්‍යු
kya	**kyaa**	**kyu**

dya and **dyaa** are written ද්‍ය and ද්‍යා respectively

In combination of consonants involving **r** and **ya** together, the **reepha** sometimes stands above the **yansee,** e.g. මර්ත්‍ය martya (mortal). **trya** etc. are written ත්‍ර්‍ය, but the simple **rya (ryya)** is often written ර්‍ය.
ආචාර්‍ය aacaaryya (teacher)
(ර්‍ය is never written.)
ද්ව is a special symbol used to represent **dva** in Sanskrit loanwords. ට්ඨ represents **ṭṭha.**

In Sanskrit there are no short **e** and **o**, and in Pali the short **e** and **o** only stand in certain places where the long **e** and **o** are not permitted. It has therefore been customary when writing loanwords from Sanskrit and Pali not to use the long vowel symbols in these cases; thus දෙවතා may be written so, but read as **deevataa** (god). Ambiguities may sometimes arise from this convention, which might well be abandoned.

ස්‍යාමෝපසම්පදවත	ආරූප්‍ය	බ්‍යාමප්‍රභා
ශ්‍යාමායමාන	වෛචිත්‍ර්‍ය	මෞදගල්‍යායන
ශාක්‍යසිංහ	සාමග්‍රීය	අභ්‍යවකාශ
ව්‍යක්ත	අනර්ඝ්‍ය	අද්වීප
මධ්‍යම පුරුෂ	සෞභාග්‍ය	අට්ඨකථා
මද්‍යපාන	ව්‍යාපෘත	වෛශ්‍රවණ
ආර්‍ය	වෛතුල්‍ය	ස්මෘත්‍යුපස්ථාන
අනිත්‍ය	ඖචිත්‍ය	ජ්‍යෝතිශ්ශාස්ත්‍ර

මුඛ්‍ය	ඓශ්වර්‍ය	අනවශ්‍ය
පෝෂ්‍ය	අද්වෛත	අත්‍යවශ්‍ය
සභ්‍ය	චන්ව	උදක්ෂෙප
සෞම්‍ය	වෛවර්ණ්‍ය	
වෛෂ	වේශ්‍යාව	
ච්‍යුත	ජ්‍යෙෂ්ඨ[1]	
	මධ්‍යාහ්න	

1. The first vowel-sound here is long, but it is not easily possible to mark it so.

LESSON 17

lassana	beautiful, beauty
napuru	ferocious, cruel
pirisidu	clean
kiluṭu	dirty
kiikaru	obedient
leesi	easy
yasa	fine (usually used sarcastically)
aḍipaara	footpath
puusaa	pussy
hændææva	afternoon, evening
hayiya	strength
magadi	while on the road
kolee	leaf (also of paper)
andama **hæṭiya** **vidiha**	manner
ehema **ohoma** **mehema**	thus
etakoṭa **itin**	then, thereafter
aayet, aayi(t) aayimat	again
ekka	with
koccaravat[1]	all the time
aniddaa	the day after tomorrow
pereedaa	the day before yesterday

1. Sometimes realized as [koccərat].

nikam	just; free of charge
nikamma	of itself, automatically

(a) **Adverbs** do not form a recognizable formal class in Sinhalese, but instrumental or dative case-endings (as we have seen) often give the effect of English adverbs.

yasa	fine
yasaṭa	finely
hoňda	good
hoňdin / hoňdaṭa	well
hayiya	strength
hayiyen	strongly (hard, fast, loud, tight)
leesi	easy
leesiyen	easily

Or words meaning 'manner' may be added, in the dative case-form, after the adjectival word.

lassana hæṭiyaṭa / lassanaṭa[1]	beautifully
hoňda vidihaṭa / vidiyakaṭa[2]	well
napuru andamaṭa	cruelly

There are also adverbial words which do not fall into these catgories, e.g. aayi, again.

(b) **Adjectives** are also not a recognizable formal class. Adjectival words are the 'stem-forms' of nouns, i.e. adjectival words can be made into a noun by the addition of a termination **-aa** (to give an animate noun) or **-a** (to give an inanimate noun). Conversely any noun can, in its stem-form, be used adjectivally, i.e. immediately before another noun. Such stem-forms are also used in forming conjunct verbs with karanavaa and venavaa (lesson 14 **d**), e.g. narak venavaa. It

1. Often realized as [lassənṭə].

2. In this word, -h- is usually replaced by -y- in the case forms after an indefinite suffix.

has been pointed out earlier (lessons 5 **c** and 12 **c**) that verbs such as tiyenavaa and innavaa cannot be used wih a complementary noun in Sinhalese; but they can be combined with venavaa, or an adverbial form may be used, e.g.:

kiikaruva kiikaru velaa kiikaruven kiikaruvaṭa	inna,	be obedient! (lit. 'exist obediently')

Here **-va** and **velaa** also give the effect of English adverbial endings, and **karalaa** sometimes does the same: eeka pirisidu karalaa tiyanna, keep it clean(ly).

The stem-form of an inanimate noun is usually the same as its plural (omitting **-val**); with animate nouns, stem-forms should for the present be noted individually.[1]

loku	big	lokkaa (for lokuvaa, loku + aa)	big man, boss
ratu	red	rattaa (for ratuvaa)	red one[2]
pohosat	rich	pohosataa	rich man
mooḍa	foolish	mooḍayaa	fool
hapan	clever	hapanaa	clever man

And conversely –

ballaa	dog	balu væḍee	dirty piece of work[3]
Gaalla	Galle	Gaalu koocciya	the Galle train (11 A 8)
paaṭa	colour	paaṭa pænsalee	coloured pencil
pota	book	pot almaariya	book-case (cupboard)

1. See lesson 24.
2. Of animals,; sometimes also of objects such as balls (in a game).
3. 'Dog' is a term of high abuse in Ceylon.

Many adjectives can be used as nouns of quality without further alteration, e.g. sudu, særa, hoňda, usa, diga (see 7 A 24 note and lesson 13 c). **lassana** is a word of this type: meevaa lassanayi, these are beautiful; meeke lassana, the beauty of this, meeke lassanak[1] nææ, there is no beauty in this.

(c) **etakoṭa** and **itin** are both used inferentially (what will you do, then?) as well as in the meaning 'thereafter' (what did you do **then**?). etakoṭa may also mean 'at that time, by that time'. etakoṭa is often realized as [etooṭə].

ehema contains the emphasizing particle **ma**; when followed by **nam**, 'if', this particle may be omitted: ehema nam or ehenam, 'if so' (lesson 14).[2] ehema itself may be emphasized by a further **ma**, in which case it is usually pronounced [ehemmə]. Similarly [ohommə, mehemmə].

ehema (or **hema, heema**) is frequently used to give slight additional emphasis or additional politeness to the word preceding it. Sometimes it may be roughly equivalent to 'etcetera'; often it is untranslatable.

tavat ehema yanne nææ	don't go again (lesson 15 **b**)
sæpa-saniipa ehema kohomada?	how are you?

ekka,[3] 'with', functions as a postposition, being used with both animates and inanimates; the preceding word usually takes a final **-t**.

apit ekka	with us

ekka-yanavaa, 'to go with', is used as a transitive verb, 'to take (a person) with one'.

taattaa lamayaava Kolaňba ekka-yanavaa,
father takes the child to Colombo

Where it follows a dative case-form or a verbal infinitive (usually also with **-t**), **ekka** can be translated 'also'.

taattaa Kolaňba yannat ekka lææsti vunaa
father made ready to go to Colombo also.

(d) **di** is an enclitic particle which is sometimes added after locative case-endings.

gedaradi	(while) at home (often pronounced [gedəddi])
ehedi	(while) there
Kolaňbadi	(while) at Colombo

maga is a locative case-form in -a; in the direct case the word is hardly used. **metanadi**, 'while here', is usually realized as [metendi] (cf. lesson 4 **d**).

---

1. In formal contexts, also **lassanayak.**
2. But **not** ohonam, mehenam.
3. For ek-va; cf. ekkalaa (lesson 15).

A.
aayit ehema kiluṭuvaṭa aňdinna epaa
ape gedara pirisiduvaṭayi tiyenne
kaar-ekaṭa yaṭa venna gihin lamayaa ehemmama gal gæhilaa hiṭiyaa
monavaayeda mee kola?
maŋ hæmadaama kantooruvaṭa kææm paarsalayak geenavaa
ee væḍee maŋ ape lokkaaṭa kiyalaa balannam
ee mahattayaa karannema gon væḍa
ee naakiyaa bat kanna hari hapanaa
mee kaňdu paara naginna ape kaar-eka parana væḍi
Nuvaradi Tirikunaamalee paaraṭa hærenna, etaninut dakunu ataṭa hærilaa yanna
dolahaṭa kææma kanna bat kaḍeeṭa maŋ ṭikakaṭa duvalaa ennam
Yaapanee koocciya enna tava velaa tiyenavaa
eeka taattat ekka kiyanna epaa
aayit ehema mee vidihe væḍa karanna epaa
etakoṭa tamayi ammaalat aave
bæri velaa vat ehema aayit mehe enna epaa
iskooleedi ada ee lamayaa maṭa gæhævvaa
tava ṭikakadi oya puusaa maava huuranavaa
itin kohomada mahattayaa?
eyaa maava Kolam̆ba ekka-yanavaa
mee lamayaa koccaravat nikam inne nææ
mage meesee lokuvaṭa hadanna epaa
kuḍee ehema bas-eke tiyalaa yanna epaa
ara kavda atana usaṭa inne?
hæmadaama mahattayaa ee lamayaage hoňda kiyanavaa maṭa
ohomama inna ṭikak
lassana væḍee ee minihaaṭa vune
koocciyen ehemat enna puluvan
ammaa ee gollanṭat ekka bat ivvaada?

B.
Who's that that came in that white car?
Is the lady at home?
That wristwatch of yours is **very** beautiful.
My smallest boy goes to a **girls'** school.
In our village there is neither a railroad nor a bus route.

I must go to Colombo tomorrow to buy a new sarong-cloth.

At home I look at the paper every morning.

Yesterday we went to Kandy very early, had (our) meal in Kandy, and returned to Colombo in the afternoon.

(They) don't let (you) go free on buses and trains.

10 This time our mangoes were many of them spoilt.

This is a real jungle road.

The dog is now really clean.

Our master told (us) to do that job this way.

What did father ask the teacher?

15 There is one good thing about this dog; he likes bathing.

What did the teacher hit that boy with?

You almost gave that man my parcel.

I haven't much work tomorrow (or) the next day.

He too arrived just then.

20 This dog is very ferocious; he's not at all obedient.

Did it rain hard here too these last few days?

That man is very rich, but there isn't even a footpath to his house.

Don't spoil the child.

An awful thing nearly happened to me!

25 I'll give you a cup of tea at 5.0.

Those [few] mangoes went bad.

That table is too long.

Do (it) however is easiest.

The 10 o'clock train is not due out yet.

Notes:

A. 1 kiluṭuvaṭa, dirtily. kiluṭuva is a noun-form, 'dirt', of which kiluṭu is the stem or adjectival form. aňdinna = 'dress'.

2 pirisiduvaṭa, cleanly (noun-form, pirisiduva). **gedara pirisiduyi** gives a similar sense, but tiyenne = 'is kept'; tiyenavaa is the involitive counterpart of tiyanavaa.

3 gihin, see n. on 13 A 8. gal gæhenavaa, to be struck motionless (turned to stone), thunderstruck. ehemmama, 'just as he was'; **ma** is sometimes doubled in this way.

4 'What do these pages belong to?' See n. on 12 A 22. 'Of what value are these notes?' would be **mee kola kiiye eevaada**?

5 'Food parcel' in English gives a wrong impression. This is equivalent to 'my sandwiches'. **paarsalee** is often used of packages of food. kææm paarsalee or kææma paarsalee.

6 balannam, 'see (what he says)', 'try (telling the boss)'. **balanavaa** is frequently added after an absolutive, e.g. mee saariya æñdalaa balanna, try this sari on. **vædee** here means 'thing, matter'.

7 **ma** here should be translated 'only', 'always'. gon væḍa means 'stupid actions' (lesson 3 **g**).

8 hapanaa or hapanek or hapan. This means 'he is a good eater'.

9 paara naginna: cf. kanda naginna, climb the hill; gas naginna, 9 A 20.

10 dakunu ataṭa or dakunaṭa. etaninut = 'and then'.

11 'I will hurry out to the cafe for my lunch.'

12 Yaapanee koocciya enna (or just Yaapanee koocciyaṭa) tava(ma) velaa tiyenavaa; lit., 'there is still time for the Jaffna train (to come)', i.e. the Jaffna train is not due yet, it is not yet time for the Jaffna train. **Yaapanee** is used adjectivally here (like Tirikunaamalee in 10 above). velaa: see n. on 16 A 9, and compare Yaapanee koocciya yanna dæn velaava hari, where the sing. form is required. In some sentences of this kind ('for someone to do something') containing a noun and an infinitive verb-form, even an animate noun (cf. note on 16 A 15) does not need **-ṭa**.

13 taattat ekka or taattaaṭa.

14 For the case-form **vidihe**, see lesson 5 **e**. væḍa = actions.

15 ammaalaa = mother and others. Pronounce [ammalat].

16 bæri velaa vat ehema = even accidentally, i.e. 'whatever you do'.

17 gæhævvaa = gæhuvaa. Similarly **æhævvaa** often replaces æhuvaa, and **væhævvaa** replaces væhuvaa.

18 'Pussy nearly scratched me'. Notice this idiom; more literally, 'in another minute the pussy scratches me'. There is no equivalent in Sinhalese to 'almost' with a verb. After tava ṭikakadi/ṭiken/poḍḍen in this usage, normally the present tense is used of past events, or else the inifinitive with **giye** (13 A 8 note).[1] Cf., of the future, tava ṭikakin

1. Or with **tiyunaa**, 'would have been possible' (lessson 29 **b**).

huurayi, will scratch (you) in a minute, and 14 A 2.

20 A similar sense would be given by: eyaa maŋ ekka Kolam̃ba yanavaa.

21 nikam innavva (usually pronounced [nikãã innəva]), to keep quiet. koccaravat ... nææ, won't ever ('won't **always**' would require **hæmatissema**, lesson 22 **f**).

22 lokuvaṭa or lokuven hadanna = to make big(ger). Also **loku karalaa hadanna** – but not simply loku hadanna (see **b** above).

24 'Who is that who is (so) tall over there?' Sinhalese cannot say simply 'usa innavaa' (**b** above).

25 **hoñda** is a noun here, 'good qualities'.

26 'Just stay as (= where) you are'. ohoma = in your fashion, as v. mehema, 'in my fashion'. Cf. 8 A 28.

27 'A fine (i.e. curious) thing happened to him', viz. what he deserved. **væḍee** is preferable to **væḍak** here, cf 10 B 17.

28 koocciyen ehemat = koocciyenut. Note the position of the **-t**.

B. 1 White: use **kiri paaṭa**, cream (milk)-coloured. **sudu** is not generally used of cars.

3 Say 'hand-watch' (using stem-form of **ata**).

4 Say 'woman-school' (**gæænu** is the stem-form of gææni).

7 Cf. 15 B 29.

8 In the afternoon – hændææve or hændææva ṭa. Cf. note on 12 A 5. Returned: say 'came'.

10 This time: mee paara (direct case).

12 Compare the pattern of A 2 above. **sudu**, white, can also be used here. Really = hoñdaṭa(ma); in this metaphorical sense (as in Eng. 'a jolly good cleaning'), **hoñdin** is not used.

13 (In) this way: see **a** above.

15 Say: 'there is one good quality (A25 above) of this dog'. 'He', see lesson 11.

17 See A 18 above.

18 Tomorrow or the next day, **heṭa aniddaa**. So **iiye pereedaa**, in these last few days, **ada heṭa** (lesson 2 notes). **ada iiye** means 'very recently'.

21 See note on B 18 above.

22 Rich, cf. A 8 above.

24 Cf. A 27 above and 10 A 24n.
28 'However is easiest': say 'in an easy way' (dat. or instr.).
29 Cf. A 12 above. The 10 o'clock train = dahaye koocciya.

Script

Handwriting naturally involves certain modifications of the letter as printed. In particular, the **i** vowel-sign is usually joined on to the consonant character, e.g.  will be written 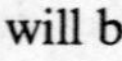, or  as . The u vowel-sign, which is printed , is normally written ; thus , 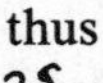. (In handwriting it will not normally be possible to distinguish , pu from 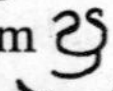, pra). The ælapilla () is also usually joined to the preceding consonant: 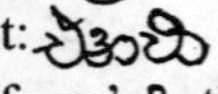.

Where letters begin with a 'platform' , this is also usually joined on to the rest of the letter in one continuous stroke, and often flattened out, eg.  for .

The first of the following two examples of handwriting is reasonably careful, the second is less so.

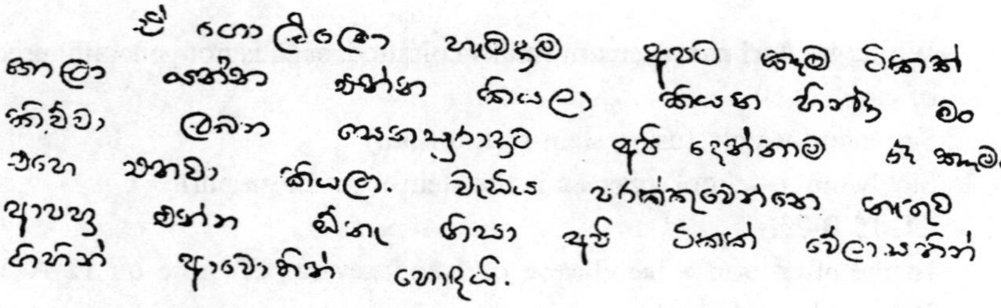

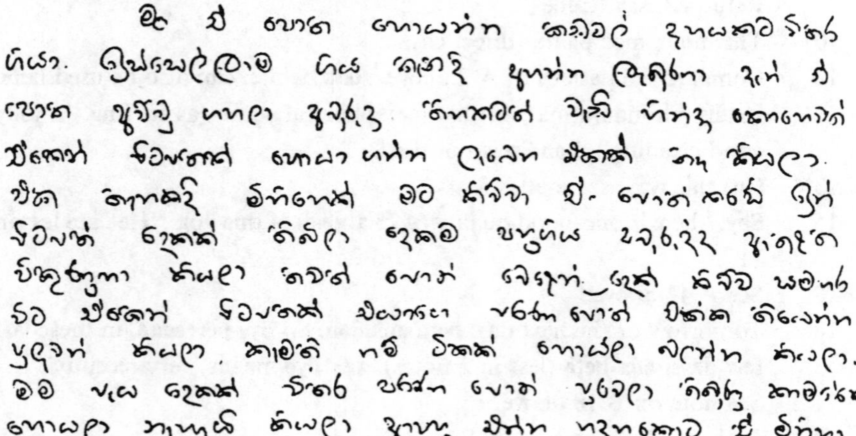

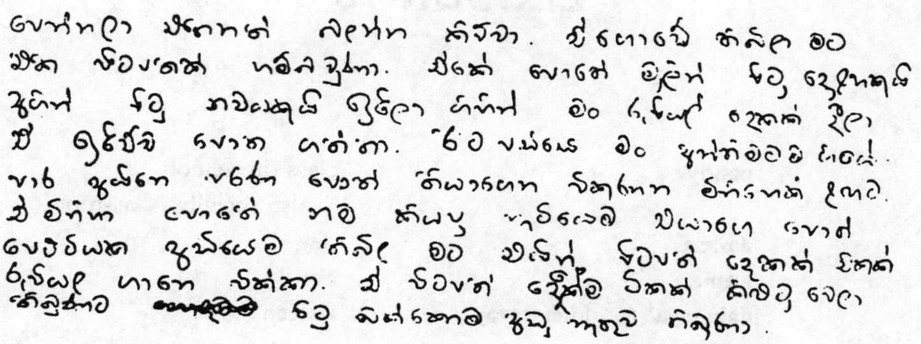

Transcription:

A. ee gollo hæmadaama apaṭa kææma ṭikak kaalaa yanna enna kiyalaa kiyana hindaa maŋ kivvaa labana senasuraadaaṭa api dennaama rææ kææmaṭa ehe enavaa kiyalaa. væḍiya parakku venne nætuva aapahu enna oonæ nisaa api ṭikak veelaasanin gihin aavotin hoňdayi.

B. maŋ ee pota hoyanna kaḍaval dahayakaṭa vitara giyaa. issellaama giya tænadi ahanna læbuṇaa dæn ee pota accu gahalaa avurudu tihakaṭat væḍi hindaa kohevat eeken piṭapatak hoyaa ganna læbena ekak nææ kiyalaa. eka tænakadi minihek maṭa kivvaa ee pot kaḍee in piṭapat dekak tibilaa dekama pahugiya avurudda æṭuḷaṭa vikuṇunaa kiyalaa. tavat pot veḷen – dek kivva[1] samahara viṭa eeken piṭapatak eyaage paraṇa pot ekka tiyenna puluvan kiyalaa, kæmati nam ṭikak hoyalaa balanna kiyalaa. mama pæya dekak vitara paraṇa pot puravalaa tibuṇu kaamareeka hoyalaa næhæyi kiyalaa aapahu enna hadanakoṭa ee minihaa almaariyak uḍa goḍagahalaa tibuṇu pot gonnak pennalaa eṭenat balanna kivvaa. ee goḍee tibilaa maṭa eka piṭapatak hamba vuṇaa. eekee potee mulin piṭu doḷahakuyi agin piṭu navayakuyi irilaa gihin. maŋ rupiyal dekak diilaa ee iricca pota gattaa. iiṭa passe maŋ antimaṭama giyee paara ayine paraṇa pot tiyaagena vikuṇana minihek ḷaňgaṭa. ee minihaa potee nama kiyapu hæṭiyema eyaage pot peṭṭiyaka aḍiyema tibila[2] maṭa eyin piṭapat dekak ekak rupiyala gaane vikkaa. ee piṭapat dekeema ṭikak kiḷuṭu velaa tibuṇaṭa piṭu okkoma aḍu nætuva tibuṇaa.

See further p. 348.

1. kivvaa.
2. tibilaa.

LESSON 18

pantiya	class (in school; also socially); classroom
davasa	day
hæma	every
dahasaya[1] (pr. [**dahasəyə**])	sixteen
dahahata[1]	seventeen
daha-aṭa	eighteen
dahanamaya	nineteen
issellaama særeeṭa (usually pr. [**issellamə**])	for the first time
palaveni	first
deveni	second
tunveni	third
kiiveni (+ **-da**)	"how-many-eth?"
kii særayak (+ **-da**)	how many times?
særayak / **paarak** / **varak**	once
desarayak (pr. [**desərəyak**]) / **depaarak** / **devarak**	twice
kæňdavanavaa	summon
goravanavaa	thunder; growl, groan
væṭenavaa	fall

(a) **Causative verbs**. Every verb can, by inserting **-va-** immediately before **-navaa**, become causative, i.e. having the sense of causing the action to be done, rather than doing it.

---

1. Also written **daasaya, daahata**.

karanavaa, do — karavanavaa, cause to be done

The sequence **-ava-** in causative verbs is often realized as **-oo-**. The past tense of a causative verb usually ends in **-evvaa (-evuvaa)**: karavanavaa – kerevvaa.

An **i** vowel preceding -navaa is changed to **a** in the causative.

hiṭinavaa, stand — hiṭavanavaa, plant, place.

Some verbs assimilate the sequence **consonant + ava** to **double consonant + a**; in such cases, a further **-va-** may be added.

vaṭavanavaa→vaṭṭanavaa or vaṭṭavanavaa, fell, drop deliberately (past tense, væṭṭuvaa or væṭṭevvaa)

gahavanavaa→gassanavaa or gassavanavaa, cause to beat or to shake (alternation h/s lesson 9 **a**)

Where a half-nasal occurs in the verbal root, the sequence **half-nasal + ava** may become **full nasal + consonant + a**; here also, a further -va- is often added.

iňdavanavaa (caus. of iňdinavaa or innavaa)→indanavaa, place, plant.

naňgavanavaa (caus. of naňginavaa)→naŋvanavaa, naŋganavaa, lift

gennanavaa – for genvanavaa – serves as a causative form of **geenavaa**.

The following causatives are irregular in form:

bonavaa, drink	povanavaa, give to drink
tiyanavaa,[1] place	tibbavanavaa / tabbavanavaa — cause to place

Some causative verbs, such as **kæňdavanavaa** and **goravanavaa**, have no corresponding non-causative form in use. Some have only an involitive non-causative form in use.

væṭenavaa, fall	vaṭṭanavaa, fell, drop deliberately
penenavaa / peenavaa — appear	pennanavaa (for penvanavaa), show (past tense. pennuvaa)

The intermediary through whom the action is caused to be done is usually introduced in the dative case followed by **kiyalaa**, 'having said', or in the direct case followed by **lavvaa**, 'having placed'.

maŋ puusaaṭa kiyalaa eyaava hiirevvaa
I got the cat to scratch him

maŋ Caarli lavvaa gennanavaa
I'll get Charlie to bring (it).

---

1. In books, this word is written **tabanavaa**.

The causative form may also have its involitive counterpart.

kiyavanavaa	'cause to be spoken', i.e. read (strictly speaking, to read **aloud**)
kiyavenavaa	get read; get said (lesson 13**a**).
yavanavaa	cause to go, i.e. send (past tense yævuvaa)
yævenavaa	get sent, happen to go
evanavaa	cause to come, i.e. send
evenavaa	get sent, happen to come

Note the difference between sending to me or to you (**evanavaa**) and sending to a third party (**yavanavaa**).

(b) palaveni, deveni etc., when referring to animates, are not used predicatively alone. In such cases, nominal forms are substituted, made by adding the termination **-yaa**.

eyaa palaveni minihaa	he is the first man[1]
eyaa palaveniyaa	he is the first

Before **-veni**, and before **særayak**, **paarak**, **varak**, the numerals have the same slightly modified (stem) forms as they do before **denaa**. The forms for '13 people' etc. are: dahatundenaa, dahahataradenaa, pahalosdenaa, dahasayadenaa, dahahatdenaa, dahaaṭadenaa, dahanamadenaa.

varak, devarak etc. are used in official contexts such as the multiplication tables. Notice the difference between **ekapaara(ka)ṭa**, 'at one time', and **ekapaaraṭama**, 'all of a sudden'.

(c) A noun following **hæma** adds the particle **ma** (as in **hæma-daa-ma** (lesson 1), every day), and sometimes also the indefinite suffix **-k**. hæma paarama, every time – hæma tænama, everywhere – hæma potakama, in every single book. **hæmooma** (also **hævoma**) means 'everybody', with case-forms **hæmooṭama**, **hæmoogema**, **hæmoogenma**.

A.

oya parana kaar-eka tavamat paare duvavanna puluvanda?
væḍakaarayaaṭa kiyalaa oya pot ṭika dænaṭa meesee uḍa tibbavanna
ape lamayaa dæn ṭika ṭika loku pot kiyavanavaa
nitarama mee lamayaaṭa ammaa bat kavanna oonæ
am̆bagaha kappavanna minihekuṭa enna kiyanna

1. This usually means 'he is my first choice'.

ballaava naavannaṭ ekka vatura tiyenavaada?
kaar-eka ibeema hiṭavunaa
maŋ gedaraṭ ekka-yanavaa
mahattayaage kiiveni lamayaada mee?
10 ee minihaa balanna maŋ dæn tunsærayak giyaa
davasakaṭa kii særayak tee bonavaada?
maŋ Kolam̆baṭa ævit adaṭa davas pahak venavaa
mee lamayaa pantiye kiiveniyaada? mee særee pantiye kiiveniyaaṭada aave?
maŋ kaḍeeṭa gihin kiri bootaleekuyi hon̆da pihiyakuyi araŋ enna yanavaa
15 hæma ekenma mee lamayaa tamayi palaveniyaa
tava dahapahalosdenek innavaa enna
maŋ Yaapanee issellaama særeeṭa giye dahahateedi
dahaaṭeedi maŋ gedarin yanna giyaa
dolosvarak paha kiiyada?
20 ammaa okkoṭama ekka tee vækkerevvaalu
tava eka paarayi karanne!
liyuma kohe-koheda bæluve? hæma potakama bæluvaada?
otanaṭa hon̆daṭa peenavaada?
ekak vat vaṭṭanne nætuva araŋ enna
25 maṭa mee meesee tavat poḍiyaṭa hadalaa oonæ

B. I got father to write the teacher a letter.
The boy is getting the servant to pick the mangoes.
The boy swallowed a lot of water.
I got the shopkeeper to wrap up the parcel properly.
5 The teacher wrote to father and got (him) to beat me.
The mother feeds the little child with milk.
I got that man to make a beautiful cupboard.
How many more shall (we) pour tea for?
I am giving a supper for ten tomorrow.
10 I went to Colombo yesterday morning with two or three other boys.
This boy is the first of (them) all.
I have now told the boy more than five times to come, but he **still** hasn't come.

Father wrote to that man six times.
I sent that boy to the shop to fetch a cup of tea.
15 I have no way of sending that book at the moment.
Who did (you) get to do that job?
I have no money to order that book.
What did father ask the teacher when he had summoned him?
It was (my) son who came first in the class this time.
20 Twice eight is sixteen.
(I) can't bring (them) all at once; I'll try to fetch (them) in two lots.
That man was just going to fall out of the bus.
Yesterday afternoon it was thundering and raining in our area.
What were the 10-rupee notes in?
25 This boy is third in the class.

Notes:

A. 3 ţika ţika or ţiken ţika, little by little.

4 Note that with kavanavaa and poṿanavaa, the food is the object of the verb, and the person who is caused to eat or drink it – who is fed – is in the dative case. Several other causative verbs are, or may be, associated with a dative case of the person in this way, e.g. **dannanavaa** (for danvanavaa), to inform, **anda(va)navaa**, to dress (tr.): maŋ eeka eyaaţa dænnuvaa, I informed him of that, aayaa lamayaaţa (or lamayaava) ændevvaa, the ayah[1] got the child dressed.

5 **kapanna** would do as well as kappavanna here (so also **duvanna** in A1).

6 naavanavaa (past **nææ̈vvaa**) is used of washing animates, hoodanavaa of washing inanimates, or portions of animates, e.g. the feet.

7 **hiţiyaa** would do as well as hiţavunaa here.

8 'I'm taking (him) home too'. 'I'm going home as well' would rather be **maŋ gedara yannat ekka yanavaa.**

11 davasakaţa: the dative case is always used in expressions of this kind; twice a day = davasakaţa desarayak.

12 See note on 16 A 9.

13 pantiye kiiveniyaaţada aave = where did he come in the class (= kiiveniyaada vune).

1. Nurse.

14 yanavaa = intend, see note on 13 A 8. araŋ enna = to buy.
15 hæma ekenma = in everything. **eken** is preferable to **eke** here.
16 'There are still 10 to 15 people to come.' (Cf. 11 B 19).
17 dahahateedi = 'in 1917', or 'at the age of 17'. Similarly dahaaţeedi in the next sentence. **-e** is lengthened before **-di**; cf. 11 A 17 note.
19 More colloquially, dolahe eevaa pahak (pahe eevaa dolahak) kiiyada? dolahe eevaa = 'those of 12', i.e. twelves.
20 See note to 17 A 17.
21 'You just do it once more!' (a threat).
22 kohe-koheda, 'where (and) where', i.e. in which places.
23 'Does it appear well to there?', i.e. Can you see all right from there?
25 poḍiyaţa hadanna, or poḍi karalaa hadanna = to make small; see note on 17 A 22. Note that **maţa hadalaa** (sc. tiyenna) **oonæ** means 'I need it made', as v. **hadanna oonæ**, need to make it.

B. 3 Swallowed – 'was caused to drink'.
5 Here **liyalaa** replaced **kiyalaa**.
6 See A4 above.
8 Lesson 14 a.
9 Supper = 'night meal'.
12 **Still**: tavamat.
15 Way of sending – 'way to send'. At the moment, this minute: **dænma** or **dænmama** (Sinhalese say 'now itself').
16 **kiyalaa** is treated postpositionally (see lesson 8 **d**), i.e. **-da** must be added **after** kiyalaa, not before it.
17 Order – gennanna (use infinitive).
18 Say 'having summoned the teacher, what did he ask?'
19 See A 13 above.
21 In two lots, at two times – desareekaţa. Try: 1 **d**.
22 See note on 17 A 18.

SINHALA SYLLABARY

Vowels		අ	ආ	ඇ	ඈ	ඉ	ඊ	උ	ඌ	එ	ඒ	ඔ	ඕ
K	ක්	ක	කා	කැ	කෑ	කි	කී	කු	කූ	කෙ	කේ	කො	කෝ
G	ග්	ග	ගා	ගැ	ගෑ	ගි	ගී	ගු	ගූ	ගෙ	ගේ	ගො	ගෝ
C	ච්	ච	චා	චැ	චෑ	චි	චී	චු	චූ	චෙ	චේ	චො	චෝ
J	ජ්	ජ	ජා	ජැ	ජෑ	ජි	ජී	ජු	ජූ	ජෙ	ජේ	ජො	ජෝ
Ṭ	ට්	ට	ටා	ටැ	ටෑ	ටි	ටී	ටු	ටූ	ටෙ	ටේ	ටො	ටෝ
Ḍ	ඩ්	ඩ	ඩා	ඩැ	ඩෑ	ඩි	ඩී	ඩු	ඩූ	ඩෙ	ඩේ	ඩො	ඩෝ
Ṇ	ණ්	ණ	ණා	ණැ	ණෑ	ණි	ණී	ණු	ණූ	ණෙ	ණේ	ණො	ණෝ
T	ත්	ත	තා	තැ	තෑ	ති	තී	තු	තූ	තෙ	තේ	තො	තෝ
D	ද්	ද	දා	දැ	දෑ	දි	දී	දු	දූ	දෙ	දේ	දො	දෝ
N	න්	න	නා	නැ	නෑ	නි	නී	නු	නූ	නෙ	නේ	නො	නෝ
P	ප්	ප	පා	පැ	පෑ	පි	පී	පු	පූ	පෙ	පේ	පො	පෝ
B	බ්	බ	බා	බැ	බෑ	බි	බී	බු	බූ	බෙ	බේ	බො	බෝ
M	ම්	ම	මා	මැ	මෑ	මි	මී	මු	මූ	මෙ	මේ	මො	මෝ
Y	ය්	ය	යා	යැ	යෑ	යි	යී	යු	යූ	යෙ	යේ	යො	යෝ
R	ර්	ර	රා	රැ	රෑ	රි	රී	රු	රූ	රෙ	රේ	රො	රෝ
L	ල්	ල	ලා	ලැ	ලෑ	ලි	ලී	ලු	ලූ	ලෙ	ලේ	ලො	ලෝ
V	ව්	ව	වා	වැ	වෑ	වි	වී	වු	වූ	වෙ	වේ	වො	වෝ
S	ස්	ස	සා	සැ	සෑ	සි	සී	සු	සූ	සෙ	සේ	සො	සෝ
H	හ්	හ	හා	හැ	හෑ	හි	හී	හු	හූ	හෙ	හේ	හො	හෝ
Ḷ	ළ්	ළ	ළා	ළැ	ළෑ	ළි	ළී	ළු	ළූ	ළෙ	ළේ	ළො	ළෝ
(ňg)	ඟ්	ඟ	ඟා	ඟැ	ඟෑ	ඟි	ඟී	ඟු	ඟූ	ඟෙ	ඟේ	ඟො	ඟෝ
(ňd)	ඳ්	ඳ	ඳා	ඳැ	ඳෑ	ඳි	ඳී	ඳු	ඳූ	ඳෙ	ඳේ	ඳො	ඳෝ
(ňḍ)	ඬ්	ඬ	ඬා	ඬැ	ඬෑ	ඬි	ඬී	ඬු	ඬූ	ඬෙ	ඬේ	ඬො	ඬෝ
(m̆b)	ඹ්	ඹ	ඹා	ඹැ	ඹෑ	ඹි	ඹී	ඹු	ඹූ	ඹෙ	ඹේ	ඹො	ඹෝ
F	ෆ්	ෆ	ෆා	ෆැ	ෆෑ	ෆි	ෆී	ෆු	ෆූ	ෆෙ	ෆේ	ෆො	ෆෝ

The simplified Sinhala syllabary is illustrated above. The complete alphabet, incorporating Pali and Sanskrit characters, includes: FOUR additional inflections derived from two diphthongs, ai ඓ and au ඖ plus ṛ ඍ and ṛṛ ඎ, illustrated by: කෛ, කෞ, කෘ and කෲ respectively; TEN aspirated consonants: ඛ, ඝ, ඡ, ඣ, ඨ, ඪ, ථ, ධ, ඵ and භ; TWO nasals: ඞ and ඤ; TWO sibilants: ශ and ෂ; අං and අඃ. Of these, ං (non-initial) is in common use.

LESSON 19

vissa	20
visi-eka	21
visi-deka	22
tiha	30
tis-eka	31
hataliha	40
hatalis-eka	41
panaha	50
panas-eka	51
iridaa	Sunday
saňdudaa	Monday
aňgaharuvaadaa	Tuesday
badaadaa	Wednesday
brahaspatindaa	Thursday
sikuraadaa	Friday
senasuraadaa	Saturday
allanavaa	hold, catch
illanavaa	ask for
hitanavaa	think
aňduranavaa	recognise, know (a person)
tooranavaa	choose; explain
teerenavaa	be understood; be chosen
mahat venavaa	get fat
ahu venavaa	get caught
æti karanavaa	bring up, create
kælee karanavaa	make into a wilderness
gal venavaa	go solid
kaamaree	room

maḍa	mud
æti	is enough
madi	is not enough
samahara	some
melahakaṭa, melahaṭa	by this time[1]
særen, særeeṭa	fiercely

(a) **Compound tenses**. Besides the tense-forms hitherto mentioned, additional verb-forms are supplied by the use of the absolutive followed by **tiyenavaa** as an auxiliary verb.

tiyenavaa following an absolutive refers to a state in which a person or thing is, was or will be, as a result of the action under consideration; this will usually correspond to English periphrases with 'have' (e.g. 'have done' as opposed to 'did'). When used in this manner, **tiyenavaa** itself is usually either omitted or put in the incomplete form. Thus the absolutive in such cases may stand alone as a main verbal form. In such cases it can be negatived by adding **nææ**.

Alternatively, this mode of expression may refer (1) to a fact not directly experienced by the speaker; here **tiyenavaa** is usually kept. This meaning is of course not usually possible in 1st-personal sentences. (2) to a previous habit; here also **tiyenavaa** is required (in a positive statement).

eyaa iiye mærunaa	he died yesterday
eyaa mærilaa	he is dead
eyaa mærilaa nææ	he is not dead
eyaa iiye mærilaa tiyenavaa	he died yesterday (I hear)
maŋ Kolam̆ba giyaa	I went to Colombo (on a past occasion)
or	I have been to Colombo (today)
maŋ Kolam̆ba gihin tiyenavaa	I have been to Colombo (on one or more occasions)
maŋ Kolam̆ba gihillaa nææ	I have not been to Colombo

'maŋ Kolam̆ba gihillaa' would have to give the idea of a one-way trip, I have arrived in Colombo and am still there – and would therefore never be said, since **ævillaa** would be used instead in such a context. maŋ Kolam̆ba gihillaa aavaa is of course possible.

1. **elahakaṭa**, by that time, is less common.

The correspondence with English 'have done' etc. is not absolute; e.g., in asking and answering questions which refer to one particular occurrence, the plain past tense is often used in Sinhalese, although in English the auxiliary verb may be used.

koo, taattaa giyaada?	giyaa
oh, has father gone?	Yes, he has

The use of the absolutive alone in a direct 2nd-personal question implies either a) that the action is occurring unexpectedly soon (here the English will contain the word 'already'), or b) that the primary emphasis is on the action or its object rather than on the actor or subject (here the Eng. may express the sentence passively). In a 3rd-personal question, the use of the absolutive alone may also imply that the person being questioned cannot answer from direct experience.

Thus in the example quoted above, **taattaa gihillaada**? will imply either that the speaker supposes that the man he is addressing did not **see** his father go, or that his father has gone unexpectedly soon.

When an absolutive is used alone in a question, **-da** must follow the absolutive; if it follows any other word, **tiyenne** must be added. In other words, an absolutive cannot replace an **incomplete** verb-form here.

ee minihaa ævillaada?	has that man come?
but	
ee minihaada ævit tiyenne?	is that the man who has come?

(b) **illanavaa** is associated with an ablative case of the person from whom one asks.

maŋ eyaagen tee ṭikak illuvaa

I asked him for some tea

ahu venavaa is associated with a dative case of the person or thing one is caught by.

eyaa kaar-ekaṭa ahu vunaa

he was run over by the car

teerenavaa is similarly associated with a dative case of the person who understands.

eeka maṭa teerenavaa

I understand that

This word is the involitive counterpart of **tooranavaa**, to explain, which is now used in this sense only in the compound form **tooralaa denna**. **tooranavaa** however also has the meaning 'choose' or 'sort'.

allanavaa has additional meanings 'serve (food etc.)' to someone, and 'be attractive' to someone (with dative cases: meeke lassana maṭa allanne nææ, I am not attracted by the beauty of this).

(c) The incomplete form of **æti** is **ætte**. æti + da gives the form **ædda**? **madi** has no incomplete form: it is necessary here to say **madi venne**. **madi** is used (like vædi, lesson 16 **c**) after adjectival words: usa madi, not high enough, too low. **ætte nææ** cannot be used in the sense of **madi**.

æti can be used adverbially ('sufficiently') if followed by **venna**, '(so as) to become'. 'That's enough' is **ee æti** (not eeka æti).

(d) **daa** (day) remains unaltered in the locative case, and does not usually take a **-k** suffix, or have a plural form. Thus 'on Sunday' is just **iridaa**; **iridaaṭa** means 'for (the day on) Sunday' or 'up till Sunday' (cf. heṭaṭa, etc.). 'On Sundays', 'on a Sunday' are expressed by **iridaa davasvala** and **iridaa davasaka**.

daa is also used after numerals in expressing dates: palaveni daa, (on) the first of the month. Be careful not to obscure the first vowel sound in **badaadaa** (**ba-** not **bə-**). Final **-daa** is usually pronounced very short (as in kavadaada).

(e) The numerical forms for '20 people' etc, are visidenaa, visiekdenaa (not visiekkenaa), etc.[1] The ordinal forms are visiveni, 20th, visiekveni (not visipalaveni), tisveni etc.

(f) **samahara** is usually used before a plural noun.

samahara minissu	some men
samahara pot[2]	some books

A.

ape karattee genihin tiyenne ee minihaa venna oonæ
minihaa ada hoňdaṭama arakku gahalaa
paara vaturaṭa heedilaa gihillaa nemeyi, etana paaraṭa kanda kaḍaa væṭilaa, eekayi kaarvalaṭa yanna denne nætte
eyaava maṭa dæn epaa velaa tiyenne
hæmadaama tee biilaa biilat tavama nææ epaa velaa
poḍi lamayaaṭa væḍiya vatura allanna denna epaa
maava aayi itin allanna hitanna epaa
lamayaa kaamaree kælee karalaa

---

1. With 20 and numbers above, **denaa** is sometimes omitted, and e.g. vissak, visi-ekak (not -ekek) may be used of people.

2. Sometimes the form **samaharak** is used, which may also stand **after** the noun (pot samaharak). **samaharun** is used for 'some people'.

lamayaa dæn sudu velaa
paarsalee gal velaa
taattaa iiye maava ee mahattayaaṭa aňduravalaa dunnaa
pota illalaa maṭa liyumak evalaa (tiyenavaa)
ape lamayaa ada pota kiyavalaa nemeyida iskoolee aave?
ballaa maḍa naalaada?
melahakaṭa ee mahattayaa gedara gihillaa
iiye hændæævet Kolam̆baṭa væhælaa tiyenavaa
ee bas-eke minissu hatalisdenekuṭa vaḍaa hiṭiyaa
almaariya ganna dora usa palala madi
iridaa davasema væssaa
samahara davasvala Kolam̆baṭat særeeṭa vahinavaa
lamayaa ballekut æti karanavaa balalekut æti karanavaa
sikuraadaa api Jaapanee yamu
lamayaa kiri madi velaa aňḍanavaa
iiye æti venna væssaa
Tirikunaamalee paare dæn vatura bæhælaa; dæn kaar-bas-valaṭa yanna enna puluvan
mahattayaa dæn huňgak vayasaṭa gihin
hoňda geḍi ṭika tooralaa araŋ pættakin tiyaa tiyanna
apiṭa dæn mehe iňdalaa æti velaa, gedara yannamayi hitenne
minihaa yanne næti veyi

B. Can (you) catch me?
A gentleman has come to look at the car.
Have (you) washed the dog?
The road has got washed away by the water.
Don't ask me for money.
Some small children often cry.
This road has now become real jungle (got very overgrown).
My children have grown big now.
Rs. 5/- is quite enough for this book.
They don't want us any more.
He must have come yesterday too.
Have (you) read this book?
The cupboard door is shut.

By constantly eating rice (he) has got fat.
15 By constantly drinking toddy I have grown to dislike (it) now.
There aren't enough chairs for this table.
Is this enough?
That's enough now.
The dog has been run over by the car.
20 Father has drunk my tea.
This boy has come by **bus** (I hear).
Is today Saturday? What day is it today?
Is there enough tea for me too?
One side of this mango has gone bad.
25 There is still one chair lacking for this table.
By this time tomorrow we shall be in Kandy.
This tea is not enough for me.
Did our dog come your way, perhaps?
I don't understand that at all.

Notes:

A. 1 Cf. lesson 10 **d**. Here, the emphasized word is followed by **venna oonæ**, instead of by **-yi** or **tamayi**.

2 gahanavaa has many idiomatic usages. Here it means 'drink'. hoňdaʈama, see n. on 17 B 12.

3 heedilaa gihillaa, 'washed and gone', i.e. washed away. The absolutive **kaɖaa** is used before certain verbs where a sudden violent action is in question. Thus kaɖaa væʈenavaa (fall down – of things), kaɖaa biňdenavaa (get broken),[1] kaɖaa paninavaa (give a sudden leap). **eekayi** in connection with a phrase containing an incomplete verb-form has the idiomatic meaning 'that's the reason why'.

5 Notice the effect of **-t** after an absolutive; 'even though constantly drinking' (lesson 15 **a**). See note on A 23 below.

6 vatura allanavaa = play with water. This refers to children playing in puddles etc. **væɖiya**, see 16 A 28.

7 'You'll never catch me now' or 'You won't get me involved again'. Think to do = think of doing (cf. the use of dannavaa in 6 B 13).

---

1. See lesson 20.

9 'Has got fair(er)', see 7 A 24 note.

10 This doubtless refers to a **kææma paarsalee** (17 A 5 n). **hayi velaa** would have the same meaning as gal velaa here.

11 aňduravalaa denavaa = introduce. **aňduravalaa** is often pronounced as if written aňduralaa. **aňdunnalaa** (for aňdunvalaa) is a variant form.[1]

12 See n. on duvalaa, 15 A 22. In Eng. we say 'send and ask for' rather than 'ask for and send', but **illanna** is not possible here.

14 See n. on 12 B 1. **maḍa naanavaa** is treated as a conjunct verb; so sometimes **vatura naanavaa** – but cf. vature piinanavaa, maḍe piinanavaa. **maḍe naanavaa** is also possible.

15 gedara gihillaa = has got home.

16 iiye-hændæævet or iiyet hændææve, yesterday afternoon also. væhælaa, for væhalaa, absolutive of vahinavaa. The sound-sequence **æhə** is avoided.

17 minissu can be omitted.

18 usa palala madi = too low and too narrow. No word for 'and' is required. ganna: 'to take'.

19 davasema = all day. The loc. case is usual here.

21 Or lamayaa ballekuyi balalekuyi æti karanavaa. **-t** . . . . **-t** can only be used for 'both . . . and' **if the verb is repeated**, as here.

23 Although what is insufficient is not the subject of the main verb, the connection here is sufficiently close for the absolutive to be used. Cf. A5 above.

25 bæhælaa, see n. on 16 above. kaar-bas, cars and buses, cf. meesa puṭu, tables and chairs, pææn pænsal, pens and pencils.

26 vayasaṭa gihin, has got old.

27 araŋ can be omitted. tiyaa tiyanna = keep (as opposed to 'put'). See 15 A 29 n. and 15 B 23.

28 'Having been here and (it) having been enough, it is only going home we think of'; i.e. we are tired of being here now, and only think of getting home. There is little difference between **api hitanavaa** and **apiṭa hitenavaa** (involitive).

29 Here **næti veyi** is a less emphatic equivalent of nææ.

---

1. But **aňdunanavaa** is less often used.

B. 4 Washed away, see n. A 3 above.

9 Quite: yasaṭa.

10 Here 'any more' means 'now'.

11 **ævit tiyenavaa** is more positive than **aavaa venna oonæ.**

13 Say 'the door of the cupboard'. The door was shut by somebody, not accidentally; the involitive form should not be used here.

15 The absolutive is grammatically unattached, as in A23 above (and cf. 18 A 25).

17, 18 This: **mee, oya** are more common than meeka, ooka here.

22 What day: kavadaada (**koyi davasada** is more particularized, 'which day?').

23 Say 'is there tea sufficiently for . . .'

24 Say 'a side' (cf. A 27 above).

26 'Shall be' needs no equivalent in Sinhalese.

28 Your way: 3 A 24. Perhaps: lesson 17 c.

LESSON 20

bañdinavaa	tie; get married, build
adinavaa	drag, pull
biñdinavaa	break (tr.)
damanavaa, daanavaa (irreg. past tense, **dæmmaa**)	place; post (letter)
sumaanee	week
avurudda (pl. **avurudu**)	year
gee (pl. **geval**)	house
liñda (pl. **lin**)	well
viidiya	street
raattala	pound (lb.)
baagee	half
siini (pl.)	sugar
lunu (pl.)	salt
luunu (pl.)	onions
hæṭa	60
hæṭa-eka	61
hættææva	70
hættæ-eka	71
asuuva	80
asuu-eka	81
anuuva	90
anuu-eka	91
aluten	afresh, newly; (with past tense) recently
edaa	that day; in the past
uḍadi	ago

væradi	wrong, mistaken
varada / **værædda**	fault
paas	passed (of an examination)
kehel, **kesel** (pl.)	bananas

(a) The past tenses of bañdinavaa and biñdinavaa are **bændaa**, **bindaa** (for bæñdiyaa, biñdiyaa). Notice here how the sequence half-nasal consonant + iyaa becomes full nasal + consonant + aa. So **ændaa** from añdinavaa (lesson 16). (Compare the similar development in the formation of causatives, lesson 18 **a**). Similarly, besides **næggaa** from naginavaa there is also the form **næŋgaa** from the form nañginavaa.

biñdinavaa is used of smashing objects of glass or china (see lesson 11 **d** on kaɖanavaa), or of breaking open fruits, e.g. coconuts (where kaɖanavaa means picking the fruits); also of breaking **into** a house.

(b) **Participles**. There is no relative pronoun 'who, which' in Sinhalese. Instead, a verbal participle is used. Every verb has two participles, present and past. These are used before nouns as verbal adjectives, e.g. 'the man who eats' will appear as 'eating man', kana minihaa.

The present participle can be arrived at by leaving out the final **-vaa** of the present tense.

Present tense	Present participle
kanavaa	kana
naginavaa	nagina
dænenavaa	dænena
innavaa	inna
naanavaa	naana

The past participle has several forms. One form can be arrived at by shortening the final **-aa** of the past tense.

næggaa	nægga
bæluvaa	bæluva
dænunaa	dænuna
hiʈiyaa	hiʈiya

A more literary variant is obtained by leaving out the final **-vaa** of the past tense of verbs ending in **-anavaa**, or the final **-yaa** of the past tense of verbs in **-inavaa** (remember that this **-yaa** is usually lost in a double consonant). This form however is not much used in speech, except in a few words such as **hiṭi**.

bæluvaa	bælu
hiṭiyaa	hiṭi
næggaa (for nægiyaa)	nægi

The corresponding form in the case of verbs in **-enavaa** ends in **-u**.

dænunaa	dænunu

In ordinary speech, however, the usual form is obtained by adding **-pu** to the short form of the absolutive. A vowel **aa** preceding **-pu** is usually shortened.

balaa	balapu (balaapu)
næga	nægapu
hiṭa	hiṭapu

These forms are not used in connection with verbs in **-enavaa**. Such verbs, however, often use a past participle ending in **-icca**.

væṭenavaa	væṭicca

Notice

tiyenavaa	tiyicca (pron. [tiiccə])[1]

Among verbs with irregularly formed absolutives, the following past participial forms occur:

enavaa	aapu, aava (literary, aa)
yanavaa	giya
denavaa	diipu, dunna, dunnu (literary, dun)
bonavaa	biipu, bivva (literary, biv)
venavaa	vecca, vuna (literary, vunu, vuu)
gannavaa	gatta, gattu, aragatta (literary, gat)
karanavaa	karapu, kala (**pr.** [kələ])
geniyanavaa	genicca (literary, genagiya)

(c) A phrase such as 'the men who eat the rice' is represented by **bat kana minissu**. Here the order is important. The participle forms the last item in an adjectival phrase, which may be expanded at will provided the participle stands immediately before the noun it qualifies.

gedara hæmadaama udeeṭayi rææṭayi bat kana minihek

a man who eats rice at home every day, morning and evening

---

1. Also tibicca, abs. tibilaa and past tense tibunaa; the corresponding present tense-form **tibenavaa** however is only used in writing.

There are no specifically passive verb-forms in Sinhalese. Accordingly the participles may sometimes need to be translated passively in English.

kaḍana jambu væṭenavaa

the jambu-fruits which are being picked are falling down

(Compare an English sentence such as 'the house is building' – i.e. is being built).

A phrase such as 'the rice which the man is eating' is represented by **minihaa kana bat**. Here minihaa is a direct case-form. Similarly: maŋ eyaaṭa diipu salli, the money which I gave him.

A participle can be repeated to give the idea of a repeated action.

ee lamayaa maŋ kiyana kiyana hæma ekama karanavaa

that boy does everything I (ever) tell him (lit., 'each one thing')

The words **puluvan**, **kæmati**, **oonæ** and **bæri** can all be used as participles (but not **epaa** or **madi**, which need a participial form of **venavaa** after them). **oonæ**. . . **-k** means 'any(thing) **you** want', and can therefore usually be translated 'any', especially when followed by **-ma**.

oonæ(ma) potak maṭa denna

give me any book

kæmati and **bæri** (used participially) can also be followed by the emphasizing particle **-ma**.

næti is the participial (adjectival) form corresponding to **nææ**. Negative forms of participles can be made 1) by adding **næti** to the incomplete verb-form: kanne næti (present) and kææve næti (past) 2) by prefixing **no-** to the participle: nokarana, nokarapu.

ee minihaa nokarana væḍak nææ

there is nothing he does not do

Tissa kææve næti eevaa tavama tiyenavaa

what Tissa did not eat still remains

Participles are extremely commonly used.

(d) 'A pound of sugar' in **siini raattalak**; no case-form is used here. 'Half a pound' is **(raattal) baagayak**. Notice that **hamaara** is only used after other numerals, e.g. 2½ lbs., **raattal dekahamaarak**. It is not much used in composition with the higher numerals 20, 30 etc.: '20½' would be **vissakut hamaarak** rather than vissa-hamaarak.

geval, the plural of **gee**, is also used to mean 'one's own (single) house'; **ape geval** is the same as **ape gedara**. The dative and locative singular of this word are **geṭa** and **geyi**; the indefinite form is **geyak** (but usually **geekaṭa**, see lesson 5 **a**).

uḍadi (uḍa + di) usually follows a dative case denoting a space of time.

avuruddakaṭa uḍadi, a year ago.

(e) Bread is normally asked for by the pound in shops, but paan geḍiyak is used to mean 'a loaf'. **geḍiya** is also used of vegetables, e.g. **luunu geḍiyak**, an onion. **sudu luunu** means garlic.

Bananas, which grow in great variety in Lanka, are referred to in English as 'plantains'.

Wells are common, piped water supplies being confined to large towns.

A. api bænde giya avurudde
iskoolee dænaṭa væḍa balana guruvarayaa mamayi
bona vatura-ekaṭa ata hoodanna epaa
taattaa gihin gattu kaar-eka maṭa allanne nææ
hiṭapu guruvarayaa dæn Maatalee
paanuyi kehel geḍiyi kanavaada?
gedara luunu geḍiyak ehema ganna tiyenavaada?
kaḍakaarayaa ara otana paarsalee mona-monavaada tiyenne?
ballanṭa maŋ kæmati nææ
giya paara maat ee gollan ekka Nuvara giyaa
maŋ mee meesee uḍa æralaa tiyalaa giya pota kavda væhævve?
mee kaḍee tiyena baḍu vikunana eevaa nemeyi
ee minihaa maava maranna ædalaa gatta pihiya meekayi
ee lamayaa ate evapu liyuma læbunaada?
dæn davas pahakaṭa uḍadi daapu liyuma adayi læbilaa tiyenne
oya paarsalaye gahalaa tiyena nama mokakda?
taattaa puṭuva uḍa iňdaŋ ee aluten gahalaa tiyena pot ṭika kiyavanavaa
ara usa kanda uḍat geyak tiyenavaa
oya kæḍicca pææenaṭa mona sallida?
mee paara væṭenne kohaaṭada?
lamayaa kæmatima pota mokakda?
oya monavaada kiyanne – ee minihaa væḍa dannavaa; oonæ ekak kiyanna, karanavaa
mee pææna puluvan hoňda vidiyakaṭa maṭa hadalaa denna
maṭa bæri velaa væradi koocciyaṭa nægunaa
tava ṭikak havas velaa enna
sallivalaṭa nemeyi ee minihaa maṭa eeka denna hæduve
edaa iňdaŋ eyaava maṭa epaa vunaa

arina arina siini paarsalee lunu
ekat ekaṭa vahii
varadak nææ, ohe innavaa; mahattayaaṭa dæn kohomada?
mee ballaaṭa kiyana nama mokakda?
kiyana eevaa kiiyen kiiyakda kerenne?
taattaa enna tava havas veyi
lamayaa uḍinma paas mee paara
væḍiya loku næti geḍiyak tooralaa araŋ enna

B.

What are the days of the week?
Mother doesn't like to drink the tea I pour out.
Who's that boy who's always coming here?
The bread (they) give (you) in that shop is not good.
(You) must tell a washerman to wash the clothes.
That gentleman still hasn't received the letter I wrote last week.
They're going to pull down all those three old houses in our street.
The boy who went to the shop to get a loaf of bread and a pound of onions hasn't got back yet.
Has the bookbinder come today?
Where does the clockmaker live?
Here is the dog that scratched my arm.
He will eat the bread I am cutting.
The child hasn't given (back) the pen (he) borrowed from me yet.
The man who was sent to get a bottle of arrack isn't here yet.
Did (you) bring the **broken** umbrella?
I just told that boy to go and look at (=read) a book.
Go wherever you like.
Come to the village as quickly as possible.
Are you (all) coming past our house tomorrow?
What are they made of?
Mother is five years younger than father.
This is not a job which mother or father can (do).
Which boy did (you) send the letter by?
There is nothing which that man cannot (do).
I got fed up with constantly eating mangoes.
Don't bother about him.

A pound of bread is far too little for ten.
Where is your house, sir?
Father will be late home tonight.
30 It's two years since I bought the car.
He must have brought the **wrong** book.
Give (me) a quarter of sugar.
There is nothing this child doesn't want.
He doesn't much like to bathe from the well.
35 Come on a Sunday – we are at home every Sunday afternoon.

Notes:

A. 1 giya = gone, i.e. last. Similarly **ena** = coming, i.e. next. **labana**, participle of **labanavaa**, which is formally the volitive counterpart of **læbenavaa**, is also used for 'next' in this sense. avurudde is locative.

2 dænaṭa væḍa balana = temporarily in charge.

3 vatura-eka = container full of water (like **tee-eka**, lesson 2). Notice the use of the dative case here: into, i.e. in, the drinking water. **vaturen** might mean just 'with the drinking water', i.e. not **in** it.

4 **allanavaa** with the dative case can mean either to please (as here), or to hold towards, serve.

5 hiṭapu = former. Maatalee is a town near Kandy, centre of a cocoa-growing area.

6 **paanuyi** will often be pronounced [paaŋuyi] (see Introduction), but cannot be so written in the conventional Sinhalese script. kanavaa-da = will you have...?

7 ganna, '(for us) to take', cf. 15 A 30. 'Have you an onion for us?'

8 Here **otana** does not mean 'there', but is the present participle of **otanavaa**. mona-monavaada, 'what (and) what things?', i.e. what various things?

11 æralaa tiyalaa giya = left open ('having opened and placed and gone').

12 vikunana eevaa nemeyi, 'are not things which are for sale.' **vikunanne nææ** gives the same meaning. Though **tiyena** need not be translated in English ('the goods in this shop'), it is normal in Sinhalese, where a noun cannot be qualified by a prepositional phrase. (Cf. lesson 13 **b**).

13 pihiya meekayi or pihiya mee or pihiyayi mee(ka). ædalaa gatta is much the same as **ædagatta** (for which, see lesson 23 **a**).

14 ee lamayaa ate, 'by the hand of that boy'. **ate** (or **ata**) is used as a postposition; with involitive verbs, **atin** is used in this sense, see lesson 13 **a**.

15 dæn or miiṭa – but not dænaṭa.

16 gahalaa tiyena means 'typed'. Here we would just say 'the name on the parcel', but something further is required in Sinhalese (as in 12 above).

17 puṭuva uḍa (as v. **puṭuve**) gives the idea of reclining with the feet up – a position commonly adopted in the long easy cane chairs with which most verandas are equipped. Here gahalaa means 'printed'.

19 Sc. **læbenne**, 'could one get?' or **denne**, 'would they pay?' This form of question is rhetorical, implying 'very little'; an actual request for an offer would be expressed with **kiiyada**.

20 See n. on 15 B2. **væṭenne** is alternative to **yanne** here.

21 **-ma**, see lesson 10 **c**. mokakda or koyi ekada (mona eka, however, is not used).

22 **ekak** may often be realized as [eyak] (Introduction, p. 4).

23 puluvan hoñda vidiyakaṭa = as well as you can ('in a possible good way', cf. 17 B 28).

24 Here **maṭa nægunaa** means not 'I got angry' (8 A 29), but 'I (accidentally) got into' (lesson 13 **a**).

25 'When it has become more afternoon', i.e. a little later in the afternoon. For the detached absolutive, cf. n. on 16 A 9.

26 hæduve, 'tried' (lesson 1).

27 edaa, see 19 **d**.

28 'In every packet of sugar (I) open'. paarsalee or paarsalvala or paarsaleeka.

29 See 9 A 27.

30 This means 'No complaints, I'm all right, how are you?' **ohe**, see n. on 7 A 10.

31 ballaaṭa kiyana is commoner than **ballaage** here.

32 eevaa or eevaayin, cf. 10 A 26. kiiyen kiiyak, see 12 A 22.

33 'Father will be a little later (still)'. Cf. 25 above. **enna** is not necessary: taattaa ada havas veyi, father will be late this afternoon; if the dative form **taattaaṭa** is used, the delay is involitive: father will get late, be delayed (cf. 17 A 12 n.). According to the time of day, **daval venavaa**,

havas (hændææ) venavaa and **ræææ venavaa** may all be translated 'be late'. **heṭa venavaa** is 'to be very late'.[1]

34 paas or paas vunaa (conjunct verb, see lesson 14 **d**). uḍinma = very high(ly); **usa** cannot be used here. 'He passed well this time'.

B. 1 What – plural.

4, 7 This indefinite 'they' (French **on**) need not be translated into Sinhalese.

5 Say 'a man who washes clothes'.

7 All three, lesson 11 A 12. See also note on A 12 above.

8, 14 Hasn't got back yet, isn't here yet = (just) **tavama nææ.**

9 Say 'the man who binds (ties up) books'.

10 Say 'the man who mends watches'.

11 'Here is', cf. 11 B 14.

13 Borrow = take away.

16 Just (= simply): nikam or nikamaṭa.

17 Say 'in a direction which (you) like'.

18 As quickly as possible: cf. A 23 above.

19 Past: dihaave (see note on 8 A 12).

20 What: use **monavaa** for 'what material'. **mokak** means rather 'what particular object'. The instr. case-form is usually **monavaayin** (cf. 12 A 22), though **monavaavalin** is also used.

21 Five years – direct case, cf. 13 B 8.

22, 24 **karanna** can be omitted; cf. **maṭa Siŋhala puluvan**, I can (do, speak) Sinhalese.

23 By: cf. A 14 above, also lesson 8 **d**. The final **-e** of **ate** is lengthened before **-da**. (Cf. dekeema, 12 A 1 note).

24 Nothing: no job.

25 Constantly: lesson 15 a.

26 See 12 A 21.

27 'Far' – **hoňdaṭama.**

28 Your: use plural.

29 See A 33 above.

30 'Since', see 16 A 9 note.

---

1. For **daval**, see lesson 25.

32 "lb." is not necessary in Sinhalese any more than in English.

33 Want = oonæ (kæmati = like). Nothing: use **ekak**.

34 'Much' in a negative sentence must be rendered by **eccara**, 'so much', 'to such an extent', or **vædiya** (lesson 16 **c**). **huňgak** should not be used here. 'To bathe from the well': liňden naanavaa is enough, but Sinhalese will probably say 'having taken water from the well to bathe'. See lesson 11 **d**.

35 Every Sunday afternoon – say 'every Sunday in the afternoon'.

LESSON 21

hamba karanavaa	earn, acquire
hamba venavaa	meet, visit; be earned, be found
kataa karanavaa	speak, call; speak about
pirenavaa	be full
kuuddanavaa (past tense, **kiidduvaa**)	wake (tr.)
haravanavaa	turn (tr.)
parakku venavaa	be late
ivara karanavaa	finish (tr.)
næti karanavaa	lose, destroy
hari gassanavaa	put in order, put right
salakanavaa (with dative case)	treat well, respect
kan	until
hindaa / **nisaa**	because (of)
koṭa	when, while
hæṭiyema	just as, as soon as
bicciya[1]	wall (of building)
taappee	wall (as fence)
eliya	light; outside (n.)
ayiyaa	'elder brother'
malli	'younger brother'
akkaa	'elder sister'
naŋgi	'younger sister'
siiyaa	grandfather
aacci	grandmother
rassaava	job, employment
tanakola (pl.)	grass

1. More elegantly, **bittiya**.

ṭayar-eka	tyre
saddee	noise
santoosee	delight
aparaadee	misfortune
bima (loc., **bima**)	ground

(a) The relationship between the participial verb and its noun is not always one of subject and object (as e.g. kana minihaa, where the man is the eater, or kana tanakola, where the grass is the eaten); sometimes other case relationships are involved, which in English must be expressed by prepositional or conjunctional words.

api aapu davasa
    the day when (**on** which) we came
api inna gedara
    the house where (**in** which) we live
api liyana pææna
    the pen we write **with**
putek læbuna santoosee
    joy **at the** birth of a son
minihaa kaar-eka haravana ata
    the direction **in** which he is turning the car
hayiya tiyena kenek
    a strong man (**of** or **to** whom there is strength)
almaariya væṭicca saddee
    the noise **of** the cupboard falling

(b) Participles are also used in a number of expressions which in English involve conjunctions such as 'until', 'while', 'because', 'when', 'as soon as'. In Sinhalese a participial form is used here, followed by a word which may be considered as a particle, of which five are listed above.

kan (sometimes **kal**) is usually preceded by a present participle. It may usually be translated 'until', but sometimes 'as long as' (of time) depending on the context. **hindaa** and **nisaa** follow present or past participles, and can also be preceded by an absolutive (with a participial form understood). The form **handaa** is sometimes used for **hindaa**.

maŋ ena kan inna
    wait until I come; wait for me (n.b. **inna maṭa** cannot have this meaning: cf. 7 A 25).

eyaa maŋ ena kanma hiṭiyaa
he waited till I actually came
maat kana kan inna
wait till I've eaten too
eyaa apiṭa salakana kan, apit eyaaṭa sælakuvaa
as long as he was treating us well, we also treated him well
vahina hindaa api yanne nææ
since it is raining we will not go
vahina nisaa maŋ geṭa aavaa
because it was raining I came indoors
taattaa aapu hindaa api yanne nææ
because father has come we won't go
taattaa aapu hindaa api giyaa
because father came/had come, we went
taattaa ævit hindaa maat enavaa
because father has come, I'm coming too

hindaa and **nisaa** are also used postpositionally after nouns, and after **madi, epaa** and similar verbal substitutes.

eeka hindaa]
eeka nisaa] therefore

kan however requires a participle **vena** in such contexts.

namaya vena kan inna
remain until (it is) 9.0.

hæṭiyema (lit. 'in the very manner') following a past participle may usually be translated 'as soon as'.

Joon aapu hæṭiyema vahinna gattaa
as soon as John arrived it began to rain (notice this use of **gannavaa**)

koṭa[1] usually follows a present participle,[2] and refers to one of two simultaneous actions. It cannot be used as an equivalent to 'when' if the actions are not simultaneous. If the **koṭa**-clause refers to a past occasion, the **main** verb may be either past or, where a continuous action is indicated, present.

---

1. In books **viṭa**, as **koṭa** is the usual literary form of the absolutive karalaa.

2. A past participle occurs in restricted contexts, e.g. **eyaa naapu koṭa**! he has indeed had his bath.

api yana koṭa ṭayar-ekak giyaa

while we were on our way, a tyre burst ('went')

edaa api kana koṭa vahinavaa

it was raining that day as we ate

vahina koṭa api naannam

when it rains we will bathe

ammaa mærena koṭa api okkoma gedara

when mother died we were all at home (**hiṭiyaa** may be added here)

An absolutive standing alone as a main verb may imply not only **tiyenavaa**, but also **tiyunaa**, especially after a clause containing **koṭa**.

eyaa ena koṭa maŋ gihillaa

when he came, I was gone (**tiyunaa** is to be supplied)

But in a sentence like 'When father comes back, we'll all have tea', the two actions will be consecutive, not simultaneous. **koṭa** therefore will not be used.[1]

Notice that **yana koṭa** may mean either 'when departing' or 'while on the road' or 'upon arrival'. (Cf. in English the possible meanings of a sentence such as 'When we went to London, it was raining.') In the first two cases, the subject of the main sentence may be the same, and if the main verb is in the simple-past tense, one of the first two meanings must be given. In the third meaning, in the absence of a simple past tense verb the two verbal actions remain simultaneous. **ena koṭa** has similar ambiguities.

(c) hamba venavaa (often heard as **hambu venavaa**) in the sense of a planned meeting or interview is used with a direct object case-form; in the case of an accidental meeting, it is used with a dative case, and there is an implication that the party expressed in the dative case caught sight of the other first. In this case it may not involve a real meeting at all, but just catching sight of.

balanavaa in the sense of visiting is usually used of social calls ('I'm going to see my friend'), but in the sense of business interviews ('I'm going to see my boss'). hamba venavaa is preferred.

(d) There is no general word for 'brother' or 'sister' which applies exclusively to these relationships. Instead, distinction is made between those who are older and those who are younger than oneself in age. The terms also include, however, cousins descended from a father's brother or from a mother's sister, since those

---

1. See below, lesson 26 **b**.

relatives, and their wives or husbands, are also addressed as 'father' or 'mother' and not by the terms usually translated as 'uncle' or 'aunt'. (See note on lesson 3 A 16). Similarly **aacci** and **siiyaa** refer not only to grandparents but also to brothers and sisters of certain grandparents and their respective husbands or wives. In Kandyan districts these two words are replaced by **kiri-ammaa** and **aataa** or **attaa**.[1] The (English) words **ankal** and **ænţi** may be used for any kind of uncle or aunt. All these terms of relationship form their plural in **-laa** (mallilaa, etc.). The plural is often used respectfully to indicate a single person, or that person's household.

(e) **ţayar** is pronounced [**ţayər**], not [**ţayar**]. Loan-words of this kind are exceptions to the general rules about the pronunciation of **a**. Similarly **rabar** (pr. [**rabər**]), rubber (pl.).

A.
taattaa inna kan lamayaa hon̆daţa hiţiyaa
maŋ iiye æti vena kan am̆ba kææva
ena sumaanee maţa salli hamba vecca hæţiyema maŋ ee pota gannavaa
ee ballaa maŋ kataa karapu hæţiyema enavaa
minihaa koocciya aapu hæţiyema pænnaa
mee lamayaa kæmati kæmati hæţiyaţa iskoolee yanna enna hadanavaa; ehema karanna denna hon̆da nææ
maŋ Kolam̆ba gihillaa ena koţa redi ţikak geenavaa
nitara bas yana paarakda mee?
eyaa ena koţa heţa veyi
vahina koţa redi ţika geţa ganna
taattaa Kolam̆ba yana koţa minihaa mærilaa
eyaa Kataragama inna koţa apiţa redi araŋ aavaa
siiyaa hindaa api vædiya hayiyen aave nææ
rassaavak karana nisaa ee lamayaaţa dæn ape dihaave enna vædiya velaa nææ
potvalin pirilaa hindaa ee meesee vædak karanna bææ
taattaa kantooru yanna hadana koţa kaar-eka hiţiyaa
ammaa kataa karana koţa kohaaţada ara lamayaa mallit araŋ divuve?
taattaa ena koţa maŋ naanavaa
maŋ giya avurudde hiţavapu gahe dæn geḑi

1. Kandyans also use **appacci** instead of **taattaa**.

20 minihaa kaar-eka haravana ata hari nææ
ee redi ṭika vahina koṭa maŋ geṭa gannam
koocciya addapu hæṭiyema maŋ næggaa
api ena koṭa parakku venavaa: oya gollo kææma kanna
maŋ yana koṭa koocciya ennam
25 api ena koṭa ibeema rææ vunaa
maŋ ee orloosuvaṭa rupiyal hættæpahak denna æhævvaa
orloosuve velaava tiyalaa maava heṭa udee hariyaṭa hayaṭa kuuddanna
edaa genicca pota maṭa tavama genat denna bæri vunaa
aparaadee maŋ ee potaṭa eccara salli dunne
30 maŋ udee daanna diipu liyuma tavama ate!
oya dæn æhena saddee næti karanna puluvanda?
mahattayaaṭa puluvanda mee pææna maṭa hari gassalaa denna?

B. Wait a bit until grannie comes.
I didn't drink (any) tea till younger-brother came.
As soon as the man arrived he asked father for a job.
(You) can't drink tea immediately after drinking toddy.
5 A rather tall man came.
Keep well, son, till I get back.
While it was raining we stayed at home.
When mother died I (was) still small.
Father reads a book as he travels in the train.
10 The boy cries when he's beaten.
When we got to Kandy it was raining.
The child is crying because there is no milk to drink.
When it rained we ran into the house.
The boy went (away) when (his) father called (him).
15 **That** is not the book I meant.
From next year I shan't be going to school.
How many books were in the parcel (you) brought yesterday?
Father doesn't like the job I do.
It was late when we got home that day.
20 What did you drink (your) tea out of, younger brother?
He must have come yesterday too when we weren't (here).
I shall have gone by the time he arrives.

Next week we are going to stay with granny at Kandy.
Finish the work (you're) doing quickly and come.
25 There is insufficient light here to read the book (by).
The wall that man built has tumbled down now.
The bullock eats grass.
Don't draw on the walls.
We must pay proper respect to our teachers.
30 Every cent that boy earns he gives to (his) mother.
Haven't (you) found the pen you lost yet?
Tyres are made of rubber.

Notes:

A. 1 hoňdaṭa, lesson 17 **b**.

2 æti vena kan or æti venna (lesson 19 **c**).

4 kataa karanavaa here = call to. So in A 17 below.

5 aapu hæṭiyema or ena koṭama. pænnaa: jumped off. koocciyaṭa paninavaa normally means 'to jump **in front of** the train'; to jump **on** is **pænagannavaa** (lesson 23).

6 'To go to school or not, just as he pleases.'

8 'A regular bus route'. mee or meeka.

11 Sc. hiṭiyaa (Lesson 22**b**).

12 Katara-gama, a village in the remote S.E. jungles of Ceylon, is a famous centre of pilgrimage for both Buddhist and Hindu. **inna koṭa** here means when he was living there.

13 'Because of grandfather', i.e. because we had grandfather with us.

14 velaa, see n. on 16 A 9.

16 See 18 A 7.

17 See note on 4 above. (For 'speak to' it is usually necessary to say 'speak with' (using **ekka**); cf. 17 A 13.)

18 naanavaa = 'I was bathing'. To make this sentence refer clearly to future time, it would be necessary at least to substitute **naanne** (i.e. to invert the sentence).

19 geḍi, sc. **tiyenavaa**.

20 haravanavaa, causative counterpart of **hærenavaa**.

22 addanavaa, in form a causative of **adinavaa**, means 'to pull out' (of a train); 'just as the train was leaving'.

23 ena koṭa or enna; venavaa or veyi. 'When we come, it will be late', i.e. we shall be late getting back. This can also be expressed by saying **api enne parakku velayi**, cf. 16 A 27. See also 20 A 33 note.

24 ennam (lesson 14 **c**) or enavaa: 'the train was coming'.

25 'It suddenly got dark' (lit., it just got dark).

26 denna æhævvaa = offered (asked if I could give). See 17 A 17 note. These words always have this meaning; 'asked (someone) to give' is **denna kivvaa**.

27 'Having put time on the clock', i.e. having set the alarm.

28 genat denna = to bring back.

29 **aparaadee** with an incomplete verb ('it is a pity that I did') may be translated 'unfortunately (I did)'.

30 daanna = to post. It is not made clear here who is referred to – 'your hand' or 'his hand'.

31 næti karanna = stop, get it stopped.

B. 5 Rather = a little.

6 Get back = 'go and come'. Son: putaa, duu, ayiyaa, malli, akkaa, naŋgi are all used as terms of address as well as of reference. Personal names are not generally used in these relationships; they are addressed in the third person (see lesson 1 **c** and 12 A 24 note). So here in 20 below. Keep well = hoñdin inna; hoñdaṭa inna = be good.

10 Compare this with A 18 above, which, though formally similar in Sinhalese, refers to a past occasion. To make **this** sentence refer to a specific past occasion, **æñḍuvaa** would be used.

11 Got – use **yanavaa**, not **enavaa**.

12 'To drink' – tr. literally.

15 'Meant': mentioned, said.

20 See B 6 above.

21 Must have come, will have come = ævit tiyenavaa. 'When': **næti velaave** is preferable to **næti koṭa** here.

22 I shall have gone: maŋ gihillaa tiyeyi.

23 'Granny-at-Kandy' is all one title. It should be put in the plural (with **-laa**); cf. 20 B 28. With: **dihaave** (or **ekka**).

24 Quickly = soon.

26 Tumbled down: see note on 19 A 3.

28 On the walls – loc. case, not dative.

31 'The pen you lost': say 'your lost pen'. **næti karapu** or **næti vecca**; the former carries implications of criticism, deliberately lost.

32 Here, as a general statement is being made, a plain verb is enough; with **tiyenavaa**, it would refer to a particular case, e.g. these tyres . . .

LESSON 22

ælenavaa	stick (intr.)
iranavaa	tear
ituru karanavaa	save (keep a remainder)
as venavaa	resign, leave
avadi venavaa[1]	wake up (intr.)
kiʈʈu / **laŋ**] **karanavaa**	place near
laňga / **gaava** / **kiʈʈu**]	near
issara	formerly (some time ago)
tisse	throughout
boruva	lie (n.)
boruvaʈa	falsely
pol (pl.)	coconuts
maasee	month
baaldiya	bucket, bin
isʈeesama	station
viiduruva	glass
kooppee	cup
koopi (pl.)	coffee
kussiya	kitchen
nææyaa	relative (n.)
ænee	nail, screw
dostara	doctor
nivaaɖuva	holiday

1. This word is somewhat formal. The use of **æhærenavaa** (lit. 'the eye opens') is more colloquial.

beheta medicine
leḍee illness
leḍaa (pl. **leḍḍu**) sick man

(a) The names of the months (to which **maasee** is usually added) are janavaari, pebaravaari, maartu, apreel or apriyel, mæyi, juuni, juuli, agoostu, sæptæmbara, oktoombara, novæmbara, desæmbara. There are also old Sinhalese names for the twelve lunar months, which nowadays are only used in astrology or in religious contexts. These begin the year in April. The best known are Vesak (May), Poson (June), Æsala (July-Aug), Durutu (January).

(b) The use of **tiyenavaa** as an auxiliary verb has been explained above. **innavaa** (in the sense 'continue to be, remain, wait') is also found after an absolutive, of animates; in such cases, stress is laid on the physical persistence of a person after completion of an action.

eyaa mærilaa innavaa
he is lying (there) dead
mahattayek ævillaa innavaa
a gentleman has come (and is waiting)

After the double absolutive, **innavaa** gives the effect of a continuous present, 'is doing' etc.; but this form is not so frequently used in Sinhalese as the corresponding form in English.

eyaa siini kakaa innavaa
he is eating sugar
lamayaa tee-ekaṭa siini dadaa hiṭiyaa
the boy was putting sugar into the tea

(c) The auxiliary **tiyunaa** after an absolutive is used in reporting past actions which the speaker did not see, even where no time sequence is involved. **tiyunaa** should not be omitted here. (This is significantly different from the Eng. use of 'had').

giyaa maasee maŋ Gaallee inna koṭa eyaa maava hamba venna Kolam̆ba ævit tiyunaa
when I was at Galle last month he came to see me in Colombo (I hear)
lin̆de væṭilaa tiyicca baaldiya mee
this is the bucket which (I believe) fell in(to) the well

(For the order, cf. lesson 10 c).

The auxiliary **hiṭiyaa** after an absolutive is used of situations which persisted in the past, even if no time sequence is involved.

eyaa bæn̆dalaa hiṭiya ekkenek

he (is one who) has been married (but no longer is)

maŋ rææ tissema avadi velaa hiṭiyaa

I have been up all night

In sentences like this last, the present tense (**innavaa**) cannot be used; if used, it would have a future significance, 'I will keep awake all night'.

hiṭiyaa is often to be translated 'stayed'.

iiye maŋ gedaraṭa velaa hiṭiyaa

I stayed at home yesterday

iiye maŋ gedara gihin hiṭiyaa

yesterday I went home and stayed there

In some cases, especially in commands (or virtual commands), **inna** after an absolutive ('do something and wait') may be translated 'First, do...'

mee liyum ṭika æralaa inna oonæ, tava væḍak karanna ganna[1]

(you) must first post these letters, before beginning ('so as to begin') anything else

(d) **lan̆ga** and **kiṭṭu** – which may refer to time as well as place – stand post-positionally after either the dative or the direct case-form of an inanimate noun: **gaava** – which refers to place only – usually stands after a direct case only. These words may themselves (like **uḍa**, **yaṭa** etc., lesson 8) take case-endings; here **kiṭṭu**, which is a stem-form, forms cases as from **kiṭṭuva** (cf. 17 A 1–2, note).

gaha kiṭṭuvaṭa yanna

go near the tree

(not **gahaṭa** – double **-ṭa** is avoided in such contexts)

gaha / gahaṭa } kiṭṭuven inna

stay by the tree

minihaa kaḍee gaavayin[2] giyaa

he went past the shop.

lan̆ga and **kiṭṭu** (but not **gaava**) can be used predicatively with **-yi**, after a dative case. If **tiyenne** is added, the direct case-form is used.,

minihaage gedara kaḍeeṭa kiṭṭuyi / lan̆gayi]

---

1. ganna = begin.
2. Or **gaavin**.

his house is near the shop

but

minihaage gedara kaḍee [kiṭṭuvayi / lan̆ga(yi) / gaavayi] tiyenne

Notice the phrases **ii lan̆ga(ṭa), mii lan̆ga(ṭa)**, next after this/that, next; so also **ii gaavaṭa, mee gaavaṭa**. But **ee kiṭṭuva** means 'near that,' and **mee lan̆ga** 'nearby.'

When **lan̆ga, kiṭṭu, gaava** follow an animate noun, this noun is either in the direct case-form or in the genitive.

maŋ / mage] lan̆gaṭa enna — come near me, come to me

lan̆ga is also found after an infinitive.

rææ venna(t) lan̆gayi / rææ venna(t) enavaa] — it's beginning to get dark

(e) **leḍee: leḍak, leḍin** are used rather than leḍayak, leḍen, and **leḍaṭa** alternates with **leḍeeṭa. leḍa** (stem-form) is used as an attributive adjective: leḍa minihaa, the sick man (=leḍaa); 'he is ill' is **eyaaṭa leḍa**, or **eyaa leḍin** (innavaa – but no finite verbal form is necessary). 'He fell ill' is eyaa leḍa vunaa or eyaaṭa leḍa vunaa.

(f) tisse (usually followed by **-ma)** is used after expressions of time; sumaanayak tisse, for a whole week. **hæmatissema** means 'every time' or 'all the time'.

A. paare minihek væṭilaa innavaa
labana mæyi maasee maŋ Gaalu gihin innavaa
siiyaa dæn vayasaṭa gihin nitarama leḍa velaa innavaa
maŋ tee biilayi inne
maŋ ena koṭa mahattayaa tee biilaa innavaada?
taattaa tee biilaada inne?
ara kaamareeṭa daalaa vahalaa inna lamayaa kavda?
iskoolee hiṭavapu lamayaa mee davasvala gedara ævit
paare minihek biilaa væṭilaa hiṭiyaa
maŋ kantooru yana koṭa eyaa ævit hiṭiyaa
ee minihaa væssaṭa gahak yaṭaṭa velaa hiṭiyaalu
eyaa tee kooppayak biilayi hiṭiye
maŋ yana koṭa eyaa kææma kaalaa hiṭiyaa
mahattayaa ee kaamareeṭa velaa hayiyenma væḍak karakara innavaa
taattaa dæn maasa dekakin væḍaṭa giye nææ

pebaravaari maaseeṭa davas kiiyak tiyenavaada?
maartu maasee daha-aṭaveni daa iňdaŋ apreel maasee visinamaveni daa vena kan apiṭa nivaaḍu
mage vayasa dæn avurudu tis-ekakut maasa dekayi
taattaa leḍa velaa dæn maaseekaṭat væḍi
ada udee lamayaa boruvaṭa leḍa araŋ iskoolee yanne nætuva inna hæduvaa
mahattayaa gaava rupiyal pahak ganna tiyenavaada?
meesee bicciyaṭa laŋ karalaa tiyanna
ee mahattayaa ape laňga laňgin nææyek
dæn haṭaraṭa kiṭṭuyi
putaa ammaa laňgaṭa velaa innavaa
puṭu ṭika tava ṭikak laňgin laňgin tiyanna
mahattayaalaage dihaavaṭa laňgama bas-ekenda koocciyenda?
iricca næti eevaa ṭika maṭa denna
maŋ heṭat ekka nivaaḍu
mokakada mee ænee?
maaseekaṭa itin kiiyen kiiyakda ituru venne?
ee davas ṭikaṭa maŋ gedara gihin innavaa
avadi vena koṭa aṭat velaa
kavda ii laňgaṭa?
Posonvalaṭa davas kiiyak nivaaḍuda?
salli dena koṭa ganan nokara denna epaa

B. Mother has gone into the kitchen and is pouring out tea.
Father has got into the chair and is looking at the paper.
Yesterday I saw a dog lying dead in that road, run over by a car.
When I was ill, it was that gentleman who gave me medicine.
The little boy is putting tea from a cup into a glass.
The vegetable-woman has come with the vegetables.
Where is the boy who was crying here (just) now?
When I got home, father had arrived.
When I got home, the dog was tied to the chair.
Before, he was always coming our way.
A white dog has fallen into the well.

Father has got into (his) chair and is drinking coffee (and) reading the paper.

How many weeks are there in a year?

In which month is there most rain in your parts?

15 How many Sundays are there from 1st July to 30 November?

What is the best month to go to Kataragama?

There are two coconut trees near our house.

I haven't much money on me now.

Our house is near the station.

20 What is the nearest way from here to Galle?

Put the chair up to the table.

Don't let the cat come near the table when food is being eaten.

That boy doesn't want to come near me.

A gentleman has come to see the car.

25 We have left there now.

The leaves of this book are stuck to one another.

When the doctor came, the patient was dead.

How many months ago did I tell him that!

This boy tears up every single letter I write.

30 When is Vesak?

In what month is Vesak?

What is in the next bin?

When I got (there), the shop was shut.

Father hasn't come yet?

35 Give me a two-inch nail.

The paper for the second of last month is not here.

Notes:

A. 3 vayasaṭa gihin, see 19 A 26.

4 'I have had my tea already'. In the 1st person, inversion is normal here.

5 This is a polite request, 'Will you (please) have finished when I come' (as v. tee biilaada inne? Have you had tea?).

7 daalaa vahalaa = shut in, locked in.

8 iskoolee hiṭavapu lamayaa = the boy who was at boarding school.

10 i.e he was waiting for me at the office. On the other hand, maŋ

kantooru yana koṭa eyaa aavaa might mean 'He arrived at my house just as I was leaving it'. If we substitute **tiyunaa** for hiṭiyaa, the sentence will mean 'by the time I got to the office, he had arrived elsewhere.'

11 væssaṭa = against the rain, because of the rain. The dative case is not infrequently used in this way (cf. 13 A 8 n.). velaa = having got, gone (so in A 14, 25 etc.); compare the corresponding use of **karalaa** in 8 A 13.

13 'He had (already) finished eating and was waiting'; cf. eyaa kææma kaalaa tiyunaa, (just) 'he had finished eating'.

14 ee kaamareeṭa velaa – see note on 11 above; **ee kaamaree** alone would be sufficient.

15 'Hasn't been to work **for** two months'. The same meaning is given by 'maasa dekak tisse væḍaṭa giye (or **yanne**) nææ'.

16 maaseeṭa or maasee (loc.). But in 31 below, maaseeka would be avoided.

17 The name of the month must **precede** the number of the day.

18 ekakut or ekayi; dekayi or dekak venavaa. See lesson 13 **c**.

19 taattaa or taattaaṭa.

20 leḍa araŋ = leḍa velaa, having got ill. (Often translated into English as 'having taken ill').

21 ganna, see note on 20 A 7. gaava or laňga; kiṭṭu(va) is not used in the sense of 'on you'. A simple dative (mahattayaaṭa) is insufficient here.

22 Or bicciyaṭa kiṭṭu karalaa, bicciya kiṭṭuvaṭa karalaa, bicciya laňgaṭa karalaa, bicciya gaavaṭa karalaa. (For **karalaa**, see 8 A 13).

23 laňga is used adjectivally here, 'a near relative'. **gaava** is not used in this sense.

24 **gaava** cannot be used in this context. **hataraṭa hiṭii** has the same meaning. (See footnote under lesson 5 **c**).

25 laňgaṭa velaa innavaa or laňgin innavaa (for the case-form, see lesson 10 **a**); also ammaa gaava innavaa. A simple dative of the person (ammaaṭa) is insufficient in phrases such as 'come to mother'.

26 laňgin laňgin (**pron**. laňgillaňgin) = near(er) each other.

27 laňgama, the nearest (way): 'is it quickest?' Or **kiṭṭuma**, – but not **gaavama**.

28 ṭika: lesson 14 **e**.

29 Cf. 5 A 19. **maṭa** is also possible. In the direct case, the plural form

nivaaḍu is more often used than the singular.

30 mokakada (often pronounced [mohokədə]) 'of what', i.e. where from, what does it come from?

31 The repetition of **kiiya** here shows that the question is rhetorical, i.e. that nothing is in fact saved (cf. 12 A 22).

32 innavaa refers to the future here.

33 aṭat velaa, 'it was already after 8.0'. (In Ceylon, most people get up about 6.0, when it gets light).

34 **ii** and **mii** are interchangeable here.

35 Posonvalaṭa (or Poson-ekaṭa), 'for Poson'. Poson is here thought of as a Buddhist religious festival rather than as a month. So **Vesak** in B 31 below. kiiyak or kiiyaka.

36 This kind of circumlocution shows that the statement is general. Salli ganan nokara denna epaa means rather 'Don't give away **the** money without counting it.'

B. 1, 2 'has gone', 'has got', cf. A 11 above and note.

3 See lesson 13 **b**.

4 behet dunne or behet kale. behet karanavaa = give treatment.

5 'Putting' – use **daanavaa**. This word, unlike **tiyanavaa**, can be used with a dative case, as well as with a locative (cf. 15 A 29 note).

6 Vegetable-woman = elavalu ammaa.

9 puṭuvaṭa or puṭuve.

11 liňde or liňdaṭa.

13 Say 'to a year' (cf. A 31 above).

14 Most: huňgakma or væḍiya.

15 Say 'until it is (use **venavaa**) Nov. 30'. See A 17 above. Sundays: lesson 19 **d**.

16 To go: infinitive. What: kookada or mokakda. See 21 A 12 note.

18 Much: see lesson 16 **c**. On me: say 'near me' (**gaava** or **laňga** – but not **kiṭṭuva** in this sense).

20 **What**: either **mokakda** or **kohenda**. Nearest: cf. A 27 above.

25 There: **ehen**. This has the meaning of leaving a place. **illaa as venavaa** (to ask permission and leave) means 'to resign a job.'

26 To one another – ekaṭa eka or ekakaṭa ekak (usually in this order).

ælenavaa has no volitive counterpart in use: 'to stick' (tr.) is the causative form **alavanavaa**.

27 The word dostara is normally followed by **mahattayaa** – unless a criticism is implied, which may be the case here.

31 The Buddha is believed to have been born, to have become Enlightened (become a Buddha), and to have died on the full moon day of Vesak, which is therefore thrice sacred.

32 See note on A 23 above. This sentence might be said e.g. in a shop ('boutique').

35 See lesson 9 **f**.

36 For: say 'of', but **daa** does not change; see lesson 19 **d**.

LESSON 23

varadinavaa / **væradenavaa**	be wrong, be missed
varaddanavaa	mislead, make wrong
happanavaa (tr.) / **hæppenavaa** (intr.)	hit, collide
ævidinavaa	walk about
kalpanaa* karanavaa	reflect
tiiranaya karanavaa	decide
sellam karanavaa	play
viisi / **visi(k)** **karanavaa**	throw away
kooʈ-eka	coat (jacket)
ʂarʈ-eka (pr. [ʃə(r)ʈ])[1]	shirt
paaɖama	lesson
væʈa	fence
hænda (pl. **hæňdi**)	spoon
laaba	cheap
laabeeʈa	cheaply
taraha	anger, angry
rasa, raha	taste, tasty
baɖaginna (stem-form **baɖagini**)	hunger
amaaru	difficult
amaaruva	difficulty
oonækamin	deliberately
gæna (postposition)	concerning

---

*Stem-form of kalpanaava, idea.

1. Eng. **sh** is normally represented by ෂ (ʂ) in Sinhalese script, but often pronounced **s** or **ʃ**.

(a) **gannavaa** is very commonly added after the short form of an absolutive, forming a compound verb. It usually adds to the (absolutive) verb a sense approximately equal to 'for oneself' or 'mutually'; with certain verbs it adds a sense of 'with difficulty'. It can be added to causative verbs.

gahanavaa	strike
gahaagannavaa	strike each other, fight
hitanavaa	think
hitaagannavaa	think to oneself
dannavaa	know
dænagannavaa	find out
iňdagannavaa	sit down

Before -gannavaa, the **-aa** of the absolutive is usually shortened in pronunciation, except with monosyllabic verbal roots, or with dissyllabic roots where the first syllable is short, e.g.

allaagannavaa, pron. [allagannəva], catch; arrest
kiyavaagannavaa, pron. [kiyəvagannəva]

but

kaagannavaa, pron. [kaagannəva]
hitaagannavaa, pron. [hitaagannəva].

When **yanavaa** and **enavaa** are followed by **gannavaa** in this way, the forms **yaagannavaa** and **eegannavaa** are used, and the sense given is that of going or coming with difficulty. The same sense is given with the compound verbs **yavaagannavaa**, **evaagannavaa**, **biigannavaa** (sometimes),[1] **duvaagannavaa**,[2] **pænagannavaa**, **nægagannavaa**, **ævidagannavaa**, **dækagannavaa**, manage to send, drink, run, jump, climb, walk, see. (Compare koocciyaʈa paninna, to jump in front of the train (21 A 5), and koocciyaʈa pænaganna, to manage to jump **into** the train). With **venavaa**, the form used is **veegannavaa**.

Furthermore **gannavaa** itself is in such cases frequently compounded with **enavaa**, **yanavaa**, **innavaa**, **tiyenavaa**. Here **gena**, the absolutive of **gannavaa**, is usually reduced to **-gana** ([gənə]) or to -ŋ.[3] enavaa, yanavaa in such cases refer not

---

1. Also **kaagannavaa** when doubled; kaagena kaagena. Otherwise, kaagannavaa means 'to bite each other' (of dogs).

2. Usually written **duvagannavaa**, and so pronounced.

3. Except with monosyllabic roots. -ŋ also involves shortening the vowel -aa in the absolutive: balaagana → balaŋ.

to actual movement but to a **continuity of action**; in the case of enavaa, this is primarily thought of as affecting the speaker, in the case of yanavaa it is primarily thought of as not affecting the speaker. The sense 'with difficulty' may not apply here in the case of the verbs quoted above.

mee paara dæn hoňdaţama kælææ veegana enavaa
this road is getting overgrown (I find)
ee paara dæn hoňdaţama kælææ veegana yanavaa
that road is getting overgrown (you will find)

Where **innavaa** is used as an auxiliary in the present tense, there is a tendency for the preceding absolutive to be followed by **-ŋ**, or for the sentence to be inverted, i.e. for the absolutive to be followed by **-yi** and innavaa to appear as **inne**.

Compare the following and note the various shades of meaning:

api ee gæna kataa karakara innavaa
we are discussing that
api ee gæna kataa karagana yanavaa
we are contining to talk about that
api ee gæna kataa karagana enavaa
either
we will continue to talk about that (same as karagana yanavaa)
or
we will discuss that 'and come', i.e. we will go and discuss that (with him)
api ee gæna kataa karalaa tiyenavaa
we have spoken about that
api ee gæna kataa karaŋ innavaa/tiyenavaa
we are agreed about that
api ee gæna kataa karalayi inne/tiyenne
we have already finished talking about that

balaŋ innavaa may often be translated 'wait'.

(b) **daanavaa** (damanavaa), 'to place with some violence or finality' (lesson 20), when used after an absolutive gives a sense of getting an action done with.

araŋ daanna! [take away! / buy up!]

And compare –

maŋ ee vædee karagannam
I'll manage that myself
maŋ ee vædee karagana yannam
I'll carry on with that job
maŋ ee vædee karalaa daannam
I'll get that job done with.

daagannavaa also means 'to put on (clothes)'.

(c) paadam karanavaa means 'to study'; paadam gannavaa is (of the teacher) 'to hear the lesson (the homework) recited' – also paadam ahanavaa.

varaddanavaa is the causative of **varadinavaa**, which however is not used in the past tense or absolutive, where it is replaced by forms from the involitive **væradenavaa**.

(d) We have seen (lesson 17 **b**) that **lassana** can be used either as an adjective (meeka hari lassanayi) or as a noun (meeke lassana maṭa allanne nææ). **rasa** is a similar word; mee kææma hari rasayi, this food is very tasty: mee batvala rasa harima hoňdayi, the taste of this rice is very good.

taraha is also used both as a predicative adjective and as a noun. Thus maŋ ookaṭa tarahayi, 'I am angry about that'. No verb is required here; **tiyenavaa** is not possible, and **venavaa** gives a future meaning: maŋ taraha venavaa, I shall be annoyed (with him). But taraha can also be used as a noun: maṭa tarahak[1] tiyenavaa eyat ekka, I bear him a grudge; eyaa tarahen inne, he is in a bad mood.

badagini[2] is normally used without a verb in the same way, but with a dative case of the person: maṭa badagini, I am hungry. The case-form **badaginna** is found with the **-k** suffix: maṭa loku badaginnak (tiyenavaa), 'I have a great hunger.[3] badaginnen innavaa means 'to have an empty stomach' (**innavaa** can be omitted, cf. the usage with **leda**, lesson 22 **e**). maṭa badagini vunaa is 'I got hungry'.

Neither taraha nor badagini are normally used as **qualifying** adjectives, i.e. standing before a noun. We should not say badagini lamayek, taraha minihek, but rather tarahen inna minihek, or taraha giya minkhek (see n. on A 17 below).

---

1. In formal contexts, sometimes **tarahavak**.

2. Sometimes heard as **badigini**. It means literally 'belly-fire'.

3. **santoosee** in its stem-form is used similarly: maŋ santoosayi, I am glad, but maṭa loku santoosayak.

Compare the use of **vayasa** in lesson 16.

parakku (see lesson 21) can also be used predicatively: koocciya parakkuyi, the train is late, api parakkuyi, we are late. When used with **venavaa**, notice the difference between maţa parakku veyi, I may get delayed, and maŋ parakku veyi, I may (just) dally. (cf. above 20 A 33, 21 A 23, 17 A 12 nn). The case-form is **parakkuva**: eyaage parakkuva hindaa, because of his dallying.

amaaruve væţenavaa, fall in(to) difficulties, usually means 'get into debt'.

laaba is the stem-form of laabee, gain.

(e) To negate an infinitive, 1) **næti venna** may be used after the incomplete present tense-form;[1] 2) the infinitive may be preceded by **no-**. These forms are not used in negative commands (prohibitions), but often in expressing consequences, e.g.

mallita { peenne næti venna / nopeenna } almaariya uḍin araŋ tiyanna

put (it) on top of the cupboard so that younger-brother shan't see it.

A.
lamayaa koocciya dihaa balaŋ innavaa
lamayaa tava tee illa-illaa kooppee ate tiyaŋ innavaa
ammaa ena kan putaa dora gaavaţa velaa balaŋ innavaa
iskoolee yanna taattaa kaar-eka araŋ ena kan lamayaa æn̆dalaa hiţiyaa
behet geena koţa taattaa mæreyi
şarţ-ekaţa yaţin monavaada æn̆daŋ inne?
am̆ba kapanna gihin lamayaa ata kapaagana
ee minihaa lamayaa ekkaŋ enna iskooleeţa giyaa
kææma kanna at deka hoodaŋ enna
lamayaa taattaaţa kiyalaa pota kiyavaagattaa
ammaaţa maŋ tee-ekak hadaŋ aavaa
lamayaa vatura viiduruva biigena biigena giyaa
lamayaa guruvarayaaţa denna taattaaţa kiyalaa liyumak liyavaagana giyaa
vahina koţa vatura bimaţa biigannavaa

---

[1] Or sometimes after the actual infinitive.

15 eyaa mahattayaaṭa liyumak liyalaa tiyalaa giyaa
ee gollo apit ekka taraha velaa
taattaaṭa taraha yanavaa leesiyen
mee viiduruven vatura yanavaa
edaa paara væradilaa apiṭa gedara yanna tavat parakku vunaa
20 ara mahattayaaṭa allalaa inna
lamayaa puṭuva uḍaṭa nagina kan ammaa ata diigena hiṭiyaa
kantooruvala væḍa karana minissu Kolaňba hariyaṭa innavaa
lamayaa ata kapaŋ innavaa
onna ooka allalaa daanna
25 lamayaa alut orloosuvak ate bæňdaŋ innavaa
lamayaa ata kapaagana otaŋ innavaa
maŋ laňgaṭa kavda?
væhægana ennam!
mee pot ṭika ṭikakaṭa allaaganna, dora arinna
30 meevaa monavaayeda daanne?
ee minihaa oonækamin apiṭa paara værædduvaa
mee kaamareeṭa paara peenavaada?
ee væḍee amaaruva danne mama
maŋ heṭa enna hitaagana innavaa
35 eyaa ee gæna ṭikak kalpanaa karalaa amaaruven gedara giyaa

B. Who is that tall chap wearing a red-coloured cloth?
That is the boy who hit me in school yesterday.
Father is now dressed to go to the office.
The boy played while (his) father was eating.
5 When he goes out he puts on a coat.
The younger brother is waiting till the elder brother has climbed to the top of the wall.
The younger sister is waiting under the tree for (her) elder brother to pick her (some) mangoes.
The bull is waiting for the dog to drink (his) water.
The boy got (his) father to look over all the sums.
10 Go by the near(er) route so as not to be late.
I got our teacher to read (out) that book.

That poor old woman frequently comes to our house in an old cloth and jacket.

Those two men swore dreadfully at each other near the shop.

These goods are going very cheap.

15 Why didn't you come our way that day?

When I got here (my) son had (already) bathed.

I have a **son** for a child.

Mother came to see me when I was ill.

The dog came and drank the cat's milk.

20 The boy had poured himself a cup of tea and was drinking (it) in the kitchen.

The small son waited near the door for (his) father to return.

The cat has managed to climb (on) to the table.

The patient has managed to get out of bed.

Previously he had opened a shop near our house.

25 Whom did (you) ask for that pen?

It's coming on to rain now, let's walk a bit faster.

What have you decided about that?

That boy threw away the spoon [that was] in (his) hand.

There is no book on this table which I haven't read.

30 Younger brother always does his studies at night.

Yesterday younger brother didn't go to school.

Which one is the parcel of books?

Hungry boys like tasty foods.

His car crashed into our fence.

35 That's very difficult to do.

Notes:

A. 2 tiyaŋ (for tiyaagana) = 'holding'.

3 velaa, cf. note on karanna, lesson 8 A 13. dora gaava/laňga balaŋ innavaa is also enough.

4 æňdalaa or æňdaŋ, 'was dressed and waiting'.

5 'By the time (you) get the medicine, father will be dead' (mæreyi or mærilaa tiyeyi).

6 -ekaṭa yaṭin or -eka yaṭaṭa. **kamisee** is also used for 'shirt'.

7 gihin = having set out to, meant to.

8 'To come with the child', i.e. to fetch the child. **ekkaŋ** (for ekka-gena) or **ekkaraŋ** (or just ekka-enavaa).

9 'Wash your (two) hands before you come for dinner.' Notice how this is put in Sinhalese. at deka (pron. [addekə]) cannot be omitted here; **hoodaŋ** alone is not used for 'having washed (oneself)'. **hoodalaa** is not idiomatic here.

10 The syllable **-vaa** is shortened in speech. Pr. [kiyəvagattaa].

11 hadaŋ aavaa, 'made and came', i.e. brought. But **hadalaa aavaa** would mean 'made her a cup of tea before I came.'

12 vatura viiduruva, 'glass of water' (see lesson 5 **e**). **giyaa** here does not refer to actual motion; **biilaa giyaa**, on the other hand, means 'drank and went away'. The repetition of **biigena** (or the lengthening of the **bii-**) adds a sense of continuous haste, 'quickly drank up', 'gulped down.'

13 **denna** is needed to make the sentence clear; cf. ganna in 22 A 21.

14 bimaṭa biigannavaa, 'is absorbed by the earth'. For the dative case, cf. note on 13 A 8. The verb here has virtually a passive meaning.

15 'He left a letter for you.'

17 **taraha yanavaa** and **taraha enavaa** are both used in the sense of 'getting angry' (with a dative case, as here).

18 Cf. 16 A 26.

19 'We were home even later', lit. 'it was even later (for) us to get home'. paara væradilaa, (we) missed the way; for the detached absolutive, cf. 16 A 9 note. **api** is also possible here for apiṭa, see 17 A 12 note.

20 'Serve this gentleman first'; **allanavaa** sometimes means 'to serve food' (cf. 20 A 4 note).

21 'Stood giving (having given) him her hand.' Not **diilaa** here.

22 hariyaṭa = very much, in considerable numbers.

23 Or just **ata kapaŋ** (sc. tiyenavaa), which lays more stress on the cutting ('his hand has been cut') and less on the boy; so in A 7 above.

24 This means 'Give it up', 'never mind about that'.

25 ata = wrist. **aňdinavaa** is not used here.

27 'Who's (to come) after me?' Sometimes **mage laňgaṭa**.

28 'It's coming on to rain!' **væhægana yanavaa** on the other hand means 'it keeps on raining.'

29 dora arinna = so that **I** can open the door, cf 15 A 30 note. **maŋ dora arinna** is also possible, cf. 17 A 12 note. Cf. pot ṭika maṭa denna, dora arinna, 'give me the books, so that **you** can open the door'.

30 May refer to e.g. putting milk into bottles. Notice that articles of food etc. which are plural in Sinhalese are referred to by plural pronouns. monavaaye, see n. on 12 A 22.

31 apiṭa paara værædduvaa = made us miss the way (lit. made the way wrong to us).

32 'Can (you) see the road from this room?' (lit. Does the road appear (in) to this room?)

34 hitaagana innavaa = am thinking of, hoping to.

35 amaaruven here = hite amaaruven, sadly (**hita** = heart). The adverbial form here uses the instrumental ending, not the dative.

B. 3 To go: infinitive.

5 Say 'he goes having put a coat on' (15 A 10 note). **daagena** or **æñdaŋ**. out, **eliyaṭa**.

7 Pick her = 'pick and give'.

9 It is best to say 'all the few sums' (lesson 14 **e**), since **ganan** is an ambiguous word.

12 'Poor old' – either order is possible in Sinhalese. 'In': say 'wearing'.

13 Dreadfully: say 'very well'. **narakaṭa** (evilly) means 'in a **bad** fashion', rather than just 'thoroughly'. Near the shop: **lañga** alone is insufficient here. Add either **-di** or an absolutive ('having got (22 A 11) near the shop'); so in 20 and 21 below.

14 Going: translate literally. Say 'these few goods' (otherwise the meaning is general, see lesson 14 **e**).

17 For a child: translate literally.

18 You can say 'To see me being ill' (lesson 13 **b**).

19 Say 'drank the little milk (lesson 14 **e**) and went away' (lesson 15 A 10 note).

20 'In the kitchen': **kussiye** alone is insufficient here (cf. 13 above). Some other word is required before bibii hiṭiyaa. Say 'having got into the kitchen'.

21 Say 'having got (to) near the door'.

23 Get out: say 'descend'. Owing to the virtual absence of bedclothes, there is no difference in Ceylon between 'in the bed' and 'on the bed', 'out of bed' and 'off the bed'.

24 Open a shop for the first time = **daagannavaa**.

26 A little faster: tava ţikak hayiyen or miiţa vaḍaa ţikak hayiyen; see lesson 8 **b**.

27 What: tr. literally.

28 The spoon in his hand: here a participial word is esssential in Sinhalese (20 A 12 n).

30 At night: **rææţa** – not just **ræ** (n. on 14 A 24). Compare **udee ræyin,** which means 'before daybreak'.

33 Foods: A distinction is sometimes made in writing between **kææmvalaţa**, for meals, and **kææmavalaţa**, for food(s).

34 Into – use loc. case-form here, not dative.

35 'To do' – infinitive.

LESSON 24

nægiṭinavaa	get up
puravanavaa	fill
mahanavaa	sew; make, mend (clothes)
navanavaa[1]	fold
elavanavaa	drive away; drive (car)
uturanavaa	bubble, boil (intr.)
pupuranavaa	burst
peranavaa	strain (liquid)
gaanavaa	rub
ussanavaa	lift
pihidaanavaa	wipe; sweep (floor)
tuvaala venavaa	be wounded, be hurt
tuvaalee	wound (n.)
ætta	truth
ættaṭa / **ætten**] **ma**	truly
hæbææ	true
peṭṭiya	box (also compartment in a train)
una	fever
kaṭa	mouth
harakaa (pl. **harak**)	cow, bull
kollaa	lad
kella	lass
babaa	baby
piyaa	father
hita	mind (n.)
hulañga	wind
karadaree	trouble

1. In books, usually **namanavaa**.

ṭikaṭ-eka	ticket
midula	'compound', yard
vatta (pl. **vatu**)	garden, plantation
kæælla (pl. **kææli**)	piece
æn̆gilla (pl. **æn̆gili**)	finger, toe

(a) **piyaa** is a formal word for father (a term of reference, not of address). **vatta** is not usually a flower-garden (these are rare in Ceylon) but rather an orchard or kitchen-garden. The 'compound' is the area surrounding a house. It is normally covered with sand, the soil being sandy in most parts of Ceylon. **harak** is a stem-form (see below); the plural case-forms **harakun-ṭa**, **-ge**, **-gen** are used, but **harak** in the direct case (compare the use of the stem-form **ali**, elephants, lesson 11).

(b) pihidaanavaa – more correctly **pihadaanavaa** – is a compound verb, made up of **pihinavaa**, wipe, and **daanavaa**. It is now always used as a compound verb, which distinguishes it from **pihanavaa**, 'cook'. **puravanavaa** is a causative verb. **pirenavaa** (lesson 21) is involitive; the basic form **puranavaa** is used only in restricted contexts.

(c) **eka** is often used after a participle, where it may be equivalent to 'the fact of', the whole participial phrase thus becoming treated as a noun: maŋ yana eka (usually pronounced [yaneekə]), my going.

(d) **Stems**. The stem or adjectival form of a noun can usually be arrived at by removing a final **-aa**, **-vaa**, **-yaa** or **-a**, **-va**, **-ya**. In the case of inanimate nouns, therefore, the stem is usually the same as the plural; see lessons 9 **a** and 17 **b**.

gonaa – gon	haṛakaa – harak	balalaa – balal
minihaa – minis	kaarayaa – kaara	puṭuva – puṭu

Since however Sinhalese words cannot end in **-ṭ**, **-ḍ**, **-ṇ**, **-ḷ**, or **-r**, these consonants are followed by **-a** in the stem-form where the preceding vowel is **a** or **o**, and by **-u** where the preceding vowel is **u**. Where the preceding vowel is **i**, **e** or **æ**, usage varies. Since there is now no way of distinguishing between **n**, **l** and **ṇ**, **ḷ**, except in the script (see Introduction), such words must therefore be learnt as they occur.

leḍaa – leḍa	dora – dora	utura – uturu
gææni – gæænu	maḍa – maḍa	dakuna – dakunu
væṭa – væṭa		

Where the last consonant in a word is double, the stem-form has a single consonant, followed by **-u** (if the preceding vowel is **a**, **u** or **o**), or **-i** (if the preceding vowel is **æ**, **i** or **e**).

ballaa – balu   redda – redi
Gaalla – Gaalu   paapilla – paapili
kollaa – kolu   væssa – væhi
avurudda – avurudu   kæælla – kææli
vatta – vatu   ætta – æti

Where the removal of a final -aa/-a would leave a final half-nasal (which would
be unpronounceable), n̆ga becomes ŋ, n̆da becomes n and m̆ba becomes m; n̆ḍa
remains unaltered. Nouns ending in -nda, on the other hand, have stems in -n̆di
or -n̆du (according to the previous vowel), and nouns ending in -nḍa and -mba
are treated similarly.

hulan̆ga – hulaŋ   vilum̆ba – vilum (heel)
lin̆da – lin   an̆ḍa – an̆ḍa (cry)
kanda – kan̆du   danḍa – dan̆ḍu (stick)[1]
hænda – hæn̆di   gembaa – gem̆bi (frog)

(e) 'He has fever' is **eyaaṭa una**, but the parallel phrase to **leḍin inna koṭa** is **una
tiyena koṭa**.

A.   ee guruvarayaa nitarama lamayinṭa særa karalaa kataa karanavaa
         leḍaa dæn hun̆gak amaaruven kataa karanne
         ape ammaaṭa rasaṭa kææma hadanna puluvan
         kooppee bimin tiyanna epaa
5   bootal arina eka koo?
         kææma lææsti, okkoṭama dæn kææma kana kaamareeṭa enna kiyanna
         meevaa vatura bona viiduru
         mahattayaa bonne siini koopida kiri koopida?
         behet vatura biilaa ee minihaa mærilaa
10   minihaage piyaa mæricca eka hæbæyi
         enna sudaa maŋ lan̆gaṭa
         etakoṭama vahinna gattaa
         iskooleedi lamayaa gahaagena tuvaala velaa tiyenavaa
         nikam boru nætuva inna
15   viiduruvalaṭa vatura puravanna
         isteesamaṭa peṭṭi ussaŋ yanna kollaava evanna
         api dahadenaaṭa hari yanna paan geḍiya kææli dahayakaṭa kapanna

---

1. Literary.

uturana vatura viiduruvaṭa daanna epaa, pupurayi
kaḍakaarayaa illana illana gaanaṭa baḍu denne nææ
20 api ena koṭa eyaa nægiṭalaa
naŋgi kiri-eka hæňdi gaanavaa
una tiyena koṭa hulaŋ gæhenna narakayi
maŋ velaavaṭa aave næti koṭa mokakda hitaagatte?
huňgak baḍaginnen hiṭi hindaa lamayaa paan kæælla okkoma eka-paaraṭa kaṭe daagattaa
25 hænda pihidaalaada gatte?
minihaa kaar-eka happalaa daalaa pænalaa divuvaa
vatte inna harak ṭika elavalaa daanna kollaava yavanna
tee peralaa, daanna kooppavalaṭa
æňda uḍa tiyena redi ṭika navaa daanna
30 ee lamayaa aayet itin ehema karana ekak nææ
ada ee hæṭi vahina ekak nææ
eyaa dæn rassaavaka
harak ṭikak ævillaa vattaṭa
oya pætta issilaa væḍi
35 væsse ena koṭa kuḍee hulaňgaṭa giyaa

B. When are you going to the village?
Bring enough onions for the whole week.
The child is crying with hunger.
I got that book very cheap.
5 This child is really very naughty now.
Let us pack up all the glasses and cups carefully and send them (off).
This is the room younger brother does his studying in.
The vegetable-pingo broke and all the vegetables (are) on the road.
(You) must put a glass door on the book cupboard.
10 What do you want, then, sir?
The car broke (down) there and we had a lot of trouble.
The teacher got the father to beat the boy.
Elder brother chooses a pen for (his) younger brother.
Show the baby (his) mother in the yard.
15 Single to Galle, please.
Go into the garden to play.

I'm hungry, let's go to a shop and eat.
The baby will cry till (his) mother comes.
Who's the one who made this child cry?
20 Why is he meddling in my affairs?
I'll go home and have (my) tea.
How did (you) cut (your) hand?
I saw a man (who) had been drinking toddy and was lying in the road.
When (we) get to the station, the train will have gone.
25 This tea is not for you; that one is your cup.
When you get home, younger brother, father will have arrived.
When I got home, father had arrived.
It's a good thing it didn't rain yesterday.
We don't like the way it always rains.
30 It's a good thing (that) I stayed at home today.
I believe it's true the gentleman has gone to Kandy.
When I arrived, he was sewing.
The children are running to and fro in the yard.
Give this little girl too a piece of mango.
35 I can't write quicker than this without a proper pen.

Notes:

A. 1 særa karalaa is adverbial. **særen** is also possible here in this meaning; **særeeṭa** however would probably mean 'fast'.

3 rasaṭa, 'tastily'.

4 bimin **or** bima (locative), 'on the ground'; **not** bimaṭa (15 A 29 note).

5 bootal arina eka = the bottle opener.

7 **vatura viiduru**, on the other hand, means 'glasses of water' (23 A 12).

8 'Sugar-coffee' means black coffee with sugar. This is not to say that white coffee is drunk without sugar; the condensed milk which is normally used is always sweetened. White coffee is however not normally drunk in villages at all.

9 behet vatura = disinfectant. Drinking chemicals is a common method of suicide in Lanka.

10 hæbæyi = hæbææ + yi. This word, which has earlier been translated 'but', means literally 'it is true, (but)'. When final in a sentence, as here,

it can be replaced by **hæbææva**.

11 sudaa, 'white one'. This is a term of affection (m. or f.) and has no literal significance. **suddaa** on the other hand means 'white (or fair) man' (lesson 17 **b**).

12 etakoṭama = just at that moment. **gannavaa** with infinitive = begin (lesson 29 **b**).

13 Pron. [gahagenə].

14 Literally 'Just be without lies'. This means 'No false pretences: don't be shy.'

15 Alternatively one may say **viiduru vaturen puravanna**.

17 api dahadenaaṭa = for us ten. kææli dahayakaṭa = into ten pieces. hari yanavaa, see note on 11 A 14.

18 uturana = boiling. pupurayi or pipireyi.

19 illana illana gaanaṭa = at whatever price you offer (**lit**. is asked for. **ahana** will not do here).

21 hæn̆di gaanavaa, conjunct verb, 'to stir'. kiri-eka, see note on 20 A 3.

22 hulaŋ (stem-form) gæhenna, conjunct verb, 'to be wind-struck', i.e. to expose oneself to the air.

23 aave **or** enne.

24 hiṭi **or** inna; kaṭe **or** kaṭaṭa (22 B 5 note). ekapaaraṭa = at one go, at the one time.

25 'Did you wipe the spoon before you took it?' The position of **-da**, and the **-laa**, show that this is not a compound verb. Cf. hænda pihidaagattaada, have you wiped your spoon? The **-laa** is shortened in pronunciation.

26 The use of **happalaa** instead of **hæppilaa** implies a criticism of the driver. pænalaa divuvaa = ran away.

28 Straining is usually done into another vessel, rather than into the cup; 'strain the tea and then pour it out', 'strain the tea before you pour it.'

29 daanna = put them away. **navaa** is usually nasalized throughout: navãã.

30 Remember that **nææ** here may be completely unstressed (lesson 5 **b**). **karana ekak nææ** is more forceful than **karanne nææ**, but **karanne nam nææ** (lesson 8 **a** fn.) gives a similar effect. **ehema** has its full meaning here (as v.17 A 1).

31 ee hæṭi (or hæṭiyen) = as much as all that.

34   **tiyenavaa** is not necessary before **væḍi** here; the absolutive alone serves
      as finite verb. **issenavaa** is the involitive counterpart of **ussanavaa**.

35   hulaṅgaṭa giyaa = blew away.

B. 2   Whole: use **-ma**.

    3   With hunger: instr.

    6   Pack up: paarsal karanavaa (also **pæk karanavaa**). -yi . . . -yi can be used
         in this sentence, but is not necessary; certain pairs of nouns (such as
         'glasses and cups') can be put together without any connector. So
         kanna bonna. Carefully = well.

    8   Broke: use absolutive, see 19 A 23 note.

    9   Put: daanna. On: dative or locative.

    10   Then: etakoṭa **or** itin.

    11   Broke down: absolutive, as in 8 above. Say 'many troubles arose (were
         created) for us'.

    14   We must say 'be(ing) in the yard', see lesson 13 **b**.

    15   'Please' need not be translated (15 B 7 note). Single: say '(give) a ticket'.

    19   The one: lesson 11 **b**.

    20   Meddle in = **æṅgili gahanavaa** with the dative case.

    23   See note on 14 above. Lying: 22 A 1.

    24   Get – yana (**not** ena).

    26   See note on 21 B 6.

    29   The way: eka **or** hæṭiya.

    31   'I believe' = they say (lesson 9 **e**).

    32   Was sewing: as well as the simple present tense (lesson 21 **b**), the double
         absolutive with hiṭiyaa can be used.

    33   To and fro: ehe mehe (cf. 4 A 27). ehen mehen duvanavaa, on the other
         hand, would mean 'run up from all sides'.

LESSON 25

navattanavaa	stop (tr.)
beerenavaa	escape
nidaagannavaa	sleep
maaru karanavaa	change (tr.)
æn̆duma	garment
vaḍuvaa	carpenter
kukulaa	cock
pintuuree	picture (photo, film)
payippee	pipe
piṭuva, piṭa	page
daval	day-time: when the sun is high
hadissiye, hadissiyen[1]	unexpectedly, hurriedly
asaniipee	illness
tel (pl.)	oil; fat (of meat)
issaraha	in front of
venuven	on behalf of
venuvaṭa	instead of
passe	after, afterwards
issellaa	before (of time); ago
mæda	middle, in the middle
haraha	across
dige, digaṭa	along
vaṭee	around
ætule	within
mataka	memory
amataka	unremembered, unmindful
tibaha	thirst, thirsty
rasne	hot

1. **-ss-** in this word is sometimes pronounced **-s-**.

hiitala, siitala	cold, cool
kanagaaṭuva	sadness

(a) Besides meaning 'is enough' (lesson 19), **æti** also means '(there) probably is'.[1] (In this sense, it is also used without change as a participle.) When preceded by a **present-tense** verbal form, æti (ætte) combines probability with continuity, present or future.[2]

pææna meesee uḍa æti
 the pen may be on the table
taattaa naanavaa æti dæn
 father may be bathing now
taattaa naanavaa æti tava ṭikakin
 father may be having a bath shortly
taattaa naanavaa ætte liňden
 father must be bathing at (from) the well (not locative case here – father is not **in** the well)

This form is also used in questions, followed by **-da**.

taattaa naanavaa ædda?
 will father be bathing?

The corresponding negative form ends in **nætuva æti**, which may be preceded by the incomplete form of the verb.

meesee uḍa nætuva æti
 (it) may not be on the table
eyaa paan kanne nætuva æti
 he won't be eating bread

– or by an equivalent verbal phrase (lesson 24 c), eyaa paan kana ekak nætuva æti.
næti veyi (cf. 19 A 29) is rather more specific than nætuva æti.

minihaa enne næti veyi, I think he **won't** be coming
minihaa enne nætuva æti, he may not be coming.

With a **past-tense** verbal form, æti has the sense of 'enough'. This form is also used in questions, followed by **-da**. The corresponding negative form uses **madi** after the verb.

---

1. In a negative form, however, **ættema nææ** means 'certainly is not.'
2. For probability regarding the past, see Lesson 26 **c**.

ehema keruvaa æti — (you've) done enough of that

tee vækkeruvaa ædda? — [have (we) made enough tea? / has enough tea been made?

ehema keruvaa madi — haven't done enough of that

The sense 'enough' is possible also with a present-tense verb with æti.

meccara vatura enavaa æti

'enough that as much water as this is coming', i.e. this much water will do for us.

(b) The present and past tense verbal forms (karanavaa, keruvaa) can also take the case-ending **-ṭa**. This is especially common when followed by **mokada**, what (of it).

eyaa kivvaaṭa mokada karanne nææ

he may have said so (what of his saying so) but he won't do it

eyaa kiyanavaaṭa mokada karanne nææ

he may say so now but he won't do it

eekaṭa mokada?

what of that?

Without mokada, the past tense-form with **-ṭa** may often be translated concessively: giyaaṭa, although (he, one) goes/should have gone.

The present tense-form with **-ṭa** here is more restricted, and usually has a causal sense: taattaa kiyanavaaṭa(ma), (just) because father is saying so.

Sometimes there is also a further idea of **preventing** something happening.

baḍagini venavaaṭa lamayaa bat kæævaa

because of (possibly) becoming hungry, i.e. so as not to become hungry, the boy ate the rice

Tense forms with **-ṭa** often occur in conjunction with words expressing states of emotion, e.g. taraha, kanagaaṭu, kæmati.

api eyaa yanavaaṭa kæmati nææ

I don't want him to go

api eyaa giyaaṭa tarahayi

I'm angry at his having gone

apiṭa eyaa mærunaaṭa kanagaaṭuyi

we are sorry he has died

The past-tense verb-form with **-ṭa** is also used before **passe**, 'after'.

kivvaaṭa passe, — after saying.

(c) The instrumental case-ending **-in** is also found after past tense-forms before

passse.

keruvaayin passe, after doing

– and in other contexts

ehema yanavaayin / giyaayin] vædak venne nææ

there will be no use in (from) going on like that.

(d) The present and past tense-forms may also be followed by the postposition **ekka-ma**, 'with'; in such cases they add the suffix **-t**. This form indicates the simultaneous occurrence of two actions.

maŋ paarata bahinavat / bæssat] ekkama eyaa aavaa

just as I [set / had set] out, he arrived

In the present tense-form, **ma** is sometimes placed with the verb here instead of with **ekka**: bahinavaamat ekka.[1] (With the past tense-form however, **bæssaamat ekka** is better avoided).

A complete phrase containing a present or past tense verb may stand as the subject or object of another verb.

eyaa enavaa[2] maŋ dækkaa

I saw him coming

minihaa dora arinavaa mata dænunaa

I heard him open(ing) the door

(e) issellaa (contracted form for **issara velaa**; an intermediate form **issarelaa** is sometimes heard) can be preceded by an infinitive verb-form. issellaa and passe can also follow ordinary nouns in the dative or instrumental case-forms.

eyaa enna issellaa

before he [comes / came]

eevaa karannat issellaa (or karanna issellat)

even before doing that

væssata / væssen] issellaa

before the rain

---

1. Or **bahina kotama**.
2. Cf. lesson 13 **b**.

dolahaṭa
dolahen passe
dolahayin[1]

  after 12.0

iiṭa
in passe

  after that[2]

maṭa passe kavda?

  who is after me?[3]

A period of time in connection with these words is put in the dative case, before the postpositional word; here, issellaa can also be translated 'ago'.

(iiṭa) avuruddakaṭa passe

  a year afterwards

(miiṭa) sumaanayakaṭa issellaa

  a week ago, a week before

dæn ṭikakaṭa issellaa

  a little while ago

issellaama means 'first of all' (cf. also lesson 18, issellaama særeeṭa). **issaraha** means 'before' of place, i.e. in front of. It is used postpositionally after the direct case, and also after the genitive of pronouns. It can itself take case-endings.

kavda ara Vijayapaala mahattayaa issarahayin[4] inne?

  who's that in front of Mr. Wijepala?

in, min or **eyin, meyin** are instrumental case-forms corresponding to iiṭa, miiṭa. The instrumental forms **oyin, arin** are also used.

(f) venuven, venuvaṭa, mæda, haraha, dige, vaṭee, ætule can all be used postpositionally after the direct[5] case-form: ætule also after the locative. Other case-endings can be added to such of these words as do not already have a case-inflection, e.g. harahaṭa, mædin, vaṭeeṭa. digaṭa, ætulaṭa are dative case-forms corresponding with the locative forms dige, ætule.

---

1. Alternative form.

2. **dænaṭa passe**, however, is not used; 'henceforth' is **dæn (itin) aayet** or **aayet itin** (24 A 30).

3. For 'behind', see lesson 29 **c**.

4. Or **issarahin**.

5. Occasionally after the genitive of animate pronouns (eyaage venuvaṭa).

(g) **tibaha** is used like baḍagini (lesson 23 **d**):

maŋ tibahen (innavaa)	I (remain) thirsty
maṭa tibaha vunaa	I got thirsty
maṭa tibahayi maṭa vatura-tibahayi	I am thirsty
maṭa hari tibahak tiyenavaa	I'm very thirsty

The stem-forms **asaniipa** (pr. [asəniipə]) and **kanagaaṭu** are used in the same way:

maṭa saniipa nææ[1] maṭa asaniipayi maŋ asaniipen (cf. maŋ leḍin, 22 **e**)	I am unwell
maṭa loku asaniipayak (tiyenavaa)	I am very unwell
maŋ / maṭa asaniipa vunaa,	I became unwell
maṭa eekaṭa kanagaaṭuyi maŋ eekaṭa kanagaaṭuven inne	I am sad about that
minihaa kanagaaṭu vunaa	he became sad
maṭa loku kanagaaṭuvak tiyenavaa	I am very sad

These words are seldom used by themselves as qualifying adjectives: for example, 'a very thirsty boy' will be **hari tibahak tiyena lamayek**.

There is no simple verb corresponding to Eng. 'remember'. 'I remember' is translated **maṭa matakayi**. Other tense-forms can be specified by using **matak venavaa**.

meeka maṭa matakayi mee gæna maṭa matakak[2] tiyenavaa	I remember this
oyaava maṭa matakayi	I remember you

Note the use of the termination **-va** here of a personal 'subject' – as with involitive verbs (lesson 13 **a**).

---

1. But **maṭa saniipayi** means 'I am better now.' **saniipa velaa** is used idiomatically in the sense of 'mahat velaa.'

2. In formal contexts, also **matakayak**.

balana koţa maţa matak veyi
I'll remember when I see (it)

'I forget' is **maţa mataka nææ (næti venavaa)** or **maţa amatakayi** (pron. [amətəkay]).

Similarly also

maţa hiitalayi	I am cold
siitalayi	it is cold
mage ata [hiitala vunaa	my hand got cold
mage ata [hiitalayi	my hand is cold

This word can also be used adjectivally before certain nouns –

hiitala davasak	a cold day

Also

rasne davasak	a hot day

But 'I am hot' is a sentiment which is hardly expressible in Sinhalese (it should be replaced by 'my body is heated', 'my body is sweating', 'I feel the heat'). **rasne(yi)** means 'it is hot'.

(h) **ţika**, without indefinite suffix **-k**, when followed by **-yi** and used with an incomplete verb-form, means 'little, only a little' (as opposed to ţikak, **a little**).

mee tiyenne lunu ţikak
here is a little (some) salt
mehe tiyenne lunu ţikayi
there is little salt here.

(i) **piţu** (pl.) means 'pages' (of a book), but the corresponding singular form **piţuva** is rather literary and is usually replaced by **piţa** (which also means 'the back', Lesson 29).

payippee means a pipe for water, etc. It is also used where Eng. says 'tap'; no Sinhalese word for 'tap' is in general use, and the equivalent to Eng. 'turn the tap on' is 'open the pipe'. payippee is also used of a smoker's pipe, which is however not common in Lanka.

A.
api naginavat ekkama koocciya ædduvaa
eeke ætta-nætta danne mamayi
janeelee vahanna, ætulaţa hulaŋ noenna
mahattayaage pææna maŋ gaava æti ekak nææ
oyin beerunaa æti
lamayaaţa oya gæhuvaa æti

dæn væḍa keruvaa æti, rææt vunaa
eyaa giyaaṭa mokada apiṭa?
eeken apiṭa mokada?
asaniipa venna issellaa lamayaa hun̆gak mahatayi
iskoolee ærenna issellaa lamayaa gedara ævit
tibaha væḍi venna issellaa tava vatura ṭikak bonna
mataka næti venna issellaa oya pææna diilaa yanna
desæmbara maaseeṭa passe labanne mona maaseeda?
payippee dæn vatura enne nætuva æti
taattaa ada gedara ena ekak nætuva æti
dæn yana eka hon̆da nætuva æti
pintuuree gannavat ekkama minihek issarahaṭa aavaa
taattaa venuven kavda penii hiṭiye?
ee minihaaṭa pintuuree venuvaṭa salli oonælu
taappee ratu venuvaṭa sudu gaanavaaṭa maŋ kæmati
ee lamayaa kanavaaṭa væḍiya kataa karanavaa
ee mahattayaa heṭa aavaaṭa maava hamba vena ekak nææ
nikam aavaaṭa giyaaṭa væḍa karanna epaa
taattaa baninavaaṭa lamayaa ammaa gaavaṭa giyaa
kiiye koocciyeda aave?
eyaaṭa dæn ævidinna puluvan æti
viiduruva bin̆dalaa taattaa gahanavaaṭa lamayaa kussiyaṭa velaa innavaa
asaniipee hon̆da vunaaṭa passe lamayaa dæn hun̆gak mahatayi
an̆gaharuvaadaaṭa issellaa davasa kavadaada?
edaayin passe eyaa aayit mehe aave nææ
ee pota maṭa passe matak vune
pote mæda piṭaṭa haravanna
dora arina koṭa ballaa ætule
geyi ætule davalṭa rasne væḍi
taattaa gahanavaaṭa lamayaa ammaa gaavaṭa velaa innavaa
allapu kaamaree ætule kavda sadda karanne?
ee minihaa Kolam̆ba hæma paarak digeema ævidalaa tiyenavaa
uuṭa dænenna næti vennama maŋ ee nidaŋ hiṭi ballaava allalaa doraṭa bændaa
meeka harahaṭa aḍi panahayi

B. (You) have done enough work now, go and play.

Even though it's cold, all the windows are open.

The gentleman may be swearing, (but) he isn't angry.

Have a bath before (you) change (your) clothes.

5 Before the cup fell he jumped (forward) and caught (it).

I have brought (my) **pencil** instead of (my) pen.

I presented some books to the school on behalf of my father.

Instead of the old master, a new master is coming to us from tomorrow, I hear.

I now eat rice instead of bread.

10 (We) gave the child a pen for New Year, instead of money.

Who is in charge of the office today in place of the boss?

The mother was very unhappy for (her) son, who suddenly got ill and died.

He doesn't want me to come.

The carpenter is asking money for mending the chair.

15 Though I posted that letter last week (it) hasn't got (there) yet, it seems.

The boys are running round the house, playing.

That man is re-building a wall round (his) house.

They must be eating (their) meal by now.

He must be sorry for that now.

20 The child must be still playing at school.

It must be raining a lot at Galle too today.

Just as the bus stopped the man jumped (off).

As the boy left for school it began to rain.

Just as grandfather was going to fall, (I) caught (him).

25 After drinking the milk, the boy went to sleep.

After the cock had crowed in the morning, I got up.

Tell me when (you) have written the letters.

When I got there the front door was open.

Who first made a car?

30 First of all, drink (your) tea.

What did you do before this?

Just as the bus was coming, a little boy ran across the road.

A coconut tree has fallen across the road.

A little boy is running along the street crying.

35 Who is in the middle room?

Do (you) see the bus coming?

(You) have done enough crying there now.

First wash that mango before eating (it).

The cheapest bottle of oil in this shop is (Rs.) 1/25.

40 The little boy went along the road drinking milk from a bottle.

Notes:

A. 1 See 21 A 22.

2 ætta-nætta, the truth or absence of truth. 'It's me who knows whether it's true or not.'

3 See lesson 23 **e**.

4 æti ekak nææ or ætte nææ.

5 oyin, 'by that (much)'. 'Enough your having escaped by that much'. i.e. a good thing you just managed to escape.

6 oya, see lesson 3 **e**.

9 eeken or eekaṭa.

10 Here **-yi** must be translated 'was', not 'is'.

11 **iskoolee ærenavaa** means 'school finishes'. **ærenavaa** is used in this sense (the apparent opposite of its usual sense) in a few special contexts. Here the idea may be of school opening up to release its prisoners.

12 væḍi venna = become too much, increase.

14 Cf. note on 20 A 1; **labanavaa**, not **læbenavaa**, is used of the coming of time. It has, however, the same involitive sense 'receive'; for the volitional 'acquire', it is necessary to use **labaagannavaa**.

18 issarahaṭa aavaa, (just) 'came forward'; but issarahayin aavaa, 'came in front' (of the camera).

19 'Appear for', in a legal sense. **penii** is used here in preference to **penilaa**.

20 To replace the picture, i.e. perhaps to pay for damage to it. For a simple purchase, **pintuureeṭa** would be sufficient.

21 sudu gaanavaa = to paint white.

24 aavaaṭa giyaaṭa = haphazardly, any old how. Pronounce [nikaŋŋaavaṭə].

25 Because of father's (possible future) scolding, i.e. in case father should scold. So in 28 and 36 below.

27 Pronounce [puluvaŋŋæti].

29 hoñda venavaa = get cured. passe, tr. 'since'.

30 kavadaada is normal here, not **koyi davasada** or **mokakda**. issellaa davasa, the day before (also **issarin daa**). Pronounce [añgəharuvaadaṭə].

31 edaayin or edaaṭa.

34 Probably refers to past time.

35 davalṭa or daval.

37 allapu = next-door, next. sadda karanavaa = to make a noise (sadda, stem-form: lesson 17 **b**).

38 Note the position of **ma**, which usually **follows** a postpositional word (unless special emphasis is required). The -e of **dige** is lengthened here, cf. n. on 12 A 1. Kolam̃ba is loc. 'The road **to** Colombo' would be 'Kolam̃ba yana paara', cf. 9 A 28.

39 dænenna næti vennama or nodænennama. doraṭa bændaa may mean 'tied to the door' (i.e. to the hinge); in this sense **doree** is also possible. Or doraṭa (often pronounced [doṭṭə]) can mean 'outside (the door)': **doṭṭa dæmmaa**, chucked (him) out.

40 harahaṭa = crosswise. Compare this sentence with the examples in lesson 13 **c**. **meeke** can also be used here, but **-ṭa** is still needed.

B. 5, 24 Caught = allaagattaa. **ælluvaa** would give the idea of accidentally touching.

8 Old: this does not mean old in years.

10 New Year = Avurudda. This is the great domestic festival of the year in Lanka, occurring in mid-April.

11 In charge, cf. 20 A 2.

12 Suddenly = unexpectedly.

14 'For mending': section **b** above; if he has already done the job, hæduvaaṭa should be used, otherwise hadanavaaṭa.

15 'Got there': hamba venavaa or læbenavaa, but not enavaa which would mean 'come to me'.

17 Round = vaṭee or vaṭeeṭa. Rebuilding: building afresh.

22 'Stopped': say 'was stopped', i.e. use the transitive (causative) verb **navattanavaa**. Cf. addanavaa in 21 A 22.

23 'Left for': use just **yanavaa**.

24 Going to fall: translate literally (pres., not past). Cf 17 A 18 note.

26 Crow = aňɖanavaa, or **aňɖalanavaa**.

28 Front door: **issaraha dora** (sometimes called **dorakaɖa dora**). **issaraha gedara** means ‘the house opposite.’

30 First of all = before everything.

35 ‘The middle room’ is the main sitting room. Like the ‘front parlour’, it is often very little used.

37 ‘There’: cf. A 6 above.

LESSON 26

navatinavaa (for past tense and abs., use involitive forms **nævatunaa, nævatilaa**)	stop (intr.)
elanavaa	spread out (tr.)
hoyanavaa (past tense, **hevvaa**: **hoyaagannavaa** = find)	seek
koṭanavaa	dig, pound
usa yanavaa	grow tall
ganan yanavaa	get expensive
diga-arinavaa	unroll, unwrap, spread out
dañga karanavaa	be mischievous
añḍa gahanavaa	shout, summon
kelin(ma)	straight
kalin	previously
væḍiyen / **væḍiyema**	mostly, especially
vela / **kuṁbura**	rice-field
goyam (pl.)	growing rice
aanḍuva	Government
pædura	mat
piñgaana	plate
maamaa	uncle
nændaa	aunt
kos (pl.)	jak-fruit
loriya	lorry
pæṭrol / **pæṭrool** (pl.)	petrol

dee	thing
vitara	approximately; as much as; only
vage / **vaage**	like

Temporal verb-forms

(a) By replacing the verbal ending **-navaa** by **-ddi** (from innavaa, gannavaa, dannavaa the forms are **iňdiddi** or **indæddi**, **ganiddi**, **daniddi**),[1] a present-tense verbal form corresponding to the absolutive is obtained. The subject of the main sentence need not be the same as that of this present absolutive, which is often an alternative to the present participle with **koṭa**. It usually precedes the main sentence. The two actions must occur simultaneously. If the **-ddi** clause refers to a past occasion, the **main** verb may be either past or, where a continuous action is indicated, **present**. When referring to a future event, a main verb in **-navaa** is generally avoided here (cf. note on 21 A 18). See A4 and A6 below.

api yaddi ṭayar-ekak giyaa

as we were going along a tyre burst (went)

This form is sometimes repeated (**yaddi yaddi**). It also often has a concessive sense as well as a purely temporal one, i.e. can be replaced by a participle and **koṭat**, in spite of, even while. To point the contrast, **-ddi** can be followed by **-t**.

mee lamayaa una tiyeddit vatte sellam karanavaa

this childs plays in the orchard even when feverish

It can be preceded by **no-** to negative the sense.

maŋ noyaddi eyaa yayida?

will **he** go, when I'm not going?

(b) By adding **-ma** to the past verbal ending **-aa**, a meaning similar to that of the absolutive is obtained. This form usually precedes the main sentence, and the subject of the main sentence need not be the same. The form may sometimes be an alternative to the present participle with **koṭa** in particular contexts, but it refers to a time sequence – the two actions must be consecutive, not simultaneous; in other words, it involves a future perfect or pluperfect sense. When the subject of the main sentence **is** the same, a past tense in the main sentence **should be avoided**, unless the verb is inverted.

This form can be followed by **-t** to point a contrast, and can be preceded by **no-** to negative the sense.

---

1. Colloquially notice also **næddi** from **nææ**.

api gedara giyaama kanavaa

when I have got home, I (will) eat

api gedara giyaama kamu

let's eat when we get home

but api gedara gihin kææva]
api gedara giyaamayi kæævee]

when we got home, we ate

velaavaṭa kææma nokæævaamat mahat veyida?

how can (you) get fat(ter) when you don't even eat at the (proper) time?

(**nokaat** would give the same meaning).

In these verbal forms, **-aama** is sometimes realized (or even written) as **-ahamə**. It is more normally realized as **-amə** ([**bæluvamə**, **kæævamə**)]; in words with the rhythm ∪ — ∪ however, long **aa** keeps its full length (cf. **lamayaaṭa**, as v. **babaaṭa**). An alternative form is to add **-vaama** to the past participle in **-pu**: balapuvaama, diipuvaama, etc.

(c) **æti** (ætte, ædda) following an **infinitive** refers to a probable supposition regarding the past, as expressed in English by 'must have', 'will have'. **-t** may follow the infinitive.

Following an absolutive, **æti** gives much the same sense. The difference between **-laa æti** and **-nna æti** is only that -laa æti considers the completion of the action; it has the same meaning as **-laa tiyeyi**. **-t** may follow the absolutive.

lamayaa melahakaṭa bat kaalaa æti

the child must have eaten his rice by now

eevaa melahakaṭa { vikinilat / vikunalat } æti

they may (actually) have been sold by now

taattaa ee liyuma iiye liyanna æti

father must have written that letter yesterday

dæn bas-eka yannat æti

the bus must have (actually) gone already

The corresponding negative is **-nna nææ**, or { **-nna** / **-laa** } **nætuva æti** (not **-laa næti**).

tavama eyaa ee væḍa ṭika karanna nææ

he can't have done those jobs yet

kaḍee tavama æralaa nætuva æti
the shop can't have been opened (can't be open) yet

(d) **vage** can be added after any word in a sentence.

api vage	like me; as I do
galak vage	(it is)[1] like a stone
eyaa dæn enavaa vaage	he seems to be coming now
maŋ kivvaa vage	as I said
tunaṭa vage enna	come at about 3.00
nitara(ma) vage	fairly often
ee vage, oya vage (oovage)	like that
hoňdayi vage	it seems to be good
mehaaṭa væhælaa vage	it seems to have been raining here

Note –

eyaa yanna vage	he looks like going
eyaa yanna vage hæduvaa	he made as if to go

vitara (lit. 'amount') is mostly used after numerals or expressions indicating time. Here it is equivalent to 'approximately'.

tunaṭa vitara enna	come about 3.00
labana saňdudaa vitara enna	come next Monday or so

It is also used in comparisons of two quantities.

maŋ vitara usa	as tall as I (am)

vitarak (with **-yi** suffix, **vitarayi**; interrogative **vitarada**?) should be translated 'only' or 'only just'.

Siripaala vitarayi tavama aave nætte	only Siripaala has still not come
Kamanii vitarada aave?	has only Kamanii come?
Siripaala vitarak mehaaṭa enna	come here, Siripaala only!
maŋ aavaa vitarayi	I've only just come[2]
ee vitarak nemeyi	not only that (but...)

(e) **kalin** means 'before now', i.e. is equivalent to miiṭa issellaa. It is not quite the same as **issara**, which means 'some time ago' (compare B45 below with 22 B 10).

(f) **kuňbura** (pl. kuňburu) is used of rice-fields when considered as property; **vela** is used of the physical tract of ground where rice is actually growing. Thus we can say ape kuňburuvala goyam kapanna, reap our fields, but yana koṭa velaṭa

1. In writing, -yi would be added here: **vageyi**.
2. **maŋ mee aavaamayi** has the same meaning (16 A 9).

væţeyi, you may fall into the field as you go. Rice, the principal food-crop of Ceylon, grows in standing water, intersected by boundary ridges along which it is possible to walk, and from which one might slip into the water. **goyam** is rice when growing; **vii** is the seed ('paddy'), **haal** is the husked seed. When cooked (bat uyanavaa), this is called **bat**.

koţanavaa means 'to break up'. To dig over a field is kum̆bura koţanavaa.[1] vii koţanavaa is to thresh paddy. **haaranavaa** means rather 'to scrape out'; lin̆dak haaranavaa, dig a well. **viduli koţanavaa** means 'lightning is flashing'.[2]

The jak-fruit is the poor man's stand-by, when he cannot afford rice.

pædura (pl. pæduru): mats, made of coconut or other fibre, are often used for sleeping on, being in many cases cooler than a bed in the tropics.

The indefinite form of **dee** is **deyak**; the plural is **deeval**.

(g) **maamaa** is the brother of a mother, or a father's sister's husband; **nændaa**[3] is the mother's brother's wife, or the sister of a father. These words also denote father-in-law and mother-in-law respectively, since according to the traditional Kandyan system one marries the children of one's maamaa. For the use of the plural forms in **-laa**, see lesson 21 **d**. To distinguish one uncle from another, the uncle's place of residence is often prefixed to his name: Gampola maamaa, uncle from Gampola (a small town near Kandy); cf. 21 B 23.

A.
ee vayasaka minihaa paare yaddi iiye kaar-ekakaţa ahu velaa
maŋ ada iskoolee yaddi paaredi maamaava hamba vunaa
Kolam̆ba yaddi iiye hon̆daţama væssaa
taattaa ada udee yaddi hon̆daţama vahinavaa
hon̆dayi kivvaama lamayaa dora æriyaa
nændaa kos kapaddi ammaa pol gaalaa deyi
ee mahattayaa dæn kantooru gihillaa æti
midule pædurak elalaa æti, væssen issellaa geţa ganna
mee liyuma ævillaa adaţa davas tunayi
hataraţa pahaţa vitara enna
taattaa yanavat ekkama vage eyaa aave
ada hændæævaţa vahinna vage

---

1. vela koţanavaa is not used; vele koţanavaa, dig in the field, is possible.
2. In official language, **viduliya** is also used for 'electricity'.
3. nændaa must be distinguished from Nandaa, which is a proper name.

pin̆gaana væţenna vage yana koţa maŋ hon̆da velaavaţa allaagattaa
dolahamaara vitara vena koţa taattaa kææma kanna gedara eyi
ena san̆dudaa dihaava vitara aayit maava hamba venna enna
malli tavama ayiyaa vitara usa nææ
gee kaɖaa væţeddi api Kolam̆ba
am̆bageɖiya kapaddi lamayaage ata kæpilaa
kiyaddi kiyaddi lamayaa dan̆ga karanavaa
hataraţa pahak tiyeddi enna
lamayi meesee vaţee sellam karana koţa pin̆gaana bima væţunaa
Laŋkaave minissu kos kæævaaţa væɖiyen(ma) kanne bat
mee lamayaa tava tava usa yanavaa
iskoolee yana lamayek vunaama guruvarayaa kiyana kiyana hæţiyaţa karanna oonæ
aţen hayak giyaama dekayi
dæn velaava pahayi – melahakaţa ee mahattayaa gedara gihillaa
ee am̆ba(geɖi) ţika dæn narak velat æti
salli nætuva venna æti gee vikunanne
saddayak æhunaa – taattaa aavaa venna æti, gihin balanna
mee lamayaa dæn pol gahak vage usa gihin
meesee uɖa ara peţţiyak vage tiyenne mokakda?
mage hite eeka hari yana deyak nemeyi
maŋ kivvaama ahanna ko itin
naana koţa hiţi hæţiye payippee vatura nætuva giyaa
ammaa mæreddi maŋ poɖi
væssaama ape paara heedilaa yanavaa
ape pætten ţikak aavaama mokada?
mee rasne davasvala næævaama hari saniipayi
dæn bæluvaama ee væɖee hari yanne næti paaţayi
taattaa kooţ-eka bas-eke tiyeddi ævit
bonna vat vatura næti koţa koheda mee naanna kataa karanne?
meesa redda tava ţikak oya pættaţa æddaama hari
ee pota maŋ nivaaɖuvaţa gedara giyaama hoyalaa evannam
maŋ gedara yaddi putaa potak balabalaa hiţiyaa
pota evvaama salli dennam
yana koţa ada kuɖee araŋ yanna, hændææavaţa vahinna puluvan

B. The child fell down while he was running

The child drinks water while he is eating rice

While I was drawing water from the well, (my) pen fell (in)

The dog went (away) though he was being called

5 He will have come to see me while I was (away) at Galle last month

That boy came and hit me while I was doing a job

Father had an accident with (his) car on the way to the office

As the bus was stopping the man jumped (off)

The small son is watching as (his) father digs (his) field

10 My pen must have fallen near that chair; go and fetch it

The train must have gone by now

By now the shop must be shut

Aunt must have arrived in Kandy by now

He must have been picking the coconuts from our trees today

15 (They) must have cut the rice in uncle's fields by now

The two boys are fighting, although father is swearing (at them)

I will leave for Colombo about 3.00 to-morrow

In Colombo (you) can get a loaf of bread for about 24 cents

How much approximately will it cost for all of us to go and see that picture?

20 A tyre went, on the way to Galle

Where are (you) trying to go like this in the rain?

The child is watching as the men cut the tree (down)

Though they have nationalized our fields, it is still us who look after them

Though they have nationalized buses they still haven't nationalized lorries

25 When I get (the) money (I) will buy a car

When the petrol runs out, the car will stop

It must have rained in Colombo too yesterday

(That's) enough now!

Don't get out of bed when you have fever

30 Let's eat when (we) get hungry

When (we) got to the station, the train had gone

When the milkman comes to-day, tell me

Don't unwrap that parcel

When he doesn't do what (his) father tells (him), will that boy listen to what I say?

35 When I had the car I used to go to Kandy frequently

Why does that gentleman travel by train every day, when he actually has a car?

When (I) get home I will have tea

Come straight home when school finishes

What's the bread for, when (we) still have (some) rice?

40 I have eaten too much now

Goods are gradually going up in price now

How much is 28 from 30?

Father can't have come home yet

When you turn on that tap, the water will come

45 I have read this book before

Bring those [few] glasses here and don't break them

Notes:

A. 2 maamaava, see lesson 13 **a**.

3, 4 hoňdaţama, see note on 17 B 12.

4 vahinavaa means 'it was raining', as v. væssaa, 'it came on to rain'.

5 hoňdayi kivvaama = 'when approval was given'.

6 gaanavaa = scrape. The white of coconuts is scraped off on a special scraper, and the milklike liquid squeezed out of the scrapings is then used for cooking in.

7 The meaning of this will vary according to the position of the speaker. When said at the home of the gentleman in question, it will mean 'he must have reached the office by now', as opposed to **yanna æti** 'he must have left for the office'. When said at some other place, it may mean 'he must have left home for the office by now.'

9 tunayi or tunak venavaa. See note on 16 A 9.

10 hataraţa pahaţa vitara = 4.0 or 5.0 or so. Cf. on the other hand 20 below.

12 vahinna vage = it looks like raining (as v. **vahinavaa vage**, it looks as if it were raining).

13 See 25 B 24 note. **hoňda** is used here just as in English, 'in good time'.

14 Or dolahamaaraṭa vitara. Notice the form **dolahamaara**. So also **ekolahamaara**, and **pahalovamaara** (15½).

15 ena saňdudaa dihaava vitara, round about next Monday. hamba venna, to see (not 'meet' here, see lesson 21 **c**).

17 kaḍaa, see n. on 19 A 3. Kolam̆ba, sc. hiṭiyaa.

19 kiyaddi kiyaddi, in spite of repeated remonstrances.

20 hataraṭa pahak tiyeddi = at 3.55. **-k** is essential here, but **paha vena koṭa** is a permissible alternative. Similarly, pahaṭa kaalak tiyeddi, at 4.45 (cf. lesson 9 **c**).

21 bima: the locative case is often used here (cf. Eng. 'fell **on** the floor').

22 vædiyenma = more especially.

23 The double **tava** makes this statement present rather than future.

24 Probably refers to future time, or to the present ('now that you have become . . .'). In a general statement, **lamayi** would be more usual, instead of **lamayek vunaama**. The indefinite suffix **-k** is not used in making general statements.

25 '8 – 6 = 2'. **ma** here is often inaudible.

26 gihillaa, sc. æti.

28 salli nætuva = salli næti hindaa. **venna æti** replaces **-yi** here; 'it must be because . . .' Cf. 19 A 1 note.

29 aavaa here is used as the subject of venna æti: lit. 'his having come must be'. venna æti is frequently added after a finite verb in this way. saddayak æhunaa, sc. maṭa, 'I heard a noise'.

32 mage hite, 'in my heart', i.e. as I see it, in my opinion. hari yanavaa: 11 A 14.

33 **ahanna** here is virtually equivalent to 'obey'.

34 hiṭi hæṭiye = suddenly. 'The tap stopped running.'

35 poḍi(yi), see note on 25 A 10.

36 A general statement.

37 pætten, see lesson 10 **a** ('position in space'). 'What when you come?', i.e. why don't you come? mokada, or mokada venne.

39 hari yanne næti paaṭayi (or nææ vageyi) = **it seems** it isn't going right.

40 tiyeddi = while it was. **tiyeddi** (and **iňdiddi** of animates) in such contexts can in fact be translated '(accidentally) leaving'. **tiyalaa** (or **daalaa**) might also imply 'having purposely left'. The negative of this sentence

would be.. bas-eke daalaa ævillaa næhæ; notice the position of the negative – neither **nodaa ævillaa** nor **tiyeddi næævit** are possible, nor **notiyeddi**.

41 koheda, 'where'. We would say '**What** is this talk...?' næti koṭa or næti vunaama or nætuva tiyeddi.

42 meesa (adjectival), see lesson 17 **b**.

43 Here **yana koṭa** (as opposed to giyaama) would imply that the book is **here**, and not at home.

45 'When the book is sent'.

46 'When you go, go taking...' We would say 'When you go, take your umbrella **with you**'.

B. 2 Drinking while eating is considered bad in Lanka. You drink afterwards.

5 See lesson 22 **c**.

7 Say 'While father was going to the office, (his) car has collided'.

8 navatinavaa or navattanavaa can be used here.

10 And fetch = to fetch.

12 Be shut: see 19 B 13 note.

14 From our trees: use locative, **not** instrumental here.

15 See note on 21 B 23.

19 'Cost': use venavaa or yanavaa (cf. 11 A 23). Cf. 10 above.

20 'Went', translate literally: cf. lesson 21 **b**. 'On the way' = while going.

21 'Like this': lesson 3 **e**.

23, 24 Nationalize = aanḍuvaṭa gannavaa.

26 Run out (in this sense) = næti venavaa.

29 Get out: see note on 23 B 23. Fever: 24 **e**.

34 What his father tells him: say 'the thing (his) father says'. Use **koṭa** here – there is no sense of time sequence, so **nekeruvaama** will not do.

35 Used to: cf. n. on A 4 above.

36 Travel – say 'goes (and) comes'.

37 Have = drink.

41 Gradually: 18 A 3.

42 Cf. A 25 above, or 10 A 21.

45 See **e** above.

46 And don't break = without breaking (lesson 15 **a**).

LESSON 27

ahulanavaa	pick up
talanavaa (with dative of animates)	beat
dum gahanavaa	smoke (intr.)
gini gannavaa	catch fire
saayam gaanavaa	paint
(eka) velaavakaṭa	sometimes
samaharaviṭa **samaharavelaavaṭa** (pron. [samahallaaṭə])	perhaps
ikmanaṭa **ikmanin** **ikman karalaa**	quickly
paandara **paandarin**	early
veelapahin **veelaasanin**	in good time, in advance
dara (pl.)	firewood
mas (pl.)	meat
maalu	fish; curry
sissayaa[1]	pupil
vissaasa	trust, belief
naya	debt, indebted

(a) **Reported speech**. A reported statement or question can always be given in the original direct form, followed by **kiyalaa**, which literally means 'having said', but has also become merely a marker of the end of a quotation, and is therefore frequently followed by other forms of the verb **kiyanavaa**. The final word of the quotation, immediately preceding kiyalaa, may add a final **-yi** if it ends in a vowel (**-aa** being

1. This word is somewhat formal. The word **goolayaa** is more colloquial.

shortened to **-a** or **-æ**), or **-yæyi** if it ends in a consonant.

ada ennam kiyalaa kivvaa

(he) said 'I will come today'

(he) said he would come today

enavayi is also possible here instead of **ennam**, but not **eyi** in this meaning.

maŋ yanavaa kiyalaa aavaa

I came away (saying I must be off)

In this case the actual words may have been **maŋ yannam** (it is impolite in Ceylon to take one's departure without saying some such phrase).

heṭa enna puluvanda kiyalaa eyaagen æhuvaa

(I) asked him 'Can (you) come tomorrow?'

In reported questions **-da** is commonly added to the verb without here giving the sense of complaint mentioned in lesson **4 a**.

pææna kohe dæmmaada kiyalaa maṭa dæn mataka nææ

I don't now remember where (I) put the pen

Similarly **no-** may precede a finite verb where this is followed by **kiyalaa**.

api nogiyaa kiyalaa hitanavaada?

do (you) think we didn't go?

In simple quoted statements **kiyalaa** is often omitted.

kavda inne balanna

see who's there[1] (**or** who's waiting to see (it)?)

yanna epayi kivvaa

(he) said (one) mustn't go

(I) said (you) mustn't go

maŋ gedara nææ kiyannada?

shall I say (you) aren't at home?

minihaa mas kanavaada (maŋ) danne nææ

I wonder if he eats meat

Notice this use of **danne nææ**.

kiyalaa is also used in quoting thoughts (where often no equivalent in English may be required).

maŋ Gaalu yanna kiyalaa aave

it was in order to go to Galle that I came

---

1. This use of balanna is rather modernistic. It would be more strictly correct to say: kavda inne kiyalaa gihillaa balanna.

taattaa kiyalaa maŋ balanne nææ

I won't consider that (he is my) father

I won't bother about his being my father

	vecca ekaṭa	
eeka næti	vunaaṭa	kanagaaṭu venna epaa
	vunayi kiyalaa	

don't grieve about losing it

Sentences containing **kiyalaa** more than once may be confusing.

maŋ kivvaa eyaa kivvayi kiyalaa tunaṭa enna kiyalaa

I said he had told (me) to come at 3.00

Where the subject of the reported statement is also the reporter, it is not necessary to repeat it in Sinhalese.

ammaa maṭa hoňda orloosuvak araŋ denavayi kivvaa

mother said (she) would bring me a nice watch

Notice how **questions** involving a reported statement are expressed:

tava kiidenaada innavayi kivve?

how many more did (you) say there were?

cf. tava kiidenek innavayi kiyalaa kivvaada?

did (he) say how many more there were?

tava kiidenaada inne kiyalaa æhuvaada?

did (you) say (ask) 'How many more are there?'

eyaa monavaa karanavaa kiyalaada hitanne?

what do (you) think he'll do?

(b) Alternatively, a whole reported statement may be expressed as a noun, i.e. may appear as a relator-clause, with its verb in participial form followed by **bava** (fact), **vaga** (thing), or **eka** (lesson 24 **c**) – or by **hæṭi** (stem-form of **hæṭiya**, manner), where the reference is to the manner of an occurrence rather than to the mere fact. These words sometimes also have the **-k** suffix (bavak, a story that... etc.), especially in negative sentences.

	bava(k)	
eyaa mas kana	vaga(k)	maŋ danne nææ
	eka	

I didn't know he ate meat

	ekak	
gee gini gattu	bavak	maŋ danne nææ
	vagak	

I didn't know the house had caught fire

bava
gee gini araŋ vaga] eyaaţa kivvaa
tiyena eka

(I) told him that the house was on fire

Here the participial form after an absolutive can be omitted before **bava** and **vaga**, but it should not be omitted before **eka**.

maŋ ena hæţi kiyannam
I'll tell (you) how to come

maŋ ena hæţiyak kiyannam
I'll tell you a way to come

eeka næti vecca bava kiyalaa evvaa
(he) reported the loss of it

= eeka næti vunaaya kiyalaa kiyalaa evvaa

Here the apparent duplication arises from the use of **kiyalaa evanavaa** as a compound verb, 'to report'.

vaga(k)
minihaa maţa kiyapu] maţa mataka nææ
bava(k)

I can't remember if he told me

A participial form is not needed after adjectival or adverbial words.

eeka loku bava kivvaa
(he) said it was big (= eeka lokuyi kiyalaa kivvaa)

eeka ehema bava kivvaa
(he) said it was so

(c) **vissaasa** can be used, like **mataka** (lesson 25 **g**), with a further noun, in the object case if personal.

maţa eeka vissaasayi,	I believe that
maţa eyaava vissaasayi,	I trust him
meekaa vissaasa nææ	this animal (11 **b**) is not trustworthy, is not safe

Alternatively the conjunct verb **vissaasa karanavaa** can be used: maŋ eyaava vissaasa karanavaa, I trust him.

naya, like **taraha** (lesson 23 **d**), is used predicatively as well as as a noun.

maŋ eyaaţa nayayi	I am in debt to him.

nayaţa ('for debt') means 'on credit'.

(d) Many people in Ceylon do not eat meat, but almost everybody eats fish. **maalu** meaning 'fish' is the stem-form of **maaluvaa**, a whole fish (e.g. when alive), and is used of prepared food, e.g. batuyi maaluyi, rice and fish. maalu is also the plural of **maaluva**, 'curry', and batuyi maaluyi (or **bat maalu**) can thus mean 'rice and curry' in general. The Sinhalese meal par excellence consists of hot rice accompanied by varying numbers of dishes of cold curried vegetables, fruits, fish etc. Lentils are normally the only dish which is not curried. Eggs – surprisingly – are generally taboo (they are thought to be always fertile).

(e) **samahallaaţa** or **samaharelaaţa** is the common shortening for samahara-velaavaţa. **viţa** (in **samaharaviţa**) also means 'time, occasion'. (These words are often translated into English as 'sometimes', though the real equivalent of this is **(eka) velaavakaţa**). **ikmanaţa** is usually realized as [ikmənţə].

(f) **paandara** means 'early in the day', i.e. before 6.00 a.m. and can be used after the word **udee**. **veelapahin** can also mean 'earlier, rather soon', and is not used after **udee**. The **a** in the third syllable of this word must be pronounced **a**, not **ə** (even when the second syllable is written long, as it often is; it must **not** be pronounced [**velaapəhin**]).[1] **kalin** is also used in this second sense.

A.

bææ kiyanna ekko puluvan kiyanna
ee minihaaţa karanna bæri væḑak nææ kiyanavaaa
taattaa gedara hiţiyaa maŋ danne nææ
gedara ballek innavaa maŋ danne nææ
ara aliyaa mehe enne æyida dannavaada?
maŋ hitanne eyaa dæn maat ekka tarahayi
epayi kiyana koţat lamayaa dora æriyaa
eyaa edaa enavayi kivvaaţa mokada, aave nææ
taattaa epayi kiyaddi lamayaa gahaţa næggaa
epayi kiyana koţa eyaa tavat væḑi
maŋ hitanavaa dæn koocciya yannat æti
epayi kiyalat lamayaa ee kolee iruvaa
eyaa Gaalu yanna kiyalaa giyaa, samaharaviţa hate koocciya allanna æti
meeka paara kiyalaa hitanna ko
Gaalu koocciya kiyalaa lamayaa Nuvara koocciyaţa nægalaa

1. This word is rather dialectical.

ammaaṭayi taattaaṭayi kiikaruva inna oonæ kiyalaa ee vayasaka guruvarayaa apiṭa kivvaa
taattaa ada iskoolee enavayi kiyalat aave nææ
raa kiyalaa dænadæna ee minihaa ee bonne tee kiyakiyaa bivvaa
parakku velaa æti kiyalaa maŋ hituvaa
koocciya kiiyaṭada kiyalaa mahattayaa dannavaa ædda?
eka velaavakaṭa maṭa hitenavaa ee minihaaṭa ee væḍeeṭa læbena salli huňgak væḍiyi kiyalaa
ee pota maŋ kiyavalaa tiyunaaṭa, livve kavda kiyalaa maṭa mataka nææ
guruvarayaa dænaŋ hiṭiyaa ee lamayaa nitarama hariyaṭa boru kiyanavayi kiyalaa
taattaa mee dæn kiṭṭuvaṭa gihin ennam kiyalaa giyaa. ṭikak inna, tava ṭikakin eyi
etakoṭa maŋ hitaagattaa eyaa ena ekak nææ kiyalaa
iskoolee gihin væḍiya duvanna paninna yanna epayi maŋ oya lamayaaṭa kii særayak kivvaada!
mahattayaa enavayi kiyalaa maŋ huňgak velaa balaŋ hiṭiyaa
mama ikmanaṭa kiyalaa aavaaṭa, magadi bas-eka kæḍilaa parakku vunaa
ee gollange gedara aluten saayam gaanavaa kiyalaa ṭika davasakaṭa ape dihaave inna aavaa
mee geḍi talalaalu rasa
rasayi kiyakiyaa lamayaa siini okkoma kanna hadanavaa
siini ṭikak væḍiyi kiyalaa siiyaaṭa ee tee kooppee epaalu
mage deyak kiyalaa tiyenne meccaramayi
kaar hadanavaa balanna kiyalaa maŋ iiye Nuvaraṭa giyaa
ee gahen væṭena am̌ba ahulaŋ enna kiyalaa poḍi lamayaa divuvaa
aanḍuven etana geyak gahanna iḍa denne næhællu
sissayaa guruvarayaa kiyana kiyana hæṭiyaṭa karanne nææ
ee mahattayaa heṭa Tirikunaamaleeṭat yana hæṭiyak mee liyumen penenavaa
kaamaren yanna kiyapu hæṭiyen maŋ dænagattaa eyaaṭa taraha gihillaa bava
ee mahattayaa ape dihaave inna ena bava maŋ danne adayi
eyaa kivve okkoma boru bava maṭa dæn vissaasayi

ee bava maŋ veelapahin dannavaa

Kolam̆ba mee davasvala vahina bava maʈa naŋgi kiyalaa evalaa tiyunaa

ape guruvarayaa davalʈa kææma kanna enavayi kiyapu bava maʈa dænuyi matak vune

45 mee sissayaa iskoolee ena koʈa pot araŋ enne næti bava kiyalaa guruvarayaa taattaaʈa liyumak yavanavaalu

B. The child says (he) needs a coloured pencil

Why do you sometimes not want to eat rice?

The child says (he) can't go to school

Father is telling that boy not to go to school to-day

5 Mother and father said (they) would come to school to see me to-morrow

The man says (he) doesn't want (any) money for that job

That gentleman says (he) must get a good servant

Father says (he) will go to Galle too to-morrow

That gentleman says (he) will come your way to-morrow, daughter

10 The boy says (he) can't come with us

The boy says (he) needs money to get a book sent (to him)

I wonder whether that gentleman came to work yesterday or not

See if the watch is still working

Put on this blouse ('jacket') and see if it fits

15 Though he said (he) would come, (he) didn't

They also now understand that this money is insufficient for that job

Ask that child what time (his) father goes to work each morning

Say I've gone to work

Look, it says in this paper that from to-morrow many goods are going up in price

20 I can't understand how this could have happened

Tell father I've arrived

The child is falsely telling his father that someone has come to see (him)

A gentleman is asking if father has got home

Look and see why smoke is coming from that room

25 He may think I've spoken falsely

Mother must have put salt in the tea thinking it was sugar: so (we) can't drink it

Uncle came to-day, stayed a little while, and went (away) saying he'd come again to-morrow

Mother went to the shop just a little while ago saying she'd get a pound of meat

I hear he has to go to Galle very early to-morrow morning

30 The fish merchant says he can't give fish on credit

I will tell father that elder brother hit (me)

(He) says he's bought a new house and is asking us to come and see (it)

This child is sometimes very naughty

Mother and daughter went into the jungle to collect firewood

35 The boys went home even before school ended, saying the teacher told (them) to go

The child ate all the meat, saying (he) was hungry

I've been looking at one of **last week's** papers all this time, thinking it was today's paper

According to what it says in the paper, it's to-morrow that they return to Ceylon

He left in order to go to Galle

40 As soon as the pen fell, I picked it up

Father explained to me yesterday how to drive a car

That boy still doesn't really know how fish is cooked

Elder sister is explaining to younger sister how to scrape coconuts

From the way the boy eats (his) food one can say (he) isn't hungry

45 Do you know how Ceylon people cook rice?

Notes:

A. 1 See n. on 7 A 4.

2 See n. on mahattayaage, 7 A 21. According to context, however, many sentences of this type can be interpreted in a different way also; e.g. here we may translate either 'That man says there is nothing he cannot do' or 'He says there is nothing that that man cannot do'. So e.g. B 3 below (which is ambiguous in English).

3, 4 See lesson 25 **d**. kiyalaa is not essential here.

5 **æyida** is sometimes used instead of **æyi kiyalaa**.

6 **maŋ hitanne** is often used parenthetically, 'I think'. hitanavaa is also possible here, and hitanne in 11 below.

7 kiyana koṭat or kiyaddi.

10   tavat væḍi (i.e. tavat karanavaa/keruvaa væḍi), or **tava tavat karanavaa**, 'he does (it) still more'.

11   yannat æti, 'may actually have gone'.

12   epayi kiyalat, 'though he had been told not to'; independent absolutive, as also in 28, 30, 32 below. Cf. **epayi kiyana koṭat** which shows a simultaneousness, 'although he was being told not to'.

13   Gaalu yanna kiyalaa, 'saying (it was) to go to Galle', i.e. saying that he was going to Galle. **yannam** and **yanavayi** are also possible here with little difference of sense. hate koocciya, the 7 o'clock train.

14   'Pretend this is the road', 'Let's say this is the road'; said e.g. when drawing a map of the way somewhere. (Note incidentally that there is no Sinh. equivalent for the Eng. word 'pretend').

15   kiyalaa, i.e. kiyalaa hitaagana.

16   ammaaṭayi taattaaṭayi – always in this order in Sinh.   va is necessary here, see lesson 17 **b**.

18   The repetitious **bivvaa** is against the Eng. idiom. In Sinh., **kiyakiyaa hiṭiyaa** is also possible here.

19   æti or **æteyi** (= æti + yi). 'That (I) must be late'.

21   væḍiyi (pron. [væḍii], see Introd.) – the lengthening is usually audible here.

23   dænaŋ hiṭiyaa: this periphrasis is common in Sinh., and is often rendered into Eng. as 'was knowing'. **hariyaṭa** should be taken with **boru**, not with **nitarama** (but **hari boru** is not possible).

24   ennam or enavaa, but **not** eyi. Pronounce (ṭikəkiŋŋey]. kiṭṭuva = a nearby place.

26   iskoolee gihin or iskooleedi. In Eng. we must say 'when he gets to school'. yanna: much as in Eng. 'mustn't **go** running and jumping about'. oya lamayaa = you.

27   enavayi or eyi. maŋ balaŋ hiṭiyaa, 'I waited'. It can also mean 'I have been waiting', but in that case we must say **ena kan** instead of **eyi kiyalaa**.

28   ikmanaṭa kiyalaa = ikmanaṭa enna kiyalaa hitaagana, 'thinking it wouldn't take me long'. kæḍilaa = broken down.

29   gollange: see n. on 2 above. ṭika davasakaṭa = for a few days.

30   **talanavaa** of fruits is to press them gently. This is often necessary with

certain fruits such as **uguræssa**. rasa, not **rasayi** here, because of the **-lu** (lesson 9 **e**).

32 kiyalaa: here it is the grandfather who says, not the speaker.

33 'This is all that can be called mine'. The same sense is given by a dative case, mage deekaṭa tiyenne meccaramayi – or just mageyi kiyalaa tiyenne meccaramayi. here **ma** represents 'only'.

34 hadanavaa = repair. There is no necessary implication of dishonesty in such sentences; kiyalaa = 'for the purpose of', not only 'with the excuse of'.

36 aanḍuven iḍa denne nææ, 'permission will not be given by the government', 'they won't give permission from the government'. One may also say aanḍuva iḍa denne nææ, 'the government will not give permission', though here **aanḍuva** must stand immediately before **iḍa**. **gahanna** (or **daanna**) here = hadanna.

37 hæṭiyaṭa: here the dative case corresponds to Eng. 'according to': 'the way the teacher says'.

38 Here **hæṭi** would mean 'that[1] he is going to T.', whereas **hæṭiyak** means 'as if he were going', i.e. it looks from the letter **as if** he were going.

39 yanna kiyapu – he said 'get out', as v. yanavayi kiyapu – he said 'I'm going'. gihillaa: see 23 A 17.

40 adayi, i.e. **only** today. danne is past here; 'I will find out' is **dænaganne**.

42 'I know that already'. Cf. **ee bava maŋ issara dænagena hiṭiyaa**, I used to know that once.

43 kiyalaa evalaa (see **b** above) = liyalaa, but liyalaa is less usual here. (Here **tiyunaa** can have the same meaning as **tiyenavaa** (she has written), see lesson 22 **c**.) Kolam̆ba or Kolam̆baṭa.

45 iskoolee ena koṭa – just **iskooleeṭa** would do, but such a periphrasis is normal in Sinhalese (cf. n. on 22 A 36). næti bava kiyalaa or næti bavaṭa.

B. 2 Sometimes: see **e** above.

3 Can't – or won't, see n. on 6 B 14.

7 Get – ganna.

---

1. Lit. 'how' (which can often be used in Eng. also in such cases).

9 See note on 21 B 6.

11 Get sent: gennanavaa (lesson 18 **a**). (Eng. 'get down' is widely used to mean 'import'.)

12 Wonder: see **a** above.

13 Working: translate literally.

14 Fits: say 'if it is right'. (Whereas 'suits' would be translated 'is good').

17 See lesson 18 **c**.

19 'It says': kiyalaa tiyenavaa.

20 Can't understand: say 'don't understand'.

24 Smoke is coming from = it smokes (impersonal) from. Look and see = (just) balanna.

26 So: see note on 19 A 3.

27 'While' = 'time' (pl.), or omit.

28 Just a little while ago = dæn ţikakaţa issellaa.

29 Very early: paandarama, paandarinma. huñgak paandara alone is insufficient without **-ma**.

30 Fishmerchant: see lesson 13 vocabulary.

32 Asking – kiyanavaa (note on 6 A 2).

34 Collect = pick up. Cooking in Ceylon is normally done on a wood fire on the ground surrounded by three large stones on which the pans rest. This is the **lipa** or hearth. **lipa pattu karanavaa**, to light the cooking fire, is the first duty of a woman in the morning.

35 Ended: see n. on 25 A 11. Even: here **-t** must be aded to the infinitive; if added to **issellaa**, the meaning will be 'also' (i.e some went before, and some after).

36 **ţika** is needed here, see lesson 14 **e**.

37 Last week's: use locative. To-day's: (just) ada. One of = a (i.e. **-k** suffix). All this = 'this much'.

38 According to: use **hæţiyaţa** with participle, cf. A 37 above. Return: (just) enavaa.

40 Picked up: in the past tense the compound with **-gannavaa** is preferred.

41 Explain: see 15 A 24.

42 Really = properly.

45 The word 'Ceylon' is often used adjectivally like this. In Sinhalese, however, a case-form is required.

LESSON 28

mahansiya	tiredness
pissuva	madness
hadissiya[1]	hurry; accident
nicciya	certainty
purudda	habit
ivaraya	end (n.)
bara	weight, heavy
nidi / **budi**	asleep
ninda	sleep (n.)
ginipeṭṭiya	matchbox, box of matches
ispiritaalee	hospital
haal	uncooked rice
ṣook	(general term of high approval)
antaraava	danger
ahaka	aside
ææta	far off
mææta	near by; recent
lañgadi	recently; soon
vena	other
anik	other
venasa	difference
dura	far, distance
kisi	any
misa / **misak** / **misaka**	except

1. Often written **hadisiya**, or **adisiya**.

ærenna / **æra**	except
virudda	(following dat.) against; opposed
ne, novæ	you know
purudu karanavaa	(with dat. of person) train
hinaa venavaa (more colloquially, **hinæhenavaa**)	laugh, smile

(a) The stem-forms **mahansi**, **pissu**, **hadissi**, **nicci**, **purudu** and **ivara** are used in the same way as kanagaaṭu etc. (Lesson 25 **g**).

apiṭa mahansi(yi)	we are tired
væḍa karana eka mahansiyi	working is tiring
oyaaṭa pissuda?	are you mad?
væḍee ivarayi	the job is finished
meeke ivarayak[1] nææ	there is no end to (lit. of) this
oyaaṭa hadissida?	are you in a hurry?
maṭa nicci nææ eeka gæna	I'm not sure about that
api eekaṭa puruduyi	we are used to that
maṭa eeka puruduyi	I've got used to that

pissu, hadissi and purudu can also be used as attributive adjectives before a noun.

pissu ballek	a mad dog
hadissi antaraavak	a 'sudden danger', an accident[2]
purudu kenek	a known person

bara is used like diga etc. (lesson 13 **c**).

(b) ne, novæ (also **nevæ**), which are always unstressed, are frequently added at the end of a phrase in expectation of confirmation by the listener; they are roughly equivalent to 'you know', often with apologetic overtones ('I'm afraid').

meeka bara væḍi ne (**ne** replaces **-yi**)	I'm afraid this is rather heavy

In questions, **ne** may virtually replace **da**.

taattaa yanavaa ne?	are you going, father? (surely you are).

---

1. Sometimes **ivarak**.
2. This expression is rather formal. **æksiḍaŋ-ekak** is more colloquial.

But frequently there will be no English equivalent at all. **novæ** must be carefully distinguished from **neveyi**, **nevi**.

mee tiyenne bat neveyi	this is not rice
mee tiyenne bat novæ	look, this is rice

(c) **æra** (in form an absolutive, 'having left') or **ærenna** (infinitive form) can be used after a noun to translate 'except' or 'besides'.

Joon æra anik okkomalaa game giyaa
everyone except John went to the village

Joonge æra vena anik okkomalaage pot pirisiduyi
everyone else's books are tidy except John's

mahattayaa ærenna vena kavda hiṭiye?
who else was (there) besides you?

ee ærenna
besides that, furthermore

misa, **misak**, **misaka** are usually used postpositionally in a more idiomatic fashion, which may correspond sometimes with Eng. 'but only', sometimes with 'although'. These words may sometimes be followed by **nætnam**, 'if not'.

eyaaṭa ammaa misak taattaa nææ
he has no father, but only his mother

api duppat misak api hoňda minissu
we are respectable folk although we are poor

These words can also be used after present or past tense verbal forms.

eyaa kanavaa misak bonne nææ
he is not drinking, but only eating

ganan ṭikakaṭa bæssaa misak aayi næggaa
prices have risen again, though they went down for a while

(d) **ʂook**, normally pronounced **ʃook**, is used adjectivally as a term of high approval: hari ʂook, very good. As a noun, it may mean 'pretentiousness'.

(e) **mææṭak** means 'a recent time': mææṭak vena kal, until recently. **mææṭa(ka)di** means 'recently'; so also does **laňga(ka)di**. laňgadi can however refer either to the past or to the future (and so can **aluten**, lesson 20). 'Far from' is expressed either with **iňdalaa** or with a dative case: Kolaňbaṭa ææṭin, far from Colombo.

(f) **kisi** (commoner in written language than in spoken), or **kisima**, is used in negative and sometimes in interrogative sentences. The noun which follows must have the **-k** suffix.

ee minihaa ada kisi væɖak keruve nææ
 he did not do anything to-day
mee gæna kisi kenekuʈa vat kiyanna epaa
 don’t speak of this to anyone

But in positive sentences, **oonæma** must be used for ‘any’ (Lesson 20 **c**).

(g) **vena** (also **venin**) means ‘other(s) in a different category’, **anik**[1] means ‘other(s) in the same category’. Thus vena ekak, a different one; anik eka, the other one. anik may however always be preceded by vena after æra.

venas (stem-form of venasa) is used predicatively to mean ‘different’. oovaa venas, those are different. ‘Some other day’ is **aayet davasaka**.

venama means ‘separate’.

A. meeka mona vidihe ekak kiyalaa hituvaada?
mee lamayaa tavama hæmadaama daval vena kan nidaagannavaa ne
ape kaar-eka elavana minihaa ada ʂook-ekaʈa æñdagana ævit tiyenavaa
hadissi antaraavak velaa ee lamayaava ispiritaaleeʈa genihin tiyenavaa
ee iskoolee vahalaa daanavaaʈa mee minissu hari viruddayi
maŋ yana koʈa taattaa kantooruve baraʈa væɖa
puŋci malli nidiyana kaamaree kotanada?
eyaa budiyanna misak gedara enne nææ
edaa maŋ rææ velaa gedara ena koʈa taattaa nidi
api degolla vena venama inne, ekaʈa nemeyi
mee lamayaa dæn issaraʈa vaɖaa huñgak venas velaa
mee kaamara deke diga-palalin æra vena kisima venasak nææ
mee pota guruvarayaa kiyapu ekaʈa vaɖaa venas
ohoma ekak karanna mahattayaaʈa pissu væhilaa venna oonæ
malli bas-eke gihillaa tavama purudu nææ
purudu vidiyakaʈa tee-eka hadalaa geenna
mæætakadi eyaava maʈa hamba velaa nææ
mæætakadi iñdaŋ ee mahattayaa hæmadaama kantooru enne nææ
maŋ ookaʈa hari ʂook væɖak karannam ko
ee minihaage boru ʂook maʈa allanne nææ
siiyaa kiyannema hari hinaa yana kataa
taattaa Nuvara gihin ævillaa mahansi kiyalaa budi

---

1. Also **anit**.

eyaa nikamma giyaa misak kohe yanavaada kiyalaa nemeyi giye
ee minihaaṭa alut kaar-ekak tiyenavayi kiyalaa dæn hariyaṭa ṣook karanavaa
25 maṭa penena hæṭiyaṭa siiyaaṭa pissu kiyalaa hituvaaṭa pissu nææ
kaar-eka bas-eke hæppilaa ara væṭat kaḍaagana metanaṭama aavaa
maat nogihin inna eka hoňda nææ
nivaaḍu tiyena tiyena hæṭiyaṭa ee lamayaa apit ekka inna enavaa
nivaaḍuvaṭa gihin ena koṭa mee gahe geḍi hædilaa tiyeyi
30 otana mage potakut æti, eeka maṭa diilaa inna
taattaa væḍak kiyalaa dæn enna bææ kiyanavaa (kiyalaa) kiyanna
maŋ eyaava pintuurayak balannat ekka ekka-yanavaa
ee gollo ena koṭa ekat ekaṭa hændææ veyi
ekat ekaṭa mee pota iruvet ee lamayaa venna oonæ
35 Maḍakalapu yannat ekka pæṭrol tiyenavaada?
maŋ eeken væḍa araŋ ivarayi
gedarin ganan hadaagana aave nææ kiyalaa guruvarayaa lamayaaṭa gæhævvaa
pattaree kiyavalaa, nikam puṭuva uḍa daalaa yanne nætuva, hoňdaṭa navalaa meesee uḍin (araŋ) tiyalaa yanna
mee almaariyat atanin tibbaama kaamaree lassanaṭa tiyeyi
40 iiye ee gollange paara digaṭama kaar gahalaa tiyunaa

B. Younger sister has finished scraping the coconuts, she says
We have all now finished drinking (our) tea
Where did father hurry off to early this morning?
The boy has run off to the shop near by to get a pound of sugar, as the sugar is finished
5 The letter from Ceylon may have come from (my) father
This box is too heavy for me to lift, you know
What do you weigh?
I've finished reading that book now
The rice in the shop is (all) finished, so I've brought bread instead
10 That man must be mad to do such a thing
At the moment I am teaching younger brother to drive
How far is it from here to Galle?

Who is that man coming far away over there?

Is it very far to school from (your) home?

15 Your new book is very fine, you know

Seeing the old man fall down, the little child laughed heartily

The mangoes that were brought that day can't be eaten at all

Except for two or three of those coconuts, (you can) take away all the others

It is not possible to earn money here without working

20 When you get there they will all have been sold

When you have finished reading (it) fold up the paper and put it away

It must have been when that boy dropped it that that pen got broken

I saw you getting into the train to go to school

But the car may break (down) on the way

25 I saw this man stealing our things through the car window

Let's have tea after we get home

Did you see that man being run over?

The shops in our part will be shut after 12 tomorrow morning

Father must be asleep; don't make too much noise

30 Buying goods from the shop on credit is not very good

Saying the mangoes had gone bad, mother threw (them) all away

According to what he says, what's in the paper is all untrue

I believe the goods in that shop are cheaper than those in this shop

From the way (he) laughs I can tell who it is

35 When I arrived, he had gone

Do you think it will rain today?

The child went to the shop saying he would get a box of matches

It's a good thing (you) woke me up early

From the way (he) drives the car (you) can say he is still a learner

40 The boy is crying (and) saying he's lost (his) new watch

Notes:

A. 1 kiyalaa hituvaada or kiyalaada hituve – but **not** ekakda kiyalaa hituve, cf. 18 B 16 note.

2 daval vena kan, 'till late'. **daval** means any time up to about 3.00 p.m., but to stay in bed 'late' may mean say till 8.00 a.m. (see n. on 22 A 33).

3 ʂook-ekaʈa, adverbial = grandly.

4 Subject indefinite, 'they' (or it can be translated passively, cf. Lesson 13 **a** for **-va**). For the detached absolutive, cf. 20 A 25.

5 hari or hariyaʈa. This refers to a **proposed** closure: **dæmmaaʈa** would refer to a closure already accomplished.

6 baraʈa væɖa, 'heavily engaged'. Cf. 5 A 19; **baraʈa** is adverbial.

7, 8 nidiyana, budiyanna – from verbal forms **nidiyanavaa**, **budiyanavaa**, to sleep, which use past tense-forms **nidiyaagattaa**, **budiyaagattaa** (**nidiyævvaa** is dialectical). 'I went to sleep' is **maʈa ninda giyaa** (as v. maŋ nidaaganna giyaa, I went to bed).

9 rææ velaa = late; see note on 20 A 33.

10 api degolla = our two families. **vena venama** is adverbial here, 'separately'; **ekaʈa** = together.

11 Notice that 'different from' is in Sinhalese 'different (more) than'. **issara hiʈiyaaʈa vaɖaa** is also possible.

12 diga-palalin (or diga-palala) is more usual than digin palalin. Notice that 'the difference between' may be 'the difference of' in Sinh. (Lesson 29 **c**).

13 kiyapu: 'mentioned' (21 B 15).

14 **pissu væhenavaa** (to be 'mad-covered') is the common phrase (**pissu væʈenavaa** is also used, but without the dative case). ohoma ekak (or ohoma væɖak), such a thing. ehema, mehema etc. can be used adjectivally: eeka ehemayi, that is so.

15 purudu usually follows an absolutive, and not an infinitive or dative verbal form (to be used **to doing** something).

16 purudu vidiyakaʈa = as (you) usually do ('in an accustomed way') – nothing special.

18 mæætakadi or mæætaka. iňdaŋ is required here although in Eng. we say 'recently he hasn't been coming'.

19 ookaʈa hari ʂook væɖak = an ideal reply to that, just the thing. It does not mean 'to do a very fine job of work on that', for which we should rather have to say **ooka hari ʂook-ekaʈa karanavaa**.

20 boru ʂook = false pretences. allanavaa, Lesson 19 **b**.

21 kiyannema = always says. hinaa yana (not **hinaa vena** here) = at which laughter goes, i.e. which cause laughter.

23 kohe yanavaada, see Lesson 27 **a**.

24 ʂook karanavaa = boasts. For the case-ending in **minihaaʈa**, see n. on 7 A 21.

26 metanaʈama = right up to here.

27 See Lesson 9 **d** for the difference between **maat** and **mama vat**.

28 nivaaɖu tiyena tiyena hæʈiyaʈa = whenever he has holidays.

29 hædilaa tiyeyi = will be formed, will have come.

32 See Lesson 17 **c**. pintuuree means a film here.

33 hændææ: stem-form. ekat ekaʈa, 9 A 27.

34 iruvet – i.e. not to mention other damage.

35 Maɖakalapu: stem-form.

36 'I have finished with that': lit. I have got the work from that and am finished. **ivara** often follows an absolutive in this way.

37 gedarin or gedaradi. This is a normal way of saying 'he hadn't done his maths homework'.

38 araŋ tiyanavaa = put away, put in a safe place. Cf. tiyalaa tiyanavaa, to keep, store (19 A 27).

40 gahalaa = parked. (Cf. 20 A 16 for another meaning). digaʈama = all along.

B. 1, 2 Cf. A 36 above.

3 Hurry off = go hurriedly. Early: see 12 A 5 note.

4 As the sugar is finished: say 'the sugar being finished'. 'The shop near by': either lañga tiyena kaɖee or mee lañga kaɖee. Has run off: 'Has gone to run-and-come'.

5 The letter from Ceylon: Laŋkaaven liyuma is sufficient here.

7 'How much is your weight?'

9 Say 'instead **of it**' (**ee**, not eevaa; cf. n. on 19 B 17. So ee nisaa, ee kiʈʈuva, ee vage, ee vitarak, ee ærenna).

10 Cf. A 14 above, and 19 A 1 note.

11 At the moment = 'in these days'. Teaching = training. Say 'to drive cars' or 'a car'.

13 Far away: loc. or instr.

16 Down: say 'on the ground' and see note on 26 A 21. Heartily: hayiyenma.

18   Two or three: dekak tunak (not detunak).

21   See notes on A 36 and A 38 above.

22   Dropped: say 'when it fell from that boy's hand' (see Lesson 13 **a**): here **vætunaama** will imply that it did fall, while **vætilaa** implies a possibility.

25   Through: use instr. case. 'To look out of the window' is **janeelen balanavaa**.

28   Twelve in the morning is **daval dolaha**. 11 a.m. however can be **udee ekolaha**.

29   To make a noise = **sadda karanavaa** (stem-form).

30   Very: væḍiya or eccara.

31   viisi keruvaa or ahaka dæmmaa (but **ahak keruvaa** means 'removed' and **ahakaṭa dæmmaa**, 'put aside'. For pronunciation of ahakaṭa see n. on Lesson 4 **d**).

32   See note on 27 B 38. **boru** is a noun, so **-yi** is not required.

33   I believe (in this sense) = maṭa hitenavaa. maṭa vissaasayi would mean 'I insist on believing, I really trust that it is true'.

39   Be a learner = **purudu venavaa**.

40   Lost: see n. on 21 B 31.

LESSON 29

raṭa	country
baya	fear
sapattuva	shoe
kakula	leg, foot
gaňga	river
polisiya	police, police-station
paalama	bridge
tæpæl kantooruva	post office
pansala	(Buddhist) temple
vedaa (pl. **veddu**) **vedamahattayaa**	ayurvedic doctor
pilivela	order, method
hariya	area, extent
magula	festivity
sidda venavaa	happen
paṭangannavaa (abs. paṭangena or paṭan araŋ)	begin
kaalee **kala**	time
taniyama **taniyen(ma)**	alone
pahala **pallehaa**[1] **pahata**	down
ihala **uḍaha**	up
idiriye **idiripiṭa**	in presence of

1. Also written **palleha**, but pron. **-ha**, not **-hə**.

epiṭaha	further off
piṭa	outside; top, back
piṭapætta	the outside
piṭipasse	behind
passaṭa	backwards
atara **atare**	among; between
etara **egoḍa**	that side
metara **megoḍa**	this side
ehaa	that side
mehaa	this side
egoḍaha	on that side

(a) **Conditions**. Each verb has a conditional form which can be arrived at by substituting **-ot** or **-otin** for **-aa** in the past tense form.[1] This form can be used of all persons, in conditions referring to the future.

keruvot	if (I, you, he) does
eyaa aavot hoñdayi	it will be a good thing if he comes

By substituting **-at** instead of **-ot**, a concessive meaning (even if, although) is given, referring to future or to past time.

giyat	although (I, you, he) go/went

The particle **nam** (usually realized as **naŋ**) following a present or past tense verb also expresses a condition. The past tense here does not necessarily refer to past time, but only to the fact that the action will be completed before the result of the condition is realized.

eyaa ee vædee karanavaa / keruvaa] nam, salli læbenavaa

if he does (shall have done) that job, he will get paid

With the past tense **keruvaa**, the meaning can also be:

if he has done (did) that job, he will get paid

nam may also follow an absolutive in this way; **tiyenavaa** or **tiyunaa** can optionally be added. Here again the past tense **tiyunaa** will refer only to the completion of the action before the result is realized.

---

1. Occasionally **-tot** following the present tense stem, e.g. yatot (from yanavaa).

eyaa ee væḍee karalaa / karalaa tiyenavaa / karalaa tiyunaa] nam, ...

if he has done (proves to have done) that job...

bæri, not **bææ**, must be used before **nam**. **æti nam** becomes **ætnam**.

In unfulfilled conditions of the type 'If he had done that job, he **would have** got paid', the verb in the first part must be past tense, followed by **nam**; but the second part of the sentence is usually expressed vividly as a fact, 'he gets paid' (present tense). Such sentences therefore can be distinguished from the simpler type of condition above only by the context. Thus the sentence eyaa ee væḍee keruvaa nam, salli læbenavaa, besides the meanings given above, can also mean 'if he had done that job, he would have got paid'. In unfulfilled conditions, the verbal form in **-ot** is not possible.

nam, in this conditional sense, can also be found after other words in the conditional clause, where the verb is in the incomplete form. The word preceding **nam** here receives special emphasis.

eyaa nam meeka karalaa tiyenne,...

if it is he who has done this...

When **keruvot** or **karanavaa nam**, etc., are followed by **ehema**, the supposition is made less likely. The same effect is given by **nam** after **-ot**.

keruvot ehema / karanavaa nam ehema / keruvot nam] if (he) were to do

The conditional and concessive verb-forms (**-ot**, **-at**) can be negated by prefixing **no-**.

nokeruvot, nogiyat, naavot (contracted, cf. Lesson 5 **b**).

(b) The use of **tiyenavaa** and **innavaa** after absolutives has been explained in Lessons 19 and 22. After an infinitive, **tiyenavaa** in the present tense-form means 'have to, ought to' – the person concerned being either in the direct or in the dative case – and in the past tense-forms either 'had to', or (with dative case only of the person involved) 'could have'.

minihaaṭa / minihaa] eeka karanna tiyenavaa he is to do that

maṭa / maŋ] gedara yanna tiyunaa I had to go home

The sense here is of something previously prescribed.

maṭa gedara yanna tiyunaa — I could have gone home

innavaa after an infinitive means 'intend'; **hiṭiyaa** also means 'began'.

maŋ heṭa gedara yanna innavaa — I mean to go home tomorrow

but –

maŋ yana koṭa putaa aňḍanna hiṭiyaa

as I was leaving / arrived] the child began to cry

The meaning 'begin' is also given by **gannavaa** (paṭangannavaa, aragannavaa[1]) and sometimes by **venavaa** after an infinitive.

lamayaa aňḍanna gattaa / vunaa] — the child began to cry

uu duvanna aragattaa — the animal began to run

maŋ ehe yanna enna vunaa — I began to frequent the place

venavaa after an infinitive is also used in a way similar to **tiyenavaa** after an infinitive, but here the action is rather one which becomes desirable although not previously prescribed.

maṭa gedara yanna vunaa — I had to go home

sidda venavaa can also be used in this sense: maṭa[2] yanna sidda vunaa, (lit. it happened to me to go) I had to go.

læbenavaa following an infinitive can be translated 'get the chance, manage to'.

meevaa karanna apiṭa læbenne kavadaada?

when shall we get the chance of doing this?

(c) pahala, pallehaa, pahata, ihala and uḍaha are all nouns, and can take case-endings; pahatin tiyanna, keep (it) low, keep it down. **uḍaha** often has the special meaning of 'upcountry' or **uḍaraṭa**, i.e. the interior of Ceylon (not only the mountainous region): eyaa uḍahen, he is from the upcountry, uḍahaṭa vahinavaa, it is raining upcountry. pallehaa does not however mean 'low country', which is **pahata raṭa**. **pahalin** can be used postpositionally after a dative case in the sense 'down below', and similarly sometimes **ihalin**, 'above'.

vattaṭa pahalin

down below the plantation

---

1. Lesson 15 **a**.
2. Sometimes **maŋ**.

Compare

vatta pahala

in the lower part of the plantation

kanda pahalaṭa divuvaa

ran down the hill

galen pahalaṭa pænnaa

jumped down off the rock

The ending **-ha** or **-haa** (as in uḍaha, issaraha, pallehaa), which means 'area', also appears in **egoḍaha**, **epiṭaha**, and (in some districts), **yaṭaha**.[1]

api inne gaňgin egoḍaha

we live beyond the river

epiṭahaṭa karalaa tiyanna

put (it) further away

pallehaa] okkoma narak velaa
(yaṭaha[2])]

everything at the bottom has gone bad

idiriye, idiripiṭa (also issarahapiṭa), piṭipasse[3] and atara (among) are used post-positionally after direct[4] case-forms, and other case-endings are possible in the post-positional word.

maŋ Piiṭar idiriyaṭa aavaa[5]

I came before Peter (i.e. into his presence)

minihaa maŋ idiripiṭat kivvaa[5]

he said it in my presence too

almaariya/almaariyaṭa piṭipassen giyaa

(he) went behind the cupboard

meevaa atara

among these

idiriyaṭa also means 'in the future'.[5]

---

1. Also **passehaa**.
2. In this sentence, **yaṭaha** could also mean 'the inside part' (of a fruit).
3. For **passe** of time, see 25 **e** above. But in spatial contexts passe (or passen) also follows a direct case: eka ekkenaa passe ævidinavaa, chase after people, harak passe elavanavaa, chase cattle.
4. Or genitive of pronouns, as with issaraha (25 **e** above).
5. Here idiriye, idiripiṭa are formal language; idiriyaṭa is normal usage.

atara, atare (between) can also follow a pair of nouns in the dative case, if the difference is one of physical space.

iskooleeṭayi pansalaṭayi atara
between the school and the temple

In the case of a non-spatial distinction:

eekeyi meekeyi]
eekat meekat atara] venasa
the difference between this and that

piṭa (outside), egoḍa, megoḍa follow an instrumental case, and mehaa, ehaa usually follow a dative case-form (occasionally an instrumental case). Other case-endings are possible in the postpositional word.

Kolam̆bin piṭa	outside Colombo
paalamin megoḍa	this side of the bridge
api gañgin [egoḍaṭa giyaa / egoḍa vunaa	we [went across / crossed] the river
ee gollange gedaraṭa ehaa	beyond their house
tæpæl kantooruvaṭa ehaayin inne	(he) lives beyond the post office

piṭa is also used after a direct case in the sense 'on top of', but only either 1) when the same noun is repeated afterwards: ekak piṭa ekak, one on top of another, or 2) metaphorically, of responsibility: eevaa akkaa piṭin yaavi, this will all fall upon elder sister.

(d) **baya** is used like taraha (Lesson 23 **d**). The feared object is in the dative case.

maŋ bayayi eekaṭa	I'm afraid of that
api yanna bayayi	we are afraid to go
mage[1] loku bayak tiyenavaa ee gæna	I have a great fear of that
taattaaṭa baye / bayen / bayaṭa] maŋ eeka keruve nææ	I didn't do that for fear of father

But the English apologetic usage as in 'I'm afraid I can't' has no counterpart in Sinhalese.

(e) kaalee and kala usually represent a longer duration of time than velaava. Do not confuse **kaalee** with **kaala**, quarter. For **kalin**, see Lesson 26 **e**; **kalin kalaṭa** means

1. **maṭa** might be ambiguous here.

'from time to time' (also **særen særeeţa**). Phrases of this kind, consisting of a noun in the instrumental case followed by the same noun in some other case (usually dative), are quite common, e.g. **tænin tæna**, from place to place, **ţiken ţika**, little by little (18 A 3 note). The plural form **kal**[1] is often used: huňgak kal (or huňga kalak, see 16 A 9 note), for a long time.

(f) āyurvēda (the Science of Life) is a system of herbal medicine which flourishes side by side with 'western' medicine.

raţa is sometimes used to mean **'foreign** country'. eyaa raţa (or **piţaraţa**) gihin, he has gone abroad (not **raţaţa** here: Lesson 2 **a**); raţa luunu, foreign (imported) onions (also called **Bombe**[2] (= Bombay) **luunu**, as v. **ratu luunu**, red onions). uḍaraţa yanavaa (not uḍahaţa in this phrase) is 'to go upcountry'.

pansala, which literally means 'hall of cadjan' (woven coconut leaves), is strictly speaking the residence of the Buddhist monk (the 'incumbent') within the temple premises, but it is also used for the whole premises in general.

A. mage pææna oonæ nam dennam, hæbæyi eeka næti karanna vitarak epaa
usa lamayi passaţa vunot poḍi lamayinţat vena dee peneyi
malli nemeyi nam maŋ tava poḍḍen ee kaar-ekaţa ahu venavaa
vedaa ikmanaţa aavot leḍaa mærena ekak nææ
ehaa mehaa keruvot kooppee tiyena vatura bimaţa væţeyi
væţunot kiyalaa maŋ eeka allaagana hiţiyaa
adin heţin keruvot hoňdayi
væsse nætnam maŋ ada hændææavaţa ehe yanavaa
labana aňgaharuvaadaa Gaalu yanavaa nam maţat ee ekkama yanna oonæ
mahattayaa ispiritaaleeţa giyaa nam dostara melahakaţa hamba vunaa ne
meccara velaa hevvaa nam pææna hamba venna tibunaa ne
mee lamayaage væḍee, bat kææavaa nam nidaagattaa
taattaa senasuraadat væḍaţa yanna tiyena bava maamaa dænagena hiţiye nææ
polisiyaţa kivvat poḍi lamayaa baya næhælu
maţa dæn unnat ekayi malat ekayi

1. **kal** is also sometimes used instead of **kan**, until (Lesson 21 **b**).

2. Or Bombayi.

maŋ pallehaa
gaha uḍa inna lamayaaṭa pallehaaṭa bahinna kivvaaṭa ahanne nææ
uḍaha gedara gæænu lamayat yanne ee iskooleeṭamada?
ihalaṭa yanna yanna bima inna minissu peenne huňgaak poḍiyaṭa
20 puṭuvaka iňdaŋ pahalaṭa pænapæna ee lamayaa nitarama taniyenma sellam karanavaa
Laŋkaave idiriyaṭa monavaa monavaa veyida kiyalaa apiṭa hariyaṭa kiyanna bææ
ee lamayaa malli piṭa daalaa kaḍen tee bonna ammaagen salli illaagattaa
pattara ṭika ehaa mehaa karalaa balanna ee liyumat otanamada kiyalaa
paaṭin æra ee pot deka atara æti venasak maṭa peenne nææ
25 etanin api egoḍa vune huňgak amaaruven
mage kakulvalaṭa poḍi vædii mee sapattu
pilivelakaṭa væḍa karagana giyaama leesi
Laŋkaave magul gevalvala davasema kanna bonna tiyenavaa
lamayaa mage alut pææna kohe daanna ædda kiyalaa maṭa nicci nææ
30 gonaaṭa kanna denna tiyenavaa
ee hæṭiye væḍakda eeka? ehema karanna apiṭat tiyunaa
lamayaa karapu naraka væḍeeṭa taattaa bænnaa (vitarak) æti, gahannayi tiyune
mama hiṭiye ada udeema Kolam̆ba yannayi
giya saňdudaa maŋ Kolam̆ba yanna inna koṭa hayiyenma væssaa
35 kææma kaalaa maŋ Nuvara yannayi hiṭiye
maŋ meeka mahattayaaṭa denna(yi) hiṭiye
ee balalaa ape gedara hæmadaama enna hiṭiyaa
ena særee maṭa Avuruddaṭa gedara enna læbena ekak nææ
putaa iskoolee væḍa hoňdaṭa karana bava maṭa guruvarayaagen dænaganna læbunaa
40 Gaallaṭa mee davasvala vahinavaa æti

B. If (you're) not ready yet, (you) won't be able to get there in time
If (you) haven't brought (your) books, why have (you) come to school?
If the dog from the house above comes our way again, (I'll) drive (him) away

Father said if I did (my) school work well he would get me a wrist watch

5 If (you) are late, the front door may be shut

Write (it) down in case (you) forget (it)

If (she) knew I hadn't been to school today, mother would be angry

I will do so if you say

If you're going too, get in quickly

10 If (you) pour me (some) tea, I'll drink (it)

It would be a good thing if that boy studied his lessons a bit more

If (you) had come on the five o'clock bus, (you) would have seen me

If (you) posted the letter yesterday, he will get it tomorrow

What is there to do next?

15 Though the train drew out just as (I) got to the station, I managed to get on

The coconut trees in front of our house are all cut (down)

What page of the book have we got to now?

It's only the outside of these bananas which has gone bad

My book had fallen behind the cupboard

20 The doctor came to see the patient just a little while ago

I should like to join the police

The people in this country don't wear shoes much

Don't let that cat come anywhere near our house again

What a long time I've been waiting for you, ayurvedic doctor!

25 Only Siripaala is still to come

We have to go to Colombo early tomorrow morning, this matter is very urgent for me

If it rains, I'll stay at home tomorrow

I have to go home today or tomorrow

I have to send the goods to Colombo tomorrow

30 I still have to pay him Rs. 1/10 for this book

From next Monday I had better go to work every day by train

How many more to get into the bus?

I mean to go home tomorrow

Do you mean to come by car, or by bus?

35 Next August I intend to go to (my) village

Two children jumped into the road in front of the bus which had stopped

I could have gone to Galle and back too with the money it took just to get to the train (i.e. to the station)

In those days if I went out of the house I got beaten

From time to time I went to see how he was

40 The goods in this shop are not at all cheap

Notes:

A. 1 næti karanna vitarak epaa = just don't lose it.

2 vunot: see note on 22 A 11. **vena** here is a participle, from venavaa.

3 nemeyi = 'if it hadn't been for' (or **nohiṭiyaa**, if he hadn't been (there)).

4 The used of unadorned **vedaa**, instead of vedamahattayaa, shows that this is a general statement, 'if the doctor comes, the patient doesn't die'.

5 keruvot, cf. 8 A 13 note.

6 -ot kiyalaa is equivalent to Eng. 'in case'. 'In case it fell' ('saying (to myself) if it falls (, dear me!)'). Or the sentence may mean 'In case I fell'. allaagana (**pr**. [alla-gənə]) hiṭiyaa, 'held on to it'.

7 adin = by (within) today, i.e. today.

8 Probably refers to the future, but could also be an unfulfilled past condition, 'if it hadn't ...'

9 ee ekka(ma) = too. **ee** (see note on 28 B 9) is essential here, since ekka-yanavaa will otherwise be taken together ('I must take you'). labana = ena (cf. 25 A 14).

10, 11 vunaa or venavaa. The use of the past tense here is less usual, but more vivid.

11 meccara, cf. 27 B 27.

12 væḍee (here) = habit. The habit is expressed vividly by a finite verb, nidaagattaa. **nidaaganna eka(yi)** is also possible.

13 See 27 A 23.

14 The child says he's not afraid even if (you/we) tell the police. To make it clear if **-lu** referred to the opinions of someone other than the child, we could say **baya næteyi kiyanavaalu**.

15 unnat, malat are from irregular past tense forms of innavaa (lesson 5 **c**) and mærenavaa (13 A 6). ekayi = it is one, it is all the same.

16 'I am downstairs'. It is only in cities however that two-storeyed houses

('upstair houses') are common.

18 uḍaha gedara gææ̈nu lamayaa = the little girl from the house above, i.e. up the road. So **pahala gedara**, the house below. ee iskooleeṭa**ma** = to the **same** school.

19 ihalaṭa or uḍaṭa, upwards (but not uḍahaṭa here, which would give the sense 'further in, further up something'). yanna yanna = as (one) goes. An infinitive can often be doubled in this generalizing temporal sense: kal yanna yanna, as time passes/passed. huñgaak, emphatic for huñgak. poḍiyaṭa (adverbial), see 17 **a** 22 note.

20 pahalaṭa or pallehaaṭa.

21 monavaa monavaa = what various things; cf. also 20 A 8.

22 malli piṭa daalaa = putting (the responsibility) on (the back of).

23 **ma**, see 18 above.

24 æti (participial: lesson 25 **a**) or tiyicca, the difference **which exists** between them. ee pot deke venasak is also possible, cf. 28 A 12. paaṭin or paaṭa.

25 etanin, 'from that point', i.e. at that point. This sentence can also have a metaphorical meaning, 'we solved that problem with great difficulty'.

27 pilivelakaṭa = in an orderly manner, in the right order.

28 magul geval = weddings. davasema, see 19 A 19.

30 tiyenavaa = (we) have to, it's time to. This sentence can also mean 'there is (something) to give the bullock to eat'.

31 ee hæṭiye væḍak means 'something special'; cf. 24 A 31.

32 bænnaa æti = it's enough, i.e. it's **lucky**, that he only scolded him.

34 See note on 26 A 4.

37 hiṭiyaa = began to.

38 Avurudda, see note to 25 B 10.

B. 1 taama ... nætnam or dænma ... nuunot (= nu-vunot) are permissible collocations but the latter means 'If you don't get ready now'.

2 Why have you come: use past tense. **ævillaa æyi** is not possible (Lesson 19 **a**).

3 From = of.

5 Front door: see 25 B 28. The back door is **passe dora** or **pilikanne dora**.

6 In case: see A 6 above. Write **down** = liyaaganna.

7 Here **tarahayi** alone is insufficient – say 'ammaaṭa taraha yayi' (23 A

17), or 'ammaa taraha veyi'.

8 Say 'if you say, I will do so'.

9 This is not properly future; **-ot** should not be used.

11 Study: Lesson 23 **c**. It would be a good thing: 'it is good' is enough.

12 Seen: use hamba venavaa.

15 Managed to: Lesson 23 **a**.

16 In front of: say 'which were in front of'. Are cut down: use the volitive form kapalaa – otherwise the cutting would seem to be accidental.

17 Got: say 'come'.

20 Just: say 'now'. Say 'Mr. Doctor' (see note on 22 B 27). Ago: issellaa, not uḍadi, when such a short space of time is in question.

21 Join = be tied (involitive form).

22 The people in (or of) this country – the case-form alone will do here, no participle is necessary. Much: Lesson 16 **c** (not huŋgak).

23 Anywhere near our house = ape gee hariyakaṭa (vat), to the area of our house.

24 For you, ayurvedic doctor: say 'till ayurvedic doctor came' (Lesson 21 **b** and note on 7 A 25).

25 Is to come: tr. literally. tiyenne and inne are both possible here.

26 Urgent = hadissi.

30 See Lesson 13 **c**.

32 If this is translated literally, it sounds like a complaint; if innavaa or tiyenavaa is added (how many are (there) to), this is no longer so.

36 See Lesson 25 **e**.

37 It took – say 'which went', cf. 9 A 7.

38 I got (= used to get) beaten: (just) gahanavaa, (they) beat.

39 Went to see: balanna giyaa, or say 'went and saw', gihin bæluvaa.

40 As in B 22 above.

LESSON 30

sataa (pl. **sattu**)	animal
oluva	head
bæniyama	vest
lookee	world
yaaluvaa (stem form **yaalu**, friendly)	friend
bittaree	egg
talee	blade; nib
næva	ship
horaa (pl. **horu**)	thief; rascal
saappuva	shop
mala	flower
aapahu (pr. [aa-pahu], i.e. as two words)	back again (adv.)
vævenavaa	grow (intr.)
pipenavaa	blossom; rise (of food)
tattu karanavaa	knock (with dat. case); (slang) steal
gevenavaa	be worn, spent
ellanavaa	hang (tr.)
dusima	dozen
uttaree	answer
hakuru (pl.)	juggery
kiribat (pl.)	milk-rice
venaskama	difference; lack of respect
kavuru + da	who? (pl.)

(a) **hari** after an interrogative pronoun or adverb gives that word an indefinite positive sense, e.g. 'someone', 'somehow', etc. 'kavda hari' is not used; 'someone' is **kavuru hari**.[1] But in other case forms, kaaṭa hari, kaa ekka hari, etc. are used.

1. kavuru-da is also used instead of kavda when repeated; kavuru-kavuruda aave? 'who and who came?', i.e. which various people came?

mee kaage hari potak
this is a book of somebody's, somebody's book
mokak hari tiyeyi
there will be something left
monavaa hari bonna
drink something
kohoma hari karalaa enna
contrive to come (lit. 'do somehow and come')
eyaa kohe hari gihin
he has gone somewhere
kavadaa hari ape dihaave enna
come our way some day
ætule kavuru hari innavaa
there's someone inside
kavuru hari dannavaada?
does somebody (anybody) know?

Some interrogative words have this same sense when followed by **-da** but used with a **complete** verb-form or its equivalent.

kavda enavaa	someone is coming
(but kavda enne?	who is coming?)
taattaa koheda gihin	father has gone somewhere
(but taattaa [kohe gihinda? / koheda gihin tiyenne?	where has father gone?)
monavaada gæna	about something or other
(but monavaa gænada?	what about? (lesson 8 **d**))
kavda ævillaa	somebody has come
(but kavda ævit inne?	who has come?)

-do is more colloquial than **-da** here.

mokakdo peenavaa	something is visible, (I) see something
kavdo aavaa	someone came

Interrogative words followed by final **-t** instead of **-da** usually have a universalized positive significance, and in positive sentences can be translated 'everyone', 'everything', etc. The corresponding negative sentences usually contain **vat** (see Lesson 9 **d**). **vat** is really an old concessive verb-form from **venavaa**, equivalent to **vunat** which often replaces it, and meaning 'though it be'. But where a final vowel is followed by **vat**, such words are often realized, and sometimes written, as if ending in simple **-t**. **namut** is sometimes used instead of **vat**.

For **kohetma** and **koccaravat**, which have special meanings, see Lessons 12 and 17. kavuru, kavadaa and monavaa sometimes insert a **k** before **vat**: kavuruk vat,[1] kavadaak vat, monavak vat (pr. [kavurukkat], [kavədakkat] etc.) This **-k** is sometimes **written** as -t.

kavurut dannavaa	everybody knows
kavurut vage dannavaa	almost everybody knows
(but kavdat ehema kiyalaa tiyunaa	someone (had) said so)
mee vatte kohet mal pipilaa	the flowers are blooming everywhere in this garden
eyaa kavadat ohomamayi	he is always (every day) like that
eevaa kookat / monavat] hoňdayi	they are all good
eevaa kohe vat / (kohet)] nææ	they are not anywhere
etana kavuru vat / kavurut / kavuruk vat[1]] nææ	there is no one / not anyone] there
kookat / monavat[2]] hoňda nææ	none are good
kohoma vat / kohomat / kohetma / kohoma namut] bææ	it's altogether (lit. in every way, in any way) impossible
meesee uḍa mokavat[2] / mokut, mukut[2] / mokak vat / monavat[2]] nææ	there is nothing on the table

1. Or **kavuruvak vat**; cf. also **bæri velaavak vat** for **bæri velaa vat**.
2. Note these forms: **monavat** arises from **monavaa vat**.

ohoma ekak api	kavadaa vat kavadaak vat	dækalaa nææ

we have never seen such a thing

In questions, interrogative words followed by **-t** can be translated in either of these ways (e.g. 'everyone' or 'anyone'), according to the context.

kavurut dannavaada?

does anybody know? **or**
does everybody know?

mee koyivat denna puluvanda?

can (you) give (me) all these?

ee gedara koyivat hoňda nædda?

isn't there anything good in that house?

hari can often be added after **vat** or **-t**.

taattaa	mokavat mokut	hari kivvaada?

did father say anything?

When interrogative words are followed by a concessive verb-form in **-at**, we should translate 'whoever', 'whatever', etc. Here again **kavuru** is used in place of **kavda**.

kavuru hiṭiyat maṭa ekayi

whoever may be there, it's all the same to me (cf. 29 A 15)

kohe giyat vædak venne nææ

wherever (he) goes, it won't do any good

koccara keruvat oya ṭika tamayi

however much (one) does, this is the only reward (lit. 'this little itself' – a common phrase in this sense)

koovaayin gattat kamak nææ

it doesn't matter which ones you take (it) from

Interrogative words meaning **who** or **what**, followed by **-t (-da)** or **hari,** can also be used **with a noun form**; if the interrogative word stands first, the noun (if singular) is in the indefinite form. Study the following:

sissayo kavurut dannavaa

all the pupils know, the pupils all of them know

yaaluvo kavuru hari innavaada?

are there any friends here?

kavuru hari yaaluvek / yaaluvo] innavaada?

is / are] there any friend(s) here?

kavda minihek aavaa

some man or other came

mokakda koocciyak aavaa	some train or other came in
mokakda ekak peenavaa	something is visible
geval kooket	in every house
moka(k) hari potak / kooka(k) hari potak / potak mokak hari	some book or other
pot monavaa hari tiyenavaada?	are there any books (here)?
vatura mokut tiyenavaada?	is there any water?
monavaa hari deyak	something or other
salli koccara(k) dunnat / koccara(k) salli dunnat	however much money (you) give

Notice the repetition in

eevaa mona-monavat / moka-mokavat] araŋ enna — bring some of those things

Notice that **hari** and **-t** are not used immediately after the simple adjectival forms **koyi**, **mona**; but koyi can be followed by a noun (definite or indefinite) with these suffixes.

koyi geṭat / koyi geekaṭat	to every house
koyi kavurut	(absolutely) everybody

The **vat** which appears instead of **-t** in negative sentences of this type is possible also in a conditional phrase.

metana mokak vat potak / pot mokak vat] nææ — there is no book at all here

(Compare Lesson 10 A 26, above)

kuḍayak vat / hari] mokak vat / hari] araŋ aavot hoňdayi — please bring an umbrella or something

(b) **tiyaa** ('having placed') can be used after nouns or after verbal tense-forms to represent 'not to mention'. Notice the difference between æra and tiyaa.

Joon tiyaa Maaʈin vat hiʈiye nææ
even Martin wasn't there, not to mention John
Tissaʈa tiyaa lookee kaaʈa vunat ohoma ekak kiyanna epaa
you mustn't say such things to **anybody** (in the world), let alone to Tissa
potak liyanavaa tiyaa liyumak vat liyanna puluvanda?
never mind about a book, can you even write a letter?

(c) **bæniyama** is an undershirt, but is frequently worn in Lanka without anything over it. It is called in English a 'banian'.

Juggery (also written jaggery) is a kind of sugar obtained from the **kitul** palm-tree. Toddy (Lesson 15 **d**) is also obtained from this tree.

'Milk-rice' is cold rice which has been cooked in milk, and sticks together in a lump. It is often eaten at breakfast time, and is reckoned rather a delicacy.

saappuva is a shop of urban type, more substantial than kaɖee.

A. mee puʈuva kohoma vat hadanna bææ
kaar-eke vena kaaʈa vat enna iɖa næti ekaʈa maŋ monavaa karannada?
tava kiidenekda innavaa kivvaa, needa?
viiduruven vatura yanavaa nam kotanin hari biňdilaa æti
onna ohe bæniyamaʈa uɖin monavaa hari daagena enna
ee gollo mahattayaaʈa mokut venaskamak ehema keruvaada?
mage sapattuva ætulaʈa mokekda satek gihin
iskooleeʈa aava alut guruvarayaa hoňda bava sissayo kavurut dannavaa
apiʈa kookat ekayi
mahattayaa kaar-ekenda kohomada enavaa kivvaa
akkaa magul gedara yanavaada koheda
koccara hoňdaʈa væɖa keruvat ee mahattayaa maʈa salli denne ʈikayi
dora vahalaa inna, kaaʈa vat æhenne næti venna
maŋ gaava tiyicca hæma deyakma eyaa illaagattaa
eyaa kivva koyivat boru
mee davasvala væɖa karalaa ivarayak nææ, hæmadaama kavuru hari enavaa kantooruvaʈa maava hamba venna
maŋ kantooru gihin inna koʈa maava hamba venna gedaraʈa ehema kavurut aavaada?
putaada kavdat aavaa

guruvarunṭa kaaṭat mee davasvala nivaaḍu
mokak hari ekak uḍaṭa naginne nætuva mee pintuuree ellanna maŋ usa madi
koocci kooket minissu pirilaa
mee baaldiyen vatura yanne næti venna monavaa hari karalaa denna puluvanda?
oya parana pot ṭika allalaa kohaaṭa hari viisi karalaa daanna
maṭa kookaṭat tiyenne meccarayi
taattaa, nayaṭa mokut denna bæriyi kivvaa kiyalaa kaḍakaarayat ekka taraha velaa
vatura enavaada kohomada danne nææ
koocci kohomaṭa vunat, bas tiyenavaa
ahaka daana monavat tiyenavaa nam maṭa denna
kiri monavak vat oonæda?
malli enavaada koheda, kaar-eke saddee æhenavaa
eyaaṭa kaar tiyenavaa, geval tiyenavaa – maṭa ee kookak vat nææ
diipu okkomat eyaa aapahu illaagattaa
bittara dusimakda koccarada genat
yanna aave kohe vat, yævune kohe vat
hoñda hoñda tæn kohaaṭat api giyaa
eeka paareda koheda væṭilaa
mahattayaa rupiyal panahak kohoma vunat, dahayak deyi
kana eka kohoma vunat, bona eka boyi
vahinnada koheda enavaa, malli naannada koheda giyaa
iskoolee yanna venavaaṭa lamayaa taattaaṭa loku boruvak hadaŋ aavaa
eyaa sapattu æñdalat maŋ eyaaṭa vaḍaa usayi
una ehema tiyenavaa nam lamayaaṭa hulaŋ gæhenna denna epaa
mee leḍaa væḍi kal allanne nææ
ævit balana koṭa kaar-eka horu araŋ
mee pæænaṭa dæn talayak nodaa bææ

B. Somebody has taken my new pen
No one else except him does this sort of thing
Didn't (he) say (he) was going somewhere else besides Trinco?
It's not possible to do this job in any other way, this is the only way there is

5 It's a good thing there was no one there at that time
Sir, do that for me somehow
There was no one (there) except John
The door may be shut when (you) get here. When (you) knock at the door, someone will come and open it
He's asking if there isn't something to put on his hair after (his) bath
10 Though tea is poured out, there's no one to drink it
Such a thing wouldn't happen to anyone but Tissa
Did anyone come after I left?
Had anyone arrived at the office before father?
Someone has brought a large lorry and parked it in front of our house
15 Something has fallen down near your chair (, I believe)
Tell father someone's come
Is father at home, (or) has he gone somewhere?
I heard the dog growl at someone and came to see
So far, no one else in the house knows that I broke that plate
20 Grandfather has brought mangoes or something
All (my) younger brothers still go to school
All the goods in this shop are cheap
(There are) chairs everywhere in the room
Grass has grown all over the yard
25 How much do (you) want for all this?
All my friends are respectable, but poor
Everyone in this bus is for Galle
Every house has doors and windows
The child has gone to the shop without telling anyone at home
30 Someone else must have written that
(He) won't sell at any price
I can't come today at all. I have work (to do)
The child cries all the time
No answers to anything (we) ask!
35 I don't want that book at any price
Some gentleman has come
I don't take any account of him at all
Father said (he) was going somewhere early tomorrow morning

That's uncle or someone coming over there

40 When I arrived today, school had begun

That ship is not going (but) coming

That car is just like a ship

The two back tyres are extremely worn

Juggery is good with milk-rice

45 Who is (your) latest child like, mother or father?

Notes:

A. 2 enna could be omitted.

3 '(You) said there were some more people, didn't you?' **needa** = n'est-ce pas?

4 Cf. 16 A 26.

5 **onna ohe** (pr. [oŋŋohe]) is an idiomatic expression which may be translated 'just' (cf. 7 A 10 note). monavaa hari (or mokak hari), some clothing.

6 mokut venaskamak (or venaskam(ak) mokut) = some slight. (**kisi** would sound somewhat learned here.)

7 mokekda (satek) = some animal. mokaa-da = what animal? (lesson 11 **a**).

9 kookat or kooka vunat.

10 kaar-ekenda kohomada = by car or something. 'By car, or how?' would be kaar-ekenda nætnam kohomada? For similar usages, see A 11, 18, 26 below. Note that this use of -da... -da is not possible with imperative or conditional verbs (cf. last sentence in **a** above).

11 yanavaada koheda = is going or something, is going I fancy. (This is **not** a question). yanavaada mokada has a similar meaning here. magul gedara, see 29 A 28.

12 ṭikayi, lesson 25 **h**.

13 kaaṭa vat æhenne næti venna = so that no one can hear. So also in 22 below.

15 Cf. 28 B 32.

16 See note on 28 A 36.

17 kantooru gihin inna or kantooruve inna.

18 '(Your) son or somebody came too.' Cf. 10 and 11 above. kavdat or kohedat; also putaada kohedat **aave** – which is **not** a question. Notice

how **kavdat** differs from **kavurut**.

19 guruvarunṭa kaaṭat or guruvarun kaaṭat.

20 usa madi is more natural than **koṭa væḍi** here.

21 koocci kooket or kooccivala kooket. (Cf. note on A 19 above). Or

koyi koocciyakat / koocciyet

22 See 13 above.

23 allalaa or araŋ is desirable here, although not necessary in English.

24 kookaṭat (or moka(ka)ṭat, monavaaṭat) = for all purposes.

25 bæriyi (27 A 21 note) or bæ(yi). In reported speech, bæriyi is an alternative to bææ or bæyi. taattaa is the subject of this sentence.

26 kohomada or mokada; cf. 10 and 11 above. **enavaada nædda** gives much the same sense. (maŋ) danne nææ, see 27 **a**.

27 koocci kohomaṭa (or kohoma) vunat = whatever the train situation may be. **kohomaṭa** ('to what extent') can be used instead of kohoma in many places.

29 kiri monavak vat (or monavat) = any (sort of) milk; cf. 6 above.

31 Although kaar and geval are formal plurals, this does not in fact mean more than one of each here. kookak vat or kookat, or mukut or monavat – or **eevaayin ekak vat**.

33 Cf. 10 above.

34 kohe vat or koheda: '(I) meant to go somewhere, but landed up somewhere else'. In this idiom the verbal form is always incomplete; cf. karanna aave mokakda, keruve mokakda. yævenavaa, involitive causative form from **yavanavaa** (lesson 18).

35 tæn or tænvalaṭa (cf. 19 above): 'to all the best places' (9 A 3).

36 Cf. 10 above; 'on the road or somewhere' (as v. paare kohe hari, somewhere on the road).

37 Cf. 27 above.

38 Cf. ditto. bona eka (nam) boyi = he certainly drinks (a lot)! (For **nam**, see lesson 8 note 1).

40 Because he has to go – i.e. in order not to go.

41 æ̆ndalat (or daalat): see note on 19 A 23. **ændat** would give the same sense.

42 hulaŋ gæhenna, see 24 A 22.

43 kal or kalak. This means 'the patient will not last much longer'.

45 nodaa, sc. **inna**: one cannot manage without putting. The use of **bææ** after an absolutive is a common idiom; kataa nokara bææ, it is impossible to manage without (to avoid) speaking, mehema karalaa bææ, it is impossible to manage (by doing) like this. So **ehema baya velaa bææ**, you mustn't be so frightened (this meaning is also expressible by **baya velaa puluvanda**?). Cf. hadalaa oonæ, lesson 18 A 25 note. **pææenaṭa** is preferable to **pææene** here.

B. 1 **kavda gattaa** or **kavuru hari araŋ** are the best collocations of words here.

3, 4 **vena** can collate with kohe and kohoma: vena kohe vat, vena kohoma vat.

9 Hair, say 'head'. It is normal to speak of 'combing the head', though a different word is used when speaking of **cutting** the hair. His: there is no ordinary reflexive pronoun in spoken Sinhalese.

11 Wouldn't: say 'doesn't'.

14 Park: see 28 A 40. Brought: genallaa, not araŋ here.

18 Say 'hearing the dog growl, I came'.

26 Respectable: say 'good'.

28 Omit 'and'.

37 Say 'I don't reckon him at any amount' (dat. case).

39 Cf. A 18 above.

42 'Just like a ship' means 'very big'.

43 Back, as an adj.: tr. **piṭipasse** or **piṭipassa**.

44 With: say 'when eating'.

45 Latest – 'recently got', **lañgadi læbunu**. 'Mother or father?', say 'like mother (or) like father?' For 'who' here we must say **kaa** (cf. kaaṭa, kaage, kaava) or **kavuru**; kavda vage would mean 'like somebody'. Before **-da**, the final vowel of vage is lengthened.

LESSON 31

avva	sunshine
ira	sun; line (pl. **iri**)
vittiya	fact
gindara	fire (on hearth)
hembirissaava	cold (disease)
kuṭṭama	pair (of things)
aḍamaana	doubt; unsafe
molavanavaa	kindle
ravaṭṭanavaa (invol. **rævaṭenavaa**)	deceive
balaaporottu venavaa	hope
veelenavaa	get dry; be idle
paayanavaa	shine, rise (of sun)
hollanavaa	shake (tr.)
bottama	button
iňdikaṭṭa	needle
vahalee	roof
maalee	necklace
tiinta (pl.)	ink; paint
miṭiya	hammer
taalee	manner; tune
kunu	rotten; rubbish
antima	last
ganakam (stem-form)	thick

kunu as a plural noun means 'dirt': kunu ṭika araŋ daanna, take the rubbish away.

ira paayanavaa is used of the rising of the sun; **naňginavaa** is unusual here. **avva paayanavaa** means 'the sun is shining'. **væssa paayalaa** means 'the rain (weather) has cleared up.'

aḍamaana is used with the dative case of a person; meevaa maṭa aḍamaanayi, I doubt this. When used of an object, aḍamaana means ‘unsafe’: gee lañga tiyena pol gaha hari aḍamaanayi, the coconut tree near the house is very dangerous.

ganakam is used predicatively like diga etc. (Lesson 13 **c**), but when used as a noun the case-form **ganakama** is required.

meeka aḍi hatarak [ganakamayi / ganakam]] this is 4 feet thick
meeke ganakama aḍi hatarayi

antima when used adjectivally means ‘last’; as a noun it means ‘last part’: sumaanee antima,[1] the weekend.

[eyaaṭa / eyaa] dæn antimayi means ‘he is breathing his last’.

A. avva pææévvaama maŋ puṭu ṭika eliyaṭa daannam
redi gale gahalaa heeduvaama ikmanaṭa irenavaa
eyaa mona vage minihekda?
salli tiyeddi eyaa apen illanavaa
salli tiyunaama eyaa apen illanavaa
api aavaama parakku venavaa
taattaa kivvaa hariyaṭama hari
kaar-eka ṭiken ṭika yanavaa maṭa dænunaa
maṭa æti væḍak nææ eekaṭa
pæænak kiyalaa maŋ eekaṭa rævaṭunaa
putaa raa bonavaa ahu velaa taattaa hoñdaṭama gæhævvaa
ada udee lamayaa iskoolee giye paara digaṭama añda-añḍaa
lamayaa gedara aapu vele iñdaŋ digaṭama liyaagena giyaa
meeka magadi novii metanadi vunaa hoñdayi
ada gedara giyaaṭa eyaa tavama ævillaa nætuva æti
kanavaaṭa væḍiya ahaka damanavaa
harida kiyalaa balalaa inna oonæ, ganna
viiduru ṭika hoñdaṭa hoodalaa navalaa tiyanna, veelenna
eyaa nitarama apiva pahat karalaa kataa karanavaa
is-issellaa allana maalu kunu maalu
mehema vittiyak maŋ danne nææ

1. Dative case-form **antimaṭa** or also **antimeeṭa**.

mee baaldiyaṭa koccara vatura allanavaada?
ee inne maamaa bava maŋ danne eyaa kivvaama(yi)
paare yana minihek yaṭa karalaa navattanne nætuva ee minihaa gahaagena giyaa
kuḍayak genaapu eken hoňdaṭa giyaa
Kolam̆ba yanne nætuva Gaalu yaŋ
ayiyaaṭa gahanne nætuva inna kiyalaa kiyanna kiyalaa malli aňḍanavaa
meevaa avven tiyanna
hembirissaava hædeyi kiyalaa baye eyaa nonaa innavaa
mee dora arina hæṭi paarak karalaa pennanna
ee minihaava maṭa kohetma allanne nææ
mee lamayaa maṭa hoňdaṭama vissaasayi
maŋ kalpanaa karanne mee paara nivaaḍuvaṭa koheda yanna hoňda kiyalayi
mahattayaa iňdagana hiṭi tæna bima tiyilaa maṭa meeka hamba vune
siiyaa aavayi kiyalaa balanna ko mee lamayaage santoosee
iridaa senasuraadaa api gedara nææ kiyalaa ee gollanṭa sumaane davasaka enna kiyanna
nikam denavaa kiyalaa kivvaamat gatte nææ
kaar-eka hæppunaa kiyalaa taattaaṭa ehema kiyanna epaa
taattaa kataa keruvaama enavaa kiyanna
helluvaama geḍi væṭeyi kiyalaa lamayaa gaha hollanna hadanavaa
eyaa ena vaga maṭa aḍamaanayi
lamayaa hædiigena ena taalee hoňda nææ
eyaa dæn nitara nitara Nuvara yana vaga maŋ danne nææ
mee pihiyenma paanut kapana vaga maŋ danne nææ
pææna kohedi næti vunaada kiyalaa danne nææ
heṭat vahinne nætuva tiyeyida?
lamayaaṭa kiri dunne nææ kiyalaa æti venna æňḍuvaa

B. While (I was) sewing buttons (on) to the coat, the needle broke.
As the roof fell down, I ran away.
When mother is dead (we) will get the necklaces.
Correctly written!
Then will father be in the office now?

When you go, let the dog out first: I'll let him in when (I) get back.

Serve a cup of tea to that lady first of all.

I'm afraid I was late coming this evening.

Are (you) crying because father hasn't come (back)?

10 Sticks are needed to kindle the fire, he says.

This job is more difficult than we hoped.

Wash your hands before eating.

When we arrive he will have eaten.

When the children get really hungry by constant playing, (they) will come running in.

15 A car was advertised cheap in the paper on the second of last month.

It'll be tomorrow before we get back.

It's lucky that (you) were saved and not killed.

When we got there, they didn't even offer us a glass of water, let alone a cup of tea.

Father doesn't much like his coming.

20 It displeases me that the dog is always tied (up).

I've been looking (and) looking for the paper of the 15th of last month, (but) I haven't found it yet.

You must know whose (it) is?

The pupil who said he would come at 3.00 isn't (here) yet.

The mother said (her) child wanted to go home, and came to take (him) away.

25 He says he's ill and won't be coming to the office today.

Do (you) know how to fill this pen?

From the way (he) reads I know that he doesn't understand it.

I know who it is from the way he walks.

Now (I) find (my) pen is missing.

30 It said in the paper that the thief was caught.

The child has put salt into the tea thinking that it was sugar.

The child isn't at all afraid that (his) father will beat him for (his) bad behaviour.

Elder brother went to Colombo saying he would buy a new pair of shoes.

Father got ready to paint the bathroom.

35 We didn't know that you were going home at the weekend.

Father is looking for a hammer to knock in the nail.
Don't just do nothing, thinking there's (plenty of) time.
The servant is still at the shop, (I) wonder what (he's) doing.
It said in yesterday's paper that that gentleman was run over and killed by a car.
40 He said it was getting late, and left without even having a cup of tea.
The teacher knew that the child also did a lot of work at home.
The teacher is explaining to the child how to draw a cat.
Let's have the room in beautiful order before mother comes home.
Do (you) see how it's raining?
45 I wonder if it is raining?
This is five feet thick.
My watch has stopped: what's the time now?

Notes:

A. 1 eliyaṭa = (to the) outside.

2 This method of washing clothes is much practised in Ceylon.

3 mona vage = of what sort?

4 tiyeddi = when (even though) he has. **tiyaagenat** would have the same meaning. On the other hand –

5 tiyunaama (or tiyena koṭa) = when we have – unless the man is asking for **something else**. Thus

salli { tiyena koṭa / tiyunaama } eyaa apen potak illanavaa, when he has money, he asks us for a book.

6 When (if) we come, it will be late. Cf. also 21 A 23.

7 **hari** can be used with a finite verb, like **væḍi** (lesson 16 **c**). It is however never written **hariyi**, even in books. 'What father said is quite correct' (Lesson 10 **g**).

8 ṭiken ṭika (here) = scarcely (cf. 18 A 3).

9 eekaṭa or eeken. Cf. 10 A 12. æti is participial.

10 eekaṭa, 'by that'; cf. 13 A 8 note.

11 For the detached absolutive, cf. note on 16 A 9.

13 digaṭama (here) = all the time. **vele** is an alternative form of **velaave**. In this sentence **hæmatissema** would not go well with the past tense-form

giyaa, but one can say hæmatissema liyaliyaa innavaa, or hæmatissema liyana ekamayi vædee.

14 **hoňdayi** is used here with the finite verb **vunaa**: cf. note on 7 above. Cf. 24 B 30, where **hiţiyaa** would also be possible. Where hoňdayi is used with a **present**-tense finite verb, the meaning is usually sarcastic: compare ada vahinavaa hoňdayi, a pity (lit. a fine thing) it's raining to-day with ada vahina eka hoňdayi, a good thing it's raining to-day. hoňdayi need not stand at the end; it often stands as first or second word in sentences of this kind. novii or venne nætuva. Alternative ways of expressing this sentence would be (...metanadi) vuna eka/eken hoňdaţa giyaa, lit. it went (resulted) well (from) the fact that...

15 ævillaa nætuva æti = he won't have arrived. This is the negative counterpart of **ævillaa tiyeyi** (see 26 **a**). An alternative negative form is **ævillaa tiyena ekak nææ**. gedara here = his house.

16 '(He) throws away more than he eats'.

17 ganna, in order to buy (it) (cf. 15 A 30), i.e. before buying it.

18 navalaa (here) = put upside down.

19 apiva pahat karalaa = 'making us low', i.e. slightingly of us. **pahat** is the stem-form.

20 **is-issellaa** = first of all. This is a proverbial saying, meaning roughly 'keep on trying'.

21 danne nææ: did not know.

22 baaldiyaţa or baaldiye. Not baaldiya. For this impersonal use of allanavaa, cf. **mee vædeeţa pæya tunak allanavaa**, it will take three hours to do this.

23 eyaa kivvaama(yi), 'only when he told me so'. eyaa is ambiguous here in Sinh. as in Eng.; it might refer to a third party. If eyaa is omitted, the meaning must be 'when Uncle himself told me so'.

24 gahaagena giyaa = got carried off, i.e. 'made off' (in a vehicle, or by water).

25 eken or eka (cf. note on 14 above).

26 Without going, i.e. **instead of** going.

28 avven or avve; or avvaţa daanna (15 A 29 note).

29 hædenavaa, 'to be made', of a disease means 'to be contracted' (13 A 12). baye or bayen.

30 (eka) paarak karalaa = eka paarak, just once.

31 For the use of the termination **-va** here cf. also Lesson 25 **g**, oyaava maṭa matakayi.

32 **I** trust **him**.

33 hoňda kiyalayi or hoňdayi kiyalaa.

34 **tiyilaa** is necessary here (cf. notes on 23 B 13 and 20). tæna = place (Lesson 4 **c**); here it is loc. case.

35 balanna ko can be omitted. '(Look,) How glad he is that...'

36 iridaa senasuraadaa: the order is immaterial here. sumaane davasak = a weekday (!).

37 kiyalaa kivvaamat or kiyalat: 'though it was said to be given (I said I would give it) free, (he) wouldn't take it' – or, according to context, 'though he said he would.., I wouldn't...

39 kataa keruvaama, see 21 A 4. 'When (he) calls you, say "Coming!"'

42 hædiigena, see Lesson 1 **d**. Or hædilaa tiyena.

43 nitara nitara: the repetition adds very little effect.

47 æti venna, 'sufficiently', i.e. quite a lot.

B. 1 Sewing: use **allanavaa** (= fasten), not **mahanavaa** here.

2 Fell down, see 19 A 3 note (kaḍaa or kaḍaŋ).

4 See A 7 above.

6 Out(side), see A 1 above. Let him in: say 'take him into the house'.

7 Serve: Lesson 19 **b**.

8 I'm afraid: Lesson 28 **b**. This evening: cf. 20 A 33.

12 Say 'two hands'.

14 'In': say 'to the home'.

15 Advertised = daalaa. Cheap = cheaply.

16 Cf. 20 A 33 and 21 A 23.

17 And not: Lesson 15 **a**. Lucky: cf. 25 A 5.

18 Glass of water, see 23 A 12.

20 Displeases (= doesn't please): see Lesson 19 **b**.

21 Have been looking; the present tense can be used here, cf. 26 A 4 note.

24 To take away: ekka-yanna.

26 Fill: **puravanavaa** is not generally used here. Say 'put ink to'.

29 Find: say 'know'. Missing = næti.

30, 39 Said: say 'was'.

32 Behaviour: say 'works'.

35 Weekend: say 'end of the week!' (!). Did not know: say 'were not knowing' (Lesson 23 **a**).

36 Knock in (flatten) = **talanavaa**, talalaa daanavaa, as v. gahanavaa, hit.

37 Time, see 16 A 9 note. Just do nothing, cf. 17 A 21.

40 Left = went to go (6 A 1 note).

41 Knew: see on 35 above.

43 Let's have in beautiful order: say 'having put in order beautifully, let us keep (leave)'; cf. 15 **B** 23.

LESSON 32

vadinavaa	strike; enter
kææ gahanavaa	cry out (say 'kææ')
ekkahu karanavaa	add up, collect
bedanavaa	distribute, divide
gevanavaa	pay, spend
igenagannavaa	learn
tambanavaa	boil (food)
ridenavaa	hurt (intr.)
kakiyanavaa	hurt (intr.)
ehemat	occasional
ehemapiṭin	complete as it is; altogether
kaariya	matter of consequence, reason
poronduva	promise (n.)
apuuruva	remarkable thing, interesting thing
pudumee	marvel (n.)
aaraŋciya	piece of news
Eŋgalantee	England
(eka)siiya(k)	a hundred (dat. case usually **siyeeṭa**)
kalee	water pitcher
muddaree	postage stamp
keravala (pron. [keroolə])[1]	end
mu(h)uda (stem, **muudu**)	sea
goovaa (pl.)	cabbage
paḍiya	stair; salary, wages
aappa (pl.)	'hoppers'
iňdia(a)ppa	'string-hoppers'
kuum̆biyaa (pl. **kuum̆bi**)	small ant[2]

1. More elegantly, **kelavara.**
2. **hinnaa** is used in some areas.

hiree	prison
poliya	interest (on money)
suruṭṭuva	cigar ('cheroot')

a. gaman (lit. 'journey', stem-form of **gamana**) is used after a present participle in the sense of 'while'. The subject of the main verb of the sentence, if personal, must be the same as that of the **gaman** clause.

Nuvara yana gaman api mee aave
we called in here on our way to Kandy
gedara ena gaman kaḍet gihin enna
call at the shop too on your way home

After a past participle, gaman (often also followed by **-ma**) can usually be translated 'as soon as'.

api giya gaman(ma) aavaa
as soon as we had got (there), we came back again
iskoolee æricca gamanma gedara enna
come home as soon as school is over

Sometimes a participial phrase ending with gaman stands as a complete exclamatory sentence. **-mayi** may also be added here.

nidaagattu gaman!
(he's) still sleeping!
or (he's) just gone to sleep

b. paara ('way') is similarly used.

lamayaa bat kana paara jambut kanavaa
while eating rice the child is eating jambus too
tee biipu paara divuvaa
as soon as (he) had drunk his tea he hurried off

Sometimes the sense of 'blow' is more prominent.

dora oluve / dore oluva] vædicca paara taama ridenavaa
it still hurts where [the door hit (my) head / I hit my head on the door

c. gaana ('amount') is used in several idiomatic ways.

1) It stands for 'a certain amount' (of things or people).

minissu gaanakma ævillaa hiṭiyaa
quite a number of people had arrived

meeka rupiyalakut gaanayi
this costs one rupee and a bit ('one rupee something')

2) **gaana** following a noun with indefinite suffix **-k** may be translated 'in every...' The noun is usually repeated.

maŋ geyak geyak gaane[1] ee liyum beduvaa
I delivered those letters at every single house
maŋ hæma kolayak gaanema bæluvaa
I read through every page

3) **gaane** may also be translated 'at the rate of' (Lesson 12A 14 & 25).

siyeeṭa paha gaane[2] poliya gevanna oonæ
(you) must pay 5% interest

or siyeeṭa pahak venna
siyeeṭa pahak væṭenna } poliya gevanna oonæ
siyeeṭa pahak

4) After a noun or a present participle, gaane can be translated 'on the pretext of...'

pattaree balana gaane huňgak velaa maŋ dihaa balaagena hiṭiyaa
(he) was looking at me for a long time under the pretext of reading the paper

5) **gaanaṭa** after a participle may correspond to 'as if'.

mokut une næti gaanaṭa inna
pretend (lit. 'be as if') nothing has happened[3]

6) **ganan** by itself is used predicatively to mean 'expensive'.

mee kaḍee baḍu huňgak ganan
the goods in this shop are very expensive
mee pot ganan væḍi(yi)
these books are too dear

d. kaariya (be careful to distinguish from **kaarayaa** in pronunciation) is used idiomatically like **ehema** (Lesson 17 **c**) to add slight emphasis or additional politeness. It may be used together with ehema. It is usually untranslatable in these contexts.

---

1. A literary alternative is **paasaa**:geyak geyak paasaa, in every house.
2. **bægin** is a literary alternative here: siiyaṭa paha bægin.
3. Notice that Sinhalese has no direct equivalent to Eng. 'pretend'.

kaamareeṭa kaariya enna epaa
don't come into the room

e. ehemapiṭin (usually pronounced [ehempiṭin]) means 'just as things are'.

eevaa ehemapiṭin tiyanna
leave them (complete) as they are

cf. eevaa ohommama tiyanna, leave them just as they are now.
Sometimes it can be translated 'altogether'.

geḍiya ehemapiṭin narak velaa
the fruit is altogether rotten

ehemat with the meaning 'occasional' is followed by a noun with **-k** suffix, or by a plural noun.

ehemat davasaka, rarely.

f. Statements containing **nææ** as a main verbal form may be joined together by adding **-t** to each of the words preceding **nææ**.

mee meesee lokut nææ poḍit nææ
this table is neither large nor small
maŋ yannet nææ ennet nææ
I am neither going nor coming

Although two finite verb-forms are occasionally joined by **-t** . . .**-t**, or **-yi** . . .**-yi** (api kanavat bonavat, api kanavayi bonavayi), where the subject is the same and the actions are not part of a sequence (such as maŋ gihillaa ennam), it is normal in such cases to attach **-t**, **-t** to the words preceding each verb, where the sense permits (cf. 19 A 21).

mee lamayaa iskooleet yanavaa væḍat karanavaa
this child both goes to school and works

g. gevanavaa is the counterpart of the involitive verb gevenavaa (lesson 30). igenagannavaa, to learn, is a compound verb; the simple form **ugannavaa** is obsolete, but **ugannanavaa**, to teach (with dat. case of the person taught) is the causative form of it. **vadinavaa** is not used in the past tense or absolutive, where it is replaced by forms from the involitive **vædenavaa**. Basically it means 'to move with some violence': eyaa geṭa vædunaa, he burst into the house; galak maṭa vædunaa, a rock struck me (cf. maŋ galaka hæppunaa, I struck a rock, i.e. accidentally). It can also be used with a locative case, as in the example given in **b** above.

ridenavaa (sting – external pain) and **kakiyanavaa** (ache – internal pain, literally boil) are not interchangeable; they refer to different types of pain which are not always distinguished in English. Thus: ata kakiyanavaa, my arm aches, **but** ata ridenavaa, my arm hurts where I bruised it. Notice: oluva kakiyanavaa, I have a headache (**isaradayak**), but oluva ridenavaa, I've hurt my head.

h. poronduva, **apuuruva** and **pudumee**, like kanagaaṭuva etc., are often found with the indefinite suffix **-k**, as well as in stem-form. **porondu venavaa** is 'to promise'.

maŋ Gaalu yanna porondu(vak) vunaa

I promised to go to Galle

This word is stronger than Eng. 'promised', and implies a very definite undertaking.

The stemform **apuuru** means 'surprising.' So does **puduma**, stemform of pudumee; **puduma venavaa** is 'to be surprised'.

maŋ puduma vunaa eekaṭa

I was surprised at that

eevaa maṭa pudumayi

that is a surprise to me

i. hiree, like gedara, is often used without **-ṭa** with verbs such as yanavaa.[1] The stemform **hira** is used adjectivally for Eng. 'tight'.

mee sapattuva hirayi, this shoe is tight

So adverbially, hira karalaa bañdinna, tie tightly.

'Hoppers' are a sort of cold pancake made from rice flour, and often eaten for breakfast.

'String-hoppers' are a similar mixture when passed through a masher; they then look like vermicelli, and are eaten with curries.

Lesson 32 A.

කාර් එක හැප්පිච්ච පාර ලමයා බය වෙලා එහෙම්මම ගල් ගැහිලා හිටියා.

ඒ ලමයා එන්න එන්න මහතයි.

එක කාලෙකට එංගලන්තෙ ඉර බහින්නේ රෑ නමයට කියලා අපට ආරංචියි.

මේ ලමයාට එපයි කියන්න කියන්න වැඩී.

මාලුකාරයො මාලු අල්ලන්න (කියලා) මූදු ගිහින්.

මං ගානෙන් බේරුනා.

මං තිරිකුනාමලේ යමින් පාර ගෙදරත් එනවා.

අවුරුදු ගානේ ගමට එන්න.

---

1. In Up-country areas it also means 'marriage': hirayak gattaa, he got married.

ළමයා වැටිච්ච පාර පොත කොහෙවත් පෑන කොහෙවත්.
එයා ඉගෙනගන එහෙමත් තියෙනවාද?
මං ඒක වැඩි ගානකට වික්කා.
මුද්දරයක් ගන්න අපි කඩයක් කඩයක් ගානෙ ඇවිද්ද.
බර කරත්තෙ පාරෙ යන ගමන් කඩන් වැටිලා කරත්තකාරයා අන්තරා වෙලා.
ගෙදර කවුරුත් එහෙම ඉන්නවාද?
මේ ජනේලෙන් හොඳට පේනවා.
ඉස්කෝලේ යන ගමන් මතක ඇතුව පෑනත් ගෙනියන්න.
මම මේ හැම වීදියක් ගානෙම ගිහින් තියෙනවා.
මොකක් හරි ගානක් දලා එන්න.
මේසේට ඔය රෙද්ද දිග වැඩි නම් කෙරවලින් නවලා දන්න.
පයිප්පේ වතුර ඇරලා.
ඔය පොතට රුපියල් පහක් ගාන වැඩී.
සීනි එක ඇරලා තිබ්බොත් හැන්දෑ වෙන කොට කූඹි වහලා තියෙයි.
මං එයාට ගනන් කෑල්ලක් දීම්මා.
වැස්සොත් එහෙම කියලා කුඩේ අරන් ආවා.
එලවලු ටිකක් කාරිය අරන් එන්න.
කඩකාරයා එලවලු විකුනනවා ගනන් වැඩී.
මහත්තයාලා වගෙ එහෙම නෙමෙයි.
ඉඳිආප්ප ගානට තැම්බිලා.
එයා කිව්වෙ එහෙමපිටින් බොරු.
ඒවා අහලා එහෙම තියෙනවාද?
මං ගානේ තේ කෝප්පයක් බොන්න එන්න.
එහෙදි හෙම මට බනින්න එපා.
ගානෙන් ගානෙන් එයා මං ගාවට ආවා.
වෙන කාටවත් පොරොන්දුවක් එහෙම වුනාද?
පන්සල් කාරිය යන කොට මලුත් අරන් යන්න.
සිකුරාද සෙනසුරාද හරියට අපි යාපනේ යමු.
තාත්තා එහෙම කාරිය ගෙදර ඉන්නවාද?
නුවර පැත්තට එහෙම යනවා නම් මටත් කියන්න.
කුඩයක් කාරිය අරන් ආවා නම් හොඳයි.
එහෙමත් එක්කෙනෙක් තමයි බොරු නොකියන්නෙ.
කලේ වතුර බොන බව දන්නවා නම් ගන්නවානෙ.
කකුල පඩියෙ හැප්පිච්ච ගමන් එයා එහෙම්මම ඇදන් වැටුනා.

ගොහින් එන පාර මෙහෙත් එන්න.
45 තාත්තා පොත කියවන ගමන් සුරුට්ටුව කටේ.
බත් කන්න කන්න මහත් වෙනවා.

B. Father reads a book while travelling in the train
It seems he can't have gone
If (I'd) known (you) needed money, of course I'd have given it
If (you) can, come on Wednesday
5 As he was running, the child fell down
Has Mr Siripaala gone anywhere? Nowhere
Add up my bill
The cabbages are all the same price
While carrying the chair, it hit the door and a leg broke (off)
10 Cars have now got expensive
If (you) go to Colombo to-morrow, I'll come too
Catch me if (you) can
Have you got a stamp, father? If you have, may I have it?
A mad dog bit that boy in the road on his way back from school, and he came home yelling
15 Come home quickly and don't go anywhere else on the way
If (it's) difficult, please don't bother. Oh, it'll be no trouble to me
The child is now gradually getting taller
The door of that cupboard is 3 feet wide and 5 foot 10 high
If (you) have two (or) three houses in Colombo, what an income (you will get)!
20 (He) went to prison for three years and a bit
(He) was a number of years in Ceylon
Not one is red
(I) looked everywhere, (but) it was not anywhere (to be found)
If it rained yesterday, it may clear up to-day
25 It cost (us) Rs. 1/10
He doesn't look like coming

I sent the money for that book, (and) now I have neither book or money

(He) has eaten his fill and is sleeping

I sent a man yesterday to mend that gentleman's car, (but) he hasn't come (back) yet – I have neither the man nor the car

30 Father got angry and went off without even drinking (his) tea

Almost everyone dislikes children who don't listen to (= don't do) what they're told

Can't (you) stop shouting for a bit?

The child wouldn't let me go, and shut the door

I'll come for lunch by one o'clock

35 If (you're) going to Galle, mother will come too

It may rain to-morrow

Leave the milk covered, or the cat may drink it

What I did then was to begin to run a little faster

It's remarkable what you've done about it

40 He can't have gone yet

I will prescribe an unfailing remedy for that

It's wrong of you not to have posted that letter the same day

Don't just throw away the fruits which haven't gone bad

It's a wonder the watch didn't break even after falling on the ground

45 He promised to come at 3.45

Though (I) went to the office to-day, no work was done at all

Notes

A 1 Cf. 17 A 3.

2 enna enna (cf. 29 A 19) means 'gradually'. mahatayi or mahat (stem-form) venavaa.

3 eka kaaleekaṭa = eka velaavakaṭa (Lesson 27 **e**). apita aaraŋci(yi) = we hear.

5 væḍi(yi) 'the more (sc. he does it)', cf. 27 A 10.

7 **gaanen** here could mean 1) by a little bit; I just escaped (= maŋ ṭiken beerunaa), or 2) by trickery, cf. 12 A 20.

8 yamin or yana. **yamin** is a colloquial alternative to yana used by some speakers, especially in Kandyan areas, before paara, gaman, or koṭa.

emin for ena is similarly used.

9   Avurudu (stem-form) or Avurudda gaane = on the pretext of, i.e. for, New Year (as v. **avuruddak gaane**, every year). The sentence is the Sinh. counterpart of 'Come home for Christmas'.

10   See note on 30 A 34. No verb is required here.

11   igenagana ehemat or igenaganat ehema. **ehemat** does not mean 'few' here; cf. 17 A 28.

12   væḍi gaanakaṭa, at a greater figure, i.e. at a profit.

14.   For the change of subject, see note on 19 A 23. kaḍaŋ, see note on 31 B 2. A **bara karattee** is a particular kind of cart, drawn by two bullocks. **antaraa venavaa** means 'to die'.

15   kavurut ehema, 'anyone?' (cf. kavdat ehema, under Lesson 30a).

16   hoňdaṭa peenavaa = 'one can see well'.

17   **ætuva** is the opposite of nætuva, i.e. is in form an absolutive from **æti venavaa**, and can be translated 'having' or 'with'. 'Having mindfulness, take', i.e. remember to take. **matak karalaa** could be used instead of mataka ætuva.

19   gaana = pretext.

20   keravalakin (or keravalin) navalaa daanna = fold it over at (by) the end, at one end.

21   'The tap is (turned) on' – lit., the water is opened in the pipe. Alternatively, vatura-payippee æralaa, the water-tap is turned on.

22   gaana (or ganan) væḍi(yi) 'is too much'.

23   siini-eka, see note on 20 A 3. æralaa tibbot, cf. 15 B 23. 'Ants will have covered it', i.e. it will be covered with ants (**kuumbingen væhilaa tiyeyi** is also possible).

24   This means 'I cheated him' (cf. note on 7 above).

25   See 29 A 6.

28   'Rather different from you!'

29   tæmbilaa, involitive (**tambalaa** is also possible). **gaanaṭa** (or **ganan piṭa**) means 'to the right extent, properly'.

31   **ahalaa** is commonly used here, as well as **æhilaa** – though 'did you hear?' is **æhunaada?** (13 A 20), while **æhuvaada** is normally 'did you ask?'

32   maŋ gaane or mage gaane, at my expense (or **mage sallivalin**).

33 ehedi, 'when we (get) there'.

34 gaanen gaanen, by slow degrees (ţiken ţika).

35 poronduvak vunaa or porondu vunaa, made a promise (**poronduvak keruvaa** is not normal usage).

36 The stem-form **pansal** is used with yanavaa (cf. Lesson 8 **h**). 'When going to (the) temple, for instance' gives the effect of kaariya here.

37 sikuraadaa senasuraadaa hariyaţa, round about Saturday or Sunday.

40 If this refers to the future, **enavaa** would be more natural than aavaa. The sentence may also mean 'It would be a good thing if you had brought....' kuḍayak kaariya = kuḍayak vat mokak vat (Lesson 30 **a**).

41 nokiyanne, Lesson 10**d**. ekkenek tamayi may be realized as [ekkenet tamay].

42 bona bava, was drinkable. dannavaa nam, if (I) had known.

43 kaḍaa, kaḍaŋ are not used before vætenavaa when referring to **persons** (cf. A 14 above), but **ædaŋ** (not **æda**) gives a similar effect.

45 See note on 19 A 23.

46 This is a general statement: the more you eat, the fatter you get; cf. ee minihaa bat kaalaa kaalaa mahat velaa, which is specific.

B. 2 Cf. Lesson 26 **c** and **d**.

6 'Nowhere': idiomatically one can say 'There is no direction (he) has gone (in)'.

8 The same price = the one price.

9 It hit, etc. See note on A 45 above. Carry = lift and go.

13 'May I have it' – say 'Give it'.

14 Bit: kaalaa (see 19 A 23). Yelling; kææ gagahaa (for gahagahaa). 'While coming from school, in the road a mad dog having bitten (him), that child came home yelling'.

15 'And don't' – lesson 15 **a**.

16 Bother: karadara venna, trouble yourself. Please, see Lesson 15**b**. Oh: say **nææ**.

17 Gradually: A2 above.

19 'What an income you will get': we can just say 'What money!'

20 For: dative.

24 Clear up: see Lesson 31.

25 It cost: say 'Rs 1/10 went' (Lesson 11 A 23).

26 Lesson 26 **d**.

28 Eaten his fill: 'having eaten, (it) having become enough'.

30 Went off: Lesson 6 A 1.

31 no + ahana = naahana (cf. 26 A 33).

32 Stop shouting: 'be not having shouted' (kææ nogahaa), cf. Lesson 17**b**.

33 Wouldn't let = didn't let.

34 By one o'clock, eka vena koṭa (cf. A 23 above).

37. The milk: Lesson 14 **e**. Leave covered: A 23 above.

38 What I did: say 'the work I did', and compare 29 A 12.

39 Say 'the work you have done to it'.

41 Prescribe = say.

42 Say 'the fact that you didn't . . . is wrong'. The same day = that very day.

43 Just: cf. 29 A 1.

LESSON 33

temenavaa	get wet
valakkanavaa[1]	prevent
idenavaa	ripen (intr.)
ranḍu karanavaa[2]	quarrel
vaga kiyanavaa	be responsible
taman	oneself
anun (pl.)	others
bayaanaka, bayanaka	frightening
peel	fail, failed
ṣuvar	certain
his	empty
pal	worthless
hiňga[3]	scarce
pradaana	principal
tani(kara)	unalloyed
tada (adverbially, tadin/tadaṭa/tadeeṭa/tada karalaa)	firm, tight
burul	loose
pansil	Five Precepts
kara	shoulder, back of neck
paṭiya	belt, strap
beesama	basin
rattaran (pl.)	gold
baalkee	beam of wood
æhæ (pl. **æs**)	eye

1. Causative of **valakinavaa**, to refrain, which is used in restricted contexts.
2. **sanḍu** in some areas.
3. Sometimes **higa**.

karuvala (**kaluvara**)	darkness
mudda (pl. **mudu**)	ring
toppiya	hat
viyadama	expenditure
Siriipaadee	Adam's Peak
pavuma	pound (£)
avadaanama	danger
honḍaree	hundredweight
kaaranee	reason; affair, matter
paliya	revenge, unpleasant result
paahe	almost (used postpositionally)

a. paliya, literally revenge (pali gannavaa, to take revenge), has also idiomatic uses. The stem-form **pali** means 'responsible'. When negative (with **nææ**) it can be replaced by **vaga kiyanne**.

mamayi pali eekaṭa	it's me who's responsible for that
maŋ eekaṭa pali / vaga nææ	I'm not responsible for that

The case-form **paliyaṭa** when used after a participle can usually be translated 'just because'. The main sentence will refer to an undesirable happening.

nikam behet bivva paliyaṭa hoňda venne nææ
(you) won't get better just because you've taken medicine

parakku velaa aapu paliyaṭama padi kæ puvaa / padi kapana eka harida?

just because (he) arrived late, (they) cut / is it right to cut his wages

b. eevaa, plural of eeka, is often combined with a preceding adjective, or past participle in **-pu**.

ratuvaa	red ones (= ratu eevaa)
daapuvaa	those that were put

In the latter case, a noun may precede; the whole phrase then has the same meaning as a participle followed by a noun.

ṣarṭ mahapuvaa = mahapu ṣarṭ, the shirts which were made

Past participles which end in **-cca** lengthen the final vowel in such contexts.

narak veccaa	those which have gone bad

c. By the addition of **-yæ** or **-yæyi** to the final word of a sentence, the sentence becomes a question expecting the answer 'no': i.e. the sense is virtually reversed. **-kyæ** is realized as [**-kkæ**], and **-navaayæ** almost as [**-nəvæ**]. Care must be taken therefore to distinguish epaa from epaayæ (which sounds almost as [**epæ**]), etc. nætæ is used for nææ + -yæ, bæriyæ for bææ + -yæ,[1] and madææ for madi + -yæ. These endings cannot be followed by **ne**.

mee lamayaa kavadaak vat kiyana dee ahanavaayæ?
won't the child ever listen to what he's told?

mehema keruvot narakayæ?	isn't it all right to do it like this?
oya madææ dæn?	isn't that enough now?
eevaa karanna bæriyæ?	(you) can do that, can't you?

This usage is very common in speech.

d. nam, besides meaning 'if', is often used to give emphasis to the preceding word, like tamayi (Lesson 10 **d**). Unlike tamayi, however, nam does not require the sentence to be inverted and the verb in the incomplete form.

api nam randu karanne nææ api tamayi randu nokaranne	**we** don't quarrel

Notice that nam in this sense seldom stands last in a sentence, whereas tamayi frequently does.

e. There is a special 3rd-personal verb-form which we call the permissive form. This is obtained 1) by substituting **-dden** for **-navaa**, or by adding **-den** to the past participle in **-pu** or **-cca**:

kapadden	let them cut, let him cut
aapuden	let them come, let him come

2) by adding **-ve** to the past tense form, or **-(v)aave** to the past participle in **-pu** or **-cca**:

giyaave giyapuvaave	let (him) go
hitiyaave	let him be
aavaave	let him come
væticcaave	let it fall

f. hitaŋ, besides its literal meaning of 'standing up', can often be translated 'also', standing after any word in a sentence except the final verb.[2] It is also used

1. Whereas bæriya is a formal variant of bææ.

2. This use of hitaŋ is greatly extended by some English-educated speakers of Sinhalese.

like iňdaŋ, etc. (Lesson 15**a**) after a locative case-form, where it will be translated 'from' or 'since'.

Maatara maamaa hiṭaŋut[1] ævillaa hiṭiyaa
even my uncle from Matara[2] too had come
Kolam̆ba hiṭaŋ Gaallaaṭa
from Colombo to Galle

g. The stem-form **avadaanam** is used like taraha etc. (Lesson 23). peel and ṣuvar represent Eng. 'fail' and 'sure'. peel is used in the same way as paas (Lesson 20 A 34).

h. idenavaa is used of most soft fruits when ready to pick – but not of coconuts (polgeḍi), or of rice (goyam), where the word **pæhenavaa** is used.[3] idenavaa when used of food means 'to be properly cooked': bat idilaa.

rattaran (usually written **ratran**) is sometimes used as a term of endearment: mage rattaran putaa. toppiya originally meant a topee – a kind of hat[4] still occasionally worn by Ceylonese, though in general people go bareheaded in Lanka.

bayanaka is written **bayaanaka**, but in speech the second vowel is often shortened.

i. Adam's Peak is a high mountain in Lanka (over 7,000 feet, though not the highest), of striking appearance. On the rock at the summit is a large depression in the shape of a footprint (nowadays kept covered over), held to be the footprint of Adam by Muslims, and of the Buddha by Buddhists.[5] The mountain has been a great centre of pilgrimage for many centuries; it is generally climbed at night, and a striking view of the sunrise is often obtained from the top.

Pansil, the Five Precepts or basic moral commandments of Buddhism (**pancasiila** in Pali) are: to refrain from killing, to refrain from stealing, to refrain from unchastity, to refrain from lying, and to refrain from drunkenness. These are recited ('administered') by an ordained monk, and repeated by the people; this is called 'taking the precepts' (A 38 below).

---

1. This word cannot be written in Sinhalese script.

2. See Lesson 26**g**. Maatara is a town on the south coast – not to be confused with Maatale (Lesson 20 A 5).

3. pæhenavaa also means 'to go grey' (of hair).

4. Colloquially it can also mean 'something which is a nuisance': apiṭa toppi daana eka, being horrid to us.

5. And of Siva by Hindus.

Lesson 33 A.

සල්ලි තියිච්ච පලියට ඔහෙ නිකම් වියදම් කෙරුවා.

දීපුවාට වඩා තවත් මොනවාද ඕනැ?

අම්මා(ලා) තත්තා(ලා) සනීපෙන් ඉන්නවැයි?

කරුවලේ ඇවිත් දෙරේ ඔලුව වද්දගත්තාට මං පලියැ?

05 ඉදිච්චා විතරක් කඩන්න.

තමන්ට ඇති වෙන්න තියාගෙන එපායැ අනුන්ට දෙන්න.

මං නම් මේ ඉස්කෝලේ ප්‍රදන ගුරුවරයා.

කියන කියන පලියට කරන්න බැ.

මට ගහපු පාර මාත් එයාට හොඳවායින් පාරක් දුන්නා.

10 අපි යන අතරෙ තව මොනවා මොනවා වෙලා තියෙයිද දන්නෙ නැ.

ඔන්න ඔහෙ යන්න ගියාවෙ/ගියදෙන්.

හිස්වා ටික අහකින් තියන්න.

එයා ගහට නොනගින්න වැටෙන්නෙ නැ නෙ.

තාත්තා නැති එකෙ පලිය දූනුයි අපිට තේරෙන්නෙ.

15 හෙටත් එයිද දන්නෙ නැ.

මගෙ පුටුව තාත්තාගෙ පුටුවට වඩා ලොකු එක හැබැව.

ජනේලෙන් වතුර ගහලා පොත් ටික හිටන් තෙමිලා.

සල්ලි තියෙන පලියට නරක වැඩ කරලා බේරෙන්න හම්බ වෙන්නෙ නැ.

සීතල වුනාට අව්ව නම් පායනවා.

20 රාත්තලකට එකයි පනහක් නම් හොන්ඩරයකට පොඩි ගානක් යැයි?

මහත්තයා බස් එකෙන් බහිනවා හිටන් මං දක්කා.

පවුම් දෙකක් රුපියල් විසිහතක් විතර වෙනවා.

මේ මුදු රත්තරන් ගාපුවා, තනිකර රත්තරනෙන් හදපුවා නෙමෙයි.

දූන් වහින එකෙ ගෙදරට වෙලා ඉම්මු.

25 තාත්තාට තරහ ගියයි කියල අපි පලි නැ.

ලමයි ගේ ඇතුලෙ සෙල්ලම් කරලා පුටුවල හිටන් මඩ.

පයිප්පෙ දූන්මම වහන්න එපා, බේසමට තව ටිකක් වතුර පිරිච්චදෙන්.

එකකට රුපියල් පහලොවක් ගානෙ මං දුන්නා.

වැස්සට තෙමිලා ඇවිත් ඇඳුම් මාරු නොකර හිටියාම හෙම්බිරිස්සාව හැදෙන එක ඉතින් අහන්න එකක් තියෙනවැයි?

පේල් වෙන එක නම් ෂුවර්.
මං එහෙම නම් ඒ මිනිහාට හොඳ පාඩමක් උගන්නනවා.
මහත්තයාට පුලුවන් වැඩක් කරන්න එපායැ.
ඔය පෙට්ටි ටික එකක් පිට එකක් තියන්න.
කවුරු කවුරුත් දූන් පන්සිල් ගන්න ලෑස්ති වෙන්න.
එයාගෙ දූන් කොහෙත්ම ඇස් පෙනෙන්නෙ නෑ.
ලෙඩාට දූන් කොහොම වත් ඇවිදගන්න බෑ.
තාත්තා කොහොම වුනත් පුතා අලිම බොරුකාරයා.
පොත් වැඩිය තියෙනවා නම් වැඩි පොත් ටික මට දෙන්න.
තාත්තා කෑමට එන වගක් නම් කියලා නෑ මේ ලියුමෙ.
බල්ලා කාර්-එක පාරෙ දුවනවා.
තාත්තා ගෙදර ගිහින්ද කොහෙද?
මං නොහිටියා කියලා ඕවා කෙරෙන්නෙ නැතෑ?

B. (You) can't give just because you're asked
Though he offers me money (I) won't accept (it)
Teachers dislike children who don't work well
When it rains, fetch indoors the things you've put out in the sun
5 It was not only the child but even the teacher that father swore at
While we were away the house was broken into
Never mind if you're a little late, (just) come
What you've brought there is not what I said
If mother and party come while we're not at home, tell (her) to wait a bit
10 They got annoyed and went away without even saying goodbye
Very good then, you may go
You have done me a very nasty turn
That child never tells lies
It was lucky for us that younger brother was (there) to look after the baby
15 If (you) came empty-handed (you) can go empty-handed
It's frightening to go along this road after dark; there are elephants
This beam is very dangerous
Tie up this parcel a little tighter
Loosen the dog's collar a bit more
20 It's awful water in here
Seeing that the car was going to crash, the man covered (his) eyes with (his) hat, saying that what was to be could not be prevented
This shoe is too tight for me
The chief reason for his being angry with me is that (I) sold the car
A fine thing you did to say you'ld come at one: it's five o'clock now
25 When you climb Adam's Peak, you'll see the sun rise
There were no books in any of these boxes
In those days it was me who even bought books for younger brother
The son says he will do anything for (his) father
Though it rained yesterday (and) the day before, water is still short
30 All the things you told me that day are untrue
Just because (I) know (you), (I) can't let (you) go into the station without tickets

This child has been crying (ever) since he got up
Not a single box is open
I have worked and worked since morning and am quite tired now
35 Since almost everyone has come, (we) can now begin our work
Though I went to the office, no one had come, because that day was a holiday
Everyone says that man is really stupid
He has never done such a thing before [this]
It is altogether impossible to feed this child
40 What have (you) been hit with?
Children eat little rice, but drink a lot of water
What is the length (and) breadth of that?

Notes:

A 1 viyadam karanavaa, conjunct verb, to spend. ohe, see note on 7 A 27.

2 diipuvaa, passive sense.

3 This need not be sarcastic, it can be a simple question.

4 dore oluva or dora oluve. **vaddanavaa** is the causative connected with the verb vadinavaa. ævit adds the meaning 'in motion' (cf. 29 below).

6 The emphasis is on the absolutive here: 'it is only when one has left enough for oneself...' tamanṭa is a dative case connected with tamayi (Lesson 10**d**).

7 The principal teacher, the senior master. This position in Lanka is usually called 'the head master', while the person in charge of the school is called 'the principal'.

8 kiyana kiyana paliyaṭa, 'just because (they) go on asking (me).'

9 hoňdavaayin (realized as [hoňdəvæyin]) paarak, 'a blow of the good ones', i.e. a good blow.

10 api yana atare (or atara), 'by the time we have got there'. Here **atara** is used with a participle; similarly api giya atare (or api giya ṭike/ṭikaṭa), while we were away. monavaa monavaa, 29 A 21.

11 onna ohe, see 30 A 5.

12 ahakin tiyanna = put aside, cf. 24 A 4.

13 nonaňginna: a negative infinitive form often has a conditional meaning, usually of an unfulfilled condition, as here.

14 dænuyi, **pr**. [dæŋuyi].

15 'I suppose he may not come tomorrow either' – cf. heṭavat eyida danne nææ, I wonder if he'll even come tomorrow.

16 taattaage puṭuvaṭa or taattaage ekaṭa. loku eka or loku ekak bava. hæbææva, see note on 24 A 10.

17 janeelen = in through the window. gahalaa (see 19 A 23), 'water (rain) having beaten in'.

18 hamba venne = gets the chance, is able.

21 bahinavaa hiṭaŋ or bahinavat.

22 Currently (1994) about Rs.140.

23 **rattaran gaanavaa** is a conjunct verb. rattaranen or rattaranvalin; nouns which are only used in the plural in the direct case often use singular forms in other cases, e.g. kiraṭa uyanavaa, to cook with milk.

24 immu (sometimes **imu**), from innavaa, Lesson 15 **b**.

25 giyayi kiyalaa or giyaaṭa.

26 Absolutive as in 17 above.

27 dænmama is rather more emphatic than dænma.

28 This means 'I gave Rs.15 for each of them.' 'I sold them at Rs.15 each' would be **ekak rupiyal 15k gaane maŋ dunnaa**.

29 maaru nokara hiṭiyaama, cf. 32 B 32. Notice the position of **no**- in conjunct verbs. 'Is it a thing to ask?', i.e. one need hardly ask.

31 maŋ ehema nam = if (it was) me, if I were you. **maŋ oyaa nam** is also commonly used. hoñda paaḍamak, metaphorical (cf. 9 above, 'a good blow').

32 The stress is on **puluvan**: you must (only) do what you can.

34 kavuru kavurut = everyone all round. 'To take the Five Precepts' means to recite them; this is an operation which (like saying prayers) can be repeated daily, and is not like taking western monastic vows.

35 Literally 'his eyes do not appear at all now', i.e. he is totally blind now.

36 ævidaganna, Lesson 23 **a**.

37 -kaarayaa or -kaarayek. ali (lit. 'elephant') is used idiomatically to mean 'big'. **gaja**, a learned word for 'elephant', is similarly used.

40 Before verbs such as duvanavaa, elavanavaa, **paare** is used as a postposition, 'behind, after'.

41 **gihin** can be omitted.

42 maŋ nohiṭiyaa kiyalaa, because I wasn't there (cf. 27 A 15). 'Do you mean this won't be done if I'm not (there)?' A negative form such as nohiṭiyaa (no + finite verb) is only permissible when something further follows, such as **kiyalaa** (as here, see 27 **a**) or **hoñdayi** (see 31 A 14).

B. 2 This may, according to intonation and context, mean either that the money will be refused, or that some object will be refused even for money.

3 Dislike – **akamæti** may be used for kæmati nææ (cf. amataka, asaniipa).

6 See on A 10 above. Broken into, Lesson 20 **a**.

7 Never mind = it is of no consequence though.

8 There: Lesson 3 **e**.

9 Mother and party = ammaalaa (17 A 15).

10 Goodbye: see Lesson 27 **a** and 15 A 10.

12 Turn, say 'work'. The **-k** suffix is often omitted in sentences of this pattern, but the verb must then be in the incomplete form; cf. maṭa gæṭayak gæhuvaa **or** maṭa gæṭee gæhuve, he played me a trick (lit. 'knot').

14 It was lucky that: say 'it went well from the fact...'

15 Proverbial.

16 To go, **yana eka**; yanna should be avoided here. After dark: say 'after darkness has fallen' (væṭenavaa).

17 Dangerous: avadaanam (bayanaka can also be used in this sense here).

19 The dog's collar: say 'the strap which is tied on the dog's neck'.

20 Awful: **pal**. In here, i.e. in this container.

21 His eyes: say 'the two eyes' (23 A 9). 'Saying it was impossible to prevent what was going to be, the man seeing the car going to crash, with the hat covered the two eyes'.

23 'For his being' – venna or vunaaṭa.

24 See 31 A 14. Say 'the time is now **five**'.

25 Climb: see 17 A 9 (not dative).

26 In any of these boxes: mee (or meevaayin) eka peṭṭiyaka vat.

28 Says he will – **karannamlu**, whereas **karayilu** = they say he will.

33 (Not) a single box – peṭṭi ekak vat or eka peṭṭiyak vat.

37 mooḍayi or mooḍayaa or mooḍayek.

38 Such a thing: 28 A 14.
39 Altogether, see Lesson 30 a.
42 What, i.e. how much.

SINHALESE VERSIONS OF B LESSONS

Lesson 1 B.

lamayaa yanavaa
taattaa enavaa
api bonavaa
ee gollo enavaa
mama pota balanavaa
eyaa tee bonavaa
minihaa puṭuva hadanavaa heṭa
api hæmadaama tee bonavaa
ammaa hæmadaama tee hadanavaa
api dæn yanavaa

Lesson 2 B.

liyuma koo?
koo puṭuvak?
taattaa heṭa gamaṭa enavaa
lamayaa gedara yanavaa
taattaa minihaaṭa potakaṭa salli denavaa
dænaṭa mama liyumak liyanavaa
heṭaṭa api gedara yanavaa
taattaa minihaaṭa puṭuvakaṭat salli denavaa
api heṭat gedara enavaa
apit heṭa gedara yanavaa
taattaa puṭuvakut hadanavaa
minihek puṭuvak hadanavaa
minihaa mehe balanavaa
ee gollo heṭa mehe enavaa
pota nææ
ammaa lamayekuṭat tee denavaa
mama lamayaaṭat puṭuvak hadanavaa
minihaa potak liyanavaa

lamayaa hæmadaama pota balanavaa
minihekut mehe enavaa

Lesson 3 B.

mage pota ratuyi
lamayaa tee bivvaa
minihaa gamaṭa giyaa
ammaa gedara aavaa
mama ee pota bæluvaa
iiye taattaa maṭa salli dunnaa
eyaa puṭuva hæduvaa
eeka mage
meeka loku puṭuvak
ara loku sudu gonaa ape
araka taattaaṭayi
mage puṭuva koo?
lamayaage taattaa koo?
mee pota ara lamayaageyi
ee gollange gonaa mehe nææ
balalaa suduyi
ape lamayaa dæn lokuyi
mee ape taattaa
eyaa eyaage ballaava maṭa dunnaa
ammaa lamayaava balanavaa
api iiye gedara giyaa
eyaa mage taattaa
lamayaa gedara yanavaa
oya eka/(ooka) ee lamayaage
anna ara loku ballaa ape

Lesson 4B.

kavda?
mee monavaada? oya salli
ee koheda ee?
ee minihaage nama mokakda?

liyuma kotanada?
taattaa ada ee liyuma liyanavaada?
lamayaa hæmadaama iskoolee yanavaada?
ape taattaada ara enne?
oya pota mageeda?
ratu pota mageeda?
taattaa iiye koheda giye?
mage tee-eka bivve kavda?
lamayaa mokakda karanne?
lamayaa gedara giye mokada?
mokaṭada ee minihaa ape gedara(ṭa) aave?
ara potak (As an answer, ee potak)
oyada mage pota?
mee pota kaageda?
meevaa mage, oovaa mahattayaage
maŋ ada loku potak bæluvaa
ee minihaa ape ballaaṭa mokakda keruve?
mee liyuma maṭada?
kavda mee pota livve?
maṭa dænut salli nææ
mahattayaage puṭuva atana(yi)
ee æyi ee?
oya gollange ballaa mehe

Lesson 5 B.

eyaa dæn iskoolee yanne nætte æyi?
maṭa gedarak nææ
ape lamayaa ada iskoolee aave nædda?
maṭa ratu pææṇak tiyenavaa
maṭa puṭuvak nææ
maṭa loku ballek innavaa
ov, mama heṭa gedara innavaa
ammat gedara nææ
pota gedara
ammaa apiṭa tee denne nædda?
ee minihaa puṭuva hæduve nædda?

ee mahattayaaṭa ara liyuma livve nædda? ov, eeka maŋ livve nææ
taattaa ada gedara innavaa
lamayaage pææne paaṭa mokakda?
balalaa puṭuve
loku meesee koheda (tiyenne)?
taattaa heṭa væḍaṭa yanne nææ
oya liyume monavaada?
pænsalee mokakada tiyenne?
ara kavda atana (inne)?
mee meeseeṭa puṭuvak koo?
æyi, aliyek innavaada?

Lesson 6 B.

api yanavaa yanna
api gonaaṭa kanna denna oonæ
ammaa maṭa heṭa gedara enna kivvaa
mehe enna lamayaa
taattaaṭa ada liyumak liyanna
maṭa oya ratu pænsalee denna ko ṭikakaṭa
api dæn tee bonna kæmati
lamayaa væḍa karanna kæmati nææ
ee lamayaa væḍaṭa kæmati nææ
oya puṭuva maṭa epaa
balalaa tee bonna kæmati nææ
maṭa pææna dæn oonæ nææ
ee puṭuva hadanna maŋ danne nææ
maṭa tava tee bonna bææ
mahattayaage loku lamayaa tavama iskoolee yanavaada?
mama tavat iskoolee yanne nææ
ee minihaa tavama væḍa karanavaa
maṭa tava ballek hiṭiyaa
iiye maṭa tava potak aavaa
ammaa ada tava liyumak livvaa
æyi, nædda eyaa ee potaṭa tavama salli dunne?
lamayaa tavama iskooleeda?
kavda ada kææmaṭa enne?

tava bat poḍḍak kanna
taattaa ada heṭa enna puluvan
maṭa heṭat enna denna ko

Lesson 7 B.

væḍakaarayaa heṭa enavaa
taattaa puṭuva hadanavaa
lamayaa koo? lamayaa iskoolee
apiṭa balalek nææ; ballek innavaa
api ee aliyaava poḍi mahattayaaṭa dunnaa
ara nil paaṭa pææna kaageda? eeka mage
meesee usa nææ
minihaa gedara nææ
mahattayaa dæn keṭṭuyi
kavda ara enne?
oya gollo heṭa monavaada karanne?
ape game loku aliyek innavaa
maat iiye gamaṭa giyaa
taattaa iiye gedara hiṭiyaa
lamayaaṭa pæænak nædda?
ee gollo lamayekva hadanna danne nææ
mahattayaage potak mehe nææ
mahattayaa koheda dæn yanne?
ada mama ammaaṭa liyumak liyanavaa
mahattayaa ada heṭa game yanavaada?
ape loku lamayaa heṭa gedara enavaa
taattaaṭat puṭuvak koo?
mee pote poḍi!
mee lamayaa æyi ada gedara?
æyi, nædda eyaa ee potaṭa salli denne?
aayu boo van, mahattayaa! kohomada sæpa-saniipa?
maŋ ee gollange gedara yanna danne nææ

Lesson 8 B.

taattaa ammaaṭat usayi
liyuma meesee uḍa

meesee uḍa potak tiyenavaa
ballaa puṭuva yaṭa
oya gollo heṭa ape dihaave enavaada?
ee mahattayaa maṭat baalayi
ape baala lamayaa ada gedara nææ
Gaallaṭat vaḍaa Kolam̆ba lokuyi
dæn ekaṭa kaalayi
gaha yaṭa gonek innavaa
mee pææna kaageda?
puṭuva uḍa balalek innavaa
anna, taattaaṭa ara meesee uḍa liyumak tiyenavaa
oya pota yaṭa mokakda tiyenne?
taattaaṭa vijahaṭa enna kiyanna
pota meesee uḍa nææ
mage pææna mahattayaage meesee uḍada?
kavda meeka keruve?
ee minihaa hæmadaama velaavaṭa væḍaṭa enavaa
miiṭa vaḍaa tava ṭikak usa puṭuvak maṭa oonæ
mee lamayaaṭat vaḍaa lokuyi ee ballaa
tava tee oonæ kaaṭada?
mahattayaaṭa puṭuvakda nætte?
mee lamayaa hæmadaama iskoolee enne nætte æyi?
taattaa heṭa gedara enavaa
metana nama liyanna
kavda mee væḍee keruve?
ara aliyaage usa!
taattaa ee lamayaaṭa ape dihaave enna denne næ̈æ
maŋ ṭikakaṭa kaḍee dihaavaṭa yanavaa

Lesson 9 B.

maṭa meesee hari puṭuva hari denna
maṭa rupiyal pahak denna
taattaa ada ekaṭa gedara enavaa
ee lamayaaṭa hari lamayaage taattaaṭa hari mehe enna denna epaa
mee lamayaa ada hon̆dayi
taattaa ekko heṭa Gaalu yanavaa ekko Yaapaneeṭa yanavaa

ee mahattayaa usada koṭada?
mahata mahattayekda keṭṭu mahattayekda aave?
mee tee-eka kaaṭada? maṭada taattaaṭada?
heṭa maṭa Kolam̆baṭa vat Nuvaraṭa vat yanna bææ
ee lamayaage taattaa iiye Kolam̆ba giyaalu
heṭa mahattayaaṭa Kolam̆baṭa hari Nuvaraṭa hari yanna bæri æyi?
rupiyalakaṭa sata kiiyada?
mama pahamaaraṭa gedara yanavaa
dekayi kaalaṭa mehe enna
ekak tiyenavaa, mee lamayaa væḍa karanavaa
eka potak mage
ara pot deka mage
tava eka puṭuvak oonæ
meevaa rupiyalayi
mee pææna kiiyada?
maṭa rupiyalak ekko dekak hari denna ko
ee lamayaa gedara yanna tavama paara danne nææ
heṭa hatarahamaaraṭa ee gollo ape dihaave enavaa
oya meeseeṭa puṭu kiiyak tiyenavaada?
taattaa otana, maŋ metana
meeke nama mokakda?
metana eka pææṇakaṭa salli tiyenavaa

Lesson 10 B.

mama ada enavaa hæbæyi tee bonna inne nææ
suduma sudu balalaa kaageda?
puŋcima lamayaa koo?
guruvarayaa lamayaagen ada monavaada æhuve?
maŋ iiye ee minihaagen (sallivalaṭa) potak gattaa
lokuma puṭuva mage
game usama minihaa kavda?
lamayaa pææṇen liyanavaa
mahattayaaṭa mama enna kivve poḍi væḍakaṭa
mee potvalaṭa kiiyada?
mage meesen kavda pææna gatte?
rupiyal dekak(aṭa) sata kiiyada?

api mee bonne tee
lamayaa liyuma liyanne taattaaṭayi
mama nemeyi heṭa gedara yanne
ee lamayaa yanne gedara(yi)
maṭa eka pææṇayi tiyenne
ara aliyaa mehe balanne
api dæn liyanne pææṇvalin
rupiyal hatarak satavalin kiiyada?
taattaa mage tee-eken bonavaa
minihaa mehen aave nææ
mee lamayaa hari hoňdayi
ee minihaa hari hoňdalu
ee mahattayaa potvalaṭa hari hoňdalu
mee pota gatte kohenda?
mama ee liyuma livve taattaaṭa nemeyi ammaaṭa
ammaa nemeyi taattayi maṭa mee pota dunne
okkomalaa hariyaṭa pahaṭa aavaa
mee ballaa vaturaṭa paninna kæmati nææ
ehet nææ eyaa hiṭiye
api kææma kææve dænuyi
meccara naraka ekak apiṭa oonæ nææ
balalaa puṭuva uḍaṭa pænnaa
iiye maŋ liyum aṭak livvaa (**pr.** [liyuŋŋaṭak])
yanne heṭalu

Lesson 11 B.

minissu dennek paare yanavaa
lamayi dennaa bat kanavaa
putaa kælææva kapanavaa
ṭikak inna, ammaa dæn naanavaa
ara loku ratu kaar-eka kaageda?
ee gollange lamayingen ekkenek mehe aavaa
mee kælææve ali innavaa
mee iskoolee guruvarayan kiidenek innavaada?
heṭa ape gedara tee bonna mahatturu dahadenek enavaa
Nuvaraṭa hæmadaama vahinavaada?

mama heṭa koocciyen Gaallaṭa yanavaa
hoňda lamayaa væḍa karanavaa, naraka lamayaa væḍa karanne næ
ekko eyaa ekko maŋ ada Kolaňba yanna onnæ
mee tiyenne Yaapanee
eyaa Nuvarin
mee paare bas duvanavaada?
maṭa ballo dennek innavaa
ada lamayi kiidenaada iskoolee aave?
ali(n) detundenek paare hiṭiyaa
mahattayaage kaar-eke tava kiidenek aavaada?
okkomalaa bas-ekaṭa næggaada?
ara minihaa bas-ekaṭa naginna duvanavaa
mee kaar-eka tavama paare duvanavaada?

Lesson 12 B.

ballaaṭa vature piinanna puluvan
ee mahattayaa udee havasa dekeema væḍa karanavaa
mama iiye huňgak piinuvaa
mage liyum kavda æriye?
ada kaar-eka heeduvaada?
mahattayaa ada kantooru giyaada?
ammaa ee gollanṭat bat ivvaada?
ee lamayaa ada pot kiiyak bæluvaada!
mee ballaa iiye kææve næ
ee minihaa kaar-eka iiyet heeduvaada?
mage liyuma iiye ee mahattayaaṭa æriyaada?
maŋ aave bas-eken
mee pota rupiyalak venavaa
mee lamayaage væḍa kohetma hoňda næ
ee minihaaṭa paarsalayak otanna kohetma bæ
taattaa kantooru yanne namayaṭa
mahattayaa iiye udee koheda giye?
oya meesee uḍa tava paarsal kiiyak tiyenavaada?
mee kantooruva arinne kiiyaṭada?
oya okkoma maṭa denna
ṭikak ohaaṭa venna!

mahattayaaṭa iiye mokakda vune?
maṭa heṭin væḍa ivarayi/(heṭin mage væḍa ivarayi)
eyaa adaṭa gedara
25 dæn dolahayi dahayayi

Lesson 13 B.

mama ee liyuma heṭa arinavaa
guruvarayaa mage væḍavalaṭa hoňda tææggak dunnaa
iiye ape sudu balalaa mærunaa
kuḍee kalu paaṭayi
5 maṭa diga namak tiyenavaa
mee paara huňgak palalayi digayi
hoňda lamayinṭa iskoolen tæægi læbenavaa
mage paarsalee hoňdaṭa etuvaada?
hoňda pihiyak paare tiyunaa, maŋ eeka gattaa
10 mee lamayaa kohetma hoňda næ
mee lamayaa hoňdaṭa væḍa karanavaa
mage atin dora væhunaa
mee lamayaa hoňdaṭa ganan karanna dannavaa
taattaa mage aṁbageḍiyen kanavaa
15 kuḍakaraayaa ape kuḍee tavama hæduve nædda?
guruvarayaa ee pota mage atin gattaa
mahattayaage pææna mage atin bæri velaa kæḍunaa
iiye Maḍakalapuvaṭa aňgal ekahamaarak væssaalu
mee pota aňgal dahayak mahatayi
20 aḍi hayak diga meesayak apiṭa oonæ

Lesson 14 B.

bootalee tava kiri tiyenavaa
taattaa dæn tava ṭikakin eyi
oya lamayaa huňgak mooḍa væḍa karanavaa
taattaa maṭa hoňda pæænak tæægi dunnaa
5 kaar-ekaṭa aṁbageḍiya poḍi vunaa
taattaa lamayaaṭa særa keruvaa
lamayaa kiri bootalee poḍi keruvaa
lamayaa pota paaṭa karanavaa

ee mahattayaa mage kaar-eka poḍi keruvaa
oya meesee tava ṭikak loku karanna
mee poṭa tava ṭikak puŋci karanna oonæ
lamayaa kalu galak poḍi karanavaa
lamayaava nam karanne kavadaada?
mage guruvarayaa maṭa pææṇak tæægi keruvaa
balalaa kaar-ekaṭa yaṭa vunaa
maŋ yannada ehenam?
ee lamayaage særa!
maṭa puŋci potak tæægi læbunaa
kavda mee lamayaage pææna horakam keruve?
naraka lamayinva (lamayi, lamayinṭa) maṭṭu karanna oonæ
eevaa okkoma lææsti
dæn vijahaṭama rææ venavaa
dænaṭama pahayi, tavama nææ eyaa lææsti
ee geḍi ṭika okkoma api kææva
anee, monavaa karannada?

Lesson 15 B.

ee gollo Nuvara
mee paara yanne kohaaṭada?
oya gollo gedaraṭa vatura ganne kohenda?
dekayi tunayi pahayi
rupiyalaṭa tunayi
dæn tunaṭa dahayayi
Kolam̆baṭa dekak
tavat oonæda?
maŋ ada udenma kantooru aavaa
væḍakaarayaaṭa meeseeṭa kææma arinna kiyanna
maṭa enna dora arinna
bas-eke Kolam̆ba in̆daŋ Gaallaṭa kiiyada?
ee gollo apiṭa tee-ekak vat dunne nææ
lamayaa bat vat kanne nææ
ee mahattayaaṭa væḍa hamaara karalaa mehe enna kiyanna
Yaapanee minissu væḍaṭa hari hapan
ara lamayi am̆ba kaḍanna gal gahanavaa

ee mahattayaage vam ata dakunu ataṭa vaḍaa koṭayi
mahattayaa Laŋkaavaṭa aave kavadaada?
mee meesee eka pættak usayi, eka pættak koṭayi
paan geḍiya meesee uḍin tiyanna, nættam ballaa kayi
gedara iňdalaa maŋ dæn aave
kiri bootalee vahalaa tiyanna, nættam narak veyi
poḍi lamayinṭa peenna raa vikunanna epaa
mee baḍu ṭika genihillaa almaariye tiyanna
liyuma oya pota(ṭa) yaṭin tiyanna
mage tee-eka vahalaa meesee uḍin tiyanna
oya pot ṭika dænaṭa mee æňda uḍin tiyanna
taattaa hæmadaama udeeṭa Dinamina balanavaa
api Silumina pattaree ganne nææ

Lesson 16 B.

mee paare tavama bas duvanavaada?
mee lamayaa kiri bonna hari hapan hæbæyi bat kanna kæmati nææ
ee duppat naaki minihaaṭa baninna epaa
poḍi lamayi nitarama aňḍanavaa
mage atin taattaage orloosuva kæḍunaa
Laŋkaave gæænu reddayi hæṭṭeyi aňdinavaa
noonaa mahattayaa gedara nææ
ee vayasaka minihaa mee dæn ara bas-eke nægalaa giyaa
ara naaki minihaa kaaṭada baninne?
ee minihaa nitara mehe yanavaa enavaa
ee gææni ṭikak vayasayi hæbæyi tavama hari paaṭayi
mage parana pææna maŋ eyaaṭa hoňda gaanakaṭa vikkaa
taattaa ee minihaaṭa væḍiya kæmati nææ
maṭa ada væḍiya væḍa karanna bææ
lamayaa huňgak vatura bonavaa
api ee gollanṭa hoňda væḍi
maṭa væḍiya tee epaa
paara dihaave kaḍa væḍi
bas-ekaṭa minissu væḍi
mee meesee ee lamayaaṭa ṭikak loku væḍi
ballaa pænsalee kæævaa maŋ dannema nææ

lamayaa tavama keṭṭu væḍi
mee lamayaa væḍaṭa arinna tavama taruna væḍi
raa arakkuvalaṭa hærenne kohomada?
maŋ sallivalaṭa kæmati
væḍiya loku ekak epaa
kaḍakaarayaa mahattayaagen am̆bavalaṭa gattaa væḍi
mee lamayaa maṭa pota kiyavanna denne nææ

Lesson 17 B.

ara kiri paaṭa kaar-eke kavda ara aave?
noonaa mahattayaa gedarada?
mahattayaage oya at orloosuva harima lassanayi
mage puŋcima lamayaa yanne gæænu iskooleekaṭa
ape game koocci paarak vat bas paarak vat nææ
alut sarom reddak ganna heṭa maŋ Kolam̆ba yanna oonæ
gedaradi maŋ hæmadaama udeeṭa pattaree balanavaa
iiye api udenma Nuvara gihin Nuvaradi kææma kaalaa hændææavaṭa Kolam̆baṭa aavaa
basvala kooccivala ehema nikam yanna denne nææ
mee paara ape am̆ba huñgak narak vunaa
meeka hari kælææ paarak
ballaa dæn hoñdaṭa suduvaṭa innavaa
ape mahattayaa ee væḍee mee andamaṭa karanna kivvaa
taattaa mokakda guruvarayaagen æhævve?
mee ballaage eka hoñdak tiyenavaa; uu naanna kæmati
guruvarayaa mokakinda/(mokenda) ee lamayaaṭa gæhævve?
mahattayaa tava poḍḍen mage paarsalee ee minihaaṭa denavaa
heṭa aniddaa maṭa væḍiya væḍak nææ
eyat etakoṭama aavaa
mee ballaa hari napuruyi, uu kohetma kiikaru nææ
iiye pereedaa mehaaṭat hayiyen væssaada?
ee minihaa hari pohosataa hæbæyi minihaage gedaraṭa (yanna) aḍipaarak vat nææ
lamayaa narak karanna epaa
maṭa tava ṭiken hari væḍee venna giye
mahattayaaṭa maŋ pahaṭa teevatura-ekak dennam

ee am̆ba(geḍi) ṭika narak vunaa
ee meesee diga væḍi
leesi hæṭiyakaṭa karanna
dahaye koocciyaṭa tava velaa tiyenavaa

Lesson 18 B.

maŋ taattaa lavvaa guruvarayaaṭa liyumak liyevvaa
lamayaa væḍakaarayaaṭa kiyalaa am̆ba kaḍavanavaa
lamayaaṭa vatura hun̆gak pevunaa
paarsalee maŋ kaḍakaarayaaṭa kiyalaa hon̆daṭa etevvaa
guruvarayaa taattaaṭa liyalaa maṭa gæssevvaa
ammaa poḍi lamayaaṭa kiri povanavaa
maŋ ee minihaaṭa kiyalaa lassana almaariyak hædevvaa
tava kiidenekuṭa tee hadannada?
heṭa maŋ dahadenekuṭa rææ kææmak denavaa
maŋ tava lamayi detundenek ekka iiye udee Kolam̆ba giyaa
mee lamayaa okkogenma palaveniyaa
maŋ lamayaaṭa dæn paspaarakaṭat vaḍaa enna kivvaa, hæbæyi tavamat aave nææ
taattaa ee minihaaṭa hayapaarak livvaa
tee-ekak araŋ enna maŋ ee lamayaava kaḍeeṭa yævvaa
maṭa ee pota dænmama evanna hæṭiyak nææ
ee væḍee kaaṭa kiyalaada kerevve?
ee pota gennanna maṭa salli nææ
taattaa guruvarayaava kæn̆davalaa monavaada æhævve?
putaa tamayi mee paara pantiye palaveniyaaṭa aave
devarak aṭa daasayayi
okkoma ekapaarakaṭa geenna bææ; desareekaṭa geenna balannam
ee minihaa tava ṭiken bas-eken væṭennayi giye/(væṭenavaa)
iiye hændææve ape dihaavaṭa goravagoravaa væssaa
rupiyal dahaye kola mokakada tiyune?
mee lamayaa pantiye tunveniyaa

Lesson 19 B.

maava allanna puluvanda?
kaar-eka balanna mahattayek ævillaa

ballaa næævvaada?
paara vaturaṭa heedilaa gihin
magen salli illanna epaa
samahara poḍi lamayi nitarama an̆ḍanavaa
mee paara dæn hon̆daṭama kælee velaa
mage lamayi dæn loku velaa
mee potaṭa rupiyal pahak yasaṭa æti
ee gollanṭa apiva dæn epaa velaa
eyaa iiyet ævit tiyenavaa
mee pota kiyavalaa tiyenavaada?
almaariye dora vahalaa
bat kaalaa kaalaa mahat velaa
raa biilaa biilaa maṭa dæn epaa velaa
mee meeseeṭa puṭu madi
mee ædda?
oya æti dæn
ballaa kaar-ekaṭa yaṭa velaa
mage tee-eka taattaa biilaa
mee lamayaa ævit tiyenne bas-eken
ada senasuraadaada? ada kavadaada?
maṭat ekka æti venna tee tiyenavaada?
mee am̆bageḍiye pættak narak velaa
mee meeseeṭa tava eka puṭuvak madi
heṭa api melahakaṭa Nuvara
maṭa madi mee tee
ape ballaa ehema ohe aavaada?
maṭa eeka kohetma teerenne nææ

Lesson 20 B.

sumaane davas monavaada?
mama hadana tee ammaa bonna kæmati nææ
ara nitarama mehe ena lamayaa kavda?
ee kaḍee dena paan hon̆da nææ
redi hoodanna redi hoodana minihekuṭa kiyanna oonæ
maŋ giya sumaane liyapu liyuma ee mahattayaaṭa tavama læbilaa nææ
ape viidiye tiyena ee parana geval tunama kaḍanna yanavaa

paan geḍiyakuyi luunu raattalakuyi geenna kaḍeeṭa giya lamayaa tavama nææ
pot ban̆dina minihaa ada aavaada?
orloosu hadana minihaa koheda inne?
mee inne mage ata huurapu ballaa
maŋ kapana paan eyaa kanavaa
lamayaa magen genicca pææna tavama dunne nææ
arakku bootalayak geenna ærapu minihaa tavama nææ
kæḍicca kuḍeeda genaave?
maŋ nikamaṭa ee lamayaaṭa gihin potak balanna kivvaa
kæmati dihaavaka yanna
puluvan vijahaṭa gamaṭa enna
oya gollo heṭa ape geval dihaave enavaada?
monavaayinda oovaa hadalaa tiyenne?
ammaa taattaaṭa vaḍaa avurudu pahak baalayi
meeka ammaaṭa ekko taattaaṭa hari puluvan væḍak nemeyi
liyuma æriye koyi lamayaa ateeda?
ee minihaaṭa bæri væḍak nææ
am̆ba kaalaa kaalaa maṭa epaa vunaa
eyaava ganan ganna epaa
paan raattalak dahadenekuṭa hon̆daṭama madi
mahattayaalaage geval koheda?
taattaa ada (gedara enna) rææ veyi
maŋ kaar-eka araŋ avurudu dekak venavaa
eyaa araŋ ævit tiyenne væradi pota
siini kaalak denna
mee lamayaaṭa oonæ næti ekak nææ
lin̆den vatura araŋ naanna eyaa eccara kæmati nææ
iridaa davasaka enna; hæma iridaama api hændæævaṭa gedara

Lesson 21 B.

aacci ena kan ṭikak inna
malli ena kan maŋ tee bivve nææ
minihaa aapu hæṭiyema taattaagen rassaavak illuvaa
raa biipu hæṭiyema tee bonna bææ
ṭikak usa minihek aavaa

maŋ gihin ena kan putaa hoňdin inna
vahina koṭa api gedara hiṭiyaa
ammaa mærena koṭa maŋ tavama poḍi
taattaa koocciye yana koṭa potak kiyavanavaa
gahana koṭa lamayaa aňḍanavaa
api Nuvara yana koṭa vahinavaa
bonna kiri næti hindaa lamayaa aňḍanavaa
vahina koṭa api geṭa divuvaa
taattaa kataa karana koṭa lamayaa giyaa
maŋ kiyapu pota ooka nemeyi
labana avurudde iňdaŋ maŋ iskoolee yanne nææ
iiye genaapu paarsalee pot kiiyak tiyunaada?
maŋ karana rassaavaṭa taattaa kæmati nææ
api edaa gedara yana koṭa parakku velaa/(vunaa)
malli tee bivve mokenda?
eyaa iiyet api næti velaave ævit tiyenaava
eyaa ena koṭa maŋ gihillaa tiyeyi
labana sumaane api Nuvara aaccilaage dihaave inna yanavaa
karana væḍee vijahaṭa ivara karalaa enna
pota kiyavanna metana eliya madi
ee minihaa bæňdapu taappee dæn kaḍaa væṭilaa
gonaa tanakola kanavaa
biccivala aňdinna epaa
ape guruvarayanṭa api hoňdaṭa salakanna oonæ
ee lamayaa hamba karana hæma sateema ammaaṭa denavaa
mahattayaage næti vecca pææna tavama hamba vune nædda?
ṭayar hadanne rabarvalin

Lesson 22 B.

ammaa kussiyaṭa velaa tee hadahadaa innavaa
taattaa puṭuvaṭa velaa pattaree balabalaa innavaa
iiye ee paare kaar-ekakaṭa yaṭa velaa ballek mærilaa innavaa maŋ dækkaa
maŋ leḍin inna koṭa ee mahattayaa tamayi maṭa behet kale
poḍi lamayaa kooppeekin viiduruvakaṭa tee dadaa innavaa
elavalu ammaa elavalu genallaa innavaa

dæn metana aňḍa-aňḍaa hiṭiya lamayaa koo?
maŋ gedara yana koṭa taattaa ævit
maŋ gedara yana koṭa ballaa puṭuvaṭa bæňdalaa hiṭiyaa
issara eyaa nitara ape dihaave ævit ævit[1] hiṭiyaa.
sudu ballek liňde væṭilaa innavaa
taattaa puṭuvaṭa velaa koopi bibii pattaree kiyava-kiyavaa innavaa
avuruddakaṭa sumaana kiiyak tiyenavaada?
oya gollange dihaavaṭa huňgakma væssa tiyenne koyi maaseeda?
juuli maasee palaveni daa iňdaŋ novæmbara maasee tisveni daa vena kan iridaa davas kiiyak tiyenavaada?
Kataragama yanna hoňdama maasee kookada?
ape gee gaava pol gas dekak tiyenaava
maŋ gaava dæn væḍiya salli nææ
ape gee isṭeesamaṭa kiṭṭuyi
mehe iňdaŋ Gaallaṭa kiṭṭuma paara mokakda?
puṭuva meeseeṭa laŋ karanna
kææma kana koṭa balalaaṭa meesee laňgaṭa enna denna epaa
ee lamayaa maŋ laňgaṭa enna kæmati nææ
kaar-eka balanna mahattayek ævit innavaa
api ehen dæn as velaa
mee pote kola ekakaṭa ekak ælilaa
dostara ena koṭa leḍaa mærilaa
maasa kiiyakaṭa uḍadida maŋ eeka eyaaṭa kivve!
maŋ liyana liyana hæma liyumama mee lamayaa iranavaa
Vesak kavadaada?
Vesak (tiyenne) koyi maaseeda?
ii laňga baaldiye monavaada tiyenne?
maŋ yana koṭa kaḍee vahalaa
taattaa tavama nædda ævillaa?
aňgal deke ænayak maṭa denna
giya maasee deveni daa pattaree metana nææ

Lesson 23 B.

ratu paaṭa reddak æňdaŋ inna ara usa minihaa kavda?
arayaa tamayi maṭa iiye iskooleedi gahapu lamayaa

---

1. Pronounced [ævittævit].

taattaa dæn kantooru yanna æňdaŋ innavaa
taattaa (kææma) kana koṭa lamayaa sellam keruvaa
eyaa eliyaṭa yana koṭa kooṭ-ekak daagena yanavaa
ayiyaa taappee uḍaṭa nagina kan malli balaŋ innavaa
ayiyaa am̆ba kaḍalaa dena kan naŋgi gaha yaṭa balaŋ innavaa
ballaa vatura bona kan gonaa balaŋ innavaa
lamayaa taattaaṭa kiyalaa okkoma ganan ṭika balavaagattaa
kiṭṭu paaren yanna, parakku novenna
ape guruvarayaaṭa kiyalaa maŋ ee pota kiyavaagattaa
ee naaki duppat gææni nitarama parana reddakuyi hæṭṭeekuyi æňdagana ape gedara enavaa
kaḍee gaavaṭa velaa ee minissu dennaa hoňdaṭama bænagattaa
mee baḍu ṭika huňgak laabeeṭa yanavaa
mahattayaa edaa ape dihaave naave æyi?
maŋ ena koṭa putaa naalaa (hiṭiyaa)
maṭa lamayekuṭa inne putek
ammaa maŋ leḍin innavaa balanna aavaa/(maŋ leḍin inna koṭa ammaa aavaa balanna)
ballaa ævit balalaage kiri ṭika biilaa giyaa
lamayaa tee-ekak hadaŋ kussiyaṭa velaa bibii hiṭiyaa
puŋci putaa taattaa ena kan dora gaavaṭa velaa balaŋ hiṭiyaa
balalaa meeseeṭa nægaŋ/(nægalaa) innavaa
leḍaa æňden bæhægana innavaa
minihaa issara ape gee gaava kaḍayak daagana hiṭiyaa
kaagenda oya pææna illaagatte?
dæn væhægana enavaa, tava ṭikak hayiyen ævidimu
mahattayaa mokakda ee gæna tiiranaya keruve?
ee lamayaa ate tiyicca hænda viisi keruvaa
mee meesee uḍa maŋ nokiyavapu potak nææ
malli nitarama rææṭa paaḍam karanavaa
iiye malli iskoolee giye nææ
pot paarsalee koyi ekada?/(kookada?)
baḍaginnen inna lamayi rasa kææmavalaṭa kæmati
eyaage kaar-eka ape væṭe hæppunaa
eeka karanna huňgak amaaruyi

Lesson 24 B.

mahattayaa game yanne kavadaada?
sumaaneeṭama æti venna luunu geenna
lamayaa baḍaginnen añḍanavaa
maŋ ee pota hari laabeeṭa gatte/gattaa
mee lamayaa ættenma dæn hari narakayi
viiduru kooppa okkoma hoñdaṭa paarsal karalaa yavamu
malli paaḍam karana kaamaree mee/meekayi
elavalu kada kæḍilaa elavalu okkoma paare
pot almaariyaṭa viiduru dorak daanna oonæ
mahattayaaṭa etakoṭa monavaada oonæ?
etanadi kaar-eka kæḍilaa apiṭa huñgak karadara æti vunaa
guruvarayaa taattaaṭa kiyalaa lamayaaṭa gæssevvaa
ayiyaa malliṭa pææṇak tooranavaa
ammaa midule innavaa babaaṭa pennanna
Gaallaṭa ṭikat-ekak
sellam karanna vattaṭa yanna
maṭa baḍagini, kaḍeekaṭa yaŋ kanna
ammaa ena kan babaa añḍanavaa
mee lamayaava añḍavapu ekkenaa kavda?
eyaa mokaṭada mage væḍavalaṭa æñgili gahanne?
maŋ gedara gihillaa tee bonnam
ata kapaagatte kohomada?
minihek raa biigena paare væṭilaa innavaa maŋ dækkaa
isṭeesamaṭa yana koṭa koocciya gihillaa tiyeyi
mee tee-eka mahattayaaṭa nemeyi, arakayi mahattayaage kooppee
malli gedara yana koṭa taattaa ævit iñdii
maŋ gedara yana koṭa taattaa ævit tibunaa
iiye novæhæpu eka/(væsse næti eka)/hoñdayi
nitara vahina ekaṭa/(vahinavaaṭa)/api kæmati nææ
maŋ ada gedara hiṭi eka hoñdayi
mahattayaa Nuvara giya eka hæbæælu
maŋ yana koṭa eyaa mahanavaa/(mahamahaa hiṭiyaa)
lamayi midule ehe mehe duvanavaa
mee poḍi kellaṭat amba kæællak denna
hari pææṇak nætuva maṭa miita vaḍaa hayiyen liyanna bææ

Lesson 25 B.

dæn væḍa keruvaa æti, gihin sellam karanna
hiitala vunaaṭa mokada janeela okkoma æralaa
mahattayaa bænnaaṭa mokada taraha nææ
æñdum maaru karanna issellaa naalaa inna/(naanna)
kooppee væṭenna issellaa eyaa pænalaa allaagattaa
pææna venuvaṭa pænsalee maŋ genallaa tiyenne
maŋ taattaa venuven iskooleeṭa pot ṭikak tææḡi kalaa
parana guruvarayaa venuvaṭa apiṭa heṭa iñdaŋ alut guruvarayek enavaalu
dæn maŋ paan venuvaṭa bat kanavaa
Avuruddaṭa lamayaaṭa salli venuvaṭa pææнak dunnaa
ada loku mahattayaa venuvaṭa kantooruve væḍa balanne kavda?
hadissiye asaniipa velaa mæricca putaa venuven ammaa huñgak kanagaaṭu vunaa
maŋ enavaaṭa eyaa kæmati nææ
puṭuva hæduvaaṭa vaḍuvaa salli illanavaa
maŋ ee liyuma giya sumaanee dæmmaaṭa tavama hamba velaa næhællu
lamayi sellam karakara gee vaṭee duvanavaa
ee minihaa gee vaṭeeṭa aluten taappayak bañdinavaa
ee gollo melahakaṭa kææma kanavaa æti
eyaa dæn eekaṭa kanagaaṭu venavaa æti
lamayaa tavama iskoolee sellam karanavaa æti
ada Gaallaṭat hoñdaṭama vahinavaa æti
bas-eka navattanavat ekkama minihaa pænnaa
lamayaa iskoolee yanavat ekkama vahinna gattaa
siiyaa væṭenna yanavat ekkama allaagattaa
kiri bivvaaṭa passe lamayaa nidaagattaa
udee kukulaa æñḍaluvaaṭa passe maŋ nægiṭṭaa
liyum livvaaṭa passe maṭa kiyanna
maŋ yana koṭa issaraha dora æralaa
issellaama kaar-ekak hæduve kavda?
okkoṭama issellaa tee biilaa inna
miiṭa issellaa mahattayaa monavaada keruve?
bas-eka enavat ekkama poḍi lamayek paara haraha divuvaa
paara haraha pol gahak væṭilaa
poḍi lamayek viidiya dige añḍa-añḍaa duvanavaa

mæda kaamaree kavda inne?
bas-eka enavaa peenavaada?
oya æti dæn æňɖuvaa
oya am̌bageɖiya kanna issellaa hoodaŋ inna
mee kaɖee tiyena laabama tel bootalee ekayi visipahayi
poɖi lamayaa bootalayakin kiri bibii paara dige giyaa

Lesson 26 B.

duvaddi lamayaa væʈunaa
bat kaddi lamayaa vatura bonavaa
(maŋ) liňden vatura adiddi pææna væʈunaa
ballaa aňɖa gahaddi giyaa
giya maasee maŋ Gaalle indæddi eyaa maava hamba venna ævit tiyunaa
maŋ væɖak karakara indæddi ee lamayaa ævit maʈa gæhævvaa
taattaa kantooru yaddi kaar-eka hæppilaa tiyenavaa
bas-eka navatiddi minihaa pænnaa
taattaa kum̌bura koʈaddi poɖi putaa balaŋ innavaa
ee puʈuva gaava mage pææna væʈilaa æti, yanna eeka araŋ enna
koocciya melahakaʈa gihillaa æti
melahakaʈa kaɖee vahalaa æti
nændaa melahakaʈa Nuvaraʈa gihillaa æti
ada ee minihaa ape gasvala pol kaɖanna æti
maamaalaage kum̌buruvala melahakaʈa goyam kapanna æti
taattaa baniddi lamayi dennaa gahaagannavaa
maŋ heʈa tunaʈa vitara Kolam̌ba yanavaa
Kolam̌ba paan geɖiyak sata visihatarakaʈa vitara ganna puluvan
ee pintuuree balanna yanna api okkoʈama kiiyak vitara veyida?/(yayida?)
Gaalu yaddi ʈayar-ekak giyaa
vahiddi mee koheda yanna hadanne?
minissu gaha kapaddi lamayaa balaŋ innavaa
ape kum̌buru aanɖuvaʈa gattaaʈa tavama eevaa balaaganne api
bas aanɖuvaʈa gattaaʈa lori tavama gatte nææ
maʈa salli hamba vunaama kaar-ekak gannavaa
pæʈrol næti vena koʈa kaar-eka hiʈinavaa
iiye Kolam̌baʈat vahinna æti
dæn æti

una tiyena koʈa æňden bahinna epaa
baɖagini vunaama kamu
isʈeesamaʈa giyaama koocciya gihin
kirikaarayaa ada aavaama maʈa kiyanna
oya paarsalee digaarinna epaa
taattaa kiyana dee nokarana koʈa maŋ kiyana dee ahayida ee lamayaa?
kaar-eka tiyeddi maŋ nitarama Nuvara yanavaa/(giyaa)
kaar-ekakut tiyeddi mokada ee mahattayaa hæmadaama koocciyen yanne enne?
gedara giyaama maŋ tee bonavaa
iskoolee ærunaama kelinma gedara enna
tava bat tiyeddi paan monavaaʈada?
mama dæn kææva væɖi
dæn ʈika ʈika baɖu ganan yanavaa
tihen visiaʈak giyaama kiiyada?
taattaa tava(ma) gedara enna nææ
oya payippee æriyaama vatura enavaa
mee pota maŋ kalin kiyavalaa tiyenavaa
ee viiduru ʈika biňdinne nætuva mehaaʈa araŋ enna

Lesson 27 B.

lamayaa paaʈa pænsalayak oonæ kiyanavaa
mahattayaa eka velaavakaʈa bat kanna kæmati nætte æyi?
lamayaa iskoolee yanna bææ kiyanavaa
taattaa ee lamayaaʈa ada iskoolee yanna epaa kiyanavaa
ammayi taattayi maava balanna heʈa iskooleeʈa enavayi kivvaa
ee væɖeeʈa minihaa salli epaa kiyanavaa
ee mahattayaa hoňda væɖakaarayek ganna oonæ kiyanavaa
taattaa heʈa Gaalut yanavayi kiyanavaa
ee mahattayaa heʈa duulaage dihaave enavayi kiyanavaa
lamayaa apit ekka enna bææ kiyanavaa
lamayaa potak gennanna salli oonæ kiyanavaa
ee mahattayaa iiye væɖaʈa aavaada nædda (kiyalaa) maŋ danne nææ
orloosuva tavama væɖa karanavaada (kiyalaa) balanna
mee hæʈʈee æňdalaa balanna harida kiyalaa
eyaa enavayi kiyalaa kivvaaʈa aave nææ

ee væḍeeṭa mee salli madi kiyalaa dæn ee gollanṭat teerilaa/(teerenavaa)
taattaa hæmadaama udeeṭa væḍaṭa yanne kiiyaṭada kiyalaa ee lamayaagen ahanna
maŋ væḍaṭa gihillaa kiyanna
heṭa iňdaŋ huňgak baḍu ganan yanavayi kiyalaa menna mee pattaree kiyalaa tiyenavaa
meeka venna ætte kohomada kiyalaa maṭa teerenne nææ
maŋ ævit innavaa kiyalaa taattaaṭa kiyanna
hamba venna minihek ævit innavaa kiyalaa lamayaa taattaaṭa boruvaṭa kiyanavaa
taattaa gedara ævillaa innavaada kiyalaa mahattayek ahanavaa
ara kaamaren dum gahanne mokada kiyalaa balanna
maŋ boruvaṭa kivvaa kiyalaa eyaa hitanavaa æti
ammaa siini kiyalaa teevalaṭa lunu daanna æti, eekayi bonna bæri
maamaa ada ævit ṭikak (velaa) iňdalaa heṭa aayit ennam kiyalaa giyaa
ammaa mas raattalak geenna kiyalaa dæn ṭikakaṭa issellaa kaḍeeṭa giyaa
eyaa heṭa udee paandarama Gaalu yanna oonælu
maalukaarayaa maalu nayaṭa denna bææ kiyanavaa
ayiyaa gæhævvaa kiyalaa maŋ taattaaṭa kiyanavaa
eyaa alut geyak gattayi kiyalaa apiṭa balanna enna kiyanavaa
mee lamayaa velaavakaṭa harima narakayi
ammayi duuyi dara ahulanna kiyalaa kæleeṭa giyaa
guruvarayaa yanna kivvayi kiyalaa iskoolee ærennat issellaa lamayi gedara giyaa
baḍagini kiyalaa lamayaa mas ṭika okkoma kææva
ada pattareyi kiyalaa (hitaagana) maŋ meccara velaa bæluve giya sumaanee pattarayak
pattaree kiyalaa tiyena hæṭiyaṭa ee gollo heṭayi Laŋkaavaṭa enne
eyaa Gaalu yanna kiyalaa giyaa
pææna væṭicca hæṭiyema maŋ ahulaagattaa
kaar-ekak elavana hæṭi taattaa maṭa iiye kiyaa dunnaa
maalu uyana hæṭi ee lamayaa tavama hariyaṭa danne nææ
pol gaana hæṭi akkaa naŋgiṭa kiyaa denavaa
lamayaa kææma kana hæṭiyen kiyanna puluvan baḍagini nææ kiyalaa
mahattayaa dannavaada Laŋkaave minissu bat uyana hæṭi?

Lesson 28 B.

      naŋgi pol gaalaa ivaralu

      api okkomalaa dæn tee biilaa ivarayi

      taattaa koheda ada udenma hadissiye giye?

      siini ivara velaa lamayaa siini raattalak geenna mee laŋga kaḍeeṭa

        duvalaa enna giyaa

5   Laŋkaaven liyuma taattaagen enna æti

      mee peṭṭiya maṭa ussanna bara væḍi ne

      mahattayaage bara koccarada?

      maŋ ee pota dæn kiyavalaa ivarayi

      kaḍee haal ivara velaa, itiŋ maŋ ee venuvaṭa paan genaavaa

10   ehema væḍak karanna ee minihaaṭa pissu venna oonæ

      mee davasvala maŋ malliṭa kaar elavanna purudu karanavaa

      mehe iňdaŋ Gaallaṭa koccara æætada?/(durada?)

      ara ææta ena minihaa kavda?

      gedara iňdaŋ iskooleeṭa huňgak æætada?

15   mahattayaage alut pota hari ṣook ne

      naaki minihaa bima væṭenavaa dækalaa poḍi lamayaa hayiyenma

        hinaa vunaa

      edaa genaapu aṁba kohetma kanna bææ

      oya polgeḍi dekak tunak ærenna anik okkoma araŋ yanna

      mehe bææ væḍa nokara salli hamba karanna

20   mahattayaa yana koṭa eevaa okkoma vikinilaa tiyeyi

      kiyavalaa ivara vunaama pattaree navalaa araŋ tiyanna

      oya pææna ee lamayaa atin væṭilaa venna oonæ kæḍenna ætte

      mahattayaa iskoolee yanna koocciyaṭa naginavaa maŋ dækkaa

      hæbæyi magadi kaar-eka kæḍenna puluvan

25   mee minihaa kaar-eke janeelen ape baḍu horakam karanavaa maŋ

        dækkaa

      gedara giyaayin passe tee bomu

      ee minihaa yaṭa venavaa mahattayaa dækkaada?

      heṭa daval dolahen passe ape pætte kaḍa(val) vahalaa

      taattaa nidi æti, væḍiya sadda karanna epaa

30   kaḍen nayaṭa baḍu ganna eka væḍiya hoňda næ

      aṁba narak velaa kiyalaa ammaa okkoma ahaka dæmmaa

      eyaa kiyana hæṭiyaṭa pattaree tiyenne okkoma boru

mee kaḍee eevaaṭa vaḍaa ara kaḍee baḍu laabayi kiyalaa maṭa hitenavaa
hinaa vena hæṭiyen maṭa kiyanna puluvan kavda kiyalaa
maŋ ena koṭa eyaa gihin
ada vahiyi kiyalaa hitanavaada?
lamayaa ginipeṭṭiyak geenna(m) kiyalaa kaḍeeṭa giyaa
maava veelapahin kuuddapu eka hoňdayi
kaar-eka elavana hæṭiyen eyaa tavama purudu venavaa kiyalaa kiyanna puluvan
alut orloosuva næti vunayi kiyalaa lamayaa aňḍanavaa

Lesson 29 B.

tavama lææsti nætnam velaavaṭa yanna bæri veyi
pot genaave nætnam iskoolee aave æyi?
uḍaha gedara ballaa aayi ape dihaave aavot elavanavaa
iskoolee væḍa hoňdaṭa keruvot taattaa maṭa at orloosuvak araŋ denavaa kivvaa
parakku vunot issaraha dora vahalaa tiyeyi
mataka næti vunot kiyalaa liyaaganna
maŋ ada iskoolee giye næti bava dannavaa nam ammaaṭa taraha yayi
mahattayaa kiyanavaa nam maŋ ehema karannam
mahattayat yanavaa nam ikmanaṭa naginna
tee hadalaa denavaa nam maŋ bonnam
ee lamayaa tava ṭikak paaḍam karanavaa nam hoňdayi
pahe bas-eke aavaa nam maava hamba venavaa
iiye liyuma dæmmaa nam eeka eyaaṭa heṭa hamba veyi
mii laňgaṭa monavaada karanna tiyenne?
isṭeesamaṭa yanavat ekka koocciya ædd(evv)at/(ædd(evv)aaṭa) maŋ nægagattaa
ape gee issaraha tiyuna pol gas okkoma kapalaa
api dæn pote kiiveni piṭaṭada ævit tiyenne?
mee kehel geḍivala piṭapætta vitarayi narak velaa tiyenne
almaariya piṭipasse mage pota væṭilaa tiyunaa
dostara mahattayaa leḍaa balanna dæn ṭikakaṭa issellaa aavaa/(aave)
polisiyaṭa bæňdenna maŋ kæmati
mee raṭe minissu sapattu væḍiya aňdinne nææ
ee balalaaṭa aayi ape gedara hariyakaṭa vat enna denna epaa

vedamahattayaa ena kan maŋ koccara velaa balaŋ hiʈiyaada!
Siripaala vitarayi tavama enna inne
apiʈa heʈa udenma Kolam̆ba yanna tiyenavaa, maʈa mee væɖee hun̆gak hadissi
væssot maŋ gedara innavaa heʈa
ada hari heʈa hari maʈa gedara yanna tiyenavaa
maʈa heʈa Kolam̆baʈa baɖu arinna tiyenavaa
mee potaʈa tava rupiyalakut sata dahayak maŋ eyaaʈa denna tiyenavaa
ena san̆dudaa in̆daŋ maʈa hæmadaama væɖaʈa yanna venne koocciyen
bas-ekaʈa tava kiidenek naginna innavaada?
mama heʈa gedara yanna innavaa
mahattayaa enna inne kaar-ekenda (nætnam) bas-ekenda?
ena agoostu maasee maŋ gamaʈa yanna innavaa
navattalaa tiyicca bas-eka issarahayin lamayi dennek paaraʈa pænnaa
koocciyaʈa yanna (vitarak) giya sallivalin maʈa Gaalu gihin ennat tiyunaa
ee davasvala maŋ gedarin piʈa giyot gahanavaa
maŋ særen særeeʈa gihin bæluvaa eyaaʈa kohomada kiyalaa
mee kaɖee baɖu kohetma laaba nææ

Lesson 30 B

kavuru hari mage alut pææna araŋ (tiyenavaa)
eyaa æra vena kavurut mee vidihe væɖak karanne nææ
Tirikunaamalee æra vena kohe vat ehema yanavaa kivve nædda?
vena kohoma vat mee væɖee karanna bææ, meeka tamayi tiyena ekama vidiha
ee velaave kavurut etana hiʈiye næti eka hon̆dayi
mahattayaa ee væɖee kohoma hari maʈa karalaa denna
Joon æra vena kavurut hiʈiye nææ
ena koʈa dora vahalaa tiyeyi, doraʈa taʈʈu keruvaama kavuru hari ævit arii
naalaa eyaage oluvaʈa daanna mokut nædda kiyalaa eyaa ahanavaa
tee hæduvaaʈa mokada bonna kavurut nææ
Tissaʈa æra vena kaaʈa vat mehema væɖak venne nææ
maŋ giyaaʈa passe kavurut aạvaada?
taattaaʈa issellaa vena kavurut kantooru ævit hiʈiyaada?

ape gee issaraha kavda loku loriyak genallaa gahalaa tiyenavaa
mahattayaage puʈuva gaava mokakda væʈilaa tiyenavaa
taattaaʈa kavda ævit innavaa kiyanna
taattaa gedarada, kohe vat giyaada?
ballaa kaaʈada goravanavaa æhilaa maŋ aavaa balanna
ee piñgaana mage atin kæɖicca bava gedara vena kavurut tavama danne nææ
siiyaa am̃bada monavaada genat
mallilaa kavurut tavama iskoolee yanavaa
mee saappuve baɖu kookat laabayi
kaamaree kohet puʈu
midule kohet tanakola vævilaa
mee okkoʈama kiiyak oonæda?
mage yaaluvo kavurut hoñdayi hæbæyi duppat
mee bas-eke (inna) kavurut Gaallaʈa
geval(valaʈa) kookaʈat janeel doraval tiyenavaa
lamayaa gedara kaaʈa vat nokiyaa kaɖeeʈa gihin
vena kavuru hari eeka liyanna æti
kiiya(ka)ʈat denne nææ
ada maʈa kohoma vat enna bææ, væɖa tiyenavaa
lamayaa koccaravat añɖanavaa
ahapu koyivaaʈat uttara nææ
oya pota maʈa kiiya(ka)ʈat epaa
kavda mahattayek ævit innavaa
maŋ eyaava kiiyakaʈa vat ganan ganne nææ
taattaa heʈa udenma koheda yanavaa kivvaa
maamaada koheda ara enne/(enavaa)
ada maŋ ena koʈa iskoolee paʈan araŋ (tiyunaa)
ee næva yanavaa nemeyi enavaa
ee kaar-eka nikam nævak vage
piʈipasse ʈayar deka hoñdaʈama gevilaa
hakuru hoñdayi kiribat kana koʈa
lañgadi læbunu lamayaa kavuru vageeda, ammaa vageeda taattaa vageeda?

Lesson 31 B.

kooṭ-ekaṭa bottam alladdi iňdikaṭṭa kæḍunaa
vahalee kaḍaŋ væṭena koṭa/(væṭenavat ekkama) maŋ divuvaa
ammaa mærunaama maala ṭika læbeyi
livvaa hari!
taattaa ehenam dæn kantooruve ædda?
yana koṭa ballaava eliyaṭa daalaa yanna, aavaama maŋ uuva geṭa gannam
tee kooppayak allanna ara noonaamahattayaaṭa issellaa(ma)
ada maŋ enna rææ vunaa ne
taattaa naavaaṭada aňḍanne?
gindara molavanna dara oonælu
mee væḍee api balaaporottu vunaaṭa vaḍaa amaaruyi
kææma kanna issellaa at deka hoodaŋ inna
api yana koṭa eyaa bat kaalaa æti
lamayi sellam karalaa (sellam) karalaa hoňdaṭa baḍagini vunaama gedaraṭa duvaŋ enavaa
giya maasee deveni daa pattaree laabeeṭa kaar-ekak daalaa tiyunaa
api ena koṭa heṭa veyi
mærenne nætuva beerunaa æti
api ehe giyaama tee kooppayak tiyaa vatura viiduruvak vat dunne nææ
eyaa ena ekaṭa taattaa væḍiya kæmati nææ
ballaa nitara bæňdalaa inna eka maṭa allanne nææ
giya maasee pahalosveni daa pattaree maŋ hoyanavaa hoyanavaa/(hevvaa hevvaa), maṭa tavama hamba vune nææ
mee lamayaa dannavaa æti ne kaageda kiyalaa
tunaṭa enavaa kiyapu sissayaa tavama nææ
lamayaa gedara yanna kæmati kiyalaa ammaa aavaa ekka-yanna
asaniipayi kiyalaa eyaa ada kantooru enne næhællu
mee pææñaṭa tiinta daana hæṭi dannavaada?
kiyavana hæṭiyen maŋ dannavaa eeka eyaaṭa teerenne næti bava
eyaa ævidina hæṭiyen maŋ dannavaa kavda kiyalaa
pææna næti vaga danne dæn
horaa ahu vecca vaga pattaree tiyunaa
siini kiyalaa lamayaa lunu daagena/(daalaa) tee kooppeeṭa

naraka væḍavalaṭa taattaa gahanavayi kiyalaa lamayaa kohetma baya nææ
ayiyaa alut sapattu kuṭṭamak ganna kiyalaa Kolam̆ba giyaa
naana kaamaree saayam gaanna (kiyalaa) taattaa læœsti vunaa
mahattayaa sumaanee antimaṭa gedara yana bava api dænaŋ hiṭiye nææ
taattaa ænee talalaa daanna (kiyalaa) miṭiyak hoyanavaa
velaa tiyenavayi kiyalaa nikam inna epaa
væḍakaarayaa tavama kaḍee, monavaa karanavaada danne nææ
ee mahattayaa kaar-ekakaṭa yaṭa velaa malaa kiyalaa iiye pattaree tiyunaa
parakku venavayi kiyalaa eyaa tee-ekak vat nobii yanna giyaa
lamayaa gedarat huñgak væḍa karana bava guruvarayaa dænaŋ hiṭiyaa
guruvarayaa lamayaaṭa balalek añdina hæṭi kiyaa denavaa
ammaa gedara enna issellaa kaamaree lassanaṭa hari gassalaa tiyamu
vahina hæṭi peenavaada?
vahina bava maŋ danne nææ
meeka aḍi pahak ganakam
mage orloosuva hiṭalaa, dæn kiiyada?

Lesson 32 B.

තාත්තා කෝච්චියෙ යන ගමන් පොතක් කියවනවා.
එයා යන්න නෑ වගෙ.
සල්ලි ඕනෑ බව දන්නවා නම් දෙනවා නෙ.
පුලුවන් නම් බද්ද එන්න.
දුවන ගමන් ලමයා වැටුනා.
සිරිපාල මහත්තයා කොහෙවත් ගියාද? ගිය දිහාවක් නෑ.
මගෙ ගනන එක්කහු කරන්න.
ගෝවා කෝකත් එක ගාන(යි).
පුටුව උස්සන් යන ගමන් දෙරේ හැප්පිලා කකුලක් කුඩුනා.
කාර් දූන් ගනන් ගිහින්.
හෙට කොලඹ යනවා නම් මාත් එනවා.
පුලුවන් නම් මාව අල්ලන්න.
තාත්තා ලඟ මුද්දරයක් තියෙනවාද? තියෙනවා නම් මට දෙන්න.
ඉස්කෝලේ ඉඳන් එන ගමන් පාරෙදි පිස්සු බල්ලෙක් කාලා ඒ ලමයා කෑ ගගහා ගෙදර ආවා.

15 ගෙදර එන ගමන් වෙන කොහෙවත් යන්නෙ නැතුව ඉක්මනට එන්න.

අමාරු නම් කරදර වෙන්න එපා අනේ. නෑ මට කිසි කරදරයක් වෙන්නෙ නෑ.

ළමයා දැන් එන්න එන්න උස යනවා.

ඒ අල්මාරියේ දෙර අඩි තුනක් පලලයි අඩි පහකුත් අඟල් දහයක් උසයි.

කොලඹ ගෙවල් දෙකක් තුනක් ඇත් නම් මොන සල්ලිද!

20 අවුරුදු තුනකුත් ගානකට හිරේ ගියා.

අවුරුදු ගානක්(ම) ලංකාවෙ හිටියා.

එකක් වත් රතු නෑ.

හැම තැනම (කොහෙත්) බැලුවා, කොතනක වත් නෑ තියුනෙ.

ඊයෙ වැස්සා නම් අද පායයි.

25 රුපියලකුත් සත දහයක් ගියා.

එයා එන්නෙ නෑ වගෙ.

මං ඒ පොතට සල්ලි ඇරියා, දැන් පොතත් නෑ සල්ලිත් නෑ.

කාලා (කාලා) ඇති වෙලා නිදි.

ඒ මහත්තයාගෙ කාර්-එක හදන්න මං ඊයෙ මිනිහෙක් ඇරියා, තවම නෑ ආවෙ, ඒ මිනිහත් නෑ කාර්-එකත් නෑ.

30 තාත්තා තරහ වෙලා තේ-එක වත් නොබී යන්න ගියා.

කියන දේ නාහන ළමයින්ට කවුරුත් වගෙ කැමති නෑ.

ටිකක් කෑ නොගහා ඉන්න බැරිද?

ළමයා මට යන්න නොදී දෙර වැහැව්වා.

මං එක වෙන කොට දවල් කෑමට එන්නම්.

35 ගාලු යනවා නම් අම්මත් එයි.

හෙට වහින්න පුලුවන්.

කිරි ටික වහලා තියන්න, නැත්නම් බලලා බොන්න පුලුවන්.

එතකොට මං කරපු වැඩේ තව ටිකක් හයියෙන් දුවන්න ගත්තා.

මහත්තයා ඒකට කරපු වැඩේ අපූරුයි.

40 එයා තවම යන්න (ඇත්තෙ) නෑ.

ඕකට මං නොවරදින බෙහෙතක් කියන්නම්.

මහත්තයා ඒ ලියුම එදම නොදපු එක වැරදි.

නරක් නොවෙච්ච ගෙඩි ටික විතරක් විසි කරන්න එපා.

ඔර්ලෝසුව බිම වැටිලත් නොකැඩිච්ච එක පුදුමයි.

45 එයා හතරට කාලක් තියෙද්දි එන්න පොරොන්දු වුනා.

අද කන්තෝරුවට ගියාට මොකද කිසිම වැඩක් කෙරුනෙ නෑ.

Lesson 33 B.

ඉල්ලන පලියට දෙන්න බෑ.

එයා මට සල්ලි දුන්නත් ගන්නෙ නෑ.

හොඳට වැඩ නොකරන ළමයින්ට ගුරුවරු අකමැති.

අව්වේ දපුවා වහින ගමන් ගෙට ගන්න.

05 ළමයාට විතරක් නෙමෙයි ගුරුවරුන්ටත් බැන්නා තාත්තා.

අපි ගිය අතරෙ ගේ බිඳලා.

ටිකක් පරක්කු වුනත් කාරියක් නෑ, එන්න.

මං කියපුවා නෙමෙයි ඔය ගෙනල්ලා තියෙන්නෙ.

අපි ගෙදර නැති අතර අම්මාලා ආවොත් ටිකක් ඉන්න කියන්න.

10 ඒ ගොල්ලො තරහ වෙලා, යනවා වත් කියලා (යනවා කියලාවත්) නෙමෙයි ගියෙ.

හොඳයි එහෙනම් ගිහින් එන්න කො.

මහත්තයා හරි පල් වැඩක්/වැඩේ මට කෙරුවෙ.

ඒ ළමයා කවදක් වත් බොරු කියන්නෙ නෑ.

බබා බලා ගන්න මල්ලි හිටි එකෙන් අපිට හොඳට ගියා.

15 හිස් අතින් ආවා නම් හිස් අතින් යන්න පුලුවන්.

කරුවල වැටුනායින් පස්සෙ මේ පාරෙ යන එක බයානකයි, අලි ඉන්නවා.

මේ බාල්කේ හරි අවදනම්.

මේ පාර්සලේ තව ටිකක් තදට බඳින්න.

බල්ලාගෙ කරේ බැඳලා තියෙන පටිය තව ටිකක් බුරුල් කරන්න.

20 මේකෙ තියෙන්නෙ පල් වතුර.

වෙන්න තියෙන දේ වලක්කන්න බෑ කියලා මිනිහා කාර්-එක හැප්පෙන්න යනවා දැකලා තොප්පියෙන් ඇස් දෙක වහගත්තා.

මේ සපත්තුව මට තද වැඩී.

කාර්-එක වික්ක එකයි එයා මාත් එක්ක තරහ වෙන්න/වුනාට ප්‍රදන කාරනේ.

මහත්තයා හොඳයි එකට එනවා කිව්වා, දැන් පහයි වෙලාව.

25 සිරීපාදේ නැග්ගාම උදේට ඉර පායනවා පේනවා.

මේ එක පෙට්ටියක වත් පොත් තියුනෙ නෑ.

මේ දවස්වල මල්ලිට පොත් හිටන් අරන් දුන්නෙ / (පොත් අරන් දුන්නෙ හිටන්) මමයි.

තාත්තා වෙනුවෙන් පුතා ඕනෑ එකක් කරන්නම්ලු.

ඊයේ පෙරේද වැස්සාට මොකද තවම වතුර හිඟයි.

30 මහත්තයා එද මට කියපුවා ඔක්කොම බොරු.

අඩුරන පලියට ටිකට් නැතුව ඉස්ටේසමට ඇතුල් වෙන්න දෙන්න බෑ.

මේ ළමයා නැහිට්ට වෙලෙ හිටන් අඩනවා.

පෙට්ටි එකක් වත් ඇරලා නෑ.

උදේ ඉඳන් වැඩ කරලා කරලා දැන් මට හරියට මහන්සී.

35 කවුරුත් පාහෙ ඇවිල්ලා නිසා දැන් අපේ වැඩේ පටන්ගන්න පුලුවන්.

කන්තෝරු ගියාට එද නිවාඩු දවසක් හින්ද කවුරු වත් ඇවිදින් හිටියෙ නෑ.

කවුරුත් කියනවා ඒ මිනිහා හරි මෝඩයි කියලා.

මීට ඉස්සෙල්ලා කවදවත් එයා ඔහොම වැඩක් කරලා නෑ.

මේ ළමයාට කොහොමට වත් කවන්න බෑ.

40 මොකකින්ද ගහල තියෙන්නෙ?

ළමයි බත් කන්නෙ ටිකයි, හැබැයි වතුර හුහක් බොනවා.

ඒක දිග පලල කොච්චරද?

VOCABULARY

The Sinhalese order of letters followed in the vocabulary is as follows:

a aa æ ææ i ii u uu ṛ (ṛṛ) e ee o oo ai au ŋ ḥ
k kh g n̆g gh ŋ c ch j n̆j jh ñ ṭ ṭh ḍ n̆ḍ ḍh ṇ
t th d n̆d dh n p ph b m̆b bh m y r l v
ʃ ʂ s h ḷ

Figures after each word refer to Lessons where the words first occur; s = Script section.

akamæti 33 B 3 unwilling, disliking
akkaa 21 elder sister
agoostu 22 August
an̆gala 13 inch
an̆gaharuvaadaa 19 Tuesday
accara 10 that much
aṭa 9 eight
aḍamaana 31 doubt; unsafe
aḍipaara 17 footpath
aḍiya 13 foot (12″)
an̆ḍa 24 cry
an̆ḍa gahanavaa 26 shout, call
an̆ḍanavaa 16 weep
an̆ḍalanavaa 25 B 26 crow
-at 29 although
ata 12 hand, arm; direction
atana 4 there
atara 29, 33 A 10 among; between; while
atare 29, 33 A 10 among; between; while
atin 13 at the hand of; from; in respect of, 16 A 7
ate 20 A 14 at the hand of
attaa 21 grandfather
ada 1 today
ada iiye 17 B 18 recently
ada heṭa 2 today or tomorrow
adinavaa 20 drag, pull
adisiya 28 accident
addanavaa 21 A 22 pull out
an̆dinavaa 16 draw (pictures); put on (clothes), wear
an̆dunanavaa 19 A 11 recognize, know (a person)
an̆duranavaa 19 recognize, know (a person)
-an 11 (plural ending)
anik 28 other
anit 28 other
aniddaa 17 the day after tomorrow
anun 33 others
anuu(va) 20 ninety(-)
anee 7, 15b alas
ankal 21 uncle
antaraava 28 danger

antaraa venavaa 32 A 14 die
antima 31 last; last part
andanavaa 18 A 4 dress (tr.)
andama 17 manner
anna 3 look there
aparaadee 21 (A 29) misfortune
api 1 we
apuuruva 32, remarkable thing
ape 3 our
apen 10 from us
appacci 3 A 16 father
appaa 3 father
apriyel 22 April
apreel 22 April
am̆ba 10 mangoes
am̆bageḍiya 13 mango
amataka 25 unmindful, forgotten
amaaru(va) 23 difficult(y)
ammaa 1, 3 A 16, 22 B 6, 27 A 16 mother
-aya 5, 9 (nominal ending)
ayiyaa 21 elder brother
ayise 7 A 21 you
ara 3, 7 A 20 that
araŋ 15, 28 A 38 bringing
araka 3 that one (inanimate)
arakaa 11 that one (animate)
arakku 15 arrack
aragana 15 bringing
aragannavaa 15, 29 **b** take
arayaa 11 that man
aravaa 4 those things
arahaṭa 4 thither
arahe 3 there
arinavaa 12, 15 B 10 send; open; allow
alavanavaa 22 B 26 stick on (tr.)
aliyaa 4, 33 A 37 elephant
alut 16 new
aluten 20 afresh, newly; recently
alkiriima 3s (consonantal sign)
almaariya 13 cupboard
allanavaa 19, 20 A 4, 23 **a**, 30 A 43, 31 A 22, 31 B 1 catch; serve, please
allapu 25 A 37 next door
avadaanama 33 danger
avadi venavaa 22 wake up (intr.)
avurudda 20, 25 B 10 year; New Year
avva 31 sunshine
asaniipee 25 ill-health
asuu(va) 20 eighty(-)
as venavaa 22 (B 25) resign, leave
ahaka 28 aside
ahaka daanavaa 28 B 31 throw away
ahak karanavaa 28 B 31 remove
ahaṭṭa 4, 28 thither; aside
ahanavaa 10, 17 A 17, 21 A 26 listen; ask
aharaṭa 4 thither
ahare 3 there
ahulanavaa 27 pick up
ahu venavaa 19 get caught
-aa 3 (past tense ending)
aaŋ 3**e**, 14 A 5 look there
aacci 21 grandmother
aataa 21 grandfather
aanḍuva 26 Government
aanna 3 look there
aapahu 30 back again

aappa 32 hoppers
aayaa 18 A 4 nurse
aayi(t) 17, 25 again
aayuboovan 7 (a greeting)
aayurveeda 29 herbal medicine
aayet 17, 25e again
aaraŋciya 32 news
aavaa 3 came
aavaaṭa giyaaṭa 25 A 24 haphazardly
æ 14 A 5 (particle)
æksiḍaŋ-eka 28 accident
æn̆gili gahanavaa 24 B 30 meddle
æn̆gilla 24 finger
æti 19, 25 **a**, 26 **c** is enough; is probably
æti karanavaa 19 bring up; create
ætulaṭa 25 within
ætule 25 within
ætta 24 truth
ætte 19 (incompl. of æti)
ædaŋ 32 A 43 suddenly
ædda 19 (interrog. of æti)
æddaa (see adinavaa)
æn̆da 14 bed
æn̆duma 25 garment
ænee 22 nail, screw
ænjima 15 engine
ænṭi 21 aunt
ændaa 20 drew; wore
æyi 4, 27 A 5 why?
æra 28 except, besides
ærenavaa 25 A 11, q.v.
ærenna 28 except, besides
ælapilla 2s (*a*-vowel sign)
ælenavaa 22 stick (intr.)
ævit 15 having come
ævidin 15 having come
ævidinavaa 23 walk
ævillaa 15 having come
Æsala 22 (name of a month)
æhæ 33 eye
æhærenavaa 22 eyes open
æhenavaa 13 A 20 hear
ææta 28 far
ikman 27 speed
ikmanaṭa 27 quickly
ikmanin 27 quickly
igenagannavaa 32 learn
-icca 20 (participial ending)
in̆ju 8s (exclamation)
iḍa 6c space; permission, opportunity
itin 17 then
ituru karanavaa 22 save
idiripiṭa 29 in the presence of
idiriyaṭa 29 in the future
idiriye 29 in the presence of
idenavaa 33 ripen
in̆da 15 having been
in̆daŋ 15 having been, from
in̆dagannavaa 23 sit down
in̆dalaa 15 having been, from
in̆dia(a)ppa 32 string hoppers
in̆dikaṭṭa 31 needle
in̆dii 14 will be
in 25 **e** from that
-in 10, 25 (instr. case ending)
-in 11 (plural ending)
indanavaa 18 plant, place
innavaa 5, 7 A 19, 22, 29 be (of animates); wait; intend

ibeeṭama 13 automatically
ibeema 13 automatically
ira 31 sun; line
iranavaa 22 tear (vb.)
iridaa 19 Sunday
illanavaa 19 ask for
ivara 10 (28 A 36) finished
ivara karanavaa 21 end (tr.)
ivaraya 28 end (noun)
ivvaa 12 cooked
isaradaya 32 **g** headache
is-issellaa 31 A 20 first of all
iskoolee 2 school
isṭeesama 22 station
istuti 7 thanks
ispiritaalee 28 hospital
ispilla 4s (**i**-vowel sign)
issara 22 formerly
issaraha 25 (B 28) in front of
issarahapiṭa 29 **c** in presence of
issarindaa 25 A 30 the day before
issenavaa 24 A 34 be raised
issellaa 25 before
issellaama 18 firstly
ihala 29 up
iiṭa 8 **c** to that
iiye [1], 3 yesterday
iilaňga 22 **d** next
-u 11 (plural ending)
uguræssa 27 A 30 (a fruit)
uḍa 8 above
uḍadi 20 ago
uḍaraṭa 29 Up-Country
uḍaha 29 (A18) up
uḍinma 20 A 34 highly
utura 15 north
uturanavaa 24 bubble
uttaree 30 answer (noun)
udee 12 morning
un 11 they, them
-un 11 (plural ending)
una 24 fever (**also** bamboo)
unaa 12 became
unnæhæ 1, 4 A 10 he
unnæhe 1 he
unnaa 5 was (animate)
uṁba 1 you
uṁbe 10 your
uṁben 10 from you
uyanavaa 12 cook
usa 5 high, height
usa yanavaa 26 get tall
ussanavaa 24 lift
uu 11 it (of animals), he
-e 4 (incomplete verb ending)
-e 5 (11 A 17, 12 A 1, 18 A 17) (locative case ending)
Eŋgalantee 32 England
ek- 11 one-
eka 2, 3 A 9, 10 A 12, 24 one
-eka 11, 20 (A 3) (termination for loanwords)
ekaṭa 28 A 10 together
ekat ekaṭa 9 A 27 surely
ekaa 7 A 6, 11 **b**, one (animate)
ekolaha 10 eleven
ekolos- 11 eleven-
ekka 17, 25 with; also
ekkaŋ enavaa 23 A 8 bring (a person)

ekkama 25 with
ekka-yanavaa 17 take (a person)
ekkaraŋ 23 A 8 bringing
ekkalaa 15 together
ekkahu karanavaa 32 add up
ekko 9 or
ek venavaa 15 unite (intr.)
ek velaa 15 together
egoḍa 29 that side
egoḍaha 29 on that side
eccara 10 that much
etakoṭa 17 then
etana 4 there
etara 29 that side
etuvaa 12 wrapped
edaa 20 that day; in the past
-en 10 (instr. case ending)
enavaa 1, 15 A 10, 23 **a** come
enjima 15 engine
epaa 6, 15 **c** is not required; don't!
epiṭaha 29 that side
emin 32 A 8 coming
eyaa 1 he, she
elanavaa 26 spread (tr.)
elavanavaa 24 drive, drive away
elavalu 13 vegetables
elavalukaarayaa 13 vegetable seller
elahakaṭa 19 by that time
eliya 21 light; outside
ellanavaa 30 hang (tr.)
evanavaa 18 send
ehaa 29 that side
ehaaṭa 4 thither
ehe 3 there
ehedi 17 while there
ehen 24 B 33 thence
ehenam 14 if so
ehema **[1c]), 17 c**, 28 A 14 thus
ehemat 32 few
ehemapiṭin 32 as they are; altogether
ee 3 that
-ee 5 (nominal ending)
-ee 5**e** (locative case ending)
ee gollo (gollan, golla) 1 they, them
eeka 3 that one (inanimate)
eekayi 19 A 3 that's why
eekaa 11 that one (animate)
eevaa 4, 18 A 19, 20 A 12, 30 A 31 those things
-o 11 (plural ending)
okkoma 10, 14**e** all
oktoombara 22 October
occara 10 that much
-ot 29 (conditional ending)
otana 4; 20 A 8 there; wrapping
otanavaa 12 wrap
-otin 29 (conditional ending)
onna 3 look there
onna ohe 30 A 5 just
oba (tumaa) 1 you
oya 3 that (**also** river)
oya gollo 1 you (pl.)
oyaa 1 you
oyiṭa 8 **c** to that
orloosuva 15 clock, watch
oluva 30 (B 9) head
ov 5 yes
ovvaa 4 those things
ohaaṭa 4 thither
ohe 1, 3 A 24, 7 A 10 there

ohe 3 you
ohoma 17, 28 A 14 thus
ooka 3 that one (inanimate)
ookaa 11 that one (animate)
oonæ [1 **c**], 6, 15**c**, 18 A 25, 20 is necessary
oonækamin 23 deliberately
oonæma 20, 28 any
oovage 26 **d** like that
oovaa 14, 12 A 22 those things
-ŋ 23 (for -gana)
-k 2 (indefinite ending)
kakaa 15 eating
kakiyanavaa 32 ache
kakula 29 leg
kaṭa 24 mouth
kaḍakaarayaa 6 shopkeeper
kaḍanavaa 11 (A 18) break, pick
kaḍa sayanna 13s (palatal **s**)
kaḍaa 19 A 3 suddenly...
kaḍee 6 shop, 'boutique'
kataa karanavaa 21 speak, call
katkaarayaa 13 pingo-carrier
kada 13 'pingo'
kaňdu 14 hills (pl. of **kanda**)
kan 21 until
kanagaaṭu(va) 25 sad(ness)
kanavaa 6, 6 A 25 eat
kantooruva 12 office
kanda 8, 14 hill
kapanavaa 11 cut
kamisee 23 A 6 shirt
kara 15 [kərə] having done
kara 33 neck
karagana yanavaa 23 continue to
karattee 15 cart
karadaree 24 trouble
karanavaa 4, 8 A 13 do
karalaa 15, 17**b** (31 A 30) having done
karaa 12 [kəraa] did
karunaa-karalaa 7 please
karuvala 33 darkness
kal 21; 29 **e** until, as long as; time
kala 20 [kələ] done
kala 29 time
kalaa 12 did
kalin 26 earlier on
kalu 13 black
kaluvara 33 darkness
kalee 32 pitcher
kalpanaa karanavaa 23 reflect
kavadat 30 always
kavadaa-da 4 when?
kavurut 30 everybody
kavuru-da 30 who (pl.)?
kavda 4, 30 who? someone
kavdat 30 A 18 someone
kavdo 30 someone
kaa- (**see** kavda)
kaamaree 19 room
kaaranee 33 reason; affair
-kaarayaa 12 doer
kaariya 32 matter; reason
kaar-eka 11 car
kaala 8 quarter
kaalee 29 time
kaava 15 A 27 whom?
kæňdavanavaa 18 summon
kæpenavaa 13 get cut, cut
kæmati 6, 15**c**, 20 wish, like

kælææva 9 forest, jungle
kælee 9 forest, jungle
kælee karanavaa 19 make a jungle of
kææ gahanavaa 32 cry out
kææma 6, 17 A 5, 23 **B** 33 food, meal
kæælla 24 piece
kiṭṭu(va) 22 near
kitul 15**d**, 30 (kind of palm-tree)
kiyanavaa 6 (A 2), 15 A 24, 17 A 13 say
kiyalaa 18, 27 having said
kiyalaa evanavaa 27 A 43 report
kiyavanavaa 16, 18 read
kiri 14(**f**), 33 A 23 milk
kiriammaa 21 grandmother
kiribat 30 'milk-rice'
kiluṭu 17 dirty
kivvaa 12 said
kisi 28 any
kii- 18 how many?
kiikaru 17 obedient
kiidenaa-da 11 how many people?
kiiyak-da 8, 12 A 22 how much/many?
kiiyada 8, 12 A 22 how much/many?
kiivaa 12 said
kiiveni 18 how-many-eth?
kukulaa 25 cock
kuṭṭama 31 pair (of things)
kuḍappaa 3 A 16 uncle
kuḍammaa 3 A 16 aunt
kuḍaa 3 A 16 little
kuḍee 13 umbrella
kunu 31 rubbish; rotten
kum̆bura 26 rice-field
kussiya 22 kitchen
kuuddanavaa 21 wake (tr.)
kuum̆biyaa 32 ant
keṭṭu 5 thin
-kenaa 11 **in** ekkenaa, one person
kenek 2 a person
keravala 32 end (kelavara)
keruvaa 4 did
kelin 26 straight
kella 24 girl
kesel 20 bananas
kehel 20 bananas ('plantains')
ko 6, 14, 15 (exclamation)
koccara-da 10 how much?
koccaravat 17 all the time
koṭa 5 short
koṭa 15 having done
koṭa 21 when
koṭanavaa 26 pound, dig
kotana-da 4 where?
kombuva 5s (**e**-vowel sign)
koyi 10 which?
koyivaa 10 which ones?
koranavaa 12 do
Kolam̆ba 8 Colombo
kolee 17 (A 4) leaf
kollaa 24 lad
kovvaa 10 which ones?
kos 26 jak-fruit
kohaaṭa-da 4 whither?
kohet 30 everywhere
kohetma 12 at all
kohe-da 4, 18 A 22, 30 where?
koheda 30 A 11 somewhere

kohen-da 10 whence?
kohomaṭa 30 A 27 to what extent?
kohomat 30 in every way
kohoma-da 4, 30 A 11 how?
koo 2, 4, 7 A 25 where? (exclamation)
kookat 30 every one
kooka-da 10 which one? (inanimate)
kookaa-da 11 which one? (animate)
koocciya 11 train
kooṭ-eka 23 coat
koopi 22, 24 A 8 coffee
kooppee 22 cup
koovaa 10 which ones?
gagahaa 32 **B** 14 (gahanavaa)
gaňga 29 river
gaja 33 A 37 elephant(like)
gattaa 10 took
-gana 23 'having taken'
ganakam 31 thick(ness)
ganana 12 amount; sum
ganan arinavaa 12 A 20 get round someone
ganan karanavaa 13 do sums
ganan gannavaa 12 A 21 take account of
ganan yanavaa 26 get expensive
ganii 14 will take
gannavaa 10, 23, 24 A 12, 29 take; begin
gama 2 village
gaman 32**a** while
gamana 32**a** journey
gayanukitta 14s (a vowel symbol)
gala 14 stone, rock
gal gahanavaa 15 **B** 17 throw stones
gal gæhenavaa 17 A 3 be thunderstruck
gal venavaa 19 go solid
gassanavaa 19 cause to beat, shake
gaha 8 tree, bush
gahanavaa 15, 17 A 17, 19 A 2, 20 A 16, 27 A 36, 28 A 40, 31 A 24 hit
gahaagannavaa 23 fight
gaana 12, 32 **c** amount, sum; pretext
gaanavaa 24, 25 A 21, 26 A 6, 33 A 23 rub, scrape
gaane 12 A 14, 32 **c** at the rate of
Gaalu 8 Galle
Gaalla 8 Galle
gaava 22 near
gæṭee 33 **B** 10 knot
gæna 23 about, concerning
gææni 2, 16 woman
gini gannavaa 27 catch fire
ginipeṭṭiya 28 matchbox
gindara 31 fire
giyaa 3 went
gihin 15 having gone
gihillaa 15 having gone
guruvarayaa 10 teacher
-ge 3, 4 **B** 9 (genitive case-ending)
geḍiya 13, 20 fruit (and see am̆ba, paan)
gedara 2 home, house
-gen 10 (ablative case-ending)
gena 15 having taken
genat 15 having brought
genallaa 15 having brought
genæt 15 having brought

geniccaa 15 took away
geniyanavaa 15 take away
genihin 15 having taken away
genihillaa 15 having taken away
genenavaa 15 bring
gennanavaa 18 cause to bring
gembaa 24 frog
gevanavaa 32 pay, spend
gevenavaa 30 be spent, worn
gee 20 house
-gee 3 (genitive case-ending)
geenavaa 15 bring
gonaa 3 bullock
goyam 26 growing rice
goravanavaa 18 thunder; growl
golu sayanna 13s (retroflex sibilant)
gohin 15 having gone
goolayaa 27 pupil
goovaa 32 cabbage
cah 8s (exclamation)
janavaari 22 January
janeelee 14 window
jambu 20 **c** (a fruit)
Jaapanee 9 Jaffna
juuni 22 June
juuli 22 July
-ññam 14 (future termination)
-ññaa 4 (future termination)
-ṭa 2, 13 A 8, 17**a**, 17 A 22, 22 A 11, 23 A14, 24 A 35, 25**a** (dative ending)
ṭayar-eka 21 tyre
ṭika(k) 6, 7, 14, 18 A 3, 25**h** (a) little
ṭikaṭ-eka 24 ticket
ṭikadenek 14 a few people
-t 2, 19 A 21, 30, 32**f** (emphatic suffix)
taṭṭu karanavaa 30 knock
tada 33 firm (adj.)
tanakola 21 grass
tani(kara) 33 unalloyed
taniyama 29 alone
taniyen 29 alone
tabanavaa 15 place
tabbavanavaa 18 cause to place
taman 33 oneself
tamayi 10**c** self
tamunnaanse 1 you
tamuse 1 you
tambanavaa 32 boil
tara 5 fat
taraha 23 anger, angry
taruna 16 young
tal 15 **d** palmyra palm
talanavaa 27 (A 30), 31 **B** 36 beat
talee 30 blade, nib
tava 6 yet
tavat 6 yet, yet another
tavama 6, 8 A 24 still
taattaa 1, 3 A 16 father
taappee 21 wall (murus)
taama 6 still
taalee 31 tune, manner
tæna 4, 29 place
tæpæl karanavaa 29 post
tæægi karanavaa 14 A 10 present (verb)
tæægga 13 present (noun)
tibaha 25 thirst
tibenavaa 5 be

tibbavanavaa 18 cause to place
tibbaa 5, 15 was; placed
tiyanavaa 15 (A 29), 19 A 27, 20 A 11 place
tiyaa 30 not to mention
tiyunaa 5, 22, 29 was; could have
tiyenavaa 5, 19, 20 A 12, 26 A 40, 29 be
Tirikunaamalee 9 Trincomalee
tis- 19 thirty-
tisse 22 throughout
tiha 19 thirty
tiinta 31 paint, ink
tiiranaya karanavaa 23 decide
tun- 11 -three-
tuna 8 three
tuvaalee 24 wound
temenavaa 33 get wet
tel 25 oil; fat
tee 1 tea
teevatura 10 A 23 tea
teerenavaa 19 be understood
toppiya 33 hat
tooranavaa 19 choose; explain
-da 4, 8**d**, 18 B 16 (interrogative suffix); 30**a** (indefinite suffix)
dakinavaa 13 see
dakuna 15 south; right
dañga karanavaa 26 be mischievous
danḍa 24 stick
dannavaa 6 know; 27**a** (wonder)
dannanavaa 18 A 4 inform
damanavaa 20, 23**b** place
dara 27 firewood
daval 25 daytime
daval venavaa 20 A 33 be day: be late
davasa 18 day
daha- 11 ten-
dahaaṭa 18 eighteen
dahatuna 10 thirteen
dahanamaya 18 nineteen
dahaya 9 ten
dahayamaara 9 ten & a half
dahasaya 18 sixteen
dahahata 18 seventeen
dahahatara 10 fourteen
-daa 4**c**, **d**, 19 **d** day
daagannavaa 23 (B 24) put on; open shop
daanavaa 20 (15 A 29), 22 B 5, 23**b** place, put
daasaya 18 sixteen
dækkaa 13 saw
dæn 1, 6 B 16 now; mee dæn 3 A 6 just now; dæn itin 25**e** henceforth
dænaŋ 27 A 23 having discovered
dænagana 15, 23 having discovered
dænaṭa(ma) 2, 3 for now; now already
dænenavaa 13 be realized
dænma 18 B 15 at the minute, this moment
-di 17 (locative termination)
diga 13 long, length
diga arinavaa 26 unroll
digaṭa 25 along
dige 25 along
dihaa(va) 8 direction; towards
diilaa 15 having given

dunnaa 3 gave
duppat 16 poor
dum gahanavaa 27 smoke (intr.)
dura 28 far
Durutu 22 (name of a month)
duvanavaa 11 run
dusima 30 dozen
duu 11 daughter
duuru 11 daughters
de- 11 two-
deka 8 two
deka-ma 12 A 1 both
detun- 11 B 19 two or three
-den 33 (permissive ending)
denavaa 2, 6, 15 A 1 give
-denaa 11 persons
dennaa 11 two people
desæmbara 22 December
dee 26 thing
-do 30 (particle of doubt)
dora 13, 25 A 39 door
dorakaḍa 25 B 28 doorway
dolaha 10 twelve
dolos- 11 twelve-
dostara 22 doctor
-ddi 26 (temporal ending)
naŋgi 21 younger sister
na(ñ)ginavaa 8 (A 29), 9 A 20 climb
napuru 17 cruel
nam 8 **a**, 24 A 30, 29 **a**, 33 **d** if
nama 4, 14 A 13 name
nama(ya) 11, 9 nine
nam karanavaa 14 name (vb.)
naya 27 debt
naraka 10 bad
navatinavaa 26 stop (intr.)
navattanavaa 25, 26 B 8 stop (tr.)
navanavaa 24 fold
-navaa 1, 15, 25 (verbal termination)
naaki 16 old (of people)
naanavaa 11 bathe
naave 5 did not come
nægiṭinavaa 24 get up
næti 20 **c**, 23 **e** (participle of nææ); 19 A 29, 25 **a**
næti karanavaa 21 destroy, lose deliberately
nætinam 14 if not
nætilu 9 **e** is not + -lu
nætiva 15**a** without
nætuva 15, 25 **a** without
nætta 25 A 2 non-fact
nættam 14 if not
nætte 4 (incompl. of næti)
nætnam 14 if not
nædda 5 (interrog. of næti)
nændaa 26 aunt
næva 30 ship
næhæ 2 is not; no!
næhæ(l)lu 9**e** is not + -lu
nææ 2, 5, 32 B 16 is not; no!
nææyaa 22 relative (noun)
nææra 15 not having sent
næævit 15 not having come
nikam(ma) 17 (A 21) just; free; of itself
nikamaṭa 20 B 16 just
nicci(ya) 28 certain(ty)
nitara(ma) 16 (A3) often, regularly
nidaagannavaa 25 sleep

nidi 28 asleep
nidiyanavaa 28 A 7 sleep (vb.)
ninda [1**c**], 28 sleep (noun)
nil 5 blue
nivaaḏu(va) 22 holiday(s)
nisaa 21 because (of)
Nuvara 8 Kandy
nuvara 8 city
ne 28 you know
ne- 5**b** (negative prefix)
nemeyi 8 is not
nevæ 28**b** you know
nevi 8 is not
neveyi 8 is not
needa 30 A 3 is it not so?
neenne 5 does not come
no- 5 **b**, 10 **d**, 15 **a**, 20 **c**, 23 **e**, 26 **a**, **b**, 27 **a**, 29 **a** not
novæ 28 you know
novæmbara 22 November
novii 15 not having become
noveyi 8 is not
noonaa 16 lady
-nṯa 6 (infinitive termination)
-nḏa 6 (infinitive termination)
-nna 6, 14, 29 A 19, 32 A 2, 33 A 13 (infinitive termination)
-nnam 14 (future termination)
-nne 4 (incomplete ending)
paṯangannavaa 29 begin
paṯiya 33 belt
paḏiya 32 salary; stair
pattaree 15 newspaper
pattu karanavaa 27 B 34 light (tr.)
-pan 15 (imperative ending)
pan- 18 five
panas- 19 fifty-
panaha 19 fifty
paninavaa 10, 21 A 5, 24 A 26 jump
pantiya 18 class
pansala 29 monk's house, temple
pansil 33 Five Precepts
payipee 25 pipe
parakku 21 late
parana 16 old (not new)
pal 33 worthless
palayan 15 **b** go!
palala 13 broad, breadth
palaveni 18 first
pali 33 responsible
paliya 33 revenge
palleha 29 down
pavuma 33 pound(£)
pas- 11 five-
passa 29 B 5 the back
passaṯa 29 backwards
passe 25, 29 **c** (note) after, afterwards
passeha 29 **c** behind
paha 8 five
pahata 29 down; pahata raṯa, Low Country
pahamaara 9 five & a half
pahala 29 down
pahalova 10 fifteen
pahalos- 18 fifteen-
paaṯa 5, 11 A 7, 26 A 29, colour (noun)
paaṯa karanavaa 14 colour (vb.)
paaḏama 23 lesson
paaḏam gannavaa 24 hear a lesson

paan 14 bread
paan geḍiya 15 B 21 loaf of bread
paandara 27 early morning
paandarin 27 early in the morning
paapilla 7s (**u**-vowel sign)
paayanavaa 31 shine, rise (of the sun)
paara 9 way (route); time (fois); blow (coup): ee paara 14**c** ekaparaaṭa, 18**b**; while 32**b**
paare 33 A 40 behind
paarsalee 12 parcel
paalama 29 bridge
paas 20 pass (in an exam.)
paasaa 32 in every
paahe 33 almost
pæk karanavaa 24 B 6 pack
pæṭrol 26 petrol
pæṭrool 26 petrol
pætta 15 (A 29) side
pædura 26 mat
pænsala 5 pencil
pænsalee 5 pencil
pæhenavaa 33**h** ripen
pææna 5 pen
piňgaana 26 plate
piṭa 25, 29 page; outside; top, back
piṭapætta 29 the outside
piṭaraṭa 39**f** abroad
piṭipassa 30 B 43 behind
piṭipasse 29 behind
piṭu(va) 25 page(s)
pin 7 merit
pintuuree 25 picture
pipenavaa 30 blossom
piyaa 24 father
pirisidu 17 clean
pirenavaa 21 be full
pilikanna 29 B 5 back of house
pilivela 29 order, method
pissu(va) 28 mad(ness)
pihadaanavaa 24 b wipe; sweep (floor)
pihanavaa 24 **b** cook
pihidaanavaa 24 wipe; sweep (floor)
pihinavaa 24 **b** wipe
pihiya 13 knife (pl. **also** pihiyaa)
piinanavaa 12 swim
-pu 20 (past participle ending)
puŋci 3 small
puŋci karanavaa 14 make smaller
puṭuva 1 chair
putaa 11, 12 A 24 son
puduma venavaa 32 be surprised
pudumee 32 marvel (n.)
pupuranavaa 24 burst
puravanavaa 24 fill (tr.)
purudu 28 used
purudu karanavaa 28 train
purudda 28 (A 15) habit
puluvan 6, 15**c**, 20 (A 23) is possible
puusaa 18 pussy
peṭṭiya 24 box; compartment
penenavaa 13 appear
pennanavaa 18 show
pebaravaari 22 February
peranavaa 24 strain (liquids)
pereedaa 17 the day before yesterday
peenavaa 13 appear
peel 33 fail
poḍi 3 small

poḍi karanavaa 14 crush
poḍḍak 6 a little
pota 1 book
porondu venavaa 32 promise
poronduva 32 promise (n.)
pol 15 **d**, 22 coconuts
poliya 32 interest on money
polisiya 29 police(-station)
povanavaa 18 give to drink
Poson 22 (name of a month)
pohosat 16 rich
pradaana 33 principal
baŋ 1, 15**b** you
baḍagini 23 hunger
baḍaginna 23 hunger
baḍuva 13 thing, object
bat 6 cooked rice
badaadaa 19 Wednesday
bañdinavaa 20 tie; marry; build
baninavaa 16 scold, abuse verbally
babaa 24 baby
baya 29 fear
bayanaka, bayaanaka 33 frightening
bara 28 weight, heavy
balaŋ innavaa 23 wait
balanavaa 1, 17 A 6, 21**c** look (at), look for, try
balalaa 3; 15 cat; having seen
balaaporottu venavaa 21 hope
balu 17 dog-
ballaa 3 dog
bava 27 **b** fact
bas-eka 11 bus
bahinavaa 11 go down, get out
baagee 20 half
baappaa 3 A 16 uncle
baala 8 younger, inferior
baalkee 33 beam of wood
baaldiya 22 bucket
bægin 32 at the rate of
bæniyama 30 vest, 'banian'
bæri 6, 20 impossible
bæri velaa 13 accidentally
bæhæ 6 is impossible
bææ 6, 15**c**, 30 A 45 is impossible
bicciya 21 wall (of house)
bittaree 30 egg
biñdinavaa 20 break (tr.)
binduva 7s (a nasal sign)
bima 21 ground
bivvaa 3 drank
biilaa 15 having drunk
biivaa 3 drank
budi 28 asleep
budiyanavaa 28 A 8 sleep
bunnaa 12 drank
burul 33 loose
bedanavaa 32 distribute
beheta 22, 24 A 9 medicine
beerenavaa 25 escape
beesama 33 basin
bottama 31 button
bonavaa 1 drink
boruva 22 untruth
bola(ŋ) 1 you
bootalee 14 bottle
brahaspatindaa 19 Thursday
-ma 10 **c**, 11 A 11–12, 12 A 1, 16 A 9, A 25, 26 **b**, 27 A 33, 29 A 18 (emphasizing particle)

maŋ 1 I
mak 4**a** what
makanavaa 12 rub out
maga(di) 18 (on the) way
magula 29 (A 28) festivity
mage 3 my
magen 10 from me
maṭa 2 to me
maṭṭu karanavaa 14 punish
maḍa 19 mud
Maḍakalapuva 9 Batticaloa
matak venavaa 25 be remembered
mataka 25 memory; remembered
madi 19 not enough
mama 1 I
maranavaa 13 kill
mala 30 flower
malaa 13 A 6 died
malli 21 younger brother
mas 27 meat
maha 3, 8 great
mahata 5 fat
mahattayaa 1 gentleman, Mr
mahatturu 11 gentlemen
mahat venavaa 19 get fat
mahanavaa 24 sew, make clothes
Mahanuvara 8 Kandy
mahansi(ya) 28 tired(ness)
mahappaa 3 A 16 uncle
mahapraana 11s aspirated
maat 2**c** me too
maamaa 26 uncle
maaru karanavaa 25 change (tr.)
maartu 22 March
maalu(va) 27 fish; curry
maaluvaa 27 fish
maalee 31 necklace
maava 3 **f** me
maasee 22 month
mæda 25 middle; in the middle
mæyi 22 May
mærenavaa 13 die
mææta 28 near by; recent
miṭi 5 low, short
miṭiya 31 hammer
midula 24 'compound', yard
min 25 **e** from this
minihaa 1 man
misa(k) 28 except
miiṭa 8 **c** to this
miilaňga 22 **d** next
-mu 15 (exhortative ending)
mukut 30 anything
mudda 33 ring
muddaree 32 postage stamp
mu(h)uda 32 sea
muurdhaja 6s retroflex
megoḍa 29 this side
meccara 10 this much
metana 4 here
metara 29 this side
menna 3 look here
meyaa 11 this man
melaha(ka)ṭa 19 by this time
mevvaa 4 these things
mehaa 29 this side
mehaaṭa 4 hither
mehe 2 here
mehen 10 hence; this way
mehema 17, 28 A 14 thus

mee 3, 7 A 20, 7 A 21 this; er . . .
meeka 3 this one (inanimate)
meekaa 11 this one (animate)
meevaa 4 these things
meesee 5 table
mokak-da 3, 11 A 17 what?
mokakda 30 something
mokada 4, 25 what? why?
mokavat 30 anything
mokaa-da 11 which animate?
mokut 30 something
mona 10, 20 A 8, 21 which?
monavaa-da 4, 17 A 4, 20 B 20 what things?
monavaada 30 some things
molavanavaa 31 kindle
mooḍa 14 foolish
yaŋ 15 let's go
yaṭa 8 under
yaṭa karanavaa 14 run over (tr.)
yaṭaha 20 **c** underneath
yanavaa 1, 6 A 1, 13 A 8, 15 A 10, 23**a** go; arrive (21**b**)
-yanna 8s (names of letters of alphabet)
yansee 16s (a phonetic sign)
yamaŋ 15 let's go
yamin 32 A 8 going
yavanavaa 18 send
yasa 17 fine
Yaapanee 9 Jaffna
yaaluvaa 30 friend
-yæ 33**c** (interrogative ending)
yævenavaa 30 A 34 get sent
-yi 3, 8**e**, 10**c**, **d** (copula)
-yi 9 and
-yi 14 (future termination)
raṭa 29 country; foreign
ratu 3 red
rattaran, ratran 33 gold
rattaa 14 red one
ranḍu karanavaa 33 quarrel
rabar 21 rubber
ravaṭṭanavaa 31 deceive
rasa 23 taste, tasty
rasne 25 hot
rassaava 21 job, career
raha 23 taste, tasty
raa 15 toddy
raattala 20 pound (lb.)
rææ 14 (A 24) night
rææ venavaa 14 B 22, 20 A 33 get dark: be late
ridenavaa 32 hurt (intr.)
rupiyala 9 rupee
redda 16 cloth
reepha 15s (a phonetic sign)
laŋ karanavaa 22 put near
Laŋkaava 15 Ceylon, Sri Lanka
laňga 22 near
laňgadi 28 recently; soon
labanavaa 13, 20 A 1, 25 A 14, 29 A 9 obtain
labaagannavaa 25 A 14 acquire
lamayaa 1 child
lavvaa 18 having put
lassana 17 beautiful, beauty
-laa 11, 17 A 15 (animate plural suffix)
-laa 15 (absolutive ending)

laaba 23 cheap
laabeeţa 23 cheaply
læbenavaa 13, 29 be got
lææsti 14 ready
lææsti karanavaa 14 prepare
liňda 20 well (noun)
lipa 27 B 34 hearth
liyanavaa 2 write
liyuma 2 letter
liik venavaa 16 leak
liivaa 12 wrote
-lu 9 it is said
lunu 20 salt
luunu 20 onions
leḍaa 22 sick man
leḍee 22 (A 20) illness
leesi 17 easy
loku 3, 5f, 6 B 15 big
loku karanavaa 14 enlarge
lokkaa 17 boss
loriya 26 lorry
lookee 30 world
-va 3, 11, 13, 25 (accusative ending)
-va 15 having become...
-va- 18 (causative infix)
vakkaranavaa 1, 5 A 21 pour, make
   tea
vaga 27 b thing, fact; responsible, 33a
vage 26 like
vaţee 25 around
vaţţanavaa 18 fell
vaḍaa 8 more
vaḍuvaa 25 carpenter
vat 9, 30 even
vatura 10 water

vatta 24 plantation, garden
vadinavaa 32 enter
vama 15 left-hand
vayasa 16 age
vara 18 time (fois)
varada 20 mistake
varadinavaa 23 err; be missed
varaddanavaa 23 mislead, make
   wrong
-varu(n) 11 (animate plural suffix)
varen 15 b come!
-val 9 (inanimate plural suffix)
valakkanavaa 33 prevent
vahanavaa 13, 17 A 17 close
vahalee 31 roof
vahinavaa 11 rain
-vaa 33 (for eevaa)
vaage 26 like
væţa 23 fence
væţenavaa 18 fall
væḍa 4, 5 A 19, 31 A 9 work, job,
   thing
væḍakaarayaa 4 servant
væḍi 16 excessive
væḍiya 8, 16 more
væḍiye 8 more
væḍiyen 26 especially
væḍiyema 26 especially
væḍee 4 piece of work
væradi 20 wrong
væradenavaa 23 be missed
værædda 20 fault
vævenavaa 30 grow (intr.)
væssa 13 rain
væhenavaa 28 A 14 be covered

-vi 14 (future termination)
vikunanavaa 13 sell
vikkaa 13 sold
vigasaṭa 8 soon, quickly
vigahaṭa 8 soon, quickly
vijahaṭa 8 soon, quickly
viṭa 21**b**, 27 **e** time, occasion
vitara 26 approximately; as much as
vitarak 26 only
vitarayi 26 only
vittiya 31 fact
vidiha 17 manner
viduli(ya) 26 **f** lightning (electricity)
viyadama 33 expenditure
virudda 28 against
vilum̆ba 24**d** heel
visi- 19 twenty-
visi(k) karanavaa 23 throw away
vissa 19 twenty
vissaasa 27 trust
vii 26 paddy (seed)
viidiya 20 street
viiduruva 22 glass, tumbler
viisi karanavaa 23 throw away
-ve 33 (permissive ending)
vecca 20 (past participle of venavaa)
vedaa 29 herbal doctor
vena 28 other
venama 28 **g** separate
venavaa 12, 22 A 11, 28 become; begin
venas(a) 28 different (difference)
venaskama 30 insult; difference
-veni 18 (numeral ordinal suffix)
venin 28 **g** other
venuvaṭa 25 instead of
venuven 25 on behalf of
vela 26 ricefield
velaa 15, 17**b** having become
velaa 16 A 9 time
velaava 8 time (vele, 31 A 13)
velaavakaṭa 27 sometimes
velaasanin 27 in good time
Vesak 22 (name of a month)
veegannavaa 23 become
veelapahin 27 in good time
veelenavaa 31 dry (intr.); idle
ṣarṭ-eka 23 shirt
ṣuvar(a) 33 certain
ṣook 28 (A 19, 20, 24) magnificent
saññaka 8s (name for letters with halfnasal signs)
sataa 30 animal
satee 9 cent
sadda karanavaa 25 A 37 make a noise
saddee 21 noise
san̆dudaa 19 Monday
saniipa 25g, 26 A 38 healthy
sanḍu karanavaa 33 quarrel
santoosee 21, 23 pleasure, pleased
sapattuva 29 shoe
samahara 19 some
samaharaviṭa 27 perhaps
samaharavelaavaṭa 27 perhaps
saroma 16 sarong
salakanavaa 21 treat well
salli(ya) 2 money (cent, coin)
saappuva 30 shop
saayam gaanavaa 27 paint

sæpa-saniipa 7 health
sæptæmbara 22 September
særa 14 strict, strong, fierce, rude
særa karanavaa 14 scold
særen 19 fiercely
særee 18 time (fois)
særeeṭa 19 fiercely
sikuraadaa 19 Friday
sidda venavaa 29 happen
Siriipaadee 33 Adam's Peak
sissayaa 27 pupil
siitala 25 cool; cold
siini 20 sugar
siiya 32 100
siiyaa 21 grandfather
sudaa 24 A 11 dear person
sudu 3, 7 A 24 white
suddaa 24 A 11 white man
sumaanee 20 week
suruṭṭuva 32 cigar
senasuraadaa 19 Saturday
sellam karanavaa 23 play
soodanavaa 12 wash
hakuru 30 juggery sugar
hat- 11 seven-
hata 9 seven
hatara 8 four
hatalis- 19 forty-
hataliha 19 forty
hadanavaa 1, 17 A 22 make; mend; bring up; try
hadissi(ya) 28 hurry; accident
hadissiye(n) 25 unexpectedly
handaa 21 because of
hapan 14 clever
happanavaa 23 collide with
-hamaara 9, 26 A 14 and a half
hamaara karavanava 15 finish (tr.)
hamba karanavaa 21 earn, acquire
hamba venavaa 21 meet, be found
haya 9 six
hayiya 17 strength
hayi venavaa 19 A 10 become hard
harakaa 24 cow, bull
haravanavaa 21 turn (tr.)
haraha 25 across
hari 9, 30 or
hari 10 (A 24), 31 A 7 correct; very
hari gassanavaa 21 put right
hariya 29 area
hariyaṭa 10 **c**, 12 A 12, 23 A 22 properly, exactly; very much
hari yanavaa 11 A 14, 13 A 16 go right; suit
hal 8s (vowelless consonants)
havasa 12 afternoon, evening
havas venavaa 20 A 33 be afternoon: be late
haaranavaa 12 dig
haal 26**f**, 28 uncooked rice
hæṭa 20 sixty
hæṭi(ya) 17, 27 **b** manner
(ee hæṭi 24 A 31, 29 A 31 very special)
hæṭiyema 21 as soon as
hæṭṭee 16 woman's jacket
hættæ(æva) 20 seventy (-)
hædenavaa 13 A 12 form (intr.)
hæn̆di 23 spoons
hæn̆di gaanavaa 24 A 21 stir

hænda 23 spoon
hændææva 17 afternoon, evening
hændææ venavaa 20 A 33 be afternoon: be late
hæppenavaa 23 collide
hæbæyi 10, 24 A 10 but, however
hæbææ(va) 24 true (truth)
hæma 18 every
hæmatissema 22 throughout
hæmadaama 1 every day
hæmooma 18 everyone
hærenavaa 15 turn (intr.)
hævoma 18 everyone
hiňga(higa) 33 scarce
hiṭaŋ 33**f** also; from
hiṭagannavaa 15 stand up
hiṭapu 20 A 5 former
hiṭalaa 15 having stopped
hiṭinavaa 5, 22 A 24, stand, stop
hiṭiyaa 5, 29 was; waited; began
hiṭi hæṭiye 26 A 34 suddenly
hiṭii 22 A 24 must be
hita 24 (23 A 35) mind
hitanavaa [1], 19 think
hinaa venavaa 28 laugh, smile
hinæhenavaa, 28 laugh
hindaa 21 because of
hinnaa 32 ant
hira 32 tight
hiree 32 prison
his 33 empty
hiitala 25 cold, cool
huňgak 10 much, many; very
huňgadenek 11 many people
huňgaak 10 **c** much
hulaŋ gæhenavaa 24 A 22 take the air
hulaňga 24 wind
huuranavaa 12 scratch
heṭa 1 tomorrow
heṭa venavaa 20 A 33 be tomorrow: be very late
hema 17 I suppose; etcetera
hembirissaava 31 a cold
honḍaree 33 hundredweight
hoňda 9 (A3), 16 A 1, 17 A 25, 31 A 14 good; good quality
hoňdaṭa [1], 13, 21 B 6 well, properly
hoňdaṭama 20 B 27 very much
hoňda venavaa 25 A 29 get better
hoňdin 13, 21 B 6 well
hoyanavaa 26 seek
horakam karanavaa 14 steal
horaa 30 thief; rascal
hollanavaa 31 shake (tr.)
hoodanavaa 12 wash (tr.)

Note: The examples of handwriting given in Lesson 17 are for reading practice only. However, for those who would like to work out their meaning, the following words will be required.

agin	at the end
accu	print
aḍiya	bottom
aḍu	lacking
ayina	edge
goḍa	heap
gonna	pile
pahugiya	past
pæya	hour
piṭapata	copy (n.)
mulin	at the beginning
velendaa	merchant

APPENDIX
A note on transliteration and on Proper Names

Loanwords. Most foreign words and names appear in Sinhalese in an Anglicized form, based on English pronunciation and **not** on spelling. Thus e.g. Paris (the capital of France) will appear in Sinhalese as **Pæris** and not as **Paris**. In this connection it should be remembered:

1) that the sounds **t** and **d** will normally be represented in Sinh. by **ţ** and **ḑ**. There are a few exceptions to this, such as the name **Toomas**, for Thomas, which has come into the Sinh. language from Dutch, and has therefore not adopted the Eng. form, which would be **ţomas**. (Similarly **Paavulu** as one form of Paul.) But **Teems** (not **ţems**) for Thames is probably due to the Eng. spelling. Another common exception is **Indiyaava**, India. English **th** is represented by **t** or **d**.

2) that **a** in an initial syllable will normally be represented by **æ**, even where it is not usually so pronounced in English (as well as in foreign names such as Paris, quoted above). Thus the sound **æ** will be found in the Sinh. equivalents of balloon, malaria, Malaya, machine, gazette (bælun, mæleeriyaava Mælayaava, mæsin, gæsaţ). Africa, however, is **Aprikaava**. The **æ** vowel is often used for Eng. short **e**, since Sinh. **e** is a closer vowel: **pæţrool, da Mæl** (petrol, de Mel).

3) that no distinction is made between the vowel sounds in Eng. **caught** and **coat**, the pure vowel (as in 'caught') being used also for Eng. words containing the diphthongal sound of 'coat'. The appearance of a word may mislead here; **ţavar hool** = Tower Hall (not Hole).

4) that **p** is usually used for **f** (see Introduction).

5) that Sinh. **v** is used for both **v** and **w**, and **s** for **s**, **z** and even **sh**. **-iv** represents Eng. **-ew** (**Niv Yook**, New York); the name Montagu, however, is usually written **Monţeegu** (not **Monţagiv**). Several ambiguities may of course result from transcription according to these principles, e.g. **plavar** will probably first be taken to represent 'plover', but in fact probably represents 'flower'; **siiţ** may represent 'sheet', **suu** may represent 'zoo', and the very puzzling **viv** represents 'view' (the beginner will probably think first of 'with').

6) that final **-a** in proper names is nearly always written **-aa**. This is so with all

girl's names (e.g. Hilḍaa) and with names of countries (**Ooṣṭreeliyaa-va**): cf. also **mæleeriyaa-va** above. The termination **-va** is added after **aa**, except in the case of girl's names. Further examples: **Nayijiiriyaava**, **Æmarikaava** (Nigeria, America).

7) that clusters of consonants are often simplified by omitting one, usually the last. Final **-s** is particularly liable to omission here, e.g. **læyisan-eka**, licence: the difference between 'William' and 'Williams' is likely to be lost in transcription. Notice also **peeman** (pavement, not payment), **pænal** (flannel, rather than panel). English names cannot always be clearly deduced from the transliteration; **Roos** might represent Rose or Ross, **Roslin** Rosslyn or Rosalind.

In **geographical names**, -land appears as **-lantee**, but the rest of the word will be according to pronunciation **in English**. Thus Ireland appears not as **Iirlantee**, but in the curious-looking form **Ayarlantee**.

Names of towns usually use the plural terminations with **-val** in case-formation: **Pærisvala**, in Paris. Moscow is usually **Moskav**. Geneva is sometimes **Jinoovaa**, perhaps by confusion with Genoa. Egypt is usually called **Misaree**. The second part of the name Czechoslovakia is usually pronounced **sloveekiyaava**. France is **Praŋsa raṭa**: **Praŋsa** is also used for 'French'. Similarly **Japan** also means 'Japanese'. (The lack of a specific adjectival form from names of countries prevails in English also with the name 'Ceylon', which was freely used adjectivally; one spoke of Ceylon costume, Ceylon rice, Ceylon scenery etc.) The forms used for China, Burma, Siam and Russia, however, follow spelling rather than pronunciation: **Ciinee**, **Burumee**, **Siyamee**, **Rusiyaava**.

It is interesting to notice that in many cases Eng. **a**, where pronounced in southern standard English as **aa**, is represented as **æ** in Sinh. Thus the name Alexander appears as **Ælaksænḍara**, 'auntie' as **ænṭi**. This goes together with a preference for **a** (sounding as **ə**) against the **i**-sound of certain unaccented vowels in southern standard English (**kæpṭan** for captain, or the second syllable of Alexander, above), and is probably due to the presence of many Scotsmen in early colonial days in Ceylon.

An unrealized Eng. **r** is nowadays often omitted in transcription. Remember that words such as 'park' must be transcribed **paa(r)k**: **park** would represent 'perk'. The vowel **o** has a tendency to be lengthened (**Joon** for John,[1] **pæṭrool** for petrol), especially in a second syllable – thus **Oṭooman**, rather than **Oṭaman**, will seem the natural equivalent of Ottoman.

---

1. Which is thus indistinguishable from Joan.

Proper Names. Some proper names which originally appeared in Ceylon in Portuguese or Dutch forms were later refashioned to suit Eng. pronunciation, e.g. Diez, which was originally **Diyes**, is now **ḍayas**; Saram, formerly **Saram**, is now usually **Seeram**. The very common name de Silva is written in Sinh. **da Silvaa**: here **da** is pronounced **də**, and in Eng. transcription the form used in Ceylon is always 'de Silva', not 'da Silva'; but the Sinh. transcription remains **da** and not **ḍi**. (So also with de Soysa, de Mel etc.[1]) The Portuguese honorific 'Don' is always written **Don**, and its female counterpart **Doonaa**; these are common, but are used as hereditary personal names and not as titles, i.e. they will be preceded (in English) by 'Mr'[2], and will appear among a man's initials. The common name Fernando is in Sinh. **Pranaandu**.

The Sinhalese have no real system of surnames. They have personal names, of which the commonest kinds are Sanskritic, such as Ratnapaala, Preemadaasa, or European such as Joon, Viliyoŋ. (Recently, Indian-type names such as Nihaal have become fashionable.) Some people use their personal name as a surname. Many families bear Portuguese names such as de Silva, Fernando, Pereira, Pieris (da Silvaa, Pranaandu, Pereraa, Piiris), but these names are not in fact always used as surnames, and a Mr Pieris may well have a son who calls himself, say, Mr Dharmapala (Darmapaala). There are also a very large number of personal names, mostly of Dutch origin, ending in **-is** (e.g. Haramaanis, Siyadooris, Karoolis – corresponding ultimately to Jerome, Theodore, Charles).

The Sinhalese do also have true surnames, which end in **-ge**, but only a few of these, such as Liyanage, are used as such; mostly the **ge**-name appears only in the form of an initial. Indeed, family connections can often be observed by the initials which precede the final name, e.g. Mr M.G. William may be the son of Mr M.G. de Silva, the hereditary portion being the M.G.

There are also many names of a pure Sanskrit type, such as Vikramasiŋha, Kulaseekara, which are widely used as surnames. These are by original hereditary titles of honour (e.g. Vikramasiŋha = Lion Incarnate). Finally, some people use village names as a surname; such names are Ellaavala, Ratvatte (these names are usually in a locative case-form).

---

1. In transcribing from Portuguese and Dutch **t** and **d** are represented by Sinhalese **t** and **d**, and not by **ṭ** and **ḍ**.

2. Likewise the Eng. title 'Sir' also needs 'Mr' with it in Sinhalese; Sar Joon Kotalaavala mahattayaa, Sir John Kotalawala.

Because so many people may use the same final name without being in any way connected, initials are of great importance in Lanka, and are hardly ever abbreviated even when there are as many as four of them before the final name. Indeed well-known people are sometimes referred to simply by the initials which precede their final name, e.g. 'N.M.' or 'J.R.'. The Eng. names of letters are used for initials even when writing in Sinh. script; i.e. Mr Harry Ælian[1] Nicholas Gunapaala Perera will write his initials as Ec.Ee.Æn.Jii (the full stop is nearly always used, except perhaps after **ḍabliv**), and not as Hæ.Ii.Ni.Gu. (except in certain literary circles).

The foregoing applies to men's names. Women in general use only a personal name, often ending in **-aa** or **-vati** (Eng. spelling -wathie), though in the latter case the termination **-vati** may frequently be omitted. (Other names are also shortened in this way in familiar speech, e.g. Heṭṭiaaracci may be reduced to Heṭṭi, Karunaaratna to Karu). In the case of women, a European name or word is often followed by **noonaa** (lady): Jeen noonaa, Beebi noonaa. Women's names may also end in **-haami**, and large numbers end in **-in** (Roslin, Mægilin). At village level, it is not a general practice for a woman to use her husband's 'surname'.

Both men and women not infrequently bear names of an Eng. type but of an unfamiliar appearance, such as Wilbert (Vilbaṭ – for men) or Eslin (Æsilin – for women).

Buddhist monks discontinue the use of their original names altogether, and adopt the use of a Pali or Sanskrit name, preceded by the name of their village of origin (in the locative case-form), e.g. Valaane Saddaatissa (Walane Saddhatissa), Vææuḍa Deevamitta (Weuda Devamitta). In place of **mahattayaa**, a monk's name is followed by **haamuduruvo** in ordinary speech, or in formal contexts often by the Pali word **teeroo** (thero).

The Eng. spelling of a Sinh. name is a matter of personal choice. We find Pieris, Peiris and Peries: Liyanage and Leanage: Silva and Zylwa: Soysa and Zoysa: -vardana as -wardhana, -wardene etc.: Vikrama- as Wickreme-, Wickrama- etc.: Guna- as Goona-, Gune- etc. Most Sinhalese people would not notice or bother about how another Sinhalese spells his own name in English, and there is no consistency; but occasionally a difference in English spelling may connote a difference in family; this is so, for instance, with Soysa and Zoysa, though the Sinhalese pronunciation is identical.

---

1. This learned name is not uncommon in Lanka.